Teaching With Style

A Practical Guide to Enhancing Learning by Understanding Teaching and Learning Styles

Anthony F. Grasha, Ph.D.
University of Cincinnati

Alliance Publishers

To everyone over the years who took the time to listen to my ideas about teaching and learning, who sometimes took exception, suggested alternatives, and in the process helped me to sharpen my thinking as I probed the underlying components of the teaching-learning process.

Teaching With Style
Anthony F. Grasha

Cover Design: Karen Stokely, Pittsburgh, PA
Front Cover Art: David Wills, San Francisco, CA

Curriculum for Change Series
Laurie Richlin, Editor

Copyright © by ALLIANCE PUBLISHERS

Alliance Publishers
INTERNATIONAL ALLIANCE OF TEACHER SCHOLARS, INC.
414 S. Craig Street, Suite 313 * Pittsburgh, PA 15213
Telephone (800) 718-IATS * FAX (412) 362-6195

ISBN 0-9645071-1-0

Preface

About 25 years ago I wrote a twelve page essay describing the learning styles of students as part of a proposal for a paper session for the American Psychological Association's annual meetings. At the time I was not engaged in a research program on learning styles, but I was fascinated with the different ways students appeared to learn in classes. The essay was an analysis of critical incidents in my interactions with students. It was the first thing I had ever written about college teaching and thus I had no way to guage whether others would find my observations intriguing.

To my surprise, the proposal was accepted and I suddenly began to worry about the presentation. I questioned whether I could go to a professional meeting in a few months armed only with a twelve page essay. "I'll get killed by all of the empirical types," I told myself. Thus, to *protect myself*, I developed a questionnaire and surveyed students about how they learned. Their responses were then used to supplement my informal observations. In retrospect, I am not convinced the paper was better but I felt less anxious knowing I had a few numbers to support my conclusions.

The essay was well received and the editor of the prestigious *American Psychologist* asked me to submit it for publication. The subsequent article generated a considerable amount of interest in my views on learning styles and dramatically changed my career. I then began to seriously study a variety of teaching-learning issues including the role of student learning styles and teaching styles in the college classroom.

Teaching With Style represents an extension of that twelve page essay twenty-five years later. While informal observations of classroom dynamics continue to play a role in my writing, they are supplemented with information from other sources. This book also includes concepts from research using the *Grasha-Riechmann Student Learning Style Scales,* the *Teaching Styles Inventory,* extensive interviews with college faculty across disciplines, outcomes of my work consulting with instructors on problems they faced in the classroom, ideas generated from several hundred interdisciplinary workshops and seminars I have conducted with faculty and graduate students, concepts and practices described in the literature on college teaching, and my personal experiences as a teacher and as a learner.

Teaching With Style was written to enable readers to learn more about themselves as teachers, the factors that facilitate and hinder attempts to modify instructional practices, and how to use an integrated model of teaching and learning style to *teach for learning* by enhancing the nature and quality of what occurs in the classroom. To accomplish these goals, this book is organized into eight chapters.

Chapter 1 argues that teaching style is more than a set of interesting personal qualities. Rather, such qualities are related to our preferences for particular instructional processes and are often markers that students, administrators, peers, and others employ when judging our effectiveness as teachers. This chapter also notes that without a focus on the qualities that learners possess, and how they interact with our styles as teachers, changes in instructional processes will be difficult to develop and maintain.

In *Chapter 2,* the need for self-reflection and understanding as a precursor to change is developed. Factors that facilitate and hinder attempts to modify instructional practices are examined and suggestions for overcoming barriers are made. Readers will be able to determine where they stand in a cycle of change in teaching and how to think and behave in ways that promote the development of their skills as teachers.

The need for and how to develop a philosophy of teaching as part of one's efforts to change is the focus of *Chapter 3.* This philosophy of teaching functions as a roadmap and helps to guide our thoughts, behaviors, and the selection of particular instructional methods. It provides us with an explicit conceptual rationale for why particular instructional practices should be employed. The elements of a philosophy of teaching are presented and how they can be applied in our classrooms are examined.

Chapters 4-8 present the elements in an integrated model of teaching and learning style. This model examines the relationships among learning styles of Competitive-Collaborative, Independent-Dependent, and Participant-Avoidant and teaching styles of Expert, Formal Authority, Personal Model, Facilitator, and Delegator. *Teaching style, learning styles, and classroom processes are seen as interdependent.* The selection of any one element has implications for the appearance of the other two. For example, the use of the Expert/Formal Authority styles in the context of the traditional lecture-discussion method of teaching encourages and reinforces a Dependent/Participant/Competitive set of learning styles. Ways to use an understanding of style in selecting instructional strategies are presented. More than 40 methods of instruction are described in detail and ways to use them to encourage active and collaborative learning as well as critical thinking are described.

All of the chapters in this book employ a variety of reader involvement activities, checklists, self-assessment instruments and other devices to encourage self-reflection about the personal relevance of the material. Such things are directed towards helping the reader to address how the information could fit into their philosophy of teaching.

While writing is a solitary activity, publishing a book is a collective enterprise and in this case it also was a family affair. I am grateful for the support and encouragement of my friend and colleague Laurie Richlin who created Alliance Publishers to publish books with a practical orientation towards teaching and learning. Her daughters Jennifer and Karen Stokely used their professional skills behind the scenes to comment on the layout and design of the book and helped with the development of materials for the promotion and advertising campaign. Karen also worked on a number of aspects of the artwork in the book and the advertising materials.   My sons Eric and Kevin deserve a thank you for their assistance with proofreading and computer tasks as does my wife Carol for her support and patience with this project. David Wills did a marvelous job integrating ideas about self-reflection and style and created the front cover art. The graduate students in Laurie Richlin's class on faculty development at the University of Pittsburgh and those in my seminar on college teaching at the University of Cincinnati provided helpful feedback on earlier drafts of the manuscript. The comments of reviewers Milton Cox [Miami University], Barbara Fuhrmann [Louisiana State University] Joseph Lowman [University of North Carolina, Chapel Hill], and Leslie Hickcox [Rogue Community College] also were very much appreciated.

Anthony F. Grasha
January, 1996

Table of Contents

Chapter 3

Developing a Conceptual Base for Our Teaching Styles 91

Chapter 4

An Integrated Model of Teaching and Learning Style

Chapter 5

Teaching and Learning Styles in the Management of Five Basic Instructional Concerns 207

Chapter 6

Managing the Expert, Formal Authority, Personal Model Styles 233

Chapter 7

Developing Consultant, Resource Person, Active Listening, and Group Process Skills 267

Chapter 8

Managing the Facilitator and Delegator Styles of Teaching 285

1. ■ Identifying the Elements of Teaching Style

In the main, a person's values, beliefs, and philosophy can easily
be ascertained by the way he or she teaches. The instructional
strategies and techniques that are adopted by a teacher bespeak
his attitudes about himself, his students, and their respective roles
in the teaching-learning process.

-Mary Lynn Crow

While many people have argued that style is important in teaching, identifying the elements of our styles as teachers has proved to be difficult. One reason is that traditionally the concept of style has been viewed in a perjorative manner. "It has been confused with affectation, denigrated as a kind of posturing to mask a lack of substance, or tolerated as a natural manifestation of personal eccentricities" [Eble, 1980, p. 1]. Thus, to define style, to understand it, to develop it, and to use it effectively entails moving beyond the negative sense in which it is sometimes perceived. Style in teaching as in art, music, athletics, managing people, and other areas of endeavor is not something that is put on for the occasion. Otherwise it becomes a superficial covering, mask, or a collection of interesting mannerisms that are used to create an impression. Style, Eble argued, was "what one is" [p. 95]. Our teaching style represents those enduring personal qualities and behaviors that appear in how we conduct our classes. Thus, it is both something that defines us, that guides and directs our instructional processes, and that has effects on students and their ability to learn.

While the latter observations may help to illuminate the general nature of our styles as teachers, it is deficient. *If style is what a teacher is, then there are potentially as many different styles as there are teachers.* Style then becomes everything a person does and at the same time nothing that can be studied in a systematic manner. To resolve this dilemma, it would be useful to know just what personal qualities and behaviors are shared by all faculty members. This would allow us to categorize specific types of teaching styles and to show how people vary on these common qualities. Such information also would allow us to examine how particular characteristics affect students and their subsequent ability to learn.

Understanding our teaching styles would be enhanced if we had a list of the elements of style that we use as a basis for examining ourselves. There is, however, no clear consensus about the common components of style. It largely depends upon whom you ask-- or at least whom you read. Several approaches to understanding our styles as teachers appear in the literature. Various authors emphasize different aspects of how people teach and thus there is little agreement about the elements of style. Instead, various aspects of our thoughts and behaviors are highlighted by those attempting to describe teaching style. Table 1-1 outlines several contemporary approaches to identifying the elements of style.

Table 1-1
Approaches to Identifying the Elements of Style

General Modes of Classroom Behavior
Webster's dictionary defines style as "a manner or mode of acting or performing, a distinctive or characteristic manner, or a manner or tone assumed in discourse. The idea that style represents those personal dispositions people publicly display also is evident in the education literature.

Characteristics Associated with a Popular Instructor
Typically such individuals have characteristics that colleagues and students judge to be unique and interesting.

The Teaching Methods Employed
The preferred instructional practices of someone describes their style as a teacher. Thus, a person might be labeled a "lecturer," "discussion leader," or perhaps a "Socratic teacher," Here, style becomes synonymous with the methods employed in the classroom.

Behaviors Common to All College Faculty
These are identified largely through research on the characteristics associated with "effective teaching." Included here are such things as how teachers organize information, the clarity of presentations, enthusiasm, and their ability to develop rapport with students. Variations among faculty in such behaviors become markers for identifying differences in teaching style.

The Roles Teachers Play
Roles are consistent patterns of behaviors that guide and direct our thoughts and behaviors in specific situations. The processes associated with teaching demand that faculty play a number of roles. They may assume the role of a consultant, resource person, personal model, prescriptive advisor, or other roles. When teachers are flexible, they are able to assume various roles to meet the demands of particular situations.

Personality Traits
Characteristics found in a formal theory of personality are used to describe the styles of college teachers. Or, the outcomes of observations and/or interviews cluster faculty members into groups with similar characteristics. Such dispositions help us to understand the differences that exist among instructors.

Archetypal Forms
Basic yet pervasive forms or models of teaching are identified. To varying degrees, all teachers are assumed to be representations or copies of these basic forms [e.g., Teacher-centered; Student-centered]. Variations on the archetypes occur as instructors interpret each form somewhat differently. However, they are still a pervasive theme in how someone approaches their task as an instructor.

Metaphors for Teaching
Analogies, similes, allegories, and other forms of figurative language are employed to describe the behaviors of teachers [e.g., Midwife, Yoda, Coach, Matador, Gardener]. Such metaphors reflect our beliefs, attitudes, and values and thus constitute a personal model of the teaching- learning process that we use to guide and direct our actions.

Defining Style

Defining the concept of teaching style is not unlike the problem in the story of three blind individuals who were examining an elephant. Each person held different parts in his or her hands and consequently they obtained divergent descriptions of the elephant. The person holding the trunk compared it to a python, the individual holding the tail thought it was like a skinny cat, while the person holding the leg compared it to a tree.

A similar process occurs when we try to understand our styles as teachers. The style we display at any given moment in time contains the elements of several of the perspectives shown in Table 1-1. It is a multidimensional construct and the remainder of this section examines those dimensions in more detail. The presentation will explore the unique characteristics of each of the approaches, their implications for the practice of teaching and their effects on faculty and students. This information is designed to help you to gain a better understanding of the concept of teaching style and how various conceptions of style describe you as a teacher.

General Patterns of Classroom Behavior

A dictionary definition of teaching style identifies it as a manner or mode of acting or performing. Clearly there are a variety of "modes of performing" associated with our styles as teachers. This focus on the actions teachers employ is used by many authors either in whole or in part in discussing the elements of style. *For example:*

- ... a complex array of mental, spiritual and physical acts affecting others." [Eble, 1976. p. 8]

- ... choosing, preparing, speaking, listening, responding, testing, grading—the details of one's craft. [Granrose, 1980, p. 24]

- ... outstanding teachers are enablers... They are student-centered, engaging their students close-up, ... they are facilitating, encouraging, maiutic." [Macorie, 1984, p. 177]

- ...teaching is a performing art. Excellent teachers use their voices, gestures, and movements to elicit and maintain attention and to stimulate student's emotions. Like other performers, teachers must convey a strong sense of presence, of highly focused energy." [Lowman, 1984, pp. 13-14]

- Teaching calls for the trained eye to see what is actually happening, and the trained mind to decide what to do next." [Davis, 1993, p. 8]

- ....the openness we have to questions and opposing points of view, our willingness to risk change in ourselves... [McKeachie, 1994, p. 383]

The views expressed by these authors suggest that our modes of behavior as teachers include such elements as; "mental, spiritual, and physical acts"; "speaking, listening, responding"; "voice, gesture, movements"; "facilitating, encouraging; " using a "trained eye to see what is actually happening"; and "the openness we have to questions." This list is incomplete but it does indicate the diversity of the qualities associated with modes of performing.

Various components of our modes of behavior often cluster into general patterns. In a study of the teacher behaviors mentioned in 500 nomination letters for teaching awards at the University of North Carolina, Joseph Lowman [1994; 1995] found that the descriptions used fit into two categories: intellectual excitement and interpersonal rapport. Trained judges summarized the themes in the written descriptions into one word descriptors and those associated with each category in Lowman's study are shown in Table 1-2.

Table 1-2
A Classification of Descriptors
of Classroom Behavior

Intellectual Excitement

Enthusiastic	Exciting
Knowledgeable	Engaging
Inspiring	Prepared
Humorous	Energetic
Interesting	Fun
Clear	Stimulating
Organized	Eloquent
Creative	Communicative

Interpersonal Rapport

Interpersonal Concern	*Effective Motivation*
Concerned	Helpful
Caring	Encouraging
Available	Challenging
Friendly	Fair
Accessible	Demanding
Approachable	Patient
Interested	Motivating
Respectful	
Understanding	
Personable	

* Based on information in Lowman [1994]

In a follow-up study, Lowman had students select the descriptors associated with the behaviors of a more diverse set of instructors. He discovered that students applied more of the descriptors in Table 1-2 to describe teachers they considered "very good" from those they thought were "average," or "very poor." The average number of descriptors used by students in their evaluations of faculty was: Very poor; 3.3; Average; 11.1; Very Good; 21.5.

The dimensions of intellectual excitement and interpersonal rapport occur to varying degrees in the teaching styles of anyone who teaches at the college level. The general characteristics of faculty who are judged to be low, moderate, and high on each of the two dimensions are listed below:

Intellectual Excitement

- Low: Vague and dull
- Moderate: Reasonably clear and interesting
- High: Extremely clear and exciting

Interpersonal Rapport

- Low: Cold, distant, highly controlling, unpredictable
- Moderate: Relatively warm, approachable, and democratic
- High: Warm, open, predictable, and highly student-centered

The degree to which teachers are able to exhibit intellectual excitement and interpersonal rapport has implications for the teaching conditions where they are likely to be most effective [Lowman, 1995]. Teachers who are strong on both dimensions are generally excellent for any group of students and teaching situation. Those who are deficient on both dimensions tend to be ineffective and unable to present material or to motivate students. Those teachers with moderate levels of interpersonal rapport and who exhibit a high degree of intellectual excitement are generally skilled at teaching large introductory classes. To teach smaller, more advanced courses, Lowman argues that teachers need at least moderate levels of intellectual excitement and must be strong in the area of interpersonal rapport.

Characteristics Associated with a Popular Instructor

Every campus has several professors whose styles as instructors earn them respect, admiration, and popularity. It is also true that there are people whose styles have just the opposite effects on students and colleagues. The concern here is with the former and not the latter teachers. The qualities that endear respected teachers differ, but one thing is clear: *Whatever they do, they do it well and they do it better than other teachers.* A number of instructors fit this mold and are described in the literature. Consider the synopsis below of two individuals who were both respected and popular on their campuses and the qualities that made them so.

• *Giovanni Costigan.* This great teacher's self-awareness probably exceeds most of ours. He watches himself, with 'other eyes,' from sundry vantages in the classroom as he lectures, and he adjusts his delivery as he deems necessary, readily and fluidly . . . His greatness never departed completely from a species of highbrow entertainment: not entertainment in the usual sense, but, rather, impassioned engagement with ideas that stirs an audience . . . he looks at students often, continually beckoning their tacit participation and inviting their judgments...his teaching modeled a commitment to interdisciplinary reach as well as disciplinary depth." [Weltzien, 1994, p 126.]

• *Margaret.* Her relationships with students were both personal and professional, and much of the satisfaction that she gained from teaching came from the personal connections . . . By offering structured assignments and specific suggestions for revision, Margaret sought to instill in her students discipline, listening skills, and, ultimately, independence . . .Another goal was to give her students a positive experience, because she believed positive experiences such as becoming acquainted with students, knowing the instructor cared about you— motivated students to stay in school." [Dahlin, 1994, pp. 58.59].

Such qualities are not always easy for others to duplicate. They are integrated into the personal makeup of the individuals involved and thus are difficult to copy. Yet, elements of what they do are often instructive and informative. Such models tell us something about the teaching styles of good teachers. Also, it is possible to select aspects of their qualities that we might admire for our own use. Most of us, for example, could read the descriptions above and incorporate an interdisciplinary perspective into at least one topic in a course. We also could provide more structure for students and work to build more effective interpersonal relationships with students. Doing such things would not magically transform us into a Giovanni Costigan or a Margaret . Such actions only would add something to the qualities we already possess.

Teaching Methods and Teaching Style

Sometimes people become associated with a particular teaching method. Thus, all of us know colleagues whom we would describe as a *dynamic lecturer, charismatic discussion leader*, quiet but effective *Socratic teacher*, or who are known for their effective use of *case studies, role plays* and *simulations, peer assisted instruction, film and video, computers*, and many other methods. In such cases, the particular method becomes synonymous with their style as a teacher.

This approach to style type casts a faculty member. And, like an actor or actress who is type cast, it is sometimes difficult to break out of this mold. One reason is that colleagues, students, and administrators are apt to comment on their perceived prowess with particular methods. While a compliment such as "I hear you are an excellent lecturer" is usually appreciated, it sometimes has, in my experience, two unintended after effects. *One is that such comments help to bond the teaching methods to a person's self-image as a instructor. As a result, they may become unwilling to explore alternate styles of teaching.* A participant in one of my workshops captured the latter point nicely when she said, "Everyone seems to think I'm already pretty good at what I do. I'm not sure what I could do to teach in other ways so I'll just continue doing what everyone appreciates about my teaching style."

The second unintended consequence is that a method driven teaching style may become a master key that is applied regardless of course content, number of students, and the physical environment. This is sometimes seen in people who enjoy reputations as *dynamic lecturers.* The lecture quickly becomes the method of choice regardless of the type of course and the number and maturity levels of the students involved. I have witnessed "dynamic lecturers" exclusively using a presentation mode in small seminars of 4-6 students, with advanced doctoral students, and in other courses where extensive student input and discussion would have appeared to be necessary components of the class. By the same token, I also have observed those with excellent reputations as teacher-centered discussion leaders [e.g.., teacher leads discussion with entire class] in courses of 20-40 students unsuccessfully try this technique in groups of 400-500 students in auditoriums. They are to be applauded for trying to generate participation in large groups but there are other discussion processes that have been shown to be more effective. Unfortunately, when one becomes locked into a particular instructional process it is difficult to change.

When using instructional methods to define teaching style, Charles Bonwell and James Eison [1991] suggest that methods can be classified according to the amount of risk they entail and how much they facilitate active learning. *Risk involves such things as the potential for particular methods to fail, generate controversy, take up too much class time, become unpopular with students and colleagues, or to not accomplish the goals for which they were designed.* Bonwell and Eison argue that low risk strategies are relatively short, well structured and concrete, and very familiar to both students and faculty. Those that are high risk have just the opposite characteristics. Examples of each type suggested by Bonwell and Eison as well as those generated by participants in a recent workshop I conducted are listed in Table 1-3.

Mary Lynn Crow's earlier point suggested that our methods tell us something about our personal qualities as well as the qualities of the teaching-learning process. Thus, the methods described in Table 1-3 effectively define the degree to which our teaching styles reflect risk as well as our attitudes and values regarding active learning. As a group, college faculty are not noted for their willingness to engage in instructional strategies that involve risk taking. It would appear, however, that movement in the direction of embracing active learning strategies is a better bet. And, progress in that area is slowly developing [Bonwell & Eison, 1991; Davis, 1993].

Table 1-3
Active Learning and Risk Associated
with Teaching Methods

High Active Learning-High Risk	High Active Learning-Low Risk
Role playing Skits that illustrate content points designed by students Simulations Presentations by students to the entire class Free form class session Partners teach each other Presentations by students in small groups Guided imagery exercise Unstructured small-group discussion Students interview guest speaker Students design and run session Students interview each other on content for an entire class Case discussion with large group after students prepare case outside of class	Structured group activity Pairs of students discuss ideas Demonstrations Self-assessment activity Brainstorming activities Student debates on issues that are prepared in advance In-class writing assignments Prepare case outside of class and discuss ideas in class Lecture with small-group discussions Structured small group discussion Students list new ideas they learned in coverage of topic Field trips
Low Active Learning-High Risk	**Low Active Learning-Low Risk**
Invite guest lecturer of unknown quality Have students ask questions at the beginning of class to use to organize a lecture for the session Show a film or video that you have not previewed	Show a film or video for class period Lecture for the entire class period Use a computer slide show to present a topic Read Important passages from the text to class Give a lecture to summarize important points covered during the term

* Based in part on information in Bonwell & Eison [1991]

Behaviors Common to All College Faculty

This approach to style assumes that similarities exist in the behaviors of faculty within and across disciplines. The proficiency with which teachers use such behaviors defines their teaching style. Assessment forms typically are developed to allow students and others to evaluate faculty performance in order to give teachers feedback and to allow comparisons among faculty to be made. In the research literature, the items used to identify and evaluate the elements of teaching style fall into several categories. Those that appear most frequently across a number of studies are described in Table 1-4. [cf., Grasha, 1977; Seldin, 1984; and Mckeachie, et. al., 1994].

There are several advantages as well as disadvantages to this approach to identifying the elements of style. On the positive side:

• *Everyone in a department or college is measured against the same yardstick.* This makes it possible to detect the degree to which everyone is *organized, enthusiastic,* or has good *teacher-student rapport.* It also allows everyone to see the extent to which dimensions of their style differs from the norms of their department and college.

• *The use of numerical data allows statistical techniques such as factor analysis to be used to identify the behaviors that determine a style of teaching.* Thus, the information obtained is not thought to be based upon personal whim or bias. The outcomes of this quantitative research has consistently produced clusters like those shown in Table 1-4. Those categories are robust enough to be applied across a diverse set of institutions, disciplines, and student populations.

• *One can be confident in the reliability of the information obtained.* Student ratings of faculty are typically consistent over time. This is true of measurements taken within 7-10 day periods and with comparisons of alumni ratings to judgments they made about the same instructors as students.

• *The ratings of teaching style allow one to discriminate between teachers that students perceive as relatively good to those they consider relatively poor.* Such judgments are not idiosyncratic to students and are shared by others. For example, colleague and alumni ratings of the same teachers generally agree with students.

• *The qualities of teaching style assessed by student ratings of faculty performance are related to important student outcomes.* Such ratings of teaching style predict the degree to which students report they are satisfied with a class and the likelihood of their meeting course objectives and wanting to take additional courses in the same area of study.

Table 1-4
Categories of Teaching Style

Analytic/Synthetic Approach
Ability to present and discuss theoretical issues and new developments
area from several points of view
For Example:
        Discusses points of view other than his/her own.
        Contrasts implications of various theories.

Organization/Clarity
Has clear course objectives and organizes the information for students to learn
For Example:
        Explains material clearly and is well prepared.

Teacher-Group Interaction
Extent to which discussions and a mutual sharing of ideas on issues occurs
For Example:
        Encourages class discussions and invites criticism of own ideas.

Teacher-Individual Student Interaction
The instructor is approachable, interested in students, and respects them
For Example:
        Relates to students as individuals and is accessible outside of class.

Dynamism/Enthusiasm
Degree to which the instructor is energetic, stimulating, and enjoys teaching
For Example:
        Is able to demonstrate that he/she enjoys teaching the content.

General Teaching Ability
Abilities that form a consistent pattern across different instructional styles
For Example:
        Able to stimulate intellectual curiosity of students.
        Presents material in an interesting manner.

Overload
Difficulty of course requirements and the amount of assigned course work
For Example:
        Assigned very difficult readings.

Structure
Ability of teacher to plan the details of class sessions and to organize a course
For Example:
        Has everything organized according to a schedule.

Quality
Concern teacher has for the quality of student work and their performance
For Example:
        Tells student when they have done a good job.

Student-Teacher Rapport
The nature and quality of teacher-student interaction within the classroom
 For Example:
        Listens attentively to what class members have to say.

On the negative side, students' ratings of instruction have generated controversy almost everywhere they have been used for several reasons:

• *Ratings of teaching style have been employed to do more than give faculty feedback on their performance.* The evaluations by students have played a role in decisions made about promotion, reappointment, and tenure. Legitimate concerns about the use of the ratings of teaching style for making such important decisions have been raised.

• *The information obtained has not been perceived as helping faculty to enhance their teaching styles.* Specific steps faculty could take to improve a particular element of their style [e.g., organization / clarity; student-teacher rapport; enthusiasm] and financial and other resources to do so often are not available. To counter this criticism, no item representing an element of teaching style should appear on such forms unless there are clear suggestions about how someone deficient on that item could improve and resources available to allow this to happen. Otherwise, the ratings of style are perceived as identifying defects without giving individuals the opportunity to improve.

• *Some individuals believe that teaching style cannot be quantified.* A member of a committee I consulted with on faculty evaluation recently remarked, "Teaching is an artform with qualities that numbers can never capture." Another member of this committee asked, "Where is there room for students to assess the truly unique things that happen in class if everyone is assessed on the same yardstick?"

• *Students are not perceived as knowledgeable enough to make such judgments.* College faculty members live in a hierarchical system where they are clearly in charge. Many perceive themselves as well trained and knowledgeable professionals and their students as less so. As one person I worked with on this issues said, "They just don't have the insight and experience to tell me whether or not I'm doing a good job."

• *Some critics have argued that students will try to "get even" with their teachers through the ratings.* "It's about the only way they have to get back at us," another member of a teacher evaluation committee remarked. Or, as others have said to me, "It's nothing more than a popularity contest." In discussions with faculty in workshops, some have singled out the weak -to- moderate relationship between student ratings and grades in a course as evidence for such ratings being invalid. One person said, "If the ratings of our styles as teachers aren't strongly related to the grades students receive, then what's the point of using them?"

The latter issue ignores the fact that several factors are important for academic success. The research shows that student motivation to achieve, general academic ability, time management skills, and study habits are often better predictors of academic performance than the classroom behaviors of teachers [Kirschenbaum, 1982; Hoff-Macan, 1990; Britten & Tesser, 1991]. This does not mean that what we do in class is unimportant. Rather it simply means that *aspects of our styles as teachers in traditional classroom settings are only one part of a very complicated prediction equation that accounts for student achievement in academic settings.* In my experience, sometimes teachers want to take more credit for their students' successes than is warranted.

Perhaps the most neutral interpretation of student ratings of teaching style is that they depict *consumer satisfaction.* The information provides an indication of those teacher behaviors liked and disliked by students. This latter point is not a trivial one nor should it be taken lightly. *Student satisfaction is one indicator of the emotional climate in a classroom.* That is, the degree to which students feel the environment is pleasant and that they are nurtured by their instructors and peers. In a variety of academic, training, and laboratory settings, positive emotional climates have been associated with: higher degrees of learning; individual's motivation to succeed; the willingness of students to seek out advice and help from faculty members; and the capacity of students to take a problem- focused approach to dealing with course related problems versus avoiding or denying them [Ashcraft, 1994; Ellis & Hunt, 1993; Grasha, 1996; McKeachie, et. al., 1994]. Use student ratings to identify your style in Self-Reflection Activity 1-1.

The Relationship of Ratings of Style to Emotional Climate and Student Self-Image

Specific elements of our teaching styles described in Table 1-4 affect not only the emotional climate in the classroom but the self-image of students. Information on this latter point occurs in studies using the *Grasha-Ichiyama Psychological Size and Distance Scale* [Grasha & Ichyiama, 1990; Salzmann & Grasha, 1991]. This instrument employs circle drawings as a metaphor to represent our thoughts and feelings about relationships with others. Participants in these studies are told to use the size of the circles they draw for themselves and the other person, the distance between them, and where they place them on a $8^{1/2}$ x 11 sheet of paper to represent their thoughts and feelings about the relationship. Once the drawings are completed, participants respond to a 22-item *Status-Affect Rating Scale* that allows them to determine the specific aspects of the relationship responsible for their drawings. Examples of dimensions covered on the rating scale include how much knowledge and expertise one had relative to the other person and the degree to which someone was impatient, assertive, affectionate, and friendly.

Psychological size represents how much interpersonal status relative to another person someone possess while *psychological distance* represents the amount of positive and negative affect someone believes is present in a relationship. The size of the circle drawings represents psychological size, while the separation between the two circles represents psychological distance. The larger people draw themselves, the more status, knowledge,

Self-Reflection Activity 1-1
Using A Rating Scale to Evaluate Your Style

Part I

The faculty rating scale shown below will allow you to obtain a traditional perspective on your teaching style. Rate yourself from the perspective of how you believe the average student in your class would see you. Use the information in Part II of this activity on the next page to help you analyze the results.

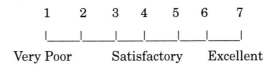

```
        1   2   3   4   5   6   7
        |___|___|___|___|___|___|
     Very Poor      Satisfactory   Excellent
```

_____ 01. Discusses points of view other than his/her own.
_____ 02. Contrasts implications of various theories.
_____ 03. Discusses recent developments in the field.
_____ 04. Explains material clearly.
_____ 05. Is well-prepared.
_____ 06. States objectives clearly.
_____ 07. Encourages class discussions.
_____ 08. Invites criticism of his/her own ideas.
_____ 09. Knows if the class is understanding him/her or not.
_____ 10. Has genuine interest in students.
_____ 11. Respects students as persons.
_____ 12. Is accessible to students out of class.
_____ 13. Behaves in a dynamic and energetic manner.
_____ 14. Ability to demonstrate that he/she enjoys teaching.
_____ 15. Displays self-confidence when teaching.
_____ 16. Presents material in an interesting way.
_____ 17. Ability to stimulate intellectual curiosity in students.
_____ 18. Is skillful in observing student reactions.
_____ 19. Assignments were very difficult.
_____ 20. Requires more than students could get done.
_____ 21. Assigns a considerable amount of reading.
_____ 22. Follows an outline closely.
_____ 23. Has everything organized according to a schedule.
_____ 24. Plans the activities of each class period in detail.
_____ 25. Tells student when he/she has done a good job.
_____ 26. Compliments students in front of others.
_____ 27. Gives positive feedback.
_____ 28. Listens attentively to what class members have to say.
_____ 29. Is permissive and flexible when dealing with students.
_____ 30. Explains the reasons for criticism.
_____ 31. Overall, rate the quality of the teaching/learning process used in this class.

Self-Reflection Activity 1-1 [Continued]

Part II

1.] Sum your scores for each of the teaching style categories described earlier in Table 1-4 and place your total score in the space provided below. The categories of style and items associated with them are:

		Teacher Total	Student Total
Analytic/Synthetic Approach	Items 1-3	[____]	[____]
Organization/Clarity	Items 4-6	[____]	[____]
Teacher/Group Interaction	Items 7-9	[____]	[____]
Teacher/Individual Student Interaction	Items 10-12	[____]	[____]
Dynamism/Enthusiasm	Items 13-15	[____]	[____]
General Teaching Ability	Items 16-18	[____]	[____]
Overload	Items 19-21	[____]	[____]
Structure	Items 22-24	[____]	[____]
Quality of Work	Items 25-27	[____]	[____]
Student-Teacher Rapport	Items 28-30	[____]	[____]
Overall Teaching Ability	Item 31	[____]	[____]

2.] To determine whether the total scores you obtained for each group of items are relatively high, moderate, or low, use the following guidelines.

Low Score: [3-9] Moderate Score [10-14] High [15+]

3.] Examine your total scores for each category and look at how you responded to individual items. What do you see as your strengths and weaknesses? In what areas do you need to improve?

4.] Obtain the average total score for your students on each of the clusters of items shown above. Place your total in the space provided. I often ask 3-4 students in class to help me obtain the scores or I ask the students to calculate them before turning the forms in. I always report back to the class a summary of what I have obtained and what I think I need to do differently in the future. I also ask them to share their perceptions of my analysis.

5.] Have people select 2-3 items they gave high ratings [6 or 7] and low ratings [1 or 2] and share the reasons why. This will provide additional insights into the reasons for the ratings.

6.] If you have time, check your individual item scores against the responses of your students. You can do this informally by comparing your scores to those of selected students or you might want to compute the average score for each item in the class.

and expertise they report possessing relative to someone else. The larger the distance between the two circles, the more they perceive the emotional climate of the relationship as tension- arousing and negative. As this distance becomes closer, the emotional climate is perceived as much more positive.

Figure 1-1 reports the results of one of our studies comparing first- year students and senior social science and math/engineering majors [Grasha, Ichiyama & Kelley, 1986]. Evidently, both the emotional climate and students' self-images vary between first- year and senior students, and such changes depend in part upon a student's academic major. Social science majors showed the least amount of change on both dimensions while math/engineering majors displayed the largest variations in psychological size and distance.

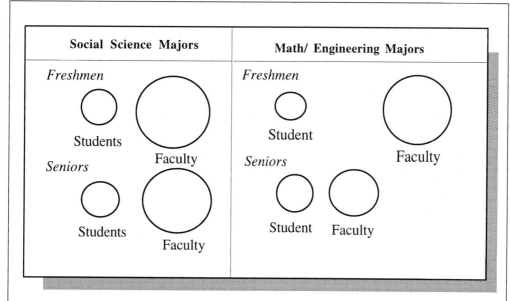

Figure 1-1: Psychological size and distance in faculty-student relationships. [Drawn to 1/4 scale] Social science freshmen and seniors' perceptions of their relationship with faculty were similar. The distance was viewed as friendly and the status-affect rating scale information also showed that both groups held similar perceptions of their knowledge and expertise. Math/Engineering majors viewed their relationship with faculty as much less friendly as freshmen and their psychological size was smaller. As seniors, Math/ Engineering majors rated their own knowledge and expertise higher than freshmen, they were not as much in awe of their faculty, and the psychological distance or emotional climate was friendlier. [Grasha, Ichiyama, & Kelley, 1986]

Other research shows that specific elements of our styles as teachers influence psychological size and distance. In a recent study [Grasha & Gardener, 1991; also reported in Grasha, 1996], college students rated the teaching styles of a faculty member and completed the *Grasha-Ichiyama Psychological Size and Distance Scale* to evaluate that relationship. Faculty members were randomly selected from a list of the names of teachers students were currently taking a course from that term. Multiple regression analysis was used to examine how well the student ratings of faculty behaviors predicted variations in psychological size and distance [measured in millimeters]. The results of this analysis showed that several behaviors in the teaching styles of faculty were associated with changes in psychological size [amount of status, knowledge, & expertise students believed they possessed] and distance [how much positive and negative affect was present in the relationship]. A summary of the results of this study is presented in Table 1-5

Table 1-5
Teaching Style and Student Perceptions of Psychological Size and Distance

The elements of teaching style listed below were associated with increases and decreases in the psychological size of college students and the distance they drew in the relationships they had with faculty.

Elements of Style that Increase Psychological Size

Instructor-Group Interaction	*Instructor Individual Student Interaction*
Encourages discussion Invites students to share ideas Pays attention to whether class is understanding material	Shows interest inn students Relates to students as individuals Respects students

Elements of Style that Decrease Psychological Size

Structure

Followed an outline closely
Proceeded according to schedule
Planned activity of each class in detail.

Elements of Style that Decrease Psychological Distance

General Teaching Ability	*Dynamism/Enthusiasm*
Makes material interesting Stimulates intellectual curiosity Skillful in observing interactions	Behaves in an energetic way Enjoys teaching Displays self-confidence

Instructor-Individual Student Interaction

Shows genuine interest in students
Relates to students as individuals
Respects students

The Roles Teachers Play

Roles are the consistent patterns of thoughts and behaviors we adopt in situations such as the classroom. Roles can be viewed broadly such as when we use the terms teacher, student, father, mother, minister, banker, or police officer. Or, a more general role under close examination often consists of multiple roles occurring together to produce consistent themes in our lives. Thus, the general role of teacher serves as an umbrella term for a network of roles that include such behaviors as advisor, lecturer, evaluator, discussion leader, resource person, and others needed in academic settings.

The thoughts and actions associated with our roles follow certain guidelines that were learned through our past experiences, the expectations others have for our behaviors, and the direct instructions we receive about how to behave. [Grasha, 1987a]. The guidelines for the general role of a student, for example, includes: attending class, taking notes, asking questions, discussing course content inside and outside of class, studying and preparing for exams, and following the requirements and rules of particular courses, majors, and academic institutions. The guidelines for the general role of an instructor includes: selecting the content to teach, designing ways to deliver that content, leading discussions, evaluating the progress of students, and meeting with students to answer questions and to provide guidance in obtaining course requirements.

The Interpretation and Execution of Role Guidelines Vary

The unique ways we interpret and execute role guidelines define our styles as teachers. Two people may try to follow the general guideline that "teachers present information in the classroom." This guideline is clear, but variations exist in how it is executed. One person decides to give a lecture while the other has students present important ideas in a small group format. Afterwards, the groups develop questions about the content that remain and additional points they would like to have clarified. The instructor then uses the remaining class time to respond to student queries. Or, perhaps two instructors decide to lecture. One does so in a dry but well-organized fashion while the other is highly animated but not as well organized. In each case, the guidelines were interpreted and executed differently, thus creating variations in teaching style.

Teachers Play Multiple Roles in the Classroom

Not only do people interpret role guidelines differently, but they also adopt one or more consistent, but distinct, ways of doing so. In effect, these multiple interpretations reflect distinct patterns of thoughts and actions that effectively make the task of teaching one of displaying and managing multiple roles. *The particular roles we play also define our teaching style.*

In a classic research study, Richard Mann and his colleagues [1970] identified the multiple roles teachers play in the classroom. Using thematic analyses of audio tapes and observations of teacher-student interactions, they identified several different roles. Included in the analysis were the teacher as *expert* and *formal authority*. These roles highlighted the content transmitting and the setting of structure and standards functions of college faculty. The *socializing agent role* captured our tendencies to act as guides and gatekeepers to a field of study. When faculty did more listening and less telling and set goals based upon student definitions of their own needs and goals— they were viewed as *facilitators*. The *ego-ideal* role was directed toward getting students to share in the excitement and value of the intellectual inquiry that instructors felt about their field of study. When teachers share their life experiences and other aspects of themselves with students, they had moved into the *teacher as person* component of their role.

Another way to understand the multiple roles teachers play is to examine those needed in order to use specific classroom methods. Table 1-5 describes several roles that my colleagues Barbara Fuhrmann, Susan Montauk, and I have observed in a variety of settings [Fuhrmann & Grasha, 1983; Grasha, 1975; Montauk and Grasha, 1993].

The manner in which the specific roles in Table 1-6 are combined also helps to define our styles as teachers. Typically this occurs because different instructional methods require that teachers assume various modes of thinking and behaving. In effect, to use them successfully, various combinations of these roles must occur. *The demands of the teaching strategy then serve as guidelines for what roles in Table 1-6 are needed and how they should be executed.* For example, the role of content expert will get played out differently in various course designs. In a lecture-discussion format, it occurs in combination with the role of lecturer. In a class that emphasizes small group work, the content expert role will appear through the role of the instructor as a consultant and resource person.

The examples that follow to examine how various instructional processes pull together different roles. Notice how combinations of those roles begin to form different teaching styles.

• Traditional Lecture-Discussion Class

   Focus: Teacher centered with presentations and occasional questions directed toward the class. Exams are the primary determiners of student grades.

   Primary Roles Emphasized: Assigner; Content Expert; Lecturer; Grader; Questioner

Table 1- 6
Roles Needed to Execute Instructional Methods

Activity Designer
Designs activities such as role plays, group projects, simulations, trigger tapes and problems for students to solve.

Active Listener
Listens to the content and feeling of what students are saying to get beneath the surface of issues they are raising.

Actor/Director
Uses dramatic techniques in class to illustrate points and/or to set up role plays to help students simulate the applications or implications of important content points in class.

Assigner
Provides students with explicit and detailed instructions on what each person is required to do to complete course requirements, activities, and projects.

Case Designer/Organizer
Develops new cases and/or pulls together existing materials and cases for students to analyze and discuss.

Coach
Directly observes students in various tasks while giving them advice, encouragement, and feedback to become more effective.

Consultant
Works with students to help them explore appropriate ways to resolve a problem. The consultant role demands that the tendency to offer direct advice be set aside in favor of giving information and suggesting options to assist students in making informed choices for resolving issues and concerns.

Content Expert
Possesses knowledge of essential concepts and facts and organizing it in ways that help students to acquire the information.

Coordinator
Manages and oversees multiple student projects and course activities.

Discussion Facilitator
Uses a discussion to review important information, to discuss issues of clarification or application of points, to stimulate creative and critical thinking about content, or to explore the broader implications of information.

Formative Evaluator
Provides students with timely feedback on an ongoing basis about their strengths and weakness on course assignments and activities.

* Continued on next page

Table 1- 6 [Continued **]**

Grader
Assigns students based to a general performance or proficiency category.

Lecturer
Gives presentations directed toward organizing and exploring critical content points. Presentations in this format are designed for an entire class period.

Materials Designer/Organizer
Develops and gathers handouts and audio, video, and computer materials.

Mini-Lecturer
Gives short presentations to clarify a point or to help students organize and explore an issue. Presentations occur for 5-10 minutes and are supplemented with discussion questions or the use of other activities [e.g., cases, role plays, small group activities].

Negotiator
Explores with students options for how course requirements, assignments, and goals can be achieved. The goal is to find ways to meet teacher and student needs and to resolve differences. Often used when students get behind but also important when alternate ways to finish assignments exist.

Nondirective Facilitator
Encourages students to think for themselves, to develop their own solutions to issues, and to take initiative and accept responsibility for their learning.

Prescriptive Advisor
Gives direct answers to meet student needs for immediate information.

Process Observer
Observes and/or categorizes the interaction patterns in class, the outcomes of course activities, and how well course goals are achieved. Observations are shared with students and the lessons learned are used in future classes.

Questioner
Uses questions to encourage creative and critical thinking and the further exploration of course themes, concerns, and problems.

Resource Manager
Pulls together and effectively uses available resources to teach a course [e.g., outside speakers, videotapes, outside readings, special equipment]

Resource Person
Shares knowledge about how, when, and where students can obtain information or acquire particular skills. Employed when the teacher does not have the information or skill needed and/or when other resources would enhance the student's knowledge.

Role Model
Sets an appropriate example for ways to think about course content, how to solve problems, and how to apply skills.

• Modular Instruction

Focus: Course content broken-up into discrete units. Each module is a package designed for self-study. It may be a case study, a set of readings, a laboratory assignment, a set of problems to solve, or a paper to be completed. A set of modules may be completed in a particular sequence or students may choose from various modules at any particular time. Class time usually reserved for answering questions and helping students to deal with concerns and issues raised in the module. Suggestions for additional readings and resources to help students effectively manage a module are provided as needed.

Primary Roles Emphasized: Assigner; Content Expert; Consultant; Coordinator; Formative Evaluator; Materials Designer; Nondirective Facilitator; Resource Person

---

• Small Group Designs

Focus: Rely on active and collaborative learning experiences. Small groups of students might be given a series of questions, topics, or problems to resolve. Work on tasks may occur within a given session or across multiple sessions. Sharing of the outcomes of assignments with the larger group typically occurs. The instructor then has an opportunity to clarify issues, to answer questions, and to raise additional points for discussion.

Primary Roles Emphasized: Active Listener; Assigner; Consultant; Content Expert; Discussion Facilitator; Evaluator; Mini-Lecturer; Nondirective Facilitator; Process Observer; Questioner

---

• Contract Teaching

Focus: Students contract or form agreements with the instructor about how much work they will do in a course. The contract is often written and it has a clearly understood set of specific responsibilities for both the student and the teacher to fulfill. The amount of work and the types of activities required for particular grades are clearly specified in the contract.

Primary Roles Emphasized: Activity Designer; Content Expert; Coordinator; Evaluator; Materials Designer/ Organizer; Negotiator

---

• Case Studies

Focus: Teaching occurs through case studies that students are required to analyze and discuss in class. Typically students prepare their reactions to cases before class. The instructor helps them to clarify how course ideas apply to a case and encourages students to think critically about the issues raised. Short presentations often used to organize and clarify important outcomes of the case analysis and/or to stimulate new directions for the discussion to take.

Primary Roles Emphasized: Case Designer/Organizer; Listener; Discussion Facilitator; Nondirective Facilitator; Mini-Lecturer; Questioner;

As the examples above illustrate, various instructional processes require that faculty adopt different combinations of roles. From this perspective, the interpretation of role guidelines, as well as the way various teaching related roles are combined and emphasized, define our teaching style. The style that evolves might be considered robust and subsequently applied to all of the courses we teach. For other faculty members, different combinations of roles are employed. Their methods are eclectic, and thus a diverse set of roles are employed to achieve their goals.

Playing Multiple Teaching Roles Creates Stress

Diverse roles contributes to our personal growth. They also make our lives much more complex and are one of the factors that contributes to tension and stress [Grasha, 1987b; Grasha, 1989]. Role tension occurs in three ways.

• *We have more than one role relationship to another person or group.* A colleague assumed the roles of consultant and resource person to a student on career and several classroom issues when interacting with a student. The student's classroom performance was poor and she eventually failed the course. "I felt awkward continuing to be a consultant and resource person afterwards," she said. "Somehow trying to help her decide what courses to take and what career decisions to make was frustrating when I knew she wasn't applying herself in class."

• *People disagree on how a role other than their own should be played.* Students, for example, often have expectations for how faculty members should teach. Such expectations are not always in line with how faculty members interpret their roles. Thus some students enjoy and want the lecturer role. They cannot understand why a teacher might spend so much time trying to be a discussion facilitator, questioner, process observer, and resource person by emphasizing small group projects and discussions.

- *Other people play their roles in ways that are incompatible with our own.* As one professor noted, "My biggest frustration is with students who refuse to play by the rules of the game." He was referring to students who skip class, show up late, fail to meet deadlines, refuse to participate, and otherwise ignore the general role guidelines for a student. This made it more difficult for him to successfully execute his preferred roles as a formative evaluator, consultant, and nondirective facilitator.

My observations suggest that role stress is handled in three ways. *Some teachers redefine the role so that the conflict is eliminated.* My colleague got someone else to advise the student. *Also, problematic relationships are terminated or new expectations are established.* When teachers and students disagree about how a course should be taught, it is easy to say "I'm the teacher and we will do it my way." Trying to blend teacher and student expectations, however, can enhance one's style of teaching. *Some manage to focus on one role and not let the other conflicting role bother them and a few just "grin and bear it."* This is often the strategy of choice when students play their roles in ways that interfere. To cope, most teachers handle students who do not participate by ignoring them and focussing on those who do.

Personality Traits and Teaching Style

Personal dispositions are used to describe teaching style. One approach is the use of personality dimensions identified by Carl Jung [1960; 1976] and the elaborations developed in the work of Isabel Myers and Katherine Briggs [Myers, 1987; Myers, 1990]. A brief description of each dimension appears in Table 1-6. *The characteristics in this table largely reflect our attitudes and interests, ways that we prefer to gather information and make decisions, and the extent to which we need order and structure in our lives.* How such qualities combine in our personality structure is used to describe our styles as teachers.

To begin to understand how these components of personality apply to you, complete Self-Reflection Activity 1-2 before reading further. It contains an instrument I developed to sensitize people to the personality dimensions inherent in Jungian theory. It is based on the research literature correlating what people think, say, and do with their scores on the Myers-Briggs Type Indicator [MBTI]. The MBTI is a well-established and formal psychological test for assessing Jungian concepts. To develop my psychological type index, two expert judges helped me cluster the data from the research literature into each of the dimension of psychological type. Comparisons of the personality profiles from the self-reflection activity to scores on the MBTI in a sample of 95 teachers and students revealed identical profiles on all four dimensions an average of 75% of the time. Identical profiles occurred on three of the dimensions an average of 85% of the time.

The test in the self-reflection activity is a "consciousness raising device" to help us understand the personality characteristics identified in Table 1-7. The MBTI, on the other hand, is a reliable and valid instrument that has several decades of research data to support the dimensions it measures.

Table 1-7
Personality Types

Interests, Attitudes, and Sources of Energy

Extraversion *[E]*
Attitudes and interests oriented towards the external world of actions, people, objects and events.

Introversion *[I]*
Inner subjective orientation towards life. Attitudes and interests are directed towards concepts, ideas, theories, and models of reality.

Preferences for Gathering Information

Sensing *[S]*
Obtaining information from sensory input associated with the immediate, real, and practical facts of experience and everyday life.

Intuition *[N]*
Gathering information by going beyond the immediate experiences of life to consider possibilities, probabilities, and other aspects of people, objects, relationships, and events that are not immediately available to our senses.

How Judgments and Decisions are Made

Thinking *[T]*
Becoming objective, impersonal, logical, looking for causes of events, and the pros and cons of various approaches.

Feeling *[F]*
Subjectively and personally weighing the values of choices and how points of view and decisions affect other people.

Lifestyle Orientations

Judgment *[J]*
Living in a decisive, planned, and orderly manner with strong needs to regulate and control events.

Perception *[P]*
Living in a spontaneous, flexible manner, aiming to understand life and to adapt to the changes that occur in as efficient a manner as possible.

Self-Reflection Activity 1-2
Identifying Your Teaching Style Through Your Personality Type

Turn to the *Psychological Type Index* on pages 27 and 28. Place the edge of a sheet of 8 1/2 x 11 inch paper across the two columns of items on the *Psychological Type Index* beginning at the top of the first page [e.g., the column of E items and I items] Lay the edge so that you can see only one pair of items at a time. *Select the member of each pair that is most like you.* [Do not try to make an absolute judgment about how each item applies to you.] *Select only one member of each pair.*

Scoring

Sum the number of items in each pair of blocks that you checked. To identify your psychological type, use the letter associated with the highest number of items checked in each dichotomy. The letters in each block of items correspond to each of the personality dimensions described in Table 1-7; E [Extravert] - I [Introvert]; S [Sensing] -N [Intuition]; T [Thinking] -F [Feeling]; J [Judgment] -P [Perception]. Thus if you checked ten E items and seven I items, you would label yourself an E. Similarly, checking nine S items and eight N items would categorize you as an S. Use this same procedure for the other pairs. Your profile would be the letters associated with the highest number of items checked [e.g., ENTP; ISFJ; ISTP; ENFJ].

Interpretation

Carl Jung believed that we are born with a preference for one member of each dichotomy. *Naomi Quenk [1993] notes that our psychological health depends upon our ability to develop a clear differentiation between each pair of characteristics.* Otherwise, it would be impossible, for example, to make consistent decisions. Trying to use logical criteria [i.e. a Thinking function] and personal values and concerns simultaneously to decide [i.e., a Feeling function] would likely produce conflict. Similarly, if the Sensing and Intuition functions were not differentiated, it would be difficult to gather information. We cannot attend to both environmental stimuli and mental processes at the same time.

Your profile or psychological type reflects the four personality dimensions you preferred across each dichotomy. There are 16 possible ways to they can be ordered [e.g., INTJ; ESFP; INTP; ENTJ; etc.] The referred or dominant member of each dichotomy is readily seen in our actions [e.g., I, N, T, J]. Such qualities become a personal signature that identifies ourselves to other people. It is important to remember that there is no ideal profile nor is one member of a dichtomy better or worse than the other. People are simply different and the dimensions in the theory help us to identify the ways they differ.

The opposite or inferior side, however, cannot be ignored [e.g., E, S, F, P]. The inferior dimensions may occasionally "slip" into our actions but they normally remain in the background and keep our dominant qualities from becoming too rigid, automatic, and stereotypical. Otherwise, someone who is overly intuitive might imagine using multimedia presentations for the first time. They may discount or ignore the inadequate wiring, lighting, seating, and other features of available rooms to use such equipment.

Self-Reflection Activity 1-2 [Continued]

Interpretation [Continued]

To simplify the interpretation in order to introduce basic ideas about psychological type, the information can be condensed in several ways [Lawrence, 1982; Kiersey and Bates 1984; Short and Grasha, 1995]

One is to focus on each dominant characteristic in the profile and examine how it occurs in your personal makeup and the classroom. To do this, develop a summary of the themes that appear in Table 1-7 and Table 1-8 that apply to you. *For example:* ENFP; [E] Oriented to external world and gives students choices ; [N] Interested in what things could become and encourages students to go beyond the facts; [F] concerned with how decisions affect others and stresses individual work in class and provides constructive feedback; [P] Spontaneous, flexible and comfortable with open ended discussions and small group work.

Another summary of our psychological type combines two of the characteristics that describe ourselves. One such approach was devised by David Kiersey and Marilyn Bates [1984] and is summarized in Table 1-9. The information in this table is based upon their work as well as additional implications of this model in educational settings identified by Lee Harrisberger [1988; 1990]. This scheme is labeled "character temperament types" and relates the Jungian dimensions to four basic temperaments-Dionysian [SP], the Epimethean [SJ], Promethean [NT], and Apollonian [NF].

The temperament model does not simply combine characteristics across the Jungian functions [i.e., E-I; S-N; T-F; or J-P]. "A person becomes an ENFJ, or INFP, or whatever, because of his given temperament rather than because, for example, extraversion somehow combined with intuition" [Kiersey & Bates, p. 28.]. In this model, temperament becomes the core of our personality and acts as a template around which a more detailed psychological type develops.

While grounded in Jungian theory, Kiersey and Bates also acknowledge the contributions of Alfred Adler, Harry Stack Sullivan, Abraham Maslow, Sigmund Freud, and others to their model.

To use the temperament shorthand, do the following:

- *If you did not complete the Psychological Type Inventory,* read the descriptions provided for each temperament in Table 1-9 and select the one you believe is most like you.

- *If you completed the inventory, use the profile obtained to identify your temperament* [i.e., SP; SJ; NT; NF]. Then consult the descriptions provided by the Kiersey-Bates model listed in Table 1-9. They will provide the *missing pieces* not found in the S, J, N, T, and F descriptors of the inventory.

- *Focus on the characteristics in Table 1-9 associated with your profile that best describe you.* Think of situations in your role as a faculty member where they tend to frequently occur. How do they facilitate and hinder your ability to adapt to the demands of teaching?

- *Identify the qualities associated with your profile that occur less frequently in your role as a teacher.* Do you need to work on developing them? What would help you to do this?

Psychological Type Index

Created by Tony Grasha, Ph.D.

Select the member of each pair of items that best describes you.

E _____

___ Prefer to be active.
___ Prefer to work with others.
___ Plunge into new experiences.
___ Relaxed and confident with people.
___ Readily offer my opinions.
___ I'm verbally proficient.
___ Short attention span on tasks.
___ Don't mind being interrupted.
___ Aware of time when working.
___ Have a large breadth of interests.
___ Guided by standards of others.
___ Have multiple relationships.
___ Tend to skip from one task to another.
___ Seek help from others with problems.
___ Act before thinking things through .
___ Use trial and error with problems.
___ Energized more by taking actions.

I _____

___ Prefer to be quiet and reflective.
___ Prefer to work alone.
___ Hold back from new experiences.
___ Less comfortable around others.
___ Ask questions before giving opinion.
___ I'm more proficient in writing.
___ Work intently on tasks.
___ Dislike interruptions.
___ Often lose track of time when working.
___ Known for the depth of my interests.
___ Guided by personal standards.
___ Have limited relationships.
___ Prefer to focus on one task at a time.
___ Try to handle problems by myself.
___ Think long and hard before acting.
___ More systematic approach to issues.
___ Energized more by thinking.

S _____

___ Prefer not to speculate.
___ I hate to wait to do things.
___ Seldom make factual errors.
___ Focus thoughts on the "here and now."
___ Seldom act on my hunches.
___ Focus on the elements of a problem.
___ Tend to be realistic.
___ Like established routines.
___ Like to memorize details and facts.
___ Prefer order and structure in my life.
___ Patient with status quo.
___ Good at checking details.
___ Tend to be practical.
___ Enjoy very stimulating activities.
___ Like a steady routine work schedule.
___ Comfortable with the pace of time.
___ Seldom think about the meaning of life.

N _____

___ Enjoy speculating.
___ I don't mind waiting.
___ Tend to make factual errors.
___ Like to project ideas into the future.
___ Frequently act on my hunches.
___ Focus on the patterns and "big picture."
___ Tend to be imaginative.
___ Impatient with routines.
___ Prefer to learn underlying principles.
___ Prefer less order and structure.
___ Impatient with status quo.
___ Poor at checking details.
___ Tend to be idealistic .
___ Prefer quiet activities in my life.
___ Prefer variations in my work schedule.
___ Uncomfortable with the pace of time.
___ Often think about the meaning of life.

Psychological Type Index

Select the member of each pair of items that best describes you.

T _____

___ Prefer to objectively analyze issues.
___ Rely on facts when deciding.
___ Use objective criteria to decide.
___ There are no exceptions to rules.
___ Prefer logical order in the world.
___ Justice more important than mercy.
___ Tend to be critical of others.
___ Have a skeptical outlook.
___ Decisions best based upon logic.
___ Do not keep diaries/scrapbooks/photos.
___ Logic tends to override my feelings.
___ Not in touch with feelings of others.
___ Brief and business like with others.
___ Offended by illogical thinking.
___ Prefer logical solutions to conflict.
___ Its important to me to be on time.
___ Prefer to plan and follow a schedule.

F _____

___ Prefer to subjectively analyze issues.
___ Focus on my values when deciding.
___ Use subjective and personal criteria.
___ Exceptions to rules must be allowed.
___ Prefer harmony in the world.
___ Mercy more important than justice.
___ Tend to be accepting of others.
___ Have a trusting outlook.
___ Impact of choice on others more important.
___ Keep diaries/scrapbooks/photo albums.
___ Feelings override sense of logic.
___ In touch with feelings of others.
___ Display personal qualities with others.
___ Offended by lack of feeling in others.
___ Seek personal ways to resolve conflict.
___ Being late is not such a big deal.
___ Dislike planning and following schedules.

J _____

___ Prefer specific plans in my life.
___ Not a very spontaneous person.
___ Prefer schedules and organization.
___ Do not handle uncertainty well.
___ Seek closure on issues.
___ Dislike unexpected events to occur.
___ Use a lot of "shoulds" and "oughts."
___ Generally good at managing my time.
___ Have enduring friendships.
___ Like to make decisions.
___ Tend to not over commit to projects.
___ Complete the projects I begin.
___ Customs and traditions are important.
___ More decisive than curious.
___ Can't wait to complete tasks.
___ Meet deadlines on tasks.
___ Believe in "the way things ought to be."

P _____

___ Prefer to leave my options open.
___ Tend to be a spontaneous person.
___ Prefer less order and flexibility.
___ Handle uncertainty well.
___ Resist closure to obtain more ideas.
___ Comfortable with unexpected events.
___ Have a "live and let live" attitude.
___ Not very good at time management.
___ Tend to change friendships.
___ Have trouble making decisions.
___ Tend to take on too many projects.
___ Have difficulty completing projects.
___ Customs and traditions not as important.
___ More curious than decisive.
___ Tend to procrastinate completing tasks.
___ Flexible in meeting deadlines.
___ Able to accept things as they are.

Table 1-8
Classroom Preferences and
Psychological Type

Introverted Types
Prefer to structure assignments and to exercise direct control over classroom proceedings and assignments. Also are somewhat inflexible in how a class session is conducted and are concerned with their personal goals for the class.

Extraverted Types
More likely to give students a broader range of choices about what to study and how to learn. Are more open with students and able to detect changes in students' attention, performance on activities, and their expectations for the course.

Sensing Types
Emphasize the facts and the acquisition of concrete skills. Use activities that allow students a narrow range of choices.

Intuitive Types
Encourage students to go beyond the facts, to gain an understanding of the relationships between different ideas, and to consider broader implications. Try to help students discover new insights into concepts and had how ideas can be transformed to become something new and different. Give students a range of activities and more likely to move freely around the room while teaching.

Thinking Types
Provide students with very little comment, praise, or critique regarding their behavior. Have very little "off task contact" with students. More attentive to their own behaviors than to those of their students and have students focusing more on what the teacher does. Deal with the class as a whole entity rather than examining the work and accomplishments of individual students.

Feeling Types
Communicate the importance of each student's individual work. Provide consistent praise as well as constructive positive and negative feedback on the work students complete. Assists students with examining their values and the role personal values play in making decisions and solving discipline related problems. Allow students to spend more time on individual work and projects. Able to focus on the needs of more than one student at a time.

Judgment Types
Repetitious, unidirectional, orderly, and controlling in their teaching methods. Emphasize adherence to structure, schedules, and deadlines. Prefer assignments and group work where a specific product or outcome is produced. Impatient with students who are not organized or who procrastinate doing assignments.

Perception Types
Employ classroom procedures that encourage student participation. They usually teach in a more flexible manner and are often spontaneous in what they do. More comfortable with open-ended discussions and asking students to engage in small group discussions and tasks.

* Information in this table represent themes abstracted from Lawrence [1993] and Firestone [1993].

Table 1-9
Identifying Your Psychological Temperament

Which one of the following temperaments best describes you?

Dionysian Temperament: Sensation-Perception (SP)

- Adventurer and likes action.
- Active and focuses on doing.
- Impulsive and uninhibited.
- Spontaneous.
- Exciting, cheerful, lighthearted.
- Bored with the status quo.
- "Easy come, easy go."
- Seeks stimulation.
- Optimistic.

Common Teaching Areas
Arts, Crafts, Sports, Drama
Music, Recreation

Preferred Teaching Methods
Group Projects, Demonstrations,
Shows, Performances, Games,
AV Materials, Practical Tests

Teaching Style

Stresses involvement of students and interested in development of freedom, spontaneity, and the creative side of learners. Can be counted on to do the unexpected. Tries to develop a "seize the moment" attitude. Does entertaining presentations and may shift gears in mid-course. Displays an unpredictable side of self in teaching.

Epimethean Temperament: Sensation-Judging (SJ)

- Responsible, dependable.
- Organized, methodical.
- Focus on outcomes.
- Parental attitude toward others.
- Believes in hierarchical structures,
- Likes rules and regulations.
- Somewhat pessimistic.
- Titles and entitlement important.
- Has a sense of duty, service, and maintains a historical outlook..

Common Teaching Areas
Agriculture, Business, History,
Political Science, Geography

Preferred Teaching Methods
Lectures, Demonstrations,
Tests/Quizzes, Recitation

Teaching Style

Wants to develop students' sense of usefulness and place in society. Views teaching as an opportunity to pass on a cultural heritage to new generations of learners. Likes obedient students and has well-established routines in the classroom. Teaching planned in advance. Typically a firm disciplinarian who gives effective feedback and criticism. Good Socratic teacher and acts as a role model for students.

Table 1- 9 [Continued]

Promethean Temperament: Intuitive-Thinking (NT)

- Independent, loner, intellectual.
- Fascinated with attempts to establish power over nature.
- Badgers self about errors.
- Pushes self to improve.
- Seldom feels they know enough.
- Likes to get things started and then turn over tasks to others.
- Future oriented, workaholic, self-sufficient, and goal oriented.

Common Teaching Areas

Philosophy, Science, Technology, Communication, Math, Linguistics

Preferred Teaching Methods

Lectures, Independent Projects, Laboratory Reports

Teaching Style

Pushes students to take course content seriously. Not as sensitive to the emotional climate of the classroom. Possesses high standards and tends to be impersonal in his or her approach to students. Does not give feedback easily and may leave some students wondering where they stand. Perceives only a few learners as working up to standards.

Apollonian Temperament: Intuitive-Feeling (NF)

- Group oriented, interactive, and communicative.
- People oriented.
- Wants to make a difference in the world.
- Values opinions and feelings of others.
- Seeks broader value issues.
- Searches for deeper meaning.
- Hypersensitive to conflict.
- Sensitive to sarcasm and ridicule.

Common Teaching Areas

Humanities, Social Science, Theater, Music, Languages, Speech, Theology

Preferred Teaching Methods

Group Projects, Discussion Modes Simulations, Self-Discovery

Teaching Style

Possesses personal charisma and commitment to teaching. Concerned about welfare of students and tries to form one to one relationships with them. Concerned with the values that underlie course content. Impatient with manufactured classroom materials and prefers to spend time to create his or her own materials. Uses large group, small group, and individualized instructional modes with equal comfort. Prefers, however, to use small group activities and workshop formats when teaching.

There are other shorthands for understanding one's personality and teaching style from a Jungian point of view than those described in Self-Reflection Activity 1-2 and Tables 1-7 and 1-8. One in particular deserves a brief mention and that is the use of what Carl Jung referred to as *cognitive orientations*. These are the four combinations of the perceptual and decision making functions in his theory [i.e., ST, SF, NT, and NF]. An excellent discussion of cognitive orientations and their implications for understanding teaching and learning styles can be found in the work of Gordon Lawrence [1982; 1993].

Jungian theory and related concepts provide a rationale for identifying and combining personality characteristics in order to describe our teaching styles. As with any approach to personality, it is important to use the descriptions obtained as general guidelines to understanding "who we are." Every perspective tries to simplify human nature in the interests of providing a useful portrait. *In the process, they inevitably miss important components of our psychological makeup.* In the final analysis, our styles as human beings and as teachers are always more than any single personality theory can hope to describe. Their approach to our personal makeup is not etched in concrete. *Thus, what particular personality theorists say about us must always be tempered with the knowledge that there is much more that could be said.*

Archetypal Forms of Teaching Style

William Reinsmith [1992;1994] notes that the important aspect of teaching is not the skills and methods employed. Instead, the idea of teacher *presence* and the *encounter* with students must be examined when trying to understand teaching style. Taking a phenomenological perspective, Reinsmith states that, "A teaching encounter is not simply a group of skills or methods assembled in a particular way. It may engender these, but the 'meeting' between teacher and student[s] has a form of being of its own [Reinsmith, 1994, p. 132]. *The relational dimension must be placed at the center of the teaching act.* It is not that the relational aspects of teaching go unmentioned during discussions of teaching in the literature. While acknowledged, they rarely hold center stage.

In effect, our presence as teachers and the responses that accompany us create a teaching encounter. Within that encounter certain predictable interaction patterns occur, and when sustained over time, the encounters become a teaching form. Based on an extensive review of the literature on teaching style, he identified nine archetypal forms that occur in the context of five modes of relating to students. These are described in Table 1-10.

Each teaching form is invested with a particular teaching presence that makes it possible for the learner to respond in a manner appropriate for that form. *This form cannot account for everything that occurs in the classroom. But it does produce recognizable patterns in how students and teachers interact and thus has a permanence to it that transcends an individual teacher.* Observing that a teacher works within a form is both to preserve the individuality of the teacher and to see beyond this to something more archetypal and enduring.

Table 1-10
Archetypal Forms in Teaching

Presentational Mode
Archetypal Forms

Disseminator / Transmitter: Passes on bits of information to the students. This form can be described as 'teaching as telling'. The most reductive form of teaching in that students and teachers become machine like and are set apart from one another.

Lecturer / Dramatist: Employs dramatic techniques in order to engage or connect with the students in a more impacting way. Teacher comes across in a vibrant manner and the performance factor is emphasized.

Initiatory Mode
Archetypal Forms

Inducer / Persuader: Aware of the students' interests and begins to suggest the possibilities of new attitudes and approaches that are different from those to which students currently adhere. Introduces an element of reciprocity and two-way communication between the teacher and the student.

Inquirer / Catalyst: Directly confronts and questions the student. Challenges students to identify and question their own basic beliefs.

Dialogic Mode
Archetypal Form

Dialogist: Teacher no longer dominates the interaction and the student and the teacher play equal parts in defining the encounter. Classroom procedures often explore student and/or teacher determined topics.

Elicitive Mode
Archetypal Forms

Facilitator / Guide: Aids the students in discovering their potential, and in gaining an understanding of the knowledge which they possess.

Witness / Abiding Presence: Active role of the teacher is diminished. Acts as a witness to students attempts to bring their knowledge to the threshold of articulation. Begins to identify with the learner yet still able to remain apart as students are given full existential freedom. Teacher seen as a role model for possibilities for their own growth.

Apophatic Mode
Archetypal Forms

Learner: Recognizes own lack of knowledge and is willing to learn along side of students. Teacher abandons the pretension to teach and views role as that of a learner. A breakdown in the distance between teacher and learner has occurred.

Absence of Teacher: The teacher has blown out the flame of his or her influence and that flame now resides within the student. Teacher has given over the teaching self in an act of pedagogical love.

The teaching forms described in Table 1-10 represent a continuum. Reinsmith sees this as an ideal sequence that teachers progress through rather than a hopscotch movement they take in response to changes in classroom situations. Phenomenologically, teaching involves a succession of encounters where particular relationships are established between college faculty and their students. Those in the earlier stages of the continuum [i.e., , the Presentational and Initiatory modes] are characterized by a strong teacher presence and less two-way communication in the exchange of ideas. Later stages [i.e., the Dialogic and Elicitive] involve much more reciprocity in the interaction while the Apophatic views the teacher as becoming a learner and the student is set free to learn independently. In effect, the nature of the *teacher presence* and the encounters change and move gradually from less intense engagements toward those that are intellectually and educationally intimate. Eventually, the teaching presence comes to reside fully in the learner. Both the instructor and the student are newly created through each of the stages in the encounter.

Each form according to Reinsmith has its own rhythm and inner dynamics. In the real world of teaching, however, they are interconnected and entwined within each other. One central form still manages to dominate depending upon the particular stage of the teacher's growth and the instructional possibilities allowed by the environment. The forms also are fictions in the sense that they allow us to examine particular aspects of teaching style but the idealized process of growth inherent in the model rarely occurs. It is likely that environmental factors may relegate a teacher to an earlier stage of the continuum for years or perhaps an entire career. Regardless of how the model applies to a given faculty member, we can only teach by inhabiting one of these archetypal forms. This form becomes the dominant structure that guides and directs our encounters with students.

Metaphors as Representations of Teaching Style

The essence of metaphor is the expression of one thing in terms of another. In this regard, a variety of analogies, similes, visual models, and other figurative devices have been used to describe the teaching styles of college faculty. For my purposes, I have grouped all of the latter entities into the category of metaphor in order to explore basic representations of everyday reality. One of my interests has been in exploring the types of metaphors college faculty and students use to describe the teaching-learning process. [Grasha, 1990b; 1990c; 1993].

My research program in this area has three goals. One is to identify the metaphors that faculty and students use to describe their roles in the classroom. The second has been to translate those metaphors into representations of the personal models college faculty and students possess about fundamental principles that underlie teaching and learning processes. The third goal is to examine how such models guide and direct their actions of teachers and students. *Thus, I employ metaphor as a means of describing teaching style, as a conceptual model that accounts for principles about teaching and learning, and as a mental construct that guides and directs the thoughts and actions of people.* The latter two uses of metaphor are presented in the discussion of developing a conceptual base for teaching in Chapter 3.

My purpose here is to outline how college faculty express their styles as teachers through metaphor. One study that was influential in stimulating my research program was conducted by Howard Pollio [1986]. He asked 800 faculty and graduate students at the University of Tennessee to send him examples of analogies, similes, and other figurative devices they used to describe the teaching learning process. He reported that a thematic analysis of this information revealed that three categories of metaphor accounted for the majority of the responses. They were:

- *Containers*

    Knowledge is viewed as a substance and the instructor is a container filled with content and facts. The student is perceived as a vessel wanting to be filled up. The metaphor of the mother robin feeding her young is one example as is the "teacher as snack machine" metaphor generated by a participant in a recent workshop. There is nothing necessarily limiting about such descriptions of teaching style. After all, teachers may contain nutritious substances that can help learners to grow and develop. On the other hand, the substance in the container may not be viewed by all students as nutrition. Two students in my research program described what they received from teachers as "junk food" and as "bad tasting medicine that you don't want to take but deep down inside you know it's good for you."

- *Journey-Guide*

    Knowledge is perceived as a perspective on the horizon. The teacher guides students on their journey. Students need to follow a course, must overcome obstacles and hurdles, and if a good course of study is designed, they will come to the end of their journey. The metaphors of a "gentle guide taking travelers through the wilderness" and "captain of the Starship Enterprise taking people through outer space to explore new universes" capture teaching styles in this category. Of course, some students do not always see such guidance as helpful. One noted that if teachers were guiding them on a "great interplanetary adventure," then they sometimes felt like they were "lost in space."

- *Master-Disciple*

    Knowledge is a skill or habit to be learned. The instructor trains students and the students ideally do what they are told without questioning the master. The master teachers list include *Socrates, Yoda, Mother Teresa,* and a wide range of others. While some faculty may view their teaching styles in this way, less than two percent of the more than 1500 metaphors students have generated in my research program touch on Master-Disciple themes. Perhaps it relates to their stage of development but undergraduates do not view themselves as disciples to great masters.

The themes of Containers, Journey-Guides, and Master-Disciple also appear in the more than 700 metaphors of teaching style that college faculty participating in workshops with me have generated. In my experience, the metaphors also go beyond the three categories. This can be seen in some of my favorite metaphors I have collected from college faculty. They include:

- Player-coach
- Matador
- Bartender
- Attorney before a jury
- Director of a play
- Fairy godmother
- Lion tamer
- Rabbi
- Swiss Army knife
- General leading troops into battle
- Mother duck leading ducklings
- Gardener
- Midwife
- Tornado
- Evangelist
- Entertainer
- Choreographer
- Tour bus driver with passengers
  who keep their window curtain closed

Self-Reflection Activity 1-3
Identifying Your Metaphor for Teaching

What metaphor describes your style as a teacher?

One of the devices I use to help people develop their metaphor for teaching is the WIF process. WIF is an acronym for **W**ords-**I**mages-**F**eelings. Describing the words-images-and feelings that your teaching elicits within you is a useful first step in discovering the "guiding metaphor" for your teaching style.

The term "guiding metaphor" is used to indicate that various needs, attitudes, values, and beliefs underlie the metaphors we create. Thus, when someone describes their teaching style as a "gardener," then there are ways that they think and behave that are different from someone who sees him or herself as a "Lion Tamer." The role of "guiding metaphors" in the teaching-learning process are described in more detail in Chapter 3. For now, complete the WIF process shown in Table 1-11 to identify the metaphor that describes your style.

Table 1-11
The WIF Process for Faculty to Generate
Guiding Metaphors

WIF Process [Words-Images-Feelings]: Think about one of the courses you teach for a moment. For the next couple of minutes, sit back and relax and imagine yourself teaching that class. Focus on what the students are like, how you behave, and important events in this course. *In the space provided below, list several words, images, and feelings that you would use to describe this course.*

Words: (e.g., traditional, cutting edge, pedestrian, innovative, etc.)

Images: (e.g., carnival, funeral, peaceful glen, exciting movie)

Feelings: (e.g., anxious, happy, excited, frustrated, etc.)

1.] Summarize what you have written above into a *guiding metaphor.* That is, an integrated/summary metaphor that includes many of the themes inherent in the words, images, and feelings that you have about the course. For example, this class was like "parents taking actions to insure that their children have what they need to get ahead in life" "working a difficult puzzle and not being able to find a solution," or "a ship visiting different ports of call where everyone on board gains from the experience." List your *guiding metaphor* below.

2.] What are the teaching techniques that support your *guiding metaphor?* For example, the parents taking actions" metaphor is seen in the fact that I tell students what they have to know, I dictate what assignments they will do, and I do this because I have more insights into what it takes to get ahead in the field than they do." *List the elements of the class that support your guiding metaphor.*

3.] Think about the ways that this class is similar and different from others that you teach. Would the same guiding metaphor apply? Or, would it have to be modified or changed? If so, indicate how.

Epilogue

Themes and Variations

There is no single satisfactory way of defining teaching style. One way to approach the issue is to define it in terms of the elements of style that appear in the words of various authors in the literature. An examination of prominent approaches in this chapter included:

- *An exploration of the distinctive general modes of classroom behavior.* Such things as the teachers ability to generate intellectual excitement and to develop interpersonal rapport with students appear to be pervasive qualities of style.

- *The characteristics associated with respected and popular teachers.* The qualities identified vary among individuals designated as models of good teaching. It appears that some people are able to put together combinations of personal characteristics and instructional practices that work exceedingly well in the classroom and that develop reputations for them as outstanding teachers.

- *Behaviors common to all college faculty.* Quantitative research on style has identified categories of classroom behaviors that occur in the behaviors of all teachers. These include such things as faculty members' ability to organize information, display enthusiasm, and to provide the structure students need to learn. Student rating scales of instructor behaviors are often used to give teachers a student perspective on how well they engage in such behaviors. Because everyone is assessed against the same yardstick, ratings also allow comparisons among individuals and groups of faculty to be made.

- *Sometimes style is synonymous with the teaching methods that a faculty member employs.* Some are called "dynamic lecturer," "effective discussion leader," "case study teacher," and other labels are used to identify their style. In each case, the definition of style reflects a particular instructional process. Such techniques, however, can tell us more about a person than what methods they prefer. Faculty members must take some risks in using them and the methods help to identify teacher attitudes about active learning.

- *The roles played in teaching also identify our styles.* Faculty roles in the classroom include such things as the expert, ego-ideal, evaluator, materials designer, and nondirective facilitator, When used alone or in various combinations, the style adopted is responsive to the needs of the classroom environment.

• *Archetypal forms of teaching appear in the interactions between students and teachers.* Examples include the teacher as disseminator, inquirer/catalyst, dialogist, witness/abiding presence, and learner. Each reflects stages of growth for teachers who ideally would move from dominating interactions with students, to sharing and discussing information, and eventually to becoming a learner themselves.

• *Various personality traits have been employed to catalogue the styles of college teachers.* Those based on ideas from Carl Jung's theory of personality are widely employed in higher education. An instructor's style in this model represents combinations of one of the poles on each of the dimensions of extraversion-introversion; sensing-intuition; thinking-feeling; and judging-perceiving. Teachers' preferred instructional methods also vary as a function of their personality type.

• *Metaphors for how faculty see the teaching-learning process also provide insights into our styles as teachers.* Faculty report seeing themselves as containers ready to fill students with knowledge, as guides taking students on a journey, and as masters with disciples to train. They also describe themselves as *matadors, evangelists, midwives, entertainers, and gardeners.* Each metaphor has particular needs, attitudes, values, and beliefs reflected within it. Thus, such metaphors for style also serve as a personal model that conceptualizes important principles of teaching and learning and that ultimately guides and directs the actions of teachers in the classroom.

There are two problems with current formulations of style. One is that they are largely descriptive of "what qualities teachers possess " and/or "what they do in the classroom." *What is missing from such models are the specific actions someone might take to adopt, enhance, or modify the style they already possess.* For example, it is possible that someone might want to become more enthusiastic, to generate intellectual excitement, to develop better rapport with students, or to become better organized and clear in their presentations. Or, they might want to experiment with the qualities of extraversion, intuition, or feeling in their approach to teaching. Some may decide that they need to be more of an *ego-ideal, dialogist, inquirer or catalyst, Yoda, or Midwife* to help their students to learn. How to make such changes, and the variables one would have to take into account to do so, generally are not included in these models.

The models discussed in this chapter largely assume that people already possess certain qualities and the model builder is simply identifying what is already there. Models based on the work of Jung's theory of personality argue that we are born with particular personality or psychological type preferences. Thus we are "hard-wired" to behave in certain ways. Other models such as Reinsmith's hold open the possibility for teachers to adopt different archetypal forms as they mature in their roles. While this is possible,

Reinsmith notes that forces in the academic environment [e.g., the reward structure, experience with various forms, expectations of students] may lock people into teaching in certain preferred archetypal forms. Presumably, if faculty members could manipulate or use such environmental forces to their advantage, numerous possibilities for growth are likely to emerge. The other models discussed in this chapter generally assume that "what is--is." Instead of dealing with issues of how to change style, they emphasize particular styles, their characteristics, and their implications for classroom processes.

This latter comment is not meant to put down or to discount the contributions of these models for understanding teaching style. They were largely designed to be descriptive and not necessarily prescriptive. Thus, they cannot be blamed for things they were not designed to do in the first place. Existing models do inform us about important elements of style and how they normally appear in people who possess such qualities. By identifying teaching methods that people who possess such qualities use, they at least point others with similar dispositions in the direction of instructional practices to consider. Modifying and changing one's style, however, turns out in my experience to be a much larger issue than simply identifying the elements of style we currently possess and then deciding what elements we might want to add. To modify, change, and to even enhance our current style involves attending to several things:

- *We need to develop a better sense of "Who I am as a teacher and what do I want to become."* This involves self-reflection directed toward getting in touch with our personal values as instructors; understanding the reasons we resist making changes in our styles; identifying how ready and committed we are to change; and the psychological factors within us that facilitate and hinder our ability to vary our styles as teachers.

- *Teaching processes should reflect a conceptual base or philosophy of teaching and thus we need to examine our teaching philosophy.* Included here are principles, concepts, and assumptions about teaching, learning, and human nature that guide and direct how we teach. Many teachers are unaware of many elements in their conceptual base. Yet, it continues to influence how they teach. Keeping it "out of sight and out of mind" does not make it go away.

  Our underlying philosophy of teaching must be explicit. Variations in current instructional practices that are designed without regard to a philosophy of teaching are intellectually hollow. Our styles as teachers must be consistent with an underlying philosophy of teaching and indeed some variations in teaching first involve modifying this conceptual base.

- *A prescriptive model for identifying, modifying, and enhancing our teaching style should be examined by anyone contemplating change.* In my experience, when people work through the issues identified above, there is still work that needs to be done. There is a need for additional guidance regarding what instructional practices to select, how to use them effectively, and what beliefs, skills, and abilities are needed to adopt particular styles.

The three issues identified above are an integral part of the content of the remaining chapters of this book. Chapters 2 and 3, for example, examine self-reflection and the considerations involved in managing personal change in teaching. How to develop a conceptual base and the elements involved in a personal philosophy of teaching are discussed in Chapter 3. The final chapters of this book present an integrated model of teaching style and what elements within the model must be manipulated in order to enhance or modify our styles.

There is one additional issue that must be explored in any attempt to examine and consider changes in our styles as teachers. This is the role of the student in the teaching-learning enterprise.

Teaching Styles and Learning Styles: "You Can't Have One Without the Other"

Information about teaching style is only one-half of the teacher-student interaction. William Reinsmith noted in his model of archetypal forms that a instructor's *"presence"* and *"encounter"* with students is essential to understanding style. Variations in such encounters in the amount of two-way communication and mutual sharing of ideas are what distinguish one archetypal form from another. The forms essentially depend upon instructors and students adopting particular styles of teaching, learning, and communicating in order to be successful. Such things do not magically appear. They develop through changes in teacher and student perceptions of each other, their actions toward each other, and the "give and take" inherent in their encounters.

Just as professors have preferred ways of teaching, students have similar preferences for how they wish to learn. *These dispositions are labeled learning styles.* This term refers to those personal qualities that influence a student's ability to acquire information, to interact with peers and the teacher, and otherwise participate in learning experiences. A variety of cognitive, social factors, motives, emotional, problem solving abilities , memory and perceptual processes, and information processing capabilities have been used to identify and label the learning styles of students [Grasha, 1993; 1990b].

Learning styles help to shape the encounters students have with teachers. In effect, the "teaching-learning interaction" is more of a "teacher-student transaction." *Both parties are involved in attempts to mold each other into mutually beneficial forms of relating.* Because of their higher status in a hierarchy, teachers often have in such encounters more of their needs met.

Yet, students are not powerless in their encounters with faculty. To get what they want, they may resist a style of teaching, avoid class, pretend to play along, plead, give rationale arguments to justify being treated differently, or directly confront teachers with examples of how their needs in the enterprise are not being met.

Fortunately, there is another approach. Teachers can explore ways to accommodate variations in student styles in their teaching. *To do this, the styles of students must be acknowledged and acted upon.* The term acknowledged is used because, in my experience, differences in learning styles are not always recognized. The result is that some faculty treat students as if they were all alike. One of my colleagues, for example, teachers his advanced graduate seminars largely by lecturing. He teaches advanced students in the same manner as those in his introductory course.

Recognition of student styles, however, is not enough. Sometimes faculty recognize differences in the personal qualities of students but fail to act upon this knowledge. One professor noted how the continuing education students she taught had considerable more life experiences and were more independent than traditional students. She was not sure how to capitalize on these differences so both groups were taught alike.

Others acknowledge variations in learning styles and take actions to modify their styles as teachers accordingly. Some people try to teach first-year classes differently than senior level or graduate seminars. Others recognize that gender and cultural-ethnic differences exist among students. Thus, they present appropriate works of male and female scholars as well as those who represent minority and other cultural-ethnic groups. Some teachers accommodate cultural differences in interaction patterns by stressing collaborative learning and work to build rapport with those students who prefer a less distant teacher.

Similarly, some faculty design their courses with a recognition that students vary in their needs for structure, independence, collaboration, empowerment, hands-on experiences, teamwork, surface and deep processing of information, as well as obtaining information through auditory, visual, and kinesthetic sensory channels. To meet student needs for structure some faculty members organize detailed syllabi, they take care to insure their presentations are well organized and they plan each class session much like a coach prepares a game plan. Small group activities and team projects are designed to meet student needs for collaboration and teamwork. Options in what assignments to complete and when they can be finished help meet student needs to feel empowered or in control over some aspects of the classroom environment. Assignments and classroom activities that stress critical and creative thinking are purposely programmed into the course to give students a chance to express such needs. Finally, presentations that emphasizes auditory, visual, and hands-on or practical exercises help to accommodate students' with different sensory preferences.

An important reason for trying to accommodate learning style differences is that discrepancies between teacher and student styles are often a source of conflict, tension , and misunderstanding. It is not so much that people are different that produces the problems. Rather, it is a failure to acknowledge differences, to understand them, and for teachers and students to look for ways to accommodate variations in their personal qualities. Unfortunately, when problems arise, the tendency to see each other as different is replaced with a perception that one person is somehow better than another. Faculty often blame students for all the difficulty and fail to recognize that both parties to any interaction are to varying degrees responsible.

An examination of how teachers and students differ on the same stylistic qualities helps us to see what happens when differences are not dealt with effectively. Earlier in this chapter, concepts from Jung's personality theory were used to describe teaching style. The same dimensions also have been used to identify the learning preferences or styles of students [Campbell & Davis, 1990; Lawrence, 1993; McCaulley, 1981]. Not surprisingly, teachers and students often vary in significant ways. This can be seen in the information presented in Table 1-11 which was compiled from data in Campbell [1986]; Cooper and Miller, [1991]; Firestone, [1993]; and Hadley, [1993].

Table 1-12
Distribution of
Personality Type in the Classroom

	Faculty	Students
Extraverted	46%	70%
Introverted	54%	30%
Sensing	36%	70%
Intuitive	64%	30%
Thinking	50%	50%
Feeling	50%	50%
Judging	63%	55%
Perceiving	37%	45%

I typically find that the discrepancies between faculty and their students on the dimensions of introversion and intuition are particularly problematic for faculty. As shown in Table 1-12, compared to the average college student, college faculty are overrepresented on these two types. In effect faculty interests and energy are largely captured by the inner world of ideas and they are more willing to consider possibilities for things that are not immediately apparent or available to the senses. Most college teachers also have the capacity to formulate hypotheses, to anticipate expected outcomes, and to formulate the implications of existing ideas and data from their disciplines.

While such qualities are ideal for scholarship, they often clash with the more extraverted and sensing qualities of students. Unlike many of their instructors, most students get their energy from the world of people, objects and events. They prefer to see, touch, and feel things in order to gather information. Their orientation is more to the hands-on experiences and the practical implications of issues. Theoretical concerns and analysis is typically one of their strong points.

Thus, when faculty become excited about theoretical and conceptual issues, most students are looking for concrete and clear examples of terms and concepts. While some faculty may be satisfied with a rich verbal description of a point, many students want to see, hear, or touch something that is a representation of the conceptual point. When teachers become too theoretical and conceptual, the majority of their students are often lost. Deep intellectual analysis is not their strong suit.

Unfortunately in my experience, college teachers often do not recognize such gaps in teaching and learning style. If anything, many believe there is something wrong with the students. "I tried my best but most of them just could not get it," is a common complaint. From the point of view of students, the situation is interpreted differently. "I don't know what's wrong with my instructors, the things they were talking about just went over my head." Some faculty come to the conclusion that "most students just don't have the intellectual capacity to be in college," while some students decide that "too many faculty have their heads in the sky."

The issue is not that some ways of thinking are better than others. Rather, all of us are simply different. It would be helpful if instructors thought more about the cognitive and other learning style differences between themselves and their students. Students are much more able to think conceptually than most college faculty think. Beverly Firestone [1993], for example, argues that what most students need are concrete examples and hands-on experiences to stimulate their conceptual thinking. She reports that this goal can be obtained by activities such as demonstrations, laboratory assignments, student research projects, building two and three dimensional models of theories, designing concept maps, analyzing cases and personal experiences, and the use of role plays and simulations. Generally any activity that turns "abstract issues into concrete realities" will help to close this gap in student and teacher styles.

How to adopt a teaching style that captures the extraversion and sensing aspects of student learning styles is an important issue in the design of classroom instruction. For those faculty who are overrepresented on the introversion and intuitive dimensions, however, this is not easy to do. *Extraverted and sensing modes of teaching are at odds with their preferred ways of thinking, so needed changes are less likely to occur.* Those modes simply are not valued as much. Instead, there is evidence that college teachers may focus their energies on those students who are most like them. Thus, the need to change is negated because a subset of the students can, as one teacher told me, "get the material in the way that I prefer to give it." One intriguing research finding shows that students learning style profiles on the Myers-

Briggs Type Indicator that matches their teachers' styles tend to get higher grades than those who are different [Hadley, 1993; Sternberg, 1993].

Similarly, teachers with a more extraverted and sensing style may have difficulty communicating with those students who are introverted and intuitive. The latter want more intellectual depth in a course, and in the words on one student, "fewer Mickey Mouse activities that are a waste of my time."

Finally, differences among faculty and students on the judging and perceiving dimensions can produce problems. Typically this occurs due to the conflict between an instructor with a judging style wanting assignments completed in a timely, orderly, and precise manner. Those students who are perceiving types, and who are not as concerned with completing assignments in a timely manner, typically find themselves at odds with such teachers.

Overall, growth in teaching and learning involves a willingness to stretch ourselves. Jung's theory noted that people have preferences on each dichotomy [e.g., E-I; S-N; T-F; J-P]. However, the other pole of each dichotomy was present at an unconscious level although not as well developed. Sometimes it slips into consciousness and we might say, "I've never acted like that before." Or, "I guess I was just beside myself" At times, experiencing our least preferred styles can become a growth producing experience provided it occurs in a nurturing and supportive environment. It gives us the opportunity to see possibilities for ourselves that the normally dominant poles of our personality prevent us from experiencing.

Thinking and intuitive teachers, for example, need to work on building the feeling and sensing sides of themselves. In much the same way, students with extraverted and sensing learning styles could benefit by activities that put them in touch with the introverted and intuitive side of themselves. *The goal is not to make one type into the other. Nor is it to gain a balance in the strength or energy devoted to each.* Rather, it is to provide experiences where people can sample and identify with the less pronounced aspects of their personal makeups. In the process, they may also begin to understand the frames of reference of others who differ from them on those qualities.

Things you can do in your teaching to stretch yourself in experiencing personal qualities you normally are unaware of can be seen in Tables 1-8 and 1-9. *Trying some of those teaching methods demands that we pay attention to processes that use aspects of the inferior or less dominant side of our personality.* In much the same way, the information in Table 1-13 highlights several personality types of students that can be translated into classroom processes. This is another way of adding variety and "stretching" yourself as a teacher. *You then could focus on using methods within and across class sessions that match the dominant qualities of your students. Or, instructional processes that made students occasionally engage the less dominant sides of their personalities could be employed.*

Table 1-13
Student Personality Type, Temperaments, and Classroom Processes

Personality Type

Extraversion
Group activities and teaching processes that engage psychomotor skills. Role plays, simulations, computer work, and interactions with peers.

Introversion
Individual work on problems, case studies, position papers, and other assignments that involve verbal reasoning. Prefers time to think about issues before being asked to offer an opinion. Thus time for private reflection should be built into classroom activities.

Sensing
Concrete tasks that stress the practical applications or implications of material. Likes problems that require linear strategies to solve them.

Intuition
Theoretical and conceptual problems and activities where the relationship among diverse elements must be drawn together.

Thinking
Likes to use rules, laws, and procedures. Prefers assignments that can be analyzed objectively and where discipline related criteria can be used to determine correct answers. Needs to feel mastery over content.

Feeling
Relationship oriented and often benefits from the use of small group discussions and team projects. Preference for tasks where the same people can be together for extended periods of time. Willing to work with peers as a tutor and to share what they know about content to help others out. Not comfortable with conflict and disagreement.

Judgment
Wants structure and order in the classroom and want to know what they are accountable for and how they will be judged. Needs specific directions on what is required and how to proceed with tasks. Prefers assignments that have clear-cut answers and dislikes activities that are open-ended. Work better with deadlines and specific time frames for activities. Need to know where they stand in a course.

Perception
Flexible, curious, and adaptive learner. Enjoys informal problem solving and dealing with issues for which there is not a single correct answer. Prefer to have choices in tasks to work on and to work autonomously. Need opportunities in class where they can be spontaneous. Dislikes repetitive teaching processes and desire variety and novelty in class.

• Ideas in in this table reflects themes in Lawrence [1993]; Campbell and Davis [1990]; Kiersey and Bates, 1984].

Table 1-13 [Continued]

Temperaments

Sensation-Perception [SP]: *Dionysian*
Needs physical involvement in learning. Hands on experiences such as practical exercises are important. Needs activity, thrives on competition and is willing to experiment with alternate teaching methods. Enjoys performing and participates well in role playing simulations. Written assignments are not enjoyed as much. Wants opportunities to talk about concrete issues and often needs help in organizing information. Prefers logically structured, efficient classroom handouts and other classroom materials.

Sensation-Judging [SJ]: *Epimethean*
Needs structure, clear directions, and will conform to it. Likes traditional learning settings. Does not thrive on long-term independent projects and is not fond of discussion groups. Takes grades and deadlines seriously and needs them to do well. Likes lectures, paperwork, Q&A sessions. Linear learner who needs clear directions. Wants to know why a task is important to do before engaging it. Appreciates authority and is open to supervision and feedback on work.

Intuitive-Thinking [NT]: *Promethean*
An independent learner who likes to pursue interests and to track down ideas. Fascinated with somewhat abstract and theoretical ideas. Tends to collect rules and principles and otherwise to give structure to the world. Wants to know how ideas are conceived, how concepts were put together and what unanswered questions exist. Tracks down information until answer is obtained but may put other assignments aside in the process. Enjoys classroom projects that foster independent inquiry. Case studies, position papers, and well constructed presentations are appreciated. Tends to be impatient with discussions.

Intuitive-Feeling [NF]: *Apollonian*
Needs personal feedback particularly positive. Enjoys group discussions and interaction activities. Likes positive written comments on papers and this is often a powerful motivator. Negative reactions can lead to resentment and inaction. Likes democratic classroom environments. Learns well from discussion methods, role playing, and enjoys reading especially fiction and fantasy.

Alternate Ways of Blending Teaching and Learning Styles

Jung's personality theory provides one frame of reference for conceptualizing style. There are others. David Kolb, for example, examines teacher and student styles in terms of their preferences for concrete experiences, reflecting on those experiences, creating concepts and theories to explain experiences, and using such concepts to solve problems and make decisions. A recent discussion of Kolb's work in teacher-student interactions and in developing a teaching portfolio can be found in Richlin and Manning [1995].

Students and teachers also can be described as field-independent [able to organize thinking and their perception independently of the context in which ideas and stimuli are embedded] and field-dependent [context in which ideas and perceptions are embedded interfere with making judgments]. Studies show that field-dependent faculty and students are much more comfortable with group oriented classroom procedures while their field-independent counterparts tend to prefer lecture-discussion formats [Fuhrmann & Grasha, 1983; Witkin, 1977]. As you might imagine, tension and misunderstandings sometimes occur among faculty and students with divergent styles.

Similarly, in his work on the qualities that promote an orientation to learning versus *getting grades,* Jim Eison [1991] reports that both students and faculty have *grade oriented* and *learning oriented* learning and teaching styles. Some faculty inadvertently place an emphasis on evaluation processes and teach in ways that encourage students to focus on "making the grade" versus *getting the content.* For some students and faculty, "this is the way it ought to be." Those with divergent styles and subsequent points of view, however, also may not get along.

The point here is not that some models of style use the same dimensions to describe teachers and students. Rather, doing so enhances our ability to understand how teaching and learning styles interact and the conditions in which they are likely to facilitate and hinder teacher-student transactions. Effective teaching undoubtedly involves accommodating differences in style as well as purposely creating discrepancies to enhance the way college faculty teach and students learn. *To meet this goal, a compatible frame of reference or model for identifying the styles of teachers and students is needed.* Otherwise, one is in the unenviable position of trying to mix apples and eggs.

A model that has compatible descriptions of teacher and student styles must accomplish several goals. It should describe such teacher and student styles, it should illustrate how they interact, and it should prescribe steps faculty can take to enhance and modify instruction to accommodate student styles. The integrated model of teaching and learning style presented in the last five chapters of this book attempts to meet these goals. It is an empirical model based on two decades of research and my work with college faculty on ways to enhance their instructional processes. The model not only allows one to describe teacher and student styles, it also suggests conditions under which certain styles will be effective and what must happen for them to change.

The teaching styles examined in the integrated model [beginning in Chapter 4] are those of the *Expert, Formal Authority, Personal Model, Facilitator, and Delegator.* Learning styles that interact with these dimensions consist of students described as *Competitive, Collaborative, Independent, Dependent, Participatory, and Avoidant.* The teaching-learning process involves the interplay of these two sets of styles in the classroom. However, before engaging this model, it would be helpful to gain a better understanding of oneself as a teacher, issues in modifying and changing teaching styles, and the role of a personal philosophy of teaching when trying to teach with style. These latter issues are covered in Chapters 2 and 3.

2. The Role of Self-Reflection in Enhancing Our Teaching Styles

Imagine a series of clear plastic domes, one within another. You only see them from the outside; from the inside they are invisible. You become aware of the environment — one of those domes that surrounds you— only when you can get outside of it. At that point you can see it. But you can't see the one which is now about you.

- Architect Howard Gossard

Obtaining New Perspectives on Our Teaching Styles

Getting outside the "domes" that surround us is an important part of enhancing our teaching style. This process involves exploring underlying attitudes, values, and assumptions about teaching and learning. It also entails challenging long-held beliefs about ourselves, our students, and the complex processes of teaching and learning. By seriously challenging those beliefs, we initiate processes for personal growth and development.

Self-reflection plays a critical role in examining other perspectives about our styles as teachers and in challenging existing beliefs. In a classic work, Donald Schon's *The Reflective Practitioner* [1983] describes the need for practitioners to "turn thought back on action." That is, to examine the relationship between what they know and what they do. Schon indicates that this process has several components.

They may ask themselves, for example, "What features do I notice when I recognize this thing? What are the criteria by which I make this judgment? What procedures am I enacting when I perform this skill? How am I framing the problem I am trying to solve?" [p. 50]

Reflection about our actions as teachers can occur during our private moments, in discussions with colleagues and students, in a journal, or perhaps as part of the statements about ourselves and our teaching that appear in teaching portfolios. The overall goal of self-reflection is to learn from our experiences in order to make ourselves better teachers. Amber Dahlin [1994] also argues that internal debates and analyses about our instructional processes "marks teachers as problem solvers and negates the concept of teachers as technicians, waiting for researchers, or legislators to tell them what they need to do in their classrooms" [p. 60]. An added benefit is that in an era in which teachers need to justify what they are doing, the insights gained from self-reflection help us communicate the mode of inquiry in which we operate to others.

Arguing for self-reflection and analysis has an "apple pie and ice-cream quality to it." It is a point with which few would take exception. *Yet, it may be the most difficult task we try to do as teachers.* There are two issues that make self-reflection difficult:

- *Our teaching styles tend to be overlearned.* Thus, we can execute the thoughts and behaviors associated with our styles in a routine manner but at a very competent level of performance. This is possible because teachers, like experts in any field, are able to use many of the elements of their skills without a high degree of conscious awareness. This is because automatic mental control processes take over and operate without conscious awareness. They include well rehearsed modes of thinking, speaking, and behaving and are labeled *autopilots, tacit knowledge, schemas, and mental scripts.* Such processes allow us to conserve our limited conscious processing capabilities for those instances when it is absolutely needed. [Baddeley, 1986; Czikszentmihalyi, 1990; Druckman & Bjork, 1991].

  One disadvantage is that functioning on "autopilot" leads to a focus upon the outcomes of our teaching but not the processes that got us there. Because many aspects of our instruction are not consciously monitored, their strengths and weaknesses are not normally examined. *Self-reflection, however, can help us to control our natural inclinations to operate without much attention to the underlying processes that guide and direct our actions as teachers.* For example, it forces us to attend to what we are saying, how we ask and answer questions, the dynamics of small group discussions, how the content was organized, the reactions of students to what we are doing, and other things that normally would not be monitored as closely.

- *Under normal conditions, self-reflection is biased.* Our attitudes, values, and other beliefs about teaching and learning act as filters for interpreting our actions. How we understand our actions is partly based upon what we initially believe about ourselves. Thus, it is important to include in our analysis of ourselves what we believe about ourselves and how such beliefs appear in our styles as teachers.

Stepping Outside of the "Domes That Surround Us"

To examine ourselves and to enhance self-understanding, we must first "step outside of ourselves." Howard Gossard's quote at the beginning of this section suggests that we must move outside of the "domes" or perspectives that surround us. Several devices can help us do this and thus allow us to come to terms with "Who am I as a teacher?" and "What do I want to become?" *They include comparing our teaching style to a divergent role model, examining our values, and asking imaginative questions about our teaching.*

Comparing Our Styles to a Divergent Role Model

Sometimes ideas about what elements to change can be obtained by examining another person's teaching style. In particular, examining the elements of style in someone who is very different than us is helpful. Such individuals often possess qualities that force us to consider approaches to instruction we otherwise never would have imagined. By exploring how to assimilate or accommodate such qualities into our teaching, new possibilities for defining ourselves emerge. Use the example of a teaching style that follows and the questions in Self-Reflection Activity 2-1 on the next page to see how this works.

A participant in a recent workshop described how she used concepts from humanistic psychology to teach a course in Contemporary Topics in American History. The class was organized around ten short books that focused on an important theme in American History. Students were required to write a 3-4 page synopsis of the book. It included specific ways they agreed and disagreed with the author's point of view and the attitudes and values the author had regarding the subject matter. Each week of the academic quarter was devoted to discussing one of the books.

"I dropped into the background in those discussions," she reported. "I began class by asking, What is it that interests you?" The group sat in silence until someone spoke. "Occasionally," she said, "I would ask for points of clarification or have students develop a broader implication of the point the author was making. Mostly, I just sat there and had them talk about their reactions. If they tried to get me to tell them what I thought, then I responded by saying that it was more important for them to know what they thought about the material. If they asked me to present, I simply said that presentations were usually a very active form of learning for the presenter and I was more interested in promoting their active involvement as learners."

She believed in ideas advocated by Carl Rogers regarding the difficulty of teaching one human being anything simply by talking to them. She also believed that having students identify the attitudes and values of the authors and then react to them led to valuable insights about the material. From her point of view, such explorations were more valuable than anything she might offer in the way of specific content. "My role as a teacher," she said, "is to facilitate the learning of my students and not to transmit content to them."

It is impossible to read an account of this historian's approach to teaching and not react to it. Participants in the workshop also had a difficult time. She violates conventional wisdom about how to conduct a discussion, how to organize a course in American History, and the role of the teacher. To react, however, we must compare and contrast the approach she takes based on Rogerian theory to our own. In effect, use of Rogerian theory and how her teaching processes are compatible with it serves as a catalyst to help us explore who we are as a teacher. In the process, we can begin to imagine aspects of how our styles as teachers might change. Such thoughts are an important step in beginning the process of exploring new directions for our instruction.

Self-Reflection Activity 2-1
Reactions to the Rogerian Classroom

1.] What words, images, and feelings summarize your reactions to her History course?

2.] Other people have reacted to her teaching by calling it creative, innovative, problematic, exciting, a cop-out , and inappropriate. Do you agree or disagree with such descriptions?

3.] What aspects of her teaching could you integrate into your courses? How would you prepare your students for this style of teaching?

Exploring Our Values

Have you given much thought to your values as a teacher? Are you aware of how many of your classroom behaviors are affected by your values? Getting in touch with what we value also can help us examine the domes that surround us. They affect our teaching styles, for example, because they influence the educational goals and instructional processes we pursue. The choice of lecturing, independent term papers, or group projects reflect our values about authority, autonomy, and collaboration. Personal values also affect our perceptions of the classroom environment. Events are often identified and perceived in line with our values [e.g., a teacher who values independence will easily identify students with similar leanings].

Our positive and negative feelings are sometimes related to whether classroom-related events correspond to our values. Faculty members who value independence, autonomy, and self-direction are typically pleased when they discover students who demonstrate such characteristics. They are less happy with students who are dependent, take little initiative, and flounder about in the classroom. And when we meet students and colleagues whose values collide or are discrepant from our own; anger, tension, and frustration typically enters the relationship.

Personal Values and Our Teaching
Self-Reflection Activity 2-2

1.] To see how this process works, select three of the personal values listed in Table 2-1 on the next page and identify how each one appears in your style as a teacher. Focus on specific behaviors you engage in that reflect these values. For example, indicators of the presence of the value freedom might be; "Students have an open reading list and read books of their own choosing." Or, "Students interact with one another on course projects without direction from the teacher."

[Value 1]

[Value 2]

[Value 3]

Also, consider how each value influences your goals and the choices you make as a teacher, your emotions, and your general perceptions of the classroom environment and your role as a teacher. For example, "I always allow time in a course for students to work independently on projects. When students resist the freedom I give them, I find myself becoming angry. The students I dislike the most are those who want me to tell them what to do. I see myself more as a consultant and resource person to them.

2.] List the classroom goals and/or choices you make for each value.

[Value 1]

[Value 2]

[Value 3]

Self-Reflection Activity 2-2 [Continued]

3.] List one way each value affects your perceptions of classroom events.

  [Value 1]

  [Value 2]

  [Value 3]

4.] Give an example of how each value influences your emotions in class.

  [Value 1]

  [Value 2]

  [Value 3]

5.] Select two new values at random from Table 2-1. Ask yourself, "How could these values become integrated into my teaching style?"

  [Value 1]

  [Value 2]

Table 2-1
A List of Values

achievement	independence	rebellion	affection
dependence	inferiority	respect	initiative
alienation	discipline	integrity	rigidity
disorder	safety	security	isolation
efficiency	intimacy	justice	autonomy
truth	honesty	knowledge	sharing
freedom	equality	success	trust
comfort	peace	variety	violence
harmony	conflict	creativity	wisdom
excitement	integrity	influence	work
inclusion	progress	love	chaos
bravery	practicality	intuition	rules
charity	choice	dignity	sharing
boredom	community	disrespect	privacy
disorder	life	play	winning
responsibility	selfishness	connection	time

Asking Imaginative Questions about Ourselves

Questions can open up possibilities for thinking about "Who am I?" as well as "What do I want to become as a teacher?" Good questions for accomplishing the latter goal are those for which we have no easy answer. Of course, imaginative questions we never believed anyone would ask us can work well too. Sorting through the complications of the question and our responses provides us with additional insights into our styles as teachers.

A Very Private Interview
Self-Reflection Activity 2-3

Imagine that a reporter for the Chronicle of Higher Education asks to interview you for a special section on the qualities of effective teachers. *In your mind's eye, how would you respond to the following questions?*

1.] What is a "personal best" achievement for you as a teacher during the past two years?

2.] What aspect of your teaching would you never give up?

3.] If your could transport your classroom anywhere on the face of the earth, where would you take it? What advantages and disadvantages would this new location have for your teaching?

4.] What plant or animal best describes you as a teacher?

5.] What plant or animal best describes your students?

6.] Imagine that you have just returned from a trip ten years into the future. How were you teaching your classes? How were your teaching methods and students different?

7.] Who is the best teacher you have ever known? What personal qualities made this person a great teacher?

8.] How do the qualities of the best teacher you knew appear in your instruction?

9.] If you could give others a gift-wrapped box that contained the best qualities of your teaching style, what items would that box contain?

10.] If you could put the worst qualities you have as a teacher in the trash, what would you throw away?

11.] What is one action you need to take to give up one or more of the latter qualities?

12.] If you could talk to anyone who has ever lived about your teaching and how to enhance it, who would you talk to?

13.] What advice would the person mentioned above likely give you?

14.] If you wrote a book about teaching, what would the title be? What are three points about instruction you would make?

The Role of Self-Reflection in Modifying Teaching Style

It would appear axiomatic that he who knows himself best stands a better chance of controlling his environment and his own fate, in the sense of recognizing more clearly means-ends relationships and being able to reach a desired goal by alternative routes.

- O.J. Harvey and H.M. Schroder

The goal of self-discovery is not to complete a journey. Rather, self-insight serves us best when it allows us to continually refine as well as elaborate our definitions of ourselves as teachers. *Without such insights, we run the risk of embracing teaching strategies that simply do not fit our personal makeup.* Or, we might adopt strategies because they are popular or there is peer pressure to do so. In both cases, the changes in style are superficial, and like most New Year's resolutions, they will be abandoned.

Self-reflection also forces us to examine our commitment and our self-confidence to enact changes in our lives. Commitment results from our analysis of the pros and cons associated with our options for change. Those alternatives with the more favorable qualities receive our attention. Also, a commitment to modify our instruction is enhanced when we believe that we possess self-discipline, the willpower to persist, an aversion to letting ourselves down, and a willingness to tolerate an occasional setback [Grasha, 1993; Grasha & Kirschenbaum, 1986].

Our sense of self-efficacy or confidence in our ability to succeed is related to two beliefs [Bandura, 1986]. One is the belief that we possess the skills and abilities needed to plan and implement change or that the means to acquire the skills needed are available to us. The second is that if we used our skills and abilities to vary our styles as teachers, for example, a successful outcome would result. Judgments about deficits in either component of self-efficacy can hold us back.

Information, training, observing others trying new things, gentle encouragement, and taking a few successful small steps can do wonders for self-confidence and our motivation. Yet all of these things must be preceded by a certain amount of comfort with our thoughts about possible new directions for our teaching. Self-reflection and analysis about "Who I am as a teacher and what do I want to become" are important parts of achieving the latter goal. *This process of self-reflection and analysis cannot be short-circuited, and in my experience, it is not valued enough.* The following critical incidents illustrate the importance of the latter point.

The Case of the Disappointed Committee

A small liberal arts college holds a faculty development day at the beginning of the school year. This is the first time the college has sponsored such a day, and it is devoted to the topic of learning styles and their instructional implications. The dean hopes the time spent will translate into specific improvements in the classroom. The program is structured so that during the morning I introduce the faculty to issues in using learning styles. I am thanked for my contribution, and after lunch I left campus.

A faculty committee runs the afternoon session action plans to incorporate information about learning styles into the classrooms. Very few detailed plans are developed and a follow-up showed that out of the sixty-five people in attendance, twelve reported that they had used information from the workshop during the term.

Analysis

The problem was that the facilitator had spent two decades thinking about learning styles and its classroom applications. Those faculty attending were given three hours of content and expected to somehow develop and implement action plans based on such information.

Learning styles provide another dome to understand ourselves, our students, and our teaching. The mistake is to assume that simply being show a new dome or perspective is enough. Time for reflection is needed before the information can be integrated.

The Case of the Faulty Faculty Development Week

A two year technical school holds a week long faculty development conference. Once again the goal is to have faculty take information from a parade of speakers and workshop leaders and integrate it into the classroom. This faculty development activity occurs the week before classes begin. Not a single hour during that week is devoted to time for the faculty to privately think about the issues raised or to plan their courses for the next term. The dean did not trust the faculty to use such time wisely yet expected that somehow information from the faculty development programs would be integrated into the classroom.

Analysis

The assumption here is that being exposed to information will somehow lead to it being used. Self-reflection time is seen as unnecessary and it is programmed out of the activities. In this case, it is done because of the dean's focus on task, a lack of trust that the faculty would use the extra-time wisely, and a lack of appreciation for self-reflection.

The Case of the Disloyal Faculty Member

A large university has a fund to support faculty development activities. Members of the faculty must write a proposal to obtain such funds. One person asks for money to attend two conferences dealing with collaborative learning processes. This particular individual is seen as needing as much help as possible. Thus, the department head enthusiastically endorses the proposal. Six months later, her department head asks what changes have been made in the classroom. The faculty member replies, "Actually, none so far. I've been thinking about what I'm doing and how collaborative learning processes might be used in my teaching. So far, I have some general ideas but nothing concrete in mind."

The department head becomes angry and replies , "I really feel betrayed by your attitude. I went out on a limb to help you get the money and you still don't have anything to show for it. I fail to see what's so difficult about adding a few new things to your classes."

Analysis

Self-reflection cannot be rushed. People need to develop some sense of intellectual comfort with new ideas about teaching before they have a chance of getting into the classroom. This process takes time and unfortunately other people do not always appreciate this fact. Those who are not making progress in changing their teaching, or who on the surface appear to be doing nothing, are in some cases still thinking about it. Some are doing so seriously while others are perhaps locked into procrastination. Yet, all too often department heads, deans, individuals involved in faculty development, and those faculty who are well into their changing their teaching are impatient with those who seem to be "standing in place."

An important point in each of the cases is that taking time to think is an integral part of any process of personal change. In my experience, the amount of time such reflection and internal debate takes is seldom appreciated nor is adequate time always put aside for it. Part of the problem is that those individuals most interested in facilitating change in others [i.e., department heads, deans, colleagues, individuals working in faculty development] are impatient for it to occur. Everyone wants to see their ideas quickly put into action. Consequently, the seemingly slow pace at which implementation occurs can become frustrating.

Furthermore, those who have already made significant changes in their approach to instruction often cannot understand why others cannot do the same thing. As one colleague said, "I made a number of changes in my teaching and what I did could be done by almost everyone. I don't know what's holding others back." In my experiences, such views occur out of the mistaken belief that people are not that much different from each other. Finally, there is a tendency to assume that the major part of the changes needed are mechanical. That is, all someone has to do is learn new techniques and to apply them to their classes.

The latter reasons tell more about what others want than they do about the needs of the individual contemplating change. *Those promoting change are sometimes insensitive to the needs of faculty who are contemplating a modification in their approach to instruction.* They fail to recognize the amount of inner turmoil associated with modifying instructional processes. They also fail to take into account how much people teach to a projected image of themselves that is difficult to discard. *Finally, there is not enough recognition that someone's style as a teacher is a part of one's personality.* Let us examine each of the latter issues in more detail.

What Others Seldom See in Faculty Considering Change

The Inner Turmoil Associated with Change

Old habits and thought patterns typically are not given up easily and a mental tug-of-war between old ways and new ways of doing things occurs. This battle is not easily won. Old ways of teaching, for example, are overlearned while new approaches must be assimilated or accommodated into mental structures that have taken a long time to develop. Unless there are very compelling reasons to change, this integration normally takes time.

In discussing this inner turmoil, William Bridges notes that several psychological processes are involved in letting go of the past. *We must disengage and stop identifying with old habits and patterns of thinking.* Perhaps this is best summed up by the New Year's Eve theme of *out with the old and in with the new.* Unfortunately, it is not that easy. We can neither wish new changes into our lives nor can we simply throw away past habits and thinking patterns without remembering the strong role they played. Rather, it typically happens only after we work through our disenchantment with such things. To do so often leads to periods of frustration, anxiety, and a certain amount of disorientation. After all, each of us needs some familiar structures to hang on to. Even if a familiar manner of teaching is no longer working well for us, at least it provides a structure for how to conduct a class.

We must of course get used to new ideas and this requires that several things happen. One is that variations in our teaching styles must first become integrated into alternate ways of thinking about ourselves as teachers. Furthermore, a variety of new rules, mental schemas, and sensorimotor scripts for executing the changes we desire must be developed. Any new thoughts and actions also must compete with their overlearned counterparts for our attention.

In effect, our old habits must be overridden and this does not happen easily. Old habits have the benefit being familiar and routine and can be executed quickly and without much conscious thought. Being less familiar, new ways of thinking and behaving require more conscious processing time and their execution initially can be awkward. Unlike old habits, the benefits of a smooth and automatic execution take time to develop. Thus, there is likely to be some discomfort while trying to employ them.

For example, a colleague recently attended a faculty development workshop and was intrigued with the idea of using case studies to help students develop critical thinking skills. He normally used a traditional lecture-discussion approach to teaching. In discussing his reactions to the workshop, he made the following comments:

> I understand that case studies can promote active learning and critical analysis. But I can cover so much more content in my lectures than I could if I used cases. I'm also not good at discussing issues I raised with a class. I don't know if I could handle a group that could go off in directions I did not want to go. It's hard enough getting them to prepare for class with what I do now, how on earth can I get them to do the preparation needed to discuss a case?"

Thoughts about new ways of doing things are contrasted with the old and the familiar. The struggle over giving up what I know I do best to encounter the unknown is evident in his reactions. After conducting this internal debate over a period of three months, he eventually decided to try using the case study method. He did so, however, only after thinking of ways his objections to this form of teaching could be managed. And, he only did so for a handful of classes in order to add a little variety to his instruction.

A Desire for Familiar Teaching Habits

Many faculty in my experience adopt teaching strategies that they would be most comfortable with if they were the students. This comes across in statements such as: "I would have loved some teacher to have given me the information I presented today. No one seemed moved by what I said." Or, "When I was a student, I would have quickly debated any teacher who said what I did. They just did not react as I did to the information." The fact that many people tend to teach as they were taught also speaks to their comfort with instructional processes that structure teacher-student interactions in familiar ways. In effect many faculty teach to a projected image of themselves and such projections are difficult to discard.

A Desire for Familiar Teacher-Student Relationships

People often want the comfort of past ways of relating to others and at times prefer to treat current relationships *as if* they reflected those from their past. Such tendencies are well documented and described in the context of object-relations theory [Cashdan, 1988]. This approach to relationships suggests that we become disappointed and frustrated when current relationships do not match expectations that largely are grounded in our past experiences. Thus, someone who was comfortable with the teacher as an authority and a rigid status hierarchy in student-teacher relationships will strive to reproduce it in the future. Anything that threatens such needs is likely to be resisted.

In effect, we tend to structure current situations and to influence others in ways that allow past wishes, desires, and needs to be expressed. Everyone is susceptible to such influences. The extent to which we can shape current relationships to reflect desirable qualities of those from our past can help us reduce stress in our interactions with others.

To change one's teaching, however, often means that new ways of relating to students must be established. This means that some of what we most desire from our past must be modified or perhaps given-up. Unfortunately, anything in our lives we invest energy in is often not easily put aside.

The Relationship of Personal Identity and Teaching Style

"Asking faculty to modify their teaching style is like asking them to change their personality," a psychotherapist friend once remarked. Her comment occurred in the context of a discussion about the problem of getting college faculty to adopt alternative modes of instruction. I initially resisted her suggestion but soon realized the valuable insight it provided.

All of us, have aspects of our beliefs, attitudes, values, motives, and other personal characteristics bundled up in our daily activities. Someone who begins a class with the statement "I'm going to cover a considerable amount of material this term as I talk about ...." is likely to have a different set of personality characteristics than an instructor who begins class by stating, "You are going to learn the content by independent study projects." The former likely prefers a more teacher centered style of instruction while the latter individual prefers more of a facilitative style to help students learn.

Getting either instructor to adopt the other's approach will involve more than simply showing them how to use each other's methods. *The choice of a teaching method is in part dictated by one's personality.* This is one reason why research comparing the relative efficacy of different teaching processes must be cautiously interpreted. For example, people who decide to teach large or small classes, who use computer assisted instruction or who employ peer assisted instructional methods have self-selected those methods. In effect, the methods and the personality of the individuals employing them are intertwined.

In my experience, people are more likely to adopt alternative teaching methods if they provide a comfortable match to their personal dispositions. Thus, someone who values control over their environment is more likely to consider an approach to involving students that also keeps the teacher in the foreground. In contrast, someone with fewer needs for personal control may opt for teaching strategies where classroom tasks are delegated to small groups of students to complete. The teacher stays in the background as a consultant and resource person to students.

It was largely my friend's comments that helped me to understand one of the sources of resistance to change. It also forced me to keep in mind the intrapersonal context in which someone's teaching style is embedded.

Self-Reflection Activity 2-4
The Side of You Others Seldom See

Complete the following sentences.

1.] The old habits of teaching I need to disengage from are ....

2.] Three words that best describe my inner turmoil when I think about making significant changes in my approach to teaching are ....

3.] Teaching to a projected image of myself does [or does not] apply to me because ... [Hint: Think of how elements of your teaching would make you you comfortable if you were a student in the class.]

4.] One aspect of this projected image I admire is ....

5.] One aspect of this projected image I need to change is ....

6.] I tend to structure my teaching in order to allow the following needs and desires to be expressed.....

7.] My approach to teaching matches my personality in that .....

Self-Reflection and the Cycle of Change in Teaching

The product of self-knowledge is to create more responsibility, more choice. Just being able to describe one's habitual patterns will not necessarily lead to more choice. Understanding, clarifying, and admitting to yourself the structure of your response pattern is a necessary, but insufficient condition for creating alternative responses.

- Richard Curwin and Barbara Fuhrmann

Self-reflection alone is not enough. It is part of a larger scheme of factors needed to initiate changes in our approaches to instruction An extension of James prochaska's model of change to modifying teaching styles integrates self-understanding with a larger set of variables responsible for personal growth [Prochaska, 1991; Prochaska et al., 1992]. The basic features of his model are described in Table 2-2.

Research suggests that it takes time for anyone to muster the courage and resolve to change. Prochaska finds that people may spend months and years in the precontemplative and contemplative stages before making at least minimal changes in their behaviors. This may be one reason why some of us recognize problems with our teaching, we sense what needs to be done, yet needed actions are not immediately taken. In effect, our cognitive network of attitudes and values must first be realigned to support a particular change. The attitudes, beliefs, and values supporting current teaching practices have in many cases taken years to develop. *Thus, there is no reason to expect that the attitudes, beliefs, and values needed to support alternative and possibly more effective modes of teaching will change overnight.*

In addition, the stages are a continuing cycle that all of us undergo in a variety of areas of our everyday lives. This cycle is illustrated in Figure 2-1. It is important to note that once a change is initiated, achieving our goal is only one outcome. It is possible for a relapse to occur or for older habits to intrude. Old habits often intrude because they are overlearned, familiar, and there is some comfort in retreating to them.

A key element in the cycle of change is how people handle relapses. They are a normal part of any attempts to vary aspects of our teaching. Taking two steps forward and one step backwards is not atypical. Thus, relapses as well as slow progress should be recognized as the norm and we should use them as learning experiences.

Unfortunately, relapses are not always used for learning what not to do next time. Instead, some individuals engage in self-criticism for not accomplishing their goals and objectives. Those who can avoid such tendencies are more successful in changing their lives. An important element here is the use of self-coaching strategies such as, "Ok, so you didn't do everything you wanted. No big deal, you still have time to improve. Let's do it this way next time." [Grasha, 1995].

The key to managing relapses is to become your own best friend and not your own worst enemy. Otherwise, a self-defeating attitude develops and attempts to produce effective changes in our lives are hampered.

Table 2-2
The Prochaska Model Applied To Teaching

Stage	Thoughts	Characteristics
Precontemplation	*I don't have any problems in my teaching that need to be changed.*	Teachers are relatively unaware of the problem. They feel no immediate and pressing need to change. Colleagues, administrators, and students are often more aware that problems exist.
Contemplation	*I know what I need to do but I'm not ready to act yet.*	Serious thought is given to making certain changes. The pros and cons as well as the costs in terms of time and energy of taking various courses of action are considered. Some individuals remain in this stage for several months or years. Someone may respond to pressures from others to change but there is very little commitment. They typically stop when the pressure is off.
Preparation	*I'm ready to do something but I want to go slowly.*	Specific plans are developed and very small changes in instruction are initiated to test the water.
Action	*I'm now doing something about the issues I'm facing.*	Intentions are converted to goals and appropriate patterns of thoughts and actions are initiated. Relapses to old habits can be a problem.
Maintenance	*I'm doing what it takes to be able to stick with it and I'm committed to these changes for a long time.*	Attempts are made to consolidate gains and to continue the changes. The prevention of relapses to old ways of doing things is also a concern.
Termination	*I've achieved the changes I wanted to make and it feels good. I have every right to feel proud of my accomplishments.*	The ability to maintain the changes has been a success and new approaches to instruction have been integrated into the classroom. Periodic feedback and reflection is still needed to fine tune one's efforts. The new approaches have been fully integrated into one's attitudes and values about teaching.

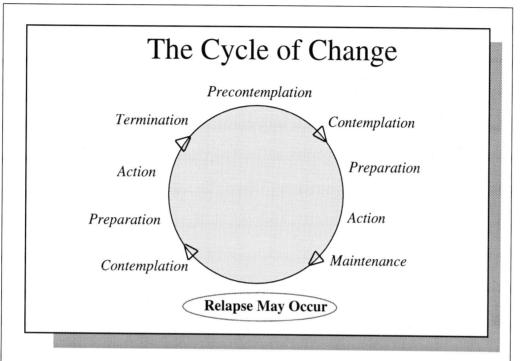

Figure 2-1: Cycles of Change in the Prochaska Model: Once initiated, changes in behavior do not always lead to an expected outcome or termination. Relapses to old habits are always a possibility. The majority of those who relapse typically revert back to the contemplation stage and the process continues from that point.

People who are successful in making changes in their lives appear to have three characteristics.

> • *They try to learn from their mistakes.*
>
> • *They do not blame themselves or overly chastise themselves for slow progress or relapses to older ways of doing things.*
>
> • *They fall back into the contemplation stage to think things over and to decide how to try again in the future.*

Prochaska's research also suggests two basic principle about personal growth. *People wanting to change need time to think. Those wanting to change others need to allow them time to think.* Rushing into the preparation and action stages too early is likely to produce two outcomes.

> • *Resistance to change.* Resistance to change in instruction is not always the old guard holding out and trying to sabotage new ideas. Such resistance might better be understood in terms of some individuals needing additional time to reframe their beliefs about the teaching-learning process. Over the years, more

than one teacher has said to me, "I like what you are saying, I can see how it might help me, but I'm just not ready to change what I'm doing yet. I need more time to think about what I want to do."

• *The results of trying to change too quickly are likely to be less than desired.* One instructor told me how he modified his English Literature course from a lecture-discussion format to one where collaborative learning activities were employed. He did this about halfway through a semester and only a few days after attending a workshop on collaborative learning strategies. The students resisted the change in the classroom procedures. They were not prepared for it and he was not particularly adept in facilitating some of the new ways of learning. In retrospect, it might have been more effective to gradually introduce collaborative learning processes into his course.

Along similar lines, follow-up data to various workshops and seminars I have conducted over the past two decades suggests that only 10-15% of the participants will take some of what they learned and use it to enhance their teaching. This data can be further understood in terms of the two categories of people who attend faculty development activities. One group were those faculty who wanted to be *reborn and invigorated.* They appeared ready for moving from contemplation to the preparation and action stages. Others attended to be *affirmed.* For the most part, they wanted their current ideas and biases acknowledged as legitimate. *My experiences suggest that the latter tend to be more numerous than the former.*

The last two outcomes typically lead to frustration among those on campuses wanting to facilitate faculty development in teaching or otherwise to promote changes in instructional processes. A predictable response is for campus change agents to view the lack of readiness as a personal deficit among those not willing to adopt new ideas. [Yes, even those in faculty development are sometimes guilty of the fundamental attribution bias; i.e., the tendency to assign blame to personal dispositions]. Based on the discussion here, however, such conclusions are probably unwarranted. It is quite possible that a number of so-called *resisters* are in the pre-contemplative and contemplative stages of change. Rather than chastised, some simply need additional time to think and activities that encourage processes of self-reflection should be developed and implemented.

Factors That Facilitate the Cycle of Change

The model for change not only describes critical processes needed to modify one's instruction, but it also suggests ideas that are helpful for engaging each of the stages in the cycle of change. Several ideas for you to consider are presented in Table 2- 3. *Perhaps the overriding point is that trying to modify one's teaching is not unlike learning any new set of skills. It basically takes time, patience, and practice.* The latter point may seem obvious but it is worth mentioning. Over the years, I have encountered faculty who have said, "I tried what you said once and it didn't work." I know of very few skills that I would subject to such a stringent criterion. After all, most of us play some sport, musical instrument, or operate a computer or other difficult piece of equipment. Most of us did not give up the first time our efforts were not successful.

Part of the problem here is that some individuals assume that teaching should not take so much work. Or, at least, its not worth it to them to spend a lot of extra time honing their skills. After all, as one colleague told me, "I'm going to get ahead in this field based on my scholarship and not my teaching." When someone with this attitude considers alternatives to current instructional practices, my experiences suggests it is often with an eye towards how much time and effort it will take. Thus, if the method fails to show immediate results, it is often abandoned in favor of older and familiar ways of behaving.

Another reason for the *I tried it once and it did not work* attitude is a tendency for some individuals to distance themselves from the particular method employed. That is, the attitude appears to be, *if the method failed, then the method failed.* Rather than question the intensity of their effort, their motivation to do well, and their skill in employing it, the failure is ascribed to the a deficiency in the teaching process.

For some, this stringent standard of immediate results is typically reserved for new teaching processes. Somehow, the need for practice, persistence, and fine-tuning one's skills are not as readily applied to matters of teaching and learning. The latter statement is not an attempt to blame others for what they should not be. Rather it forms the basis for an analogy or metaphor for what it takes to change in teaching. Namely, if one imagined what it was like to learn a new skill in some other area and how various errors, mistakes, and setbacks were overcome, then the implications become clear. *The same processes effectively used elsewhere can be employed in developing one's skills in teaching. In particular, research shows that time on task, practice, a sensitivity to feedback, a willingness to learn from one's mistakes, and a desire to meet standards of excellence produce results* [Druckman & Bork, 1991].

Proficiency in teaching, however, takes time to develop and it cannot be short-circuited. In teaching and elsewhere, it is probably 10% inspiration and 90% perspiration. This would appear to be true whether one looks at teaching as a set of skills, an art form, or some combination of the two. It seldom comes easy to anyone.

Table 2-3
Change Processes at Each Stage of the Cycle

Precontemplation/Contemplation

- Think about the positive and negative effects that current teaching processes have upon you and your satisfaction with your role.
- Read books and journal articles that describe innovations in instruction within your discipline.
- Participate in workshops and seminars where alternative approaches to instruction are discussed.
- Begin a log or journal on teaching. Write a short autobiography about your life as a teacher. Compose some poetry on teaching. Write a fictional story about the teaching-learning process.

Preparation

- Reevaluate your current practices. Imagine yourself using alternatives in a course and how you and your students would respond.
- Form a list of the pros and cons associated with specific changes you made.
- Study the teaching portfolios and syllabi of colleagues for ideas to use.
- Take the time to develop skills you believe you are deficient in. Attend workshops, read books on particular teaching methods, and ask for assistance from informed colleagues.
- Seek support by getting colleagues to join you or to discuss your ideas.

Action

- Proceed in small steps and periodically reward your effort and progress.
- Develop lists to remind yourself about what actions you need to take.
- Rehearse in your "minds eye" the things you want to try before doing so in class. Focus on what you will be saying and doing.
- Arrange your teaching environment to facilitate the changes you want to make. [e.g., seating arrangements, size of room, lighting, equipment].
- Consciously coach yourself through the thoughts and actions you want to take.

Maintenance

- Identify at least three class sessions a term you want to get feedback on. Ask students to use a 1-7 rating scale to rate the session overall where a 1 = worst session I have attended and a 7= the best session ever. Next ask them to identify 1-2 specific things you did that led them to give you the rating. Then ask for 1-2 things you could have done that would have enabled them to give you a 7. Finally ask students to list 1-2 things they could have done to have made this the best session possible.
- Reflect on how the changes appear to be working out using as a baseline how you used to teach. Ask a peer to observe and comment.
- Set a *self-destruct* date to make a decision about whether or not you will continue to employ the changes you have initiated.
- Use inevitable relapses and mistakes as an opportunity to learn. Always ask, "What did I do well and not so well?" "What changes must I make?"
- Develop a teaching portfolio to evaluate and monitor your efforts to change.
- Talk to colleagues, students, and others about what you have tried and the outcomes. Keep others informed and ask for advice and assistance.

Self-Reflection Activity 2-5
Reflections on Your Position
in the Cycle of Change

1.] What is one change you have considered making in your teaching style?

2.] Where are you currently located in the cycle of change described in Table 2-3 and Figure 2-1 with the change in teaching style identified above?

3.] Are you currently where you need to be in the change cycle? Give a reason.

4.] What are two or three ideas in Table 2-3 that you need to consider in order to move forward in the cycle and/or to maintain those variations in your teaching style that are already underway?

Factors That Hinder the Cycle of Change

Engaging in self-reflection and analysis is a necessary first step in modifying one's teaching. The trick, however, is to avoid becoming locked into analyzing a situation without taking the actions needed to correct it. This is sometimes called "analysis paralysis." At some point in time, the analysis must end and then be immediately followed by thoughts such as "I need to take the following actions now....!" This latter realization is the catalyst that allows people to engage the other elements of the change process.

To move into the action mode of modifying our teaching styles, two types of cognitive barriers must be managed.

- *Defensive patterns of thinking about ourselves must be identified and managed.* Such processes adversely affect our ability to honestly and objectively engage in the self-reflection needed. This interferes with our inability to develop a realistic appraisal of our current teaching styles. What we are currently doing receives a somewhat biased and distorted interpretation. Typically such factors operate in a self-serving manner designed to protect our preferred image of ourselves.

- *Elements of our cognitive styles and absolute and extreme modes of thinking must be countered.* Such things often prevent or stop us from initiating and following through on needed actions.

One way to short-circuit the latter factors is to follow Ellen Langer's advice and become *mindful* of them. She argues that we must consciously focus on the latter factors so that their influences are brought into conscious awareness. This involves identifying each one and to then analyze the role it plays in our ability [or inability] to make needed modifications in our instruction [Langer, 1989].

Patterns of Thinking That Affect Taking Actions to Change

All of us use a variety of conscious and unconscious thought processes to manage and to protect our preferred images of ourselves. And when it comes to assessing our teaching, few of us are willing to admit that problems exist in some aspects of what we do in the classroom. *Such tendencies can be seen in statements such as:*

- Students just aren't as interested in this topic as they were when I went to school.

- Student ratings of how well I'm doing are a waste of time. They are nothing more than a popularity contest. I'm a much better teacher than some of these students think I am.

- Teaching around here would be a lot more fun if we had better students. I wish the admissions people would do a better job.

Unfortunately, such analyses of student interest, evaluations of our performance, or the quality of the student body takes us away from asking; "How can I make a topic more interesting to students?" "In what ways are student perceptions of my teaching accurate?" "Are the problems I'm experiencing really with the quality of the students? Have I done all that I can do to "play the hand that I've been dealt?" There is a potential pitfall associated with trying to answer the latter questions. *Rather than acknowledging a problem and taking actions to remedy it, we may develop a biased view of the situation and the image of ourselves in it. We then may* fail to deal with any problems identified in a realistic manner. Effectively our understanding of what is happening, our role in the event, and what remedies are needed can become distorted.

Some people, for example, may imagine that they posses qualities that in reality seldom appear in their actions. One colleague likened his teaching style to someone who takes novice learners on a journey through the wilderness. Several of his students reported that his courses felt more like "being lost in a wilderness." Still others might deny that some personal characteristics play a role in their teaching. Few would admit that their teaching lacks excitement or that their presentation of information lacks clarity and organization. Yet such qualities are a part of the instructional practices of some faculty in every college.

A few teachers also may rationalize that their disorganized lectures, for example, have a positive influence on students. As one faculty member told me, "Students learn more when they can organize information and clarify things for themselves. Why should I have to do it for them?"

In working with college faculty, I find that several defensive patterns of thinking occur. Each interferes with self-reflection and the ability to eventually engage the action stage in the cycle of change.

Defensive Avoidance

A recognition that things are not going well emerges. Instead of taking action, people believe they have little hope of finding a solution. People affected by defensive avoidance appear to be saying, "What's the use of thinking about it, there's little that I can do about it anyway. "Understandably, *people adhering to such attitudes are likely to see further reflection and analysis as a waste of time.* Defensive avoidance takes several forms.

Some individuals rationalize the problem and make up reasons why it does not exist or they develop explanations for why they should not take action. A teacher of literature contacted me hoping I would help her discount a number of poor evaluations of her teaching. She was convinced that students were not a good judge of the quality of her instruction. Rather than try to identify the consistent themes in what the students were saying, and to think about what was accurate, she said, "I've been teaching this way for years and I must be doing something right. Just because a few students are acting out against my authority is no reason to change my methods. They are hardly in a position to judge the quality of what I am doing. "

Others may procrastinate and put off taking action. Such tendencies are understandable when someone becomes anxious and uncomfortable with some aspects of their teaching. Unsure of what to do, they choose to do nothing. One participant in a workshop told me that he was asked by his department head to teach a large lecture class on U.S. History. "Teaching 150 students in one room is not what I do best," he confided. But we were shorthanded that year so I became a good soldier and did what he asked.

His lecture style was in his own words "straightforward, it lacked emotion, and I was probably not as organized as I could be." He also noted that student responses were predictable. "Many cut class, those that showed had an air of indifference about them and getting a discussion going was nearly impossible.

"Quite frankly," he told me, I was at a loss for what to do to turn this class around. It bothered me, I was anxious and often dreaded meeting with that class. In effect, I decided that nothing could be done. I was out of my league in a large class so I opted to "grin and bear it" until a suitable replacement could be found.

Unfortunately, his department head followed a familiar unwritten rule that the last person to teach the course gets to do it again. He kept the course for four years until as he said, "they found someone more suitable."

Finally, a few people engage in defensive avoidance by trying to "pass the buck" and in effect attempt to get someone else to bail them out. Those of us who have worked closely with faculty are familiar with this strategy. Assistance is requested, the consultant shows up and is met with the following question. "I want you to tell me exactly what I need to do to turn this class around." To "tell" under such circumstances is a trap that must be avoided. The appropriate response is to engage someone through observations and discussions about their teaching where they identify issues and actions that must be taken.

In some departments, a variation on the latter strategy occurs. Some faculty members may teach a course they dislike or that is not going well and then look for opportunities to pass it on to someone else. The "someone else" is often a junior faculty member, a new hire, or an adjunct. There is nothing wrong with wanting to teach other things. Typically, however, some instructors see passing it off as preferable to engaging in the analysis and reflection to make it better.

Denial

While some recognize a problem but choose inaction, others refuse to admit that some aspect of their teaching needs to be examined. The phrase "out of sight, out of mind" describes the stance that such individuals take. *In effect, the unwillingness to recognize an issue negates the need for self-reflection.*

A College of Business Administration I visited had serious problems with a first year course required of all majors. "In theory, the course made lots of sense," one of the people involved told me. The students would be exposed to "what's it really like to enter the world of business and high finance." She explained that three faculty members were assigned to team teach the course and to select topics that "anyone entering the business world had to know about." The faculty members decided to use a large auditorium for the two-hundred students and to have junior and senior majors lead small discussion groups outside of the large group sessions.

Several problems soon emerged. The faculty members disagreed on what topics should be taught. The team teaching soon became "You take one class session and I'll take the next one." Unfortunately, lecturing to large groups was not something they did particularly well and students became dissatisfied. Rules for course grades were changed in midstream and when the students complained the faculty members choose to argue with them in the large auditorium.

Student complaints about the course were largely ignored. One of the faculty members involved told me, "We basically assumed it was, "the usual moaning and groaning of students who just didn't want to go to class." The faculty involved did not seriously ask questions such as; "What are we doing that makes the students dissatisfied?" Or, "How can we make this a better experience for everyone concerned?"

The answers to the latter questions demand self-reflection and analysis. They cannot be asked or answered as long as someone denies that a problem exists. If left alone, the problems someone refuses to admit exist typically get worse. Eventually, it becomes much more difficult to deny their existence. Indeed, this is what happened with the business course. After two months, less than one-third of the students showed up for class, those that did attend became openly hostile towards the teachers, and the dean's office was inundated with complaints. It was in the words of one faculty member, "A real mess."

So widespread was the dissatisfaction, that all administrators in the college and a significant number of faculty became concerned. The dean publicly apologized to the students, promised that their concerns would be addressed. He initiated a self-study of the course and the added reflection paid off. The course was redesigned, the students were happier, and a lesson in the "wages of denial" was acquired by all of those responsible for the initial version of the course.

Defensive Pessimism

When people begin to think about and analyze their teaching, some of their thoughts eventually come around to "what can I do differently in the future and what outcomes can I expect." Not everyone has an optimistic view of the future. Sometimes negative or inaccurate images of the future are generated as a means of self-protection. In effect, people hedge their bets and prefer to see a worst -case scenario. This tendency towards defensive pessimism is a self-handicapping strategy. *It affects someone's ability to self-reflect and analyze their teaching because it overemphasizes potential negative consequences of one's actions.* It may provide a certain amount of protection because if things go wrong, those using this strategy can say to themselves, "See, I knew modifying my teaching style would not work." Or, if things did work out for the best, they can remain pleasantly surprised.

In my experience, defensive pessimism is often associated with teachers who by any objective measure of their abilities are quite competent. For some reason, they have a difficult time allowing themselves the luxury of admitting this to themselves. I am reminded of a former client who spent 18 months trying to learn how to run discussion groups, case studies, and role plays effectively in his political science courses. Throughout this period of time, he was sure "I'll fall on my face when I try this and I'll be really fortunate if this works out as well as you think it will."

In spite of himself, his teaching improved, he was able to modify his approach to teaching, and students were impressed with his efforts. I recently heard that he was given an outstanding teaching award by his college. I'm almost convinced that when I ask he'll probably smile and say, "I guess I was lucky."

Defensive Attributions

A fundamental principle of human behavior is that our actions are always a function of personal dispositions [e. g., genetic makeup, needs and motives, intellectual capacity, personality traits] and forces in our environment. To adequately understand why a faculty member teaches a particular way, and why problems develop in a course, one must come to terms with the influence of both factors.

A related principle of human behavior is that people find it convenient to ignore the latter principle. Research indicates that most of us error in emphasizing either personal dispositions or factors in the environment to explain why we or other people take certain actions. *Attribution biases affect self-reflection because they lead us to focus on a limited number of factors responsible for issues in our teaching.*

Because we develop through experiences certain biases for interpreting events, our preferences for personal and situational responsibility for events are remarkably predictable. Two types of errors, the actor-observer bias and the fundamental attribution bias tend to dominate. Each leads us to conclude that factors outside of our own beliefs and actions are largely responsible for whatever problems are experienced in our teaching.

The *actor-observer* bias is a tendency to focus on factors in the situation to explain events for which we are personally responsible. An instructor encountering a lack of interest or involvement in students typically blames the students, the classroom facilities, the time of day, or the required nature of the course. What is usually ignored or overlooked is his or her personal responsibility for the lack of involvement.

Or, when focusing on the students behaviors, explanations for their actions are sought in real or imagined personal dispositions. Thus, they may be seen as lazy, uninterested in the material, intellectually deficient, or fatigued from taking too many classes. This *fundamental attribution* bias forces us to look for dispositional causes of student responses and to down play situational influences including instructors assuming their fair share of the problem.

Studies suggest that in western cultures, this is the default mode of our information processing system when faced with the problem of "Why did this action occur." Our experiences and cultural values emphasize individual initiative and responsibility and this naturally affects our perceptions of why people behave in certain ways. It is a deeply ingrained bias and to short-circuit it demands that we not only recognize its existence but force ourselves to consider possible situational influences for the actions we dislike in others.

The combination of the actor-observer and the fundamental attribution biases prevents the self-reflection needed to change problems in the classroom. Since the blame is largely externalized, something out there needs to change in order to make the situation tolerable. Thus, it is easy to "blame the situation" and in the process ignore personal responsibility for the problem and its solution. Complete Self-Reflection Activity 2-6 to assess the presence of the such tendencies when analyzing your teaching.

This does not mean that situational influences including student attitudes and behaviors are trivial concerns. They also must be examined in any serious attempt to analyze problems in the classroom. However, to focus exclusively on them is a mistake because students are unlikely to change unless faculty change their ways. One of the outcomes of my research on the classroom behaviors of students is that their attitudes and classroom behaviors can be modified with changes in the classroom environment. Course methods, for example, that emphasize and consistently reinforce student involvement and active learning encourage more participation and less dependence on the instructor. The intellectual excitement and interest on the part of students that many teachers want begins to emerge.

More will be said about such outcomes in a later section of this book. The important point is that teachers are finding it easier to get what they want in a course when they create a classroom environment that facilitates desired outcomes. A process of personal reflection and analysis is critical to making such changes. So too is a recognition that the attribution biases mentioned in this section only detract from obtaining the self-awareness and insight needed to initiate needed changes in the classroom.

Problematic Cognitive Styles

Our thinking processes are like a double edged sword. They help us to manage our lives effectively, but certain patterns of thinking can block our ability to take action. Graduate training tends to place an emphasis on analytical skills and values the process of intellectual insight and discovery. Studying a situation carefully and cautiously approaching a problem is a part of the training most academicians receive. It largely works and the scholarship in any discipline is a testament to the effectiveness of using such thought processes.

On the other hand, there are aspects of our thinking processes that affect our ability to analyze our teaching and to make needed changes. One way to approach this problem is to use concepts from Carl Jung's theory discussed in Chapter 1. His model of personality type emphasizes aspects of how we perceive our environment, make decisions, resolve problems, and otherwise process information. Thus, it identifies important components of our cognitive

Self-Reflection Activity 2-6
Asking What "I Do" and Not What "They Do"

Defensive ways of interpreting situations can be countered by refocusing how questions are framed about problems we experience in teaching. Thus, when the focus of attention is directed towards the students, other people, and factors in the environment, it is easy to assign blame outside of myself. A healthier perspective is to shift the focus of attention to *what I do*. When *I* is kept figural in the examination of issues in teaching, and I do not allow myself to consider what *they do,* it is possible to get beyond defensive modes of responding

While looking in a mirror, how would you answer the following questions?

1.] What attitudes and behaviors in students do my teaching methods tend to encourage and are they likely to create the excitement and interest in the content of the course I desire?

2.] How do I currently blame students for the problems that I experience in the classroom? In what ways am I being unfair to the students?

3.] What is one thing I can do to get students to take more initiative and to assume responsibility for their learning?

4] What do students think needs to happen to make this a better course for them? How can I obtain this information from from my students?

style or preferred ways of thinking. The dimensions in Jung's model have several implications for our ability to initiate changes in how we teach. [A summary of each dimension in Jung's theory appears in Tables 1-7 and 1-8 of Chapter 1] To understand how cognitive style can sometimes interfere with modifying our styles as teachers, consider the examples that follow.

A prominent trend today in higher education is the use of collaborative learning strategies. Such methods emphasize students working together in small groups on a variety of instructor-designed or self-designed tasks. *For faculty who are overrepresented on the introversion, intuition, and thinking dimensions of Jung's model [i.e., INT's], such strategies are not as easy to adopt.* The learning tasks typically involve students working on concrete examples and tasks that integrate course content. Such activities often must be designed by a faculty member. The groups work best if productive relationships among group members and with the instructor are developed and maintained. *Thus, the teacher must become a relationship expert.* Group work takes time away from the amount a traditionally oriented instructor normally has available to present conceptual issues in a lecture. Deeper intellectual concerns and issues also may not emerge as often from the groups and/or there may not be as much time to discuss them.

Many of the characteristics of collaborative learning described above are unlikely to engage the interests of someone who is a strongly introverted, intuitive, and thinking type. Collaborative forms of teaching are at odds with an INT's interests and sources of energy, modes of gathering information, and ways of making decisions and solving problems. *Changing from traditional methods to embrace collaborative approaches is less likely to occur.* Such methods are simply not valued as much. *The point is not that faculty members who are INT's cannot or will not use collaborative learning strategies.* Rather, because of their styles, they are less likely to find such methods attractive. They simply become a harder sell.

The critical issue is that our attraction to particular teaching strategies is related to whatever cognitive styles we possess [Review Tables 1-8 and 1-9 in Chapter 1 for examples of such preferences]. To change our teaching entails moving away from the comfortable and the familiar into uncharted territory. The more the methods deviate from our preferred cognitive styles, the more anxiety and tension about using them is likely to occur. *We might be better off considering teaching strategies that fit our styles or enhancing those that do.*

A related point is that we often seek out or at least pay attention to people who are like us. While some discrepancies exist between students and faculty on their cognitive styles [cf., Table 1-12 in Chapter 1], there are always some students whose styles match those of a particular teacher. It is not unusual in my experience to find some instructors gauge the appropriateness of their teaching methods upon the reactions of students whose cognitive styles are most like them. Thus, the motivation to consider options to current methods is lessened because as one colleague told me, "there are always students who manage to get the material in the way that I prefer to teach it."

Even for those willing to consider alternatives to their teaching, the styles may interfere. INT's, for example, are comfortable with reflection and contemplating ideas and future directions for themselves. Usually, they think carefully and thoroughly about their concerns before taking action. In some sense, they adhere to the adage, *Decide in haste—repent at leisure.* While sometimes helpful, they may remain overly comfortable with remaining in the contemplative and preparation stages of the cycle of change.

The latter dimensions are not the only ones that can interfere with considering and/or initiating changes in one's teaching. For *those faculty with a more extravert, sensing, and feeling style [ESF], taking actions may come easier but the analysis needed to successfully implement may be deficient or rushed.* Similarly, teachers with a more extraverted and sensing style may have difficulty communicating with those students who are introverted and intuitive. The latter want more intellectual depth in a course, and in the words on one student, "fewer Mickey Mouse activities that are a waste of my time."

Absolute and Extreme Ways of Thinking

Because the processes of change are intimately tied up with our patterns of thinking, what we think about can facilitate or hinder our attempts to change. Albert Ellis notes that people who say encouraging things about their self-concept, skills and abilities are more willing to manage and adapt to the situations they face. When people give themselves discouraging messages, their willingness to manage issues and to adapt to change decreases.

One of the important classes of beliefs that control our behaviors is irrational beliefs. According to Ellis, such beliefs are characterized by illogical and exaggerated patterns of thinking. Clues to their presence are thoughts and verbal statements that present things in extreme and absolute ways and as a result keep us from exploring options or trying more adaptive behaviors.

Extreme thoughts include words such as *all, every, always, awful, terrible, horrible, totally, and essential.* When they are used, we typically see ourselves and the world in ways that are worse than deserved. *Absolute thoughts* suggest that we have no choices. They include words such as *must, should, have to, need, and ought.* Absolute thinking patterns direct our actions and prevent us from recognizing our choices in a situation.

It is not unusual to see the use of extreme and absolute ways of thinking in the self-reflections of faculty. They become blocks to making changes in their teaching styles. Three ways such thoughts capture our attention and hold us back are listed below [Grasha, 1995]. Examples of each appear in Table 2-4, and suggestions for coping with them are discussed in Self-Reflection Activity 2-7.

- *Irrational thinking drives us away* from a reasonable pace of doing things.

- *Irrational thinking stops us from taking action.*

- *Extreme and absolute ways of thinking distort reality* and leads us to develop false impressions about our lives.

Self-Reflection Activity 2-7
Disputing Absolute and Extreme Beliefs about Change

Part I

1.] Think about a change you tried to make in your teaching that did not work out as well as you had hoped it would. List the change you tried and 2-3 things you remember saying to yourself [i.e., your self-talk] about your attempts to initiate a change and/or the outcome.
For Example:
> *Situation:* I put students into small groups to discuss a problem I had presented in class. Normally I just try to hold a discussion with the entire class.
> *Self-Talk:* Every time I try to put students into small groups for discussion, they either talk about everything but the topic I want them to discuss or only a couple of people participate in the groups." "I'm better off just doing what I normally do.

Your Situation:

Your Self-Talk:

   #1:

   #2:

   #3:

2.] Which type of belief in Table 2-4 does your self-talk fit?
For Example
> "Every time....." [Distorter/Overgeneralization]
> "I'm better off....." [Stopper/Living in the past]

Your Beliefs:
3.] For each of your beliefs you identified that fits the category of a driver, stopper, or distorter in Table 2-4, try to dispute it by doing the following.

Table 2-4
Beliefs That Interfere With Modifying
Our Teaching Styles

Drivers
Keep us from a natural pace. While often rewarded, they may lead us to
become fatigued, exhausted, and frustrated.

Perfectionism:	Be perfect in everything you do in the classroom.
Do it yesterday:	Hurry up, you have to get this done quickly.
Be Macho:	Be strong and put up a tough front. Never let students and colleagues think you are weak.
Self-sacrifice:	Please students, colleagues, and administrators at any cost, or they will not like you.
Push self to limit:	No limit to what you can do. Do as much as you can until it begins to hurt.

Stoppers
Keep us from taking actions, hold us back, and otherwise make us behave as
we always have. Give us a good excuse for doing nothing.

Catastrophizing:	This classroom situation is utterly hopeless. Nothing I do will ever correct it.
Negative thinking:	I can see nothing but gloom and doom here.
Arbitrary inference:	The new things I tried in class today did not work. I guess I should stop innovating.
Rigidity:	There is no reason to change how I teach.
Living in past:	The old ways of doing things are always best.
Waiting around:	I can't do anything until others change first.
Quitter:	I have tried everything and nothing worked.
Procrastination:	I have plenty of time to take care of this issue.

Distorters
Lead us to develop false impressions about ourselves, other people, and
events. They add confusion to our lives.

Overgeneralize:	I had a bad class today and I'll probably never have a good one again.
Blame others:	Students are responsible for what occurred.
Narrow minded:	The way I'm teaching is the only way to do it.
Denial:	This is not a problem I have to worry about.
Stereotype:	Students are basically all alike.
Either/or thinking:	This teaching method will either succeed or fail.
Overestimate:	This is the most horrible thing that has ever happened to me in the classroom.
llogical thoughts:	My colleagues must support me no matter what I do with my teaching.
Personalization	Somehow, bad things seem to happen just to me."

Self-Reflection 2-7 [Continued]

Part II

Restate that thought so that it reflects a more balanced and even-handed perspective on the situation that you could accept.
For Example:
  Not all of the groups drifted away from the topic. At most only two or three of the ten groups did so and it was in those groups that I noticed only a few people participating. Also, I'm not really sure that going back to my usual way of doing things is justified. After all, the reason I wanted to try this was because I was dissatisfied with trying to hold discussions with the entire group.

Your restatement:

  # 1:

  # 2:

  # 3:

4.] New ways of thinking without actions to back them up are largely empty thoughts. What action steps could you take to reinforce this new way of thinking about what happened?
For Example:
  I need to continue trying the small group format and examine why some groups get off of the topic. Maybe I'm giving them too much time or the instructions are not clear enough. Making the groups smaller also might help to allow everyone to participate. I just need to try some things instead of giving up.

Actions you can take that fit your restatement [s] of the situation:

  # 1:

  # 2:

  # 3:

Countering absolute and extreme beliefs involves developing a balanced perspective on what changes to make in our teaching and the expected outcomes of our efforts. *We must avoid becoming our own worst enemy.* The goal here is not to become self-delusional about the difficulties that sometimes exist whenever we try to change. Rather, the goal is to give ourselves the benefit of the doubt and to keep ourselves motivated to continue looking for ways to enhance our teaching.

A balanced perspective, unfortunately, is not enough. We also need to take actions consistent with any new way of looking at ourselves and the world around us. Otherwise, we run the risk of being "all talk and no action."

Furthermore, several lines of research suggest that our behaviors tend to reinforce underlying belief systems [Watson & Tharp, 1993; Weinberg, 1984]. Thus, if I believe my attempts to produce changes in my teaching never work, continuing to behave as I always do will only further strengthen my existing beliefs. If I can see my attempts to change as producing several positive and negative outcomes, however, then I have begun to distance myself from thoughts that it never works. By taking actions to examine what works and what does not, and to subsequently look for ways to improve, eventually helps me reinforce new beliefs about myself and my capacity to change. In effect, the process of initiating new behaviors in line with a balanced or less extreme perspective has the potential to help me redefine myself. If successful, I have taken a small step along the road of self-renewal. A succession of such *small wins* can help me to eventually make significant changes in my teaching style.

Epilogue

Themes and Variations

The information in this section was organized around several interrelated themes. *One was the emphasis on the important role that self-reflection plays in identifying, employing, and modifying our styles as teachers.* Unless we reflect and analyze our current behaviors as teachers, and try to identify the attitudes, values, and beliefs associated with our practices, our understanding of our teaching styles becomes limited. Under such conditions, we will see the outcomes of our efforts but will remain relatively unaware of the processes used to produce those results.

Also, without adequate amounts of self-reflection, people typically fail to gain a good sense of "Who Am I" as a teacher. Attempts to change under such conditions are likely to be superficial. In such cases, my experience suggests that teaching strategies and practices often fail to fit the underlying dynamics of the person trying to use them. The result is frustration, inadequate execution, and a lack of commitment to working the *bugs out of them.*

A second theme was the importance of self-reflection in a cycle of change . A model of change in teaching style was presented that includes stages of pre-contemplation, contemplation, planning, action, and maintenance. There were two important aspects of this model that are largely ignored in current thinking about faculty development. *A considerable amount of time must be spent in self-reflection before changes in our teaching styles is possible.* In the Prochaska change model discussed in this section, people need time in the reflective components of the change cycle [i.e., the pre-contemplation and contemplation stages].

Instructors must first become comfortable with the need to change before the planning and action stages can be engaged. Prematurely engaging the planning and action cycles because of pressures from others is unlikely to produce successful outcomes. Faculty wanting to initiate changes in their teaching styles, and those interested in promoting faculty development in teaching, must allow adequate amounts of time for such reflective processes to occur.

Furthermore, relapses can be expected. In my experience, they are often the rule rather than the exception when attempting to modify one's style as a teacher. Whether someone uses a relapse to learn from their mistakes or to chastise themselves ultimately determines whether that individual will experience a successful outcome. My contacts with college faculty suggest that if they decide to persist after a relapse, usually they return to the contemplative stage in the cycle of change. Most need additional time to think about it before engaging in further action steps.

The third theme in this chapter was the way various thinking processes and cognitive styles hindered and/or blocked the cycle of change. Included in the discussion were examples of defensive modes of thinking such as defensive avoidance, denial, defensive pessimism, and defensive attributions that adversely affected an objective analysis of one's teaching. Aspects of our cognitive styles such as being overly analytical, intuitive, and introverted also may clash with the styles of students as well as interfere with our ability to modify our instructional processes. Finally, the use of absolute and extreme modes of thinking about classroom issues may lead us to distort or exaggerate the problems we face and stop us from taking actions to correct them.

The Cognitive Imperative

Information presented in this chapter placed a considerable amount of emphasis on the role cognitive factors played in attempts to understand and to consider changes in our styles as teachers. *The position taken was that our patterns of thinking largely determine our ability to successfully initiate and complete such changes.* Self-understanding through actively engaging processes of self-analysis and reflection was seen as a crucial first step in this process. *One might argue, however, that such an approach is simplistic and ignores other factors such as:* the rewards [or lack thereof] for teaching in our institutions; the pressures for research and scholarly production; declining resources, large classes, unprepared students, poor faculty preparation for teaching, a lack of funds for faculty development, anti-intellectual political climates, insensitive administrators, and poor institutional leadership

Such factors have been prominent members of the *laundry list* of *why it's difficult to change things around here* for decades. *Yet analyses of the resistance to instructional change based on this laundry list have missed an important point.* When times are tough [i.e., the laundry list is in effect] some faculty still manage to find ways to enhance the nature and quality of their teaching. And, tough times in higher education have existed for at least the past decade. Yet, a variety of innovations in curriculum and teaching processes have taken hold [e.g., general education reforms, writing across the curriculum, classroom assessment processes, collaborative learning, active learning, a renewed emphasis on critical thinking.] I am also reminded that even when times were not so tough [e.g., the period of the 60's and 70's come to mind], instructional improvement and curricular reform was still a hard sell.

Thus, it does not appear to be the case that the mere presence or absence of items from the above mentioned "laundry list" are associated with the willingness of people to evoke changes in their teaching. In my work over the past two decades in higher education, I see such factors as a backdrop in which individuals and groups decide to initiate changes. They are part of the context in which change occurs and not simply forces that individually or collectively dictate the course of instructional and curriculum change.

Rather, the most important factors in my experiences are cognitive. *One is the tendency mentioned earlier for people to drift into absolute and extreme ways of interpreting events.* This leads to overgeneralizations, arbitrary inferences and exaggerations of current conditions and what is possible to do. They tend to prevent or hinder change. For example, a faculty member participating in a seminar I was running on teaching issues said, "The current fiscal and political environment for higher education is the worst thing to happen to our educational system. In such an environment, there is little reason to look for ways to become creative in my teaching. I'm better off just doing what I've always done and hope for the best."

Optimistic and Pessimistic Explanatory Styles and Processes of Change in Teaching

Maintaining an optimistic or pessimistic outlook towards the environment affects our ability to change. In my work, I find that whether faculty members interpret events in optimistic or pessimistic terms also is associated with their capacity to change. Technically, such interpretations are labeled our "explanatory style." Research by Chris Peterson [1991] and

Table 2-5
Characteristics of Optimistic and Pessimistic Explanatory Styles

Our explanations and interpretations of incidents in our teaching reflect three underlying beliefs that we have about them. They are:

- *The event was a stable / permanent or an unstable / temporary part of my life.*

- *The event was a global / pervasive experience for me or was confined to a specific situation.*

- *The event was due to personal or internal causes or was caused by external events outside of my control.*

Individuals with optimistic and pessimist explanatory styles interpret events differently. Pessimists explain bad things that happen as stable over time, pervasive across situations, and as something they influenced. Optimists cope by interpreting such events as unstable, confined to a specific situation, and due to factors outside of their control. *Just the opposite occurs when they are asked to explain why good things happened to them.*

Scenario 1: A teacher tries to use a small group collaborative activity for the first time. The small group work and discussion did not go very well.

Pessimistic: "I've always had trouble getting small groups to discuss content."

Stable/Permanent |___X___|_____|_____|_____| Unstable/Temporary
                                                                X

Optimistic: "I've learned something. That mistake won't happen the next time."

_____

Pessimistic: "Seems like I mess up small group activities no matter what I teach."

Global/Pervasive   X   Specific
Experience |_____|_____|_____|_____| Situation
                                          X

Optimistic: "This class is the only group where I've seen such problems occur."

_____

Pessimistic: "I have no one to blame but myself for doing something so foolish."

Internal Cause |___X___|_____|_____|_____| External Cause
                                             X

Optimistic: "The students were tired at the end of the week and it was difficult for them to keep their attention focused during the activity."

Table 2-5 [Continued]

Scenario 2: A teacher who normally lectures decides to try case studies as the primary teaching method for a course. After four sessions, the use of cases is working out very well.

Pessimistic: "I don't think my initial successes will last for the remainder of the term."

Stable/Permanent |_____|_____|_____|__ X __| Unstable/Temporary
               X

Optimistic: "Everything should continue to work out well this term."

_____

Pessimistic: "Cases work well but I doubt they would do so in my other classes."

Global/Pervasive |_____|_____|_____|__ X __| Specific
  Experience   X   Situation

Optimistic: "This is a great way to teach. I bet it would work in my other course."

_____

Pessimistic: "I'm either having a run of good luck or some very special students."

Internal Cause |_____|_____|_____|__ X __| External Cause
                  X

Optimistic: "The hard work and preparation for this course is really paying off."

Martin Seligman [1991] have identified the underlying components of optimistic and pessimistic explanations. These are illustrated in Table 2-5.

Peterson's and Seligman's empirical research on optimistic and pessimistic explanatory styles has identified differences between people who prefer one set of explanations to the other. Those with an optimistic mode of thinking were more willing to take control of events in their lives. They engaged in solution based problem solving and were generally happier and excited about the work they did.

Also, they were more willing to try new things and to speculate on the positive implications of ideas for the future. As a group they tended to maintain a balanced perspective on events and were not subject to exaggeration, arbitrary inferences, and overgeneralizations. Finally, they were self-confident, less anxious, and less depressed.

Their pessimistic counterparts, however, tended to believe there was little they could do to produce changes in their lives. At the extreme, they saw life as a game where they were pawns subject to the whims of outside forces. Denial and defensive approaches to managing problems were often employed. Furthermore, they did not persist as well in their attempts to initiate changes in their lives. They also tended to perceive events in much more absolute and extreme ways. Personality wise, they tended to be less confident of their skills and more anxious and depressed.

My sense of the college faculty with whom I worked with over the years who have attempted to produce changes in their teaching, and who succeeded over the long-haul, is that they possessed an optimistic outlook. As noted in Table 2-5, they were able to perceive unfavorable conditions for change in ways that did not hold them back. They also did not discount positive forces for change in their environment. Their optimistic outlook facilitated their ability to initiate the cycle of change discussed in this chapter.

In his research program, Martin Seligman [1991] has demonstrated that tendencies to be inappropriately pessimistic can be countered. He argues that people need to consider modifying pessimistic interpretations of good and bad events in order to enhance their satisfaction with aspects of their lives. One process he has examined for accomplishing this goal is similar to the one described in Self-Reflection Activity 2-7. *Because overly pessimistic ways of interpreting events often represent absolute and extreme ways of thinking, attempts should be made to dispute them.* This would be accomplished by training ourselves to adopt the optimistic modes of interpreting positive and negative events described in Table 2-5.

For positive and negative events that occur in the classroom, for example, we would counter a normally pessimistic explanation by asking several questions. *For positive events given a pessimistic interpretation we would look for ways to enhance our sense of personal optimism.* That is, to see good events as much more stable over time than we normally think, to perceive them as occurring in more than one situation in our lives, and to give ourselves more credit for producing the positive outcome. *The questions to ask are:*

- Is this pleasant event really as unstable over time as I am making it out to be? What concrete evidence do I have from my experiences that what occurred was a "fluke? At what other time periods in my teaching have I been successful in trying new things?

- What evidence do I have that this is basically the only situation where I have had such a positive experience in my teaching? What are other examples of specific classes and/or courses where I have been successful as a teacher?

- What makes me so sure that luck, chance, or other factors outside of my control produced the positive results I obtained? What are 2-3 specific thoughts and actions that I took to make what I tried in this class/course successful?

For negative events given a pessimistic interpretation, we also would look for ways to enhance our sense of personal optimism. That is, to view bad events as much more stable over time than we normally think, to perceive them as having much more limited occurrences, and to see that other people and events often contribute to things not working out as well for us. *The questions to ask are:*

- Is this unpleasant experience a good representation of how bad things always happen to me? In what ways was it unusual or different from other unpleasant events in my life. What are examples of good things that have happened in my teaching from time to time?

- What elements of what happened were confined to this particular teaching situation? What is it about this class and/or course that are unique from others I currently teach and/or have taught in my career?

- Is everything that happens in my life and in my teaching always my fault? What other factors besides my thoughts and actions played a role in what happened? In what ways did the environment, the students, colleagues, or others play a role in making this an unpleasant experience?

Booters and Bootstrappers

Self-reflection is a necessary step in the process of modifying or changing our styles as teachers. At some point in our reflection and analysis, however, the preparation and action stages of the cycle of change must be engaged. Good intentions must be translated into plans that contain specific goals and objectives for ourselves. *Taking actions and adopting patterns of thinking compatible with such plans must be initiated.* This, of course, is the most difficult part of the process. If it were easy people would seldom have problems with anxiety, depression, and stress. Whatever needed to be accomplished would be quickly initiated and life would soon return to normal.

In addition to the issues raised about overcoming thinking patterns that interfere with change, some attention also must be given to our beliefs about human plasticity. This concept refers to our beliefs about whether or not people can change and what it takes to change them. Psychologist Martin Seligman [1994] in his book titled *What You Can Change and What You Can't* argues that such beliefs enter the equation.

Seligman views people's beliefs about change as falling into the categories of booters and bootstrappers. *Booters believe that outside forces are needed for them and others to change.* This might be metaphorically a swift kick, a gentle nudge, or some desired incentive that makes the risk involved worthwhile. They believe that outside forces must intervene before people are willing to initiate changes in their lives.

Bootstrappers, on the other hand, see people as holding the keys for change within themselves. "It has to come from within or else it will not last," a participant in a workshop mentioned. If anything, bootstrappers perceive outside forces as getting in the way and as stifling creativity. They want to be their own person and resist others telling them what to do.

To determine where you stand on the latter two dimensions, answer the following questions when you arrive at a choice point where a decision to initiate some change in your life is needed.

> • Do I now have the skills and abilities to make the changes I desire? Or, could I acquire them?
>
> • If I took the desired actions, would the outcome be successful?
>
> • Can I make this change in my life happen by myself?

Those who answer *yes* to each item would fall into Seligman's category of bootstrappers. Booters would typically answer *no* to each of them. They would not see themselves as having the skills and abilities to initiate needed changes. Their chances of success also would be assessed as low. Instead, such individuals would see the need for someone else to intervene to help them change and generally to show them the way.

I suspect, however, that these are not enduring characteristics of people. Situations play an important role here. For example, my experience suggests that most college faculty members are reluctant to change aspects of their professional lives. When their scholarship and teaching are compared, variations in research programs and the types of issues studied within an area are more likely to change. *With regard to making changes in their scholarly interests, they behave more like bootstrappers.*

A stronger tendency to settle into familiar modes of instruction, however, seems to prevail. Some of the major reasons for this have been outlined in this chapter. While some do change and embrace new modes of teaching on their own, bootstrapping in modifying teaching processes is not in my experience the norm. Instead, financial and enrollment crises, institutional curriculum reform, pressure to make a good case for one's teaching in a promotion, reappointment, or tenure process, as well as expectations of administrators and colleagues often stimulate thoughts and actions directed towards change. In a sense, they function like the boot in Seligman's model of change.

While Seligman's categories might be somewhat simplistic, he does raise the issue that not everyone can become a self-initiating and self-directed change agent in everything they attempt to accomplish. At times, everyone needs some amount of outside support and encouragement to take productive action to change some aspect of their lives. In spite of this observation, *we must bear in mind that unless people have done their contemplative homework, little can be expected even with the best of outside forces intervening.*

ɟ with Style"

ling of who we are as teachers as well as
ɡness to change, a roadmap that provides specific
ɪhis roadmap might include specific goals and objectives
ɪal qualities we wish to develop, or perhaps instructional
ɕ want to use. In the normal course of things, the latter are often
ɪs of self-reflective processes on teaching. Indeed, given the content
ɪhapters 1 and 2 in this book, they would be expected.

Unfortunately, such things are not enough. What we decide to do should be compatible with a coherent philosophy of teaching. *Like scholarship, the practice of teaching must be grounded in a theoretical or conceptual base.* The methods employed in scholarly activity are often in the service of conceptual and theoretical issues. Scholarly activity often tests and develops theories, conceptual issues are used to organize and explain information, and most scholars identify themselves with one or more theoretical positions.

In much the same way, various elements of our styles as teachers should have a foundation of principles and concepts known to affect teaching and learning processes. This base can include a broad range of personal assumptions about teaching and learning, definitions of teaching, formal principles of human learning, assumptions about human nature, as well as formal and informal models about the teaching-learning process. Thus, instructors might adopt a particular teaching process because it fits an accepted principle of learning [e.g., retention is facilitated when students work in small groups and critically analyze a passage of text]. Or, perhaps experience shows that particular topics are best taught in very small steps. Self-study packets that cover discrete topics are then developed to help an instructor mold this personal assumption to particular classroom processes.

The important point is that the selection of teaching processes should not be based on personal whim or perhaps how the course was taught last time. Rather, attempts should be made to make teaching analogous to processes of scholarship. *In particular, care should be taken to ensure that our teaching is guided and directed by conceptual underpinnings that reflect more than habits we acquired for managing classes. What is needed is a consistent philosophy of teaching that helps us to make informed choices about what style of teaching to adopt.* This relationship between theory and practice, however, is not a one-way street. While theory informs the practice of teaching, what we learn from the practice of teaching also affects the development of pedagogical theory [cf., Richlin & Cox, 1991] for an excellent discussion and overview of a broader range of issues regarding the interplay of scholarship and teaching].

In Chapter 3, suggestions for how to integrate the issues raised above into your teaching are raised. In the process, the foundations for developing a personal philosophy of teaching that informs one's instruction are illustrated.

3. Developing a Conceptual Base for Our Teaching Styles

"Things are not what they seem ...."

- Mr. Miyagi to Daniel in the movie, *The Karate Kid*

I have always been fascinated with the original version of the movie *The Karate Kid*. The story is about a single mom and her teenage son who move to California. Unfortunately, her son has to deal with several bullies who use Karate to abuse other kids. Her son, Daniel, enlists the aid of Pat Morita's character [Mr. Miyagi] to teach him Karate. Daniel must promise, however, to do everything Mr. Miyagi asks without question. The latter condition, of course, is a teacher's dream.

At the crack of dawn on successive mornings, he washes and waxes Mr. Miyagi's collection of antique cars, paints his fence and the side of his home, and sands his deck with a hand- held sander. All the time, he reminds Daniel of the slow rhythmic circular and vertical hand motions needed to do each task.

In frustration one evening, Daniel rebels. He tells Mr. Miyagi that he is tired of being his personal slave and that Mr. Miyagi has not lived up to his end of the bargain. "I've done everything you've asked," Daniel says, "But you have not taught me one thing about Karate." Daniel turns and starts to walk away when Mr. Miyagi calls out, "Daniel, wait." Daniel stops and turns to face him and Mr. Miyagi tells him, "Things are not what they seem." Daniel appears momentarily puzzled when Mr. Miyagi suddenly lashes out with his arms and he instinctively uses his hands to defend against this unexpected attack. The hand motions he uses are exactly those he practiced while doing the chores.

Daniel obviously learned a tremendous amount from Mr. Miyagi without recognizing it at the time. He learned obedience, discipline, the need to focus on a task, and to respect authority. Along the way, he also learned some rudimentary movements in Karate.

Sometimes when telling this story to a group of college faculty at a workshop, someone says, "Grasha, that's a wonderful story. I've been telling people for years that students may not understand or appreciate what I'm doing now, but one day in the future, they will recognize the value of what I've taught them." Unfortunately, such statements miss an important point. Mr. Miyagi's teaching style was explicitly planned to introduce Daniel to Karate. It was not something he pulled out of a hat and secretly hoped would someday produce results. *His approach to teaching was deliberate, thoughtful, and designed to produce certain outcomes in the learner.*

Also, when workshop participants are asked what assumptions and principles about how people learn were part of Mr. Miyagi's style, the following are popular responses:

- *People learn by doing.*

- *They learn by repeating basic skills on different tasks.*

- *Individuals learn by transferring skills from one task to another.*

- *People learn by having to discipline themselves to accomplish goals they may not completely understand at the time.*

- *We learn through a process of self-discovery the knowledge and skills that ultimately will be important to us.*

In effect, there was an implicit conceptual base associated with Mr. Miyagi's teaching style. The strategies and methods employed did not exist in isolation from principles and ideas about how people learn. *And perhaps what is most important here, he undoubtedly chooses a style of teaching that would maximize the use of the above principles.*

Beyond Pedagogy

Developing a teaching style is not about selecting particular methods from a *bag of teaching tricks*. Our teaching styles, like scholarship, should be based upon a conceptual base that forms our philosophy of teaching. This philosophy of teaching acts like a roadmap and helps to guide our thoughts, behaviors, the selection of particular instructional techniques, and our general outlook on who we are and what we want to become as teachers. *Without an explicit philosophy of teaching, our teaching styles are intellectually hollow.*

The content that we teach in our disciplines is intellectually rich. It is often based on scholarly research and inquiry and typically has an underlying philosophical, theoretical, and empirical base. The facts and ideas we teach are not pulled out of a hat. Those we choose to present also are not selected randomly. Typically, there is a broader point or theme that individual pieces of information play an important role in developing. In effect, our content has an intellectual history that can be unpacked and displayed for all to see.

The selection of particular teaching methods is often not as well developed. When college faculty were asked in workshop settings and interviews about what influenced the methods of teaching they employed, a number of diverse responses were given. The most frequently cited reasons are listed in Table 3-1.

In the responses shown in Table 3-1, there is a focus on methods and a relative absence of how the methods relate to theories, principles, and accepted assumptions about the teaching learning process. Beliefs about such things are largely absent from the rationale given for using particular teaching techniques. In my experience, only a small minority of faculty list conceptual issues or a systematic philosophy of teaching as a justification for their instructional processes.

Table 3-1
Most Frequently Cited Reasons Faculty Give
For Adopting Teaching Methods

- My experiences as a student.
- How I think my colleagues and/or students expect me to teach.
- The goals that I have as a teacher.
- How I taught the course the last time I taught it.
- What I think will help me present the information best.
- Ideas I picked up talking about teaching with colleagues.
- How people I admired as teachers conducted their classes.
- Techniques I learned about reading a book or article on teaching.
- Processes I learned about attending a workshop on teaching.
- My ideas about how to best facilitate learning.
- Ideas from the research literature on teaching and learning.
- Processes my professional organization wants us to use more often.
- I'm a Rogerian, Behaviorist, Psychodynamic oriented person,
- I'm a [Rogerian, Behaviorist, Psychodynamic oriented person, Cognitive scientist, etc.,] and teach accordingly.
- I'm from the old school and use traditional methods because I've never learned how to do it any other way.
- I'm not sure, I guess I just tried a few things along the way and eventually drifted into this way of teaching.

The Instructional Method Bias

This focus on disembodied teaching methods is a pervasive bias in higher education. When asked to visit a campus to conduct a workshop or seminar, I am frequently asked to "make sure you tell us about some of your favorite teaching methods." When colleagues meet to discuss their classes, the discussion typically focuses on how well aspects of one's lecture, discussion process, role plays, or other "methods" were executed. And, when materials are assembled for promotion, reappointment, and tenure, a syllabus is often requested along with evaluations of one's teaching. What the latter emphasize are the methods employed and how well others think they were executed.

Historically, people who were perceived as "purveyors of pedagogy" were second class citizens in higher education. Teachers, instructional consultants, educators and others in the latter categories were perceived as only dealing in "technique and method." This was not scholarship and inquiry as practiced in what one person told me were "more advanced disciplines." Another said, "pedagogy lacks intellectual substance. It's about technique and nothing more." "What is often implied is that such knowledge is less complex, less understandable, and less amenable to scientific study" [Berliner, 1986, p. 13]. What is forgotten is that expertise in teaching as in anything else involves domain-specific knowledge. It can and is studied scientifically! Because it involves practical knowledge, however, it is placed lower in the hierarchy of importance by those pursuing in their minds higher and more complex interests [Berliner, 1986].

I also vividly remember early in my career an encounter with this bias in a meeting with a former provost of my university. He was a conservative individual who found it difficult to understand how faculty within a discipline could learn anything useful about teaching from anyone outside of the discipline. His idea of faculty development was to pair a new faculty member with an experienced one in the tradition of the apprentice model. He never did this, of course, he only thought it was a good idea.

After describing his apprentice model, he said to me, "You see Grasha, you deal in Ped—A—Go—Gy." The words were drawn out in a sarcastic manner. "This place is about more important things. Scholarship is what drives this institution, not pedagogy."

It was hard for me at the time to completely dismiss what he was saying. One reason was that my Faculty Resource Center reported directly to his office and he was my boss. [How I managed the resource center in the face of this bias is another story.] I was not interested in exploring his views because I did not think they could be influenced by rational argument.

The other reason for not exploring the issue was that he was right. What people could easily see in the 'purveyors of pedagogy" were the methods they endorsed. The intellectual underpinning of those techniques was not publicly displayed. Unless one knew about theories of teaching and learning within education and psychology, and was familiar with the large body of empirical data in these areas, the methods might appear to exist in a vacuum.

The reality is that strategies for teaching and learning are often based upon empirical research and/or theoretical systems about how people learn. Unfortunately, this conceptual base is not communicated as well to people outside the *inner circle* as are the details of specific teaching strategies and techniques. Thus, what most people learn about teaching is one or more methods that they can use. The fact that those methods are grounded in empirical data, that they have an underlying theoretical base, and often possess an intellectual history is seldom recognized.

In the final analysis, "teaching will be considered a scholarly activity only when professors develop a conception of pedagogy that is very tightly coupled to scholarship in the disciplines themselves" [Shulman, 1987, p. 20]. *One way to link our teaching styles to scholarship is to insure that they are guided and directed by a conceptual or theoretical base.* To do this, the selection of teaching methods should mimic the way methods of scholarship are chosen in almost any discipline. For example:

- *Methods are generally used to achieve particular goals [i.e., to test hypotheses, to answer research questions].*

- *Those goals typically come from some theoretical or conceptual base.*

- *Methods are chosen because they are compatible with the theoretical or conceptual issues studied.*

• *The adequacy of a research project is often assessed by how well the outcomes support particular goals [i.e., hypotheses, research questions].*

• *The adequacy of the methods also is determined by how well they allowed certain goals to be achieved.*

A research study, for example, would not be very interesting if the write-up said "I used x, y, and z methods to gather information and my findings appear below." Rather, it is the theoretical or conceptual base in which particular methods are couched that makes them interesting. Consider the following statement. "Because I was interested in exploring the conceptual position taken by authors in this area, methods x, y, and z helped me to answer the following questions. The findings are presented below and they are compatible with theories and ideas derived from the literature. The methods employed were adequate to answer the questions I had raised."

The Need for a Conceptual Base

In much the same way, the selection of our styles as teachers should be embedded in a conceptual context that includes principles of teaching and learning. This would help to give instructional processes a coherent theoretical structure that typically they now lack. In effect, the intellectual base would guide and direct the selection of goals to pursue, the instructional methods employed, and the desired outcomes. Evaluating processes also would examine the fit of the goals, methods, and outcomes to some underlying conceptual scheme.

For example, a history professor once told me that his goals in a survey course were: to teach his students to know basic historical facts, to think critically about historical issues, to develop positive societal values, and to have them learn to appreciate how historical themes appeared in modern life. I then asked him how he taught such things. He replied, "I give them very detailed and insightful lectures." When asked how he evaluated the students' ability to achieve such goals, he replied, "I use clever multiple choice exam items." In effect, his goals and methods were discrepant.

The latter problem could be avoided by designing a course with a philosophy of teaching and learning in mind. Such principles would allow someone to select methods that would realistically help achieve particular goals. If a teacher, for example, believed that "students learn best when actively involved in the classroom," alternatives to the lecture could be explored. Thus, attempts to achieve goals such as "teaching critical thinking" and "positive societal values" might better occur through small group discussions, position papers, and debates among students on important issues.

On the other hand, if one believed that "students learn best through very detailed and insightful lectures," evaluation processes would test that assumption. *It is unlikely that "clever multiple-choice exam items" would be a sufficient outcome measure for all of the stated goals.* Other methods of evaluation used might include whether students could write critical essays on the relationship of historical issues to modern times and their ability to list the positive societal values they acquired in the course. The outcomes of such evaluations would probably show that the lecture method helped students to acquire basic historical facts but did little to affect their ability to achieve the other goals.

In the process, a teacher would have to seriously question the principles of teaching and learning that guided the choice of instructional methods. Other ideas of how people learn and the role of the teacher would be examined. Or, the lofty goals would have to be set aside without evidence to support them. This is not an uncommon problem. In my experiences, many teachers can articulate classroom goals but typically find it difficult to assess them. Thus, they either assume their "wished for outcomes" will occur or are content to employ traditional assessment devices such as exams and term papers. The range of other possibilities for assessing student outcomes is not widely known. For those readers interested in exploring a diverse set of goals in their teaching, Table 3-2 contains ideas for assessing student outcomes that are appropriate for a variety of instructional goals.

Our course goals, the corresponding methods used to help achieve them, and evaluations of the outcomes produced are interconnected. And, each of the latter components should relate to an underlying intellectual base that guides and directs what goals, methods, and evaluation processes are selected. Figure 3-1 illustrates the basic components of a conceptual base to teaching. The role of evaluation processes in this scheme are outlined in Figure 3-2.

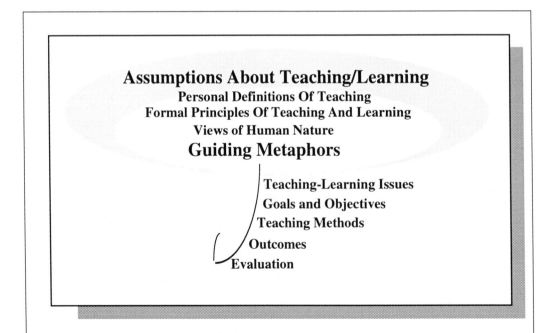

Figure 3-1: Elements in a conceptual base for teaching.

Table 3-2
Instructional Goals and Outcome Measures

General Goals	Outcome Measures
Student content achievement, including factual knowledge, competencies in using various skills, and ability to meet specific course objectives	Classroom exams and quizzes. Criterion-referenced exams. Standardized achievement exams for disciplines developed by Educational Testing Service and other sources. Professional board exams in fields like architecture and health sciences. Instructor observations and self-reports of students on their behavior in class.
Variations in learning styles of students	Use of collaborative, independent, participatory and other learning style measures [e.g., GRSLSS in Chapter 4].
Quality of student life in the classroom	Use of questionnaires and/or interviews that assess students' responses to the classroom environment, including course procedures, instructor behaviors, textbooks, other course materials and resources, relevance of course to their programs of study, overall satisfaction.
Developing skills students can use in occupational and other settings	Comments of employers on students' progress in jobs that specific classes trained them for. Evaluations of students from people familiar with their accomplishments. Significant achievements in later life that various sources agree are related in part to particular instructors or programs.
Application of concepts	Classroom exams that stress application of concepts and principles. Performance of students on simulation exercises that use course concepts. Performance of students in practicum experiences as rated by supervisors.
Writing skills	Brief in-class reaction papers. Term papers, lab reports, essay tests, literature reviews, position papers, short-stories.

Table 3-2 [Continued]

General Goals	Outcome Measures
Ability to think creatively and to improve problem-solving and decision-making skills	Classroom and/or standardized tests for creativity and problem solving skills. Ratings by peers, instructors, employers, or other sources of students' ability to develop new solutions to problems. Performance in classroom simulations and role-playing activities that demand such skills.
Variations in values and self-concept and career changes as a result of instructional processes	Self-reports of students. Information from standardized measures of values and occupational preferences. Observations of student performance in classroom simulations, role plays, and other activities that have students use personal values, beliefs, and career-related interests and skills.
Collaborative skills	Group tasks and projects [cf., teaching strategies in Chapters 7 & 8].
Quality of instructor's life in the classroom	Self-reports on perceptions of satisfaction with aspects of one's classroom role.
Instruction producing effects on beyond the immediate classroom.	Included here are new courses that were added to a curriculum, recognition the school received because of a particular course offering, willingness of people to select majors due to the quality of the instruction, and teaching methods and courses that led to outside funding. Use of self-reports or peer observations.
Creating successful variations in instructor's teaching styles	Use of teaching style measures discussed in Chapters 1 and 4.
Use of new classroom procedures and methods to accomplish instructional goals	Descriptions of course designs, syllabi, the materials used, and the evaluations of their quality and usefulness. Comparisons of teaching methods before changes with those used afterward.
Developing critical thinking skills	Class projects that emphasize analysis of information, identifying problems, examining underlying assumptions, and developing valid conclusions. Problem solving/decision making activities.

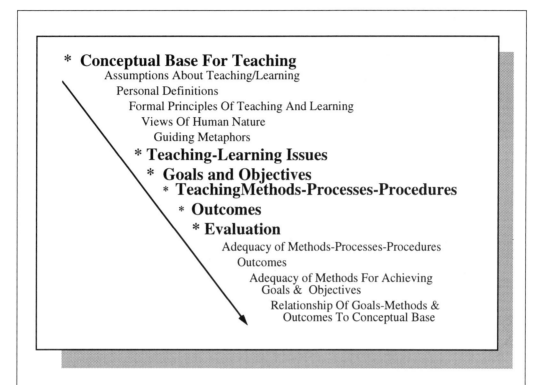

Figure 3-2: Relationship of evaluation processes to each element in a conceptual base for teaching. All of the elements listed above are interrelated.

Consciously Identifying Your Conceptual Base

It would be fair to say that a conceptual base is at least implicit in whatever teaching style someone adopts. The problem is that not everyone is aware of it. A philosophy of teaching only becomes useful when we can identify its components and then decide what aspects of it we want to keep, modify, or perhaps drop. In the process, we can then choose additions to the principles of teaching and learning we would like to see in our teaching. There are certain advantages to consciously identifying, modifying, and adding to our conceptual base. They include:

- *Consciously identifying and selecting principles of teaching and learning to guide our selection of teaching processes makes their selection more than a personal whim.* Thus, when challenged about why certain processes are used, a response other than "I like to teach this way" is possible. One can now say, for example, "Students learn best when they are actively involved in the material and can discuss their ideas with other students. This discussion technique I'm using gives me a vehicle to use the latter principles in my teaching."

- *Basing our teaching style on a clear conceptual base allows us to go beyond the content when designing a course.* If one assumes, for example, that learners possess a variety of learning styles, then course design must reflect more than considerations of what content to teach. At a minimum, one would have to address the issue of how to teach content to learners with independent, collaborative, visual, and auditory preferences. Creative solutions to such problems make the design and implementation of classroom processes much more exciting.

• *Consciously basing our teaching style on a conceptual base allows us to challenge personal beliefs about effective instructional practices.* An experience with a faculty member I worked with illustrates this point. He taught a political science course using a lecture-discussion process. He was aware of research findings showing that students who engaged in active-learning processes such as small group discussion and problem solving activities were more satisfied and had higher levels of achievement in the classroom. "What I realized," he said to me, " was that my current teaching style was incompatible with the concept of active learning. Lecturing is a wonderful active learning experience for me but does little for the students in that regard. I must find a way to bring the same benefits to my students." Exploring principles of teaching and learning allowed him to make thoughtful comparisons to his own teaching.

• *Consciously identifying and selecting the conceptual issues that underlie our teaching styles helps us to overcome "mindless" ways of designing courses.* In her research program, psychologist Ellen Langer [1989a; 1989b] defines *mindlessness* as processing information without attention to details in a familiar, routine, and predictable manner. It appears in our actions anytime we do the following:

  a.] Using categories or distinctions learned from past experience as rigid guides for current behaviors.

  b.] Behaviors are initiated without giving much conscious thought to questions such as, "Why am I doing this?" "What is the purpose of my teaching this way?" "What am I really trying to accomplish in my teaching?"

  c.] Acting from a single perspective or mindset and failing to consider alternate perspectives on issues [e.g., "What other options for thinking about the design of this course and my classroom behaviors do I have?"]

Such tendencies occurred in the responses of several faculty I once interviewed about why they employed particular teaching styles. While many responses were thoughtful and reflected an underlying philosophy of teaching, others included: "I'm more familiar with these methods." "That's the way I was told to teach in graduate school." "I've always taught this course this way." And, "this is the way I taught the course the last time I was responsible for it."

Ellen Langer argues that the best way to overcome the drift toward *mindlessness* is to recognize the signs of it and to take actions to prevent a recurrence. It is defeated when people develop, what she labels a mental state of *mindfulness.* Self-Reflection Activity 3-1 illustrates several ways to become mindful when designing a course around our teaching styles.

Components of a Conceptual Base

Each component of the conceptual base identified in Figure 3-1 undoubtedly plays at least an implicit role in our teaching styles. As noted above, an important task is to bring what implicitly guides and directs our instruction into conscious awareness. When this is done, we might discover that some aspects of our conceptual base is developed better than others. It is also possible that focusing on each component can help us modify and change the underlying intellectual rationale for our teaching. Finally, it should become clear that the components are interrelated. Each gives us a somewhat different perspective on why we teach as we do. Yet, each is ultimately needed to fully understand the intellectual underpinnings of our teaching styles. The remaining parts of this section examine in detail each of the components of a conceptual base.

Personal Assumptions about Teaching and Learning

> As we see them, assumptions are the beliefs we have about the causes of behavior. Assumptions are generally related to the things we take for granted about why we and other people behave as we do. In the context of the classroom, they represent our personal storehouse of knowledge about the teaching-learning process. Thus, personal assumptions are a collection of truths, half-truths, myths, prejudices, biases, and other opinions about why teachers and students behave as they do.
>
> - Fuhrmann and Grasha

Whatever our assumptions, they help to guide and direct our actions in the classroom. If I assume that all students are lazy and will only work if the teacher rewards their actions, my classroom procedures will probably reflect teacher control and rewards. On the other hand, if I assume that students can grow and develop in many areas with little assistance from me, then I will exert less direct control over the class.

A variety of personal assumptions about teaching and learning are possible. Some are grounded in our everyday experiences in the classroom while others are assimilated from observing and talking to others about their teaching. Our assumptions may be shared by others or they may represent our unique perceptions about teaching and learning. Regardless of their source and whether or not they are shared, such beliefs play an important role in how we design and implement a variety of classroom processes.

Self-Reflection Activity 3-1
Defeating Mindlessness in Course Design

A key to defeating mindlessness is to identify mindful considerations for why you teach in particular ways. When applied to teaching, Ellen Langer's research suggests that breaking with past habits, resisting attempts to let others control how you teach, and assuming more personal control over all aspects of the classroom environment is helpful. The activity below can help you think of ways of accomplish the latter goals. The examples used to illustrate certain points are taken from workshop participants who have responded to this process.

Select a course that you are currently teaching and respond to the following statements and questions using this course as a frame of reference.

Breaking Past Habits

1.] List 2- 3 past habits that appear on a regular basis in your current teaching.
   For Example:
      I like to talk about recent research in my field in all of my courses. I usually stand in front of the room and lecture.

   Your Response:

2.] How does each habit help you to accomplish your goals as an instructor?
   For Example:
      Talking about recent research helps me to stay current and it gives my class the new information they can use to supplement what is in the text- book. Lecturing allows me to cover a large amount of important material in a short amount of time.

   Your Response:

Self-Reflection Activity 3-1[Continued]

3.] In what ways does each of the latter habits interfere with your ability to accomplish your goals?
For Example:
> While I think that discussing current research is useful, I suspect that many students find that it is difficult enough just keeping up with the text. I may be overwhelming many of them with facts and figures. I would like to have more discussion in my class and I find that the more I lecture the less willing students seem to want to participate.

Your Response:

Resisting Control by Others

4.] Using the tactics described in Table 3-3 as a guide, select 2-3 that students colleagues, administrators, and others employ to influence your teaching.
For Example:
> I'm not tenured and thus I worry about getting poor student evaluations if I try to innovate too much in my classes. I'm responding to pressure to comply with what I believe students are most comfortable with or running the risk of getting punished for innovating.

Your Response:

5.] Besides being aware of the influence strategy, what could you could do tomorrow to begin to resist such tactics?
For Example:
> I must give the students a clear rationale for why I'm teaching a particular way. Also, they need to be involved early on with feedback and suggestions they might have for changing things.

Your Response:

Self-Reflection Activity 3-1 [Continued]

Assuming More Control Over The Classroom Environment

6.] What are 1-3 aspects of the instructional process that you feel you have less control over than you would like?

For Example

Students being prepared for class so we can have small group discussions.

Your Response:

7.] Without becoming a dictator, but using processes that would help students to learn more effectively, what can you do to gain the control you would like to have but currently don't possess?

For Example:

I could have them complete a study guide on the reading material for class so that they would have to read beforehand. The study guide would include specific content questions and also open-ended questions and/or problems and issues I would want to discuss further in class. I would give them a few points of credit for completing the study guide. This would help everyone to have something to say about the issue.

Your Response:

Table 3-3
The Way Others Try to Influence Your Teaching

The influence tactics listed below affect the selection of classroom methods. *Which ones have you experienced?*

Will of the Majority
Several people may overtly or subtly suggest we follow the lead of the majority. A workshop participant told me that a peer walked out of observing her class as soon as she put them into discussion groups. When asked, the observer replied, "I left when you quit teaching" and thus implied that teaching is lecturing.

Another example was a colleague who decided to teach her basic biology class using a modular format. Each module covered a different topic and allowed students to work independently and in small groups on a variety of content related projects. Four of the six other members of the department told her they considered the way she was teaching the basic course inappropriate. They suggested she teach like everyone else [i.e., using the lecture-discussion format]. She filed an academic freedom grievance.

Social Proof
Observations of what others think and do can influence us to follow suit. If one is unsure about how to teach and/or what content to teach, simply observing what other more experienced people do may exert subtle pressures for how to behave in the classroom.

Pressure for Compliance
Rewards and/or punishment are used to influence someone. When faced with new teaching strategies, some students may resist by complaining, skipping class, not doing the work, or otherwise making the course unpleasant for the instructor. The unstated message is "We want the old and familiar way of teaching used in this course." Sometimes teachers give into such pressure by saying, "Why bother, most of the students don't seem to care anyway."

Obedience to Authority
Typically this takes the form of people responding to some authority either to change or to justify not changing some aspect of their teaching. Common authorities include national experts on teaching issues, accreditation and professional bodies, elected officials with educational mandates, campus administrators with clout, and even a collective bargaining contract. In the latter case, I have observed participants responding to new ideas for teaching by stating, "But our union contract prevents us from doing something like that." This is typically not the case but some continue to believe in the authority of "the collective bargaining agreement" to limit their approach to teaching.

Social Power
Influence occurs through: someone's expertise about how to teach; information they possess about teaching-learning issues; the fact the other party likes them; or the other party's perception that this person could reward or punish them. Deans, faculty development consultants, department chairs, an important figure in a field, and colleagues may use one or more of these sources of social power to influence your teaching.

Listed below are several personal assumptions about the teaching-learning process generated by participants in workshops I have conducted.

- Teachers are more effective if they present information with enthusiasm.

- Learning proceeds best if students collaborate with each other.

- It is better to begin a course with a firm hand and to lighten up later on in the term.

- The use of instructional technology is a good way to motivate students to learn.

- Give students an inch and they will take a mile.

- Rewarding students for their efforts works-- sometimes.

- Time spent in small group discussions is seldom time well spent.

- A good grading system is all that you need to motivate students to do well.

- Students learn to think about issues better with case studies.

- Most students could learn quite well without having to listen to lectures.

- Variety is the "spice of classroom life."

- Students need to integrate and organize the information from class sessions, the text, and outside readings.

Whatever assumptions we make, they are like a double-edged sword. Assumptions may lead us to explore alternate ways of teaching or broaden our perspectives on what is possible. On the other hand, they sometimes are so powerful that they can lead to rigid ways of teaching. The flexibility needed when courses, technology, student populations, and our disciplines change may not be there. Thus, we fail to check our personal assumptions about teaching and learning or to test their adequacy when circumstances vary. Furthermore, our assumptions may prevent us for examining other points of view. When teaching issues are discussed, "Don't bother me with the facts because my mind is made up," is not an unusual posture that some teachers take. This is particular true of individuals who are locked into a particular style of teaching. A major contributor to such problems is a failure to examine our assumptions and to adopt new ones when needed.

Self-Reflection Activity 3-2
Exploring Personal Assumptions about Teaching

Identifying the assumptions we make about teaching and learning can help us to understand our classroom processes and stimulate us to think about what we might want to do to modify or change. The following process can help you explore your assumptions and their implications for your teaching style. The examples in the activity are from a workshop participant who used this process.

1.] What are three assumptions you make about teaching and learning?
   For Example:
      - Students learn best when rewarded for their efforts.
      - Students learn best by "doing."
      - Teachers need to keep absolute control over a classroom:

Your Response:

   Assumption 1

   Assumption 2

   Assumption 3

2.] How do each of your assumptions appear in your courses? Also state how each assumption facilitates and hinders your teaching style?
   For Example:
      Students learn best when rewarded for their efforts: I use a point system to give students credit for all course assignments. Their final grade depends upon the number of total points they earned.

      Facilitates
      Helps students to do a variety of inside and outside of class assignments. Students report they like the structure the point system provides and feel more in control of their grades.
      Hinders
      The system creates a dependence upon me to reward their efforts. It does not do much for teaching them to learn for the sake of learning.

Self-Reflection Activity 3-2 [Continued]

Students learn best by "doing:" Class sessions use demonstrations, and critical thinking activities that keep students actively involved.

Facilitates
Allows me to show how course content relates to things students see and do everyday of their lives.
Hinders
Does not allow me as much time as I would always like to clarify certain points or to present additional information on a topic.

Your Response:

Assumption 1
Facilitates/Hinders

Assumption 2:
Facilitates/Hinders

Assumption 3:
Facilitates/Hinders

Self-Reflection Activity 3-2 [Continued]

3.] What assumption[s] about teaching and learning need to be modified to enhance the nature and quality of your classes? What would you do to make this happen?
For Example:
   Teachers need to keep absolute control over a classroom: While I think I need to be in charge, I may be overdoing it a bit. I probably need to ask students how they would like to see class sessions organized to determine if changes are needed.

Your Response:

4.] What new assumption[s] would you add that might enhance the nature and quality of your classes?
For Example:
   Students can learn well through self-directed, self-initiated learning projects: Instead of always providing things for students to do on their own, I should give them the option of developing a course - related project they might like to pursue.

Your Response:

Our personal assumptions develop through our experiences in a culture that has its roots in antiquity as well as its limbs growing into the future. Consequently, our current assumptions have historical antecedents and also represent views of education that lie in the future [Fuhrmann and Grasha, 1983; Grasha, 1992]. Self-Reflection Activity 3-3 can help you to identify the time periods associated with your beliefs about teaching.

Self-Reflection Activity 3-3
Identifying the Historical Origins of Our Assumptions about Teaching and Learning

Respond to the items below using the following rating scale.

```
        1    2    3    4    5    6    7
        |____|____|____|____|____|____|
      Disagree                    Agree
```

_____ 01.] The instructor is the expert and should have the last word about the correct way to interpret course issues.
_____ 02.] Teachers can learn from their students.
_____ 03.] Education is a lifelong process that goes beyond college.
_____ 04.] Speculation about the future should be a discussion topic in any course within a discipline.
_____ 05.] Teachers must prescribe in detail the course content, assignments and methods of evaluation.
_____ 06.] Lectures have positive benefits for students.
_____ 07.] Interdisciplinary course offerings should be stressed.
_____ 08.] Students' ability to cope with change must be developed.
_____ 09.] When students are dependent upon the teacher, the ability of students to learn is facilitated.
_____ 10.] Students know what they need to learn and should be encouraged to pursue such interests.
_____ 11.] Self-awareness is an important part of what students should learn in college.
_____ 12.] To be effective, teachers must use advances in technology in the classroom [e.g., computers, CD-ROMS, Videotapes].
_____ 13.] Learning demands personal sacrifice and discipline.
_____ 14.] Specialization is an important educational goal.
_____ 15.] Teachers should be less directive and act more as facilitators of their students learning.
_____ 16.] The values that underlie a discipline must be discussed in class.
_____ 17.] Instructors know best what students need to learn.
_____ 18.] Students should be taught to think critically about issues.
_____ 19.] Teaching methods must be based upon theories of human learning.
_____ 20.] Education should develop students' abilities to deal with multi-cultural and/or multinational issues.

Self-Reflection Activity 3-3 [Continued]

Scoring Key
Sum your ratings for the items in each category.

> *Category A:* [Items 1, 5, 9, 13, 17] Total _____
> *Category B:* [Items 2, 6, 10, 14, 18] Total _____
> *Category C:* [Items 3, 7, 11, 15, 19] Total _____
> *Category D:* [Items 4, 8, 12, 16, 20] Total _____

Category A items represent beliefs about education that had their origins during the Colonial Period; *Category B* the 19th Century; *Category C* the 20th Century; and *Category D* the future.

Based on norms for this test, a high score would occur in the range of [101-140]; a medium score [61-100]; and a relatively low score [20-60].

The responses from several samples of college teachers to items in the questionnaire appear in Figure 3-3. As can be seen in this figure, the assumptions faculty reported about teaching had their origins in a variety of time periods. Those from the 20th century and those that emphasize assumptions about the future [i.e., taken from the writings of individuals speculating about future trends in higher education] tend to be somewhat more popular than assumptions from the colonial period and the 19th century.

1.] Which are 2-3 assumptions in the questionnaire items that you would like to see represented less often in your teaching?

2.] What are 2-3 assumptions described the questionnaire that you would like to see represented more often in your teaching?

3.] What instructional practices would help you to integrate the latter assumptions into your teaching?

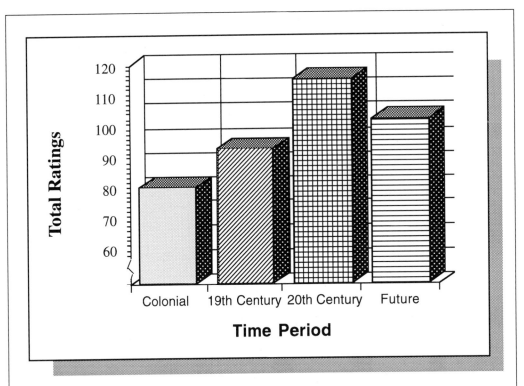

Figure 3-3: Faculty ratings on teaching-learning assumptions associated with each historical time period. Items from the 20th Century and Future time periods were endorsed to a higher degree than were those of the 19th Century and Colonial time periods. However, ideas on teaching from the colonial period and the 19th century are still present, although to a lesser degree, in the assumptions that college teachers make about teaching and learning. [n=98]

Personal Definitions of Teaching and Learning

Thanks for all of the help you gave me with my teaching when I was in graduate school. What I appreciated most over the years was your insistence that we identify our philosophy of teaching and use it to guide and direct our classroom activities. In particular I enjoyed working on a personal definition of who I was as a teacher. It helped me but I am amazed at how often colleagues of mine are unaware of their philosophy. When I periodically ask someone what is your philosophy of teaching or how do you define yourself as a teacher, most just look at me without responding. I'm not sure whether they don't understand the question or have simply not thought about it and consequently have no answer.

- A letter from a former graduate student

Some people possess a definition of the teaching-learning enterprise that helps to guide and direct their instructional processes. Personal assumptions about teaching and learning are typically embedded in such definitions. The following definitions were generated in a recent faculty seminar:

Workshop Participants' Definitions of Teaching:

- Teaching is a process of internal and external dialogue about things of importance conducted with passion and discipline.

- Teaching is an activity where one person tries to facilitate in another person an appreciation of the complexities involved within an area of study. Teaching involves getting people to think critically about such issues.

- Teaching occurs whenever someone with knowledge and expertise in a discipline purposely steps into the background. Those with less knowledge are then allowed to step forward and acquire the information needed to fill the void.

- Teaching involves course processes where the teacher and the student are able to learn something new in a course. When teachers become learners, and have to admit that they do not know everything, the artificial barriers between students and teachers begin to fall. Only when such barriers disappear is the dialogue necessary for learning possible.

- Teaching is a performance art. Like actors on a stage, faculty play their assigned roles before an audience of students. And like any good performer, teachers must prepare what they will say and do in advance to have a maximum effect on that audience. That impact, however, lasts for only a brief amount of time during the performance. What happened is soon forgotten or becomes a distant memory stripped of much of its content.

- Teaching is an imperfect attempt by one person of higher status to influence the thoughts and behaviors of someone with less status. The high status teacher influences through his or her expertise, the willingness to give positive and negative evaluations, and by the student allowing him or herself to be influenced in such a way.

These definitions of course need to be explored in more detail. One reason is that when taken alone, they do not always capture the diversity of ideas about teaching and learning that underlie such statements. Another reason is that such definitions represent personal shortcuts for individuals to express who they are as teachers. Thus, some of the terminology is idiosyncratic and needs further elaboration and explanation.

In workshop and seminar settings, I often ask participants to discuss and clarify what various terms mean and how components of their definition appears in their classroom behaviors. All of this is a prelude to exploring when modifications in their definition and subsequent approach to teaching are needed.

Self-Reflection Activity 3-4
Exploring Your Personal Definition of Teaching

Answer the following questions to explore your definition of teaching. The responses of a workshop participant are included as an example of how one person responded to each part of this activity.

1.] What is your personal definition of teaching?
   For Example:
   Teaching is a process of internal and external dialogue about things of importance conducted with passion and discipline.

   Your Response:

2.] What key phrases or words in your definition are absolutely critical for someone else to understand your approach to teaching?
   For Example:
   Teaching is a *process* of *internal and external dialogue* about things of *importance* conducted with *passion and discipline.*

   Your Response:

3.] What does each key word or phrase mean to you?
   For Example:
   Process: I see teaching as a dynamic transaction between my students and me. Clearly I do things that change how they think, feel, and behave. In turn their reactions to what I do have implications for how I think, feel, and behave. This process is never complete.

   Internal and external dialogue: I use many different types of activities in class to help students develop their ideas about course content and to talk about it with their classmates.

   Importance: If I don't think something is important for my students to learn, I don't teach it. I always hated it when I was a student and a teacher said "I have to teach this material." I'd rather not play that game with my students. I also want to find out what my students think is important for them to learn. I allow students to select topics and content they can explore.

Self-Reflection Activity 3-4 [Continued]

Passion: I know too many people who just go through the motions. I won't let that happen to me, and if it somehow does, I'm going to quit teaching.

Discipline: Plays a role because I believe what is covered, the instructional processes used, and deadlines must clearly stated. I also expect my students to complete assigned work and before a deadline.

Your Response:

4.] What would you drop, modify, or add to your current definition? Give a reason for your response.
For Example:
It occurs to me that I'm much more interested in facilitating learning. Thus, defining teaching is not sufficient. I would change the definition to read, "Teaching and learning involve internal and external dialogue about things of importance conducted with passion and discipline."

Your Response:

Formal Principles of Teaching and Learning: Theories of Learning

"There is nothing as practical as a good theory."

- Kurt Lewin

Formal principles of teaching and learning emerge from various forms of qualitative and quantitative research on teaching-learning processes. They can be found in a variety of sources. All major disciplines, for example, have journals devoted to teaching while the journals *College Teaching* and *The Journal on Excellence in College Teaching* publish empirical studies, general articles, essays, and suggestions for improving college teaching across disciplines. Other journals such as *The Journal of Educational Psychology* and *The Journal of Higher Education* specialize in empirical studies that examine a variety of theoretical and practical issues in human learning, student characteristics, and teaching styles appropriate for a variety of educational settings.

In addition, Jossey-Bass publishers have a series of monographs titled *New Directions in Higher Education* and the School of Education and Human Development at The George Washington University publishes the *ASHE-ERIC Higher Education Reports.* Jossey-Bass, Oryx Press, many university presses, and other publishers have extensive listings of books dealing with college teaching. Finally, there are newsletters on college teaching such as the *Teaching Professor* as well as available are the published proceedings of numerous national and regional conferences on college teaching.

All of the sources listed above have two things in common:

- *They contain information about formal principles of teaching and learning applicable to classrooms across disciplines.*

- *The information in these sources is largely ignored by the majority of people teaching in higher education.* Part of the problem is that most teachers do not know that such books, monographs, newsletters, and journals are available. About 15% of those attending workshops I conduct report reading such things regularly while another 25% reports occasionally reading at least part of a book or article on teaching-learning processes. The remainder of participants are not familiar with the variety of materials available on college teaching processes generally or within their disciplines.

On a number of occasions I have heard faculty members say, "It's difficult enough just keeping up with the books and journals I have to read." Those works individuals feel they *have to read* typically contain content relevant for their scholarship. Another underlying belief captured well by one workshop participant is that "research on pedagogy is something people in the College of Education need to be concerned about.

Sometimes I think some instructors believe that what they do in the classroom represents a mysterious artform that cannot be studied. And if it is studied, the results obtained would be of more interest to people in education or related fields. Also, I suspect that because teaching is generally not rewarded on par with other forms of scholarly activity, time is not devoted to looking for ways to enhance it. Or, at least, the literature is not meticulously searched for new ideas.

Finally, one way people in any discipline encounter the scholarship in their area of interest is through their graduate training programs. While the situation is improving somewhat, the overwhelming majority of those finding jobs in higher education have had little formal training in teaching. This lack of training not only has implications for the development of teaching skills but is one of the reasons most faculty are not familiar with the literature on teaching.

On a more positive note, the need to overcome such deficits appears to have become a national priority. Some of it is driven by education having become a political football in the hands of elected officials looking for "more value for their educational dollars." Campus administrators caught in a financial squeeze from fewer public monies, rising costs, and declining student bodies are looking for ways to become more efficient. While such forces push for changes in the teaching-learning process, they do not always do so in the direction of having people use formal principles of teaching and learning to adjust their instructional efforts.

On the other hand, there is interest in enhancing the nature and quality of undergraduate education through the applications of research on teaching and learning. Those in the forefront of such efforts ground their suggestions in the scholarship of teaching. Such initiatives include classroom assessment processes [Cross and Angelo, 1988], the use of teaching portfolios for growth and accountability in teaching [Seldin, 1991; Richlin and Manning, 1995], writing across the curriculum [Walvoord,1990], collaborative and active learning [Bruffee, 1993; Bonwell & Eison, 1991]; Johnson, Johnson, & Smith, 1991], the need to develop critical thinking skills in students [Halpern, 1989; Kurfiss, 1988; Zechmeister & Johnson, 1992], the use of principles of learning from a variety of sources to inform educational practice [Davis, 1993; Fuhrmann & Grasha, 1983; Lowman, 1995; McKeachie, et, al., 1994], and the employment of computers, CD-ROM's and other forms of technology to the classroom [Barrett, 1992].

To discover which formal theoretical positions your instructional practices most resemble, complete Self-Reflection Activity 3-5 beginning on the next page.

Self-Reflection Activity 3-5
The Theoretical Base For Teaching-Learning Assumptions

In spite of having little formal training in teaching and a relative lack of awareness about the literature on teaching and learning, instructional practices often fit existing theories of teaching and learning. This is not surprising. Such practices have been acquired in a culture where ideas about teaching and learning appear as a backdrop to efforts in other areas of endeavor [e.g., training programs, supervisory practices, parenting]. Once they are consciously identified, we can better understand the intellectual base of our teaching. *We then are in a position to make an informed choice about which principles fit our teaching goals.*

Use the rating scale that follows for your response to each item.

Disagree   Agree

_____ 01.] More than anything else, students need to develop their capacity to solve problems.

_____ 02.] Students learn best in small discrete steps.

_____ 03.] Teachers must teach to meet the unique learning needs of students.

_____ 04.] Students need to be taught how to solve problems.

_____ 05.] Grades are the best way to motivate all students.

_____ 06.] Emotional reactions to content should be encouraged in class and become a part of what is discussed.

_____ 07.] Course work needs to develop critical thinking abilities.

_____ 08.] Organization and structure are essential for learning.

_____ 09.] Students do not need to be pressured to learn.

_____ 10.] Instruction should take into account the natural limitations in students' information processing abilities.

_____ 11.] Teachers should allow time in a course for students to learn at their own pace.

_____ 12.] Teachers are primarily role models and facilitators of learning.

_____ 13.] It is important to present course concepts in several different contexts in order for students to learn them thoroughly.

_____ 14.] Students should be allowed to retake exams until they master the content in a course.

_____ 15.] Students should be encouraged to develop their natural capacity as self-initiated, self-directed learners.

_____ 16.] Students need to develop discipline appropriate and ways of organizing course information for themselves.

_____ 17.] Students need to be rewarded for doing course assignments and in order to develop and maintain interest in them.

_____ 18.] Students must learn to take responsibility for their learning.

Self-Reflection Activity 3-5 [Continued]

Scoring Key
Sum your ratings for the items in each category.

  Category A: [Items 1, 4, 7, 10, 13, 16] Total _____
  Category B: [Items 2, 5, 8, 11, 14, 17] Total _____
  Category C: [Items 3, 6, 9, 12, 15, 18] Total _____

Category A items represent beliefs about education that had their origins in Cognitive Based Theories of Learning; *Category B:* Behavioral Based Theories of Learning; *Category C:* Humanistic Based Theories of Learning.

Based on norms for this test, a high score would be in the range of [81-126]; a medium score [51-80]; and a relatively low score [18-50].

A brief summary of the teaching-learning concepts behind the cognitive, behavioral, and humanistic theories are presented in Table 3-4. The responses from several samples of college teachers to each theoretical position in the questionnaire are shown in Figure 3-4.

1.] Rank order the scores that you obtained on the questionnaire. What theoretical positions tend to be most and least prevalent.?

2.] What aspects of your teaching do you need to change to bring them more in line with the theoretical positions you endorsed?

3.] Are there other theoretical positions besides those described in this chapter that appear to fit your teaching style?

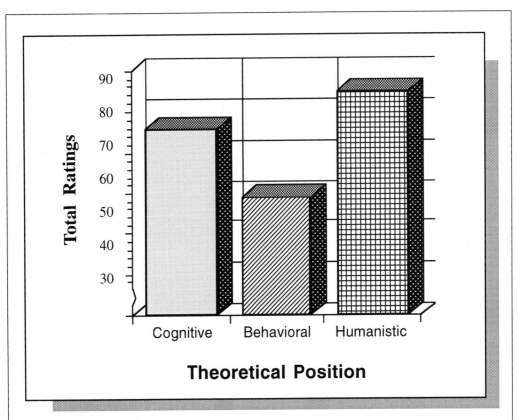

Figure 3-4: Faculty ratings to theoretical assumptions about teaching and learning. Items from the humanistic and cognitive positions tended to be endorsed stronger than were those of the behavioral position. [n=98]

Issues With Theories of Teaching and Learning

It is important to recognize the following two points about the relationship of teaching to the practice of teaching.

- *A particular theoretical point of view does not and cannot specify all aspects of the practice of teaching.* Theoretical positions on teaching and learning developed from controlled research or from philosophical positions about human nature. They were initially applied to understanding our everyday lives. Thus, some principles don't generalize well to instructional issues or one is forced to "stretch a point" to make them apply.

- *There is no single theory that will account for the complexity of the classroom learning environment.* As the data in Figure 3-4 suggests, educational practices of any teacher often reflect elements of several theoretical positions. Most of us are eclectic in our approaches. While there are people who advocate and rely upon a particular conceptual position, such "pure cases" are the exception rather than the rule in higher education.

Table 3-4
Brief Sketches of Three Theories of Teaching

Cognitive Theory

Overview
Deals with how sensory input is transformed, reduced, elaborated, stored, recovered, and used to solve problems. Information processing can occur at a conscious level of awareness but our ability to do so is typically viewed as limited. There often is too much input and too many decisions to be made for anyone to consciously think about and monitor everything that is required. *Thus, various automatic mental control processes, schemas, and other mental mechanisms help us to deal with familiar situations where routine thought and action sequences are required.*

Motivating Students
People are seen as active seekers of new information and skills. Once a problem is attended to, and the challenge of finding a solution or making a decision is acknowledged, conscious and automatic thought and action sequences are activated. *Teachers motivate students best when they provide course activities and projects that tap their natural ability and interest in solving problems and making decisions.* Students must develop confidence in their ability to think and teachers help by providing students with success experiences and by not overwhelming them with information.

Facilitating the Acquisition of Information
Teachers must actively engage students. Otherwise automatic processing takes over and students lose their interest in a task. *Tasks that provide variety and novelty will capture students' attention better but care must be taken not to overload the cognitive system with too much information.* Also, it is helpful to: provide short breaks, ask thought provoking questions, have students write short position papers where they can summarize, paraphrase, and elaborate on course content; and to emphasize no more than 5-7 major points per session. The use of concrete examples, activities, and demonstrations that stimulate the imaginations of students facilitates processing concepts. Finally, the use of case studies, and discipline related -problems develops critical thinking skills.

Humanistic Theory

Overview
Emphasizes the development of the whole person by integrating the cognitive and affective aspects of the learning experience. *Instructors are not as concerned with teaching static knowledge as they are with helping students learn how to learn.* They encourage students to explore content on their own, to work with others, to use resources when they need them, and to reflect on the joy, excitement, frustration, anxiety, and other emotions associated with learning.

Motivating Students
People are seen as active learners who possess a natural tendency towards self-actualization or achieving their potential in life. Teachers must support and help such tendencies to develop. The use of classroom procedures where students can make choices, seek new experiences, work independently, self-reflect, and have a sequence of small as well as relatively large successes assists students with achieving their potential. *Also, instructors who provide active support, encouragement, and otherwise nurture student efforts to learn from their successes and failures keep students motivated to learn.*

Table 3-4 [Continued **]**

Facilitating the Acquisition of Information
Teaching is not technique but the transmission of a philosophy of living into the classroom. For example, teachers must prize and accept the strengths and weaknesses of learners, trust students and be willing to empathize with their thoughts and feelings. This is accomplished when students participate in all aspects of course design, have opportunities to explore issues that interest them, and when teachers attend to their ideas, and reflect their thoughts and feelings. *Furthermore, teachers must nurture and help develop the self-images of students.* Teachers must select a level of performance that is in line with the skills and abilities of learners and become sensitive to whether classroom goals are too high. *Positive feedback must be emphasized* and *teachers also should act as facilitators of students' learning.* Students must be encouraged to make choices, to develop personal implications from content, and to develop their skills at personal inquiry. *Finally, instructors must see themselves as learners, they must emphasize the integration of facts, concepts, and values, and insure that a safe environment for students to express ideas and to collaborate with the teacher and peers is established.*

Behavioral Theory

Overview
Emphasizes the ways external stimuli influence learning. Thus *the manipulation of external rewards and incentives and the creation of classroom structures that guide and direct the actions of learners become important.* Also, the behavioral position allows students to learn in small steps, at their own pace, and to develop skills to competent levels. This often means giving learners extra-time to acquire material or to retake exams until a specified level of competence is obtained. While instructor- generated structures and incentives are emphasized, students are gradually taught how to self-monitor, regulate, and reward their own actions.

Motivating Students
Learners are viewed as incentive driven and thus teachers use external rewards and incentives. Course requirements and procedures help students to see that their actions have favorable as well as unfavorable consequences. Contract teaching is often used where students earn points towards a grade for successfully completing class-related activities. Or, they may contract for a certain number of activities that are later converted into letter grades. Contracts help students to learn how to self-monitor and regulate their actions.

Facilitating the Acquisition of Content
The instructor creates a structured learning environment where clear goals and objectives for students to achieve are emphasized. *Self-pacing is employed to accommodate individual differences* in the rate at which people learn. A course may be set up in distinct content modules. Before being allowed to take the next module in a series, students must demonstrate proficiency with the previous module. *Mastery of the information is stressed.* Students must be able to demonstrate that they can obtain a criterion of, say, 90 percent or better on exams or that they can demonstrate proficiency with specified skills. *Finally, immediate feedback and reinforcement of performance are provided.* This can be instructor- generated. But, often students are often encouraged to develop and monitor their progress [i.e., through journals, study schedules,] and to find ways to reward themselves for pursuing activities that help them acquire course content and skills.

Formal Principles of Teaching and Learning: Principles from Research on Human Learning

Recently, I conducted a review of the research on human learning to identify principles of learning that had a major impact on how people acquire and retain information [cf., Grasha, 1995a, Chapter 4; Grasha, 1995b]. My criterion for inclusion was that a principle of learning had to show at least a 30% benefit on learners compared to a comparison group not exposed to the concept. *As you read each of the principles listed below, consider how it could become part of your conceptual base and used in your classes.*

- *Students learn best by doing, by images of doing, and by observing others doing things.* Sometimes a useful substitute to "doing things" is mentally practicing applications of information and sequences of skills we wish to acquire. And, learning from observations is helped by: giving labels to what such models do; observing how they organize a task from the least to most difficult components; and by reminding ourselves of the payoffs in becoming proficient with the information and skills. Teachers should encourage such things in their teaching.

- *Using metaphor, charts, concept maps, pictures, illustrations, anecdotes, and other figurative devices facilitates learning.* Information is normally coded in memory in verbal and in imaginal forms. Having two codes is better, because during retrieval, one memory code can stimulate the other or take its place. The more abstract and theoretical the content, the less likely a strong imaginal code will form. Thus, theoretical information should be made appropriately concrete to help learners mentally visualize it.

- *Quality time on task is a very pervasive factor in influencing learning.* This is more than *practice makes perfect.* Research shows that when learners spend time rehearsing information, examining its implications and applications, comparing and contrasting concepts to related ones, examining the different contexts in which a concept occurs, and looking for meaningful patterns-- they learn more. Thus, teaching methods that demonstrate such things and encourage students to do them are more successful in promoting the acquisition of content.

- *Making learning a "social enterprise" facilitates the acquisition and retention of information.* Students are generally motivated to work with others, and when clear directions and interesting tasks are provided, content acquisition is facilitated. Another reason is that collaborative learning often increases the time they spend on a learning task.

- *Rewards encourage learning provided they are not overused.* This would include constantly reminding students that, "To do well on the test you have to..." Or, "These points are important and I'm going to test you on them." Research suggests that the students begin to focus more on grades rather than learning content when grades are emphasized. Also, their natural interest in learning may begin to wane as they begin to feel controlled by the rewards.

Formal Principles of Teaching and Learning: Models of Teaching Style

Chapter 1 identified several models of teaching style. The implications for how faculty teach, empirical evidence supporting the model, and some of the outcomes they produced in students were discussed. *Principles and concepts from such models of style can be integrated into our conceptual base.* There are several ways to accomplish this goal.

The work of Joseph Lowman on *general descriptors of classroom behavior* presented in Chapter 1 identified behaviors that you might want to emulate [cf., Table 1-2]. Those descriptors in this table that you find attractive, but lacking in your current behaviors, might be addressed. People who believe they are deficient in using humor, displaying energy and excitement, being helpful and encouraging to students, or being patient and respectful could work on ways to develop such qualities in their classroom teaching. Colleagues who display desired qualities might be observed or perhaps become consultants to help you learn how to do such things. Or, feedback from students might be obtained on specific ways that teachers who possess the characteristics of interest behave toward them.

Working with a teaching-learning consultant and having a videotape of several class sessions analyzed also can help. First, the tape can show what qualities you already possess. Then, as attempts are made to try new things, additional videotaped segments can highlight strengths and weaknesses of trying to add new dimensions to your teaching.

In much the same way, *you could observe respected and popular teachers* on campus and attempt to emulate desirable qualities in their teaching style. Consider taking that person to lunch and inquire how they learned to do things that interest you. Ask for suggestions that might help you. Your goal is not to try and emulate everything that person does. Rather, the goal is to find a few things that fit your personal makeup that would be worth trying.

Behaviors common to all faculty members can be integrated into a philosophy of teaching that guides one's instruction in the following manner:

- *Determine where you stand on the dimensions covered by this model.* Use the student rating scale in Self-Reflection Activity 1-1 of Chapter 1 to gather a baseline on how students perceive you on each dimension. Or, in conjunction with the latter idea, invite colleagues into your classes to make similar judgments.

- *Identify aspects of your teaching that the evaluations suggest you are strongest and weakest in.* Select specific behaviors that you would like to develop. Bill McKeachie suggests that involving a colleague or a campus teaching consultant to discuss your ratings and having them respond to your plans is typically very helpful. People who do so are more likely to initiate changes and to persist in their attempts to try new behaviors [McKeachie, et al., 1994].

- *Reevaluate your teaching and concentrate on those behaviors you want to enhance.* Gather data about your teaching from students and colleagues. Use it to identify how well others see your instructional skills. Use this information to fine tune what you do. If a student rating scale is used, ask students to supplement their ratings with written comments. In this way, they can indicate the specific reasons for their evaluations and offer concrete suggestions for improvement.

As noted in Chapter 1, some approaches to style are based on the *particular teaching methods someone uses.* Some strategies were shown to encourage active learning and to involve varying degrees of personal risk. The latter then become the intellectual issues in which the methods are grounded. Particular methods are chosen because of someone's interest in managing active learning and perhaps enhancing or avoiding risk.

The roles teachers play can be studied for those that might be added to your style as a teacher. One way to do this is to analyze your current teaching processes for the roles you currently employ. Then using the list of roles in Table 1-6 on pages 19 and 20., select those that you would like to see more often in your teaching. Develop specific teaching strategies compatible with those roles. Ideas for such strategies might come from a colleague, those in Chapters 4-8 of this book, a teaching journal in your discipline, or from an article in the interdisciplinary journals *College Teaching* and the *Journal on Excellence in College Teaching.*

The latter sources can be counted on to provide stimulating as well as practical ideas for ways to teach that use a variety of the roles described in Table 1-6. The authors of such articles describe in detail what they did and the outcomes of their efforts. Many of the methods described are interdisciplinary in nature and with a little imagination can be applied to almost any discipline.

The process of identifying teaching roles also helps to uncover the *archetypal forms* in your teaching and those forms you wish to use in the future. *The important point is to get beneath the surface of your methods and to see them as reflecting particular roles and archetypal forms.* The questions to ask to integrate this information into your philosophy of teaching are: "Am I currently satisfied with what I see? "What other roles or archetypal forms should I address?" "What approaches to teaching will help me to integrate new roles and archetypal forms into my teaching?"

Employing the *personality trait model* as a conceptual rationale for engaging in particular teaching strategies were covered in the context of the discussion of that model in the body and in the Epilogue to Chapter 1. There, ideas for matching the personality characteristics in Carl Jung's model to particular methods and approaches to instruction were illustrated. Furthermore, the particular problems presented by students with styles that differ from their teachers were noted and ways to counter them discussed. Finally, ways to employ *methods for teaching* as a conceptual rationale for your teaching is covered in the context of the discussion in the last section of the current chapter on "Guiding Metaphors" and in the Epilogue.

It is not necessary to integrate every model or even parts of every model of teaching style into our philosophy of teaching Rather, it is best to initially consider the implications of a single model and to make the ideas in that model an integral part of what you do. One payoff is that you then have a response to the question, "Why do you teach the way you do?" An appropriate answer is, "Because I'm basing my teaching on the principles and concepts from a model of teaching style." The latter answer with appropriate details supplied is much better than, "Oh, I don't know. I've always taught this way and it seems to work."

Formal Principles of Teaching and Learning: Models of Learning Style

Most of us take for granted the observation that people differ. However, this fact of human behavior was not always so well understood. It was not until the early part of the 19th century that the implications of individual differences were recognized. Edwin Boring [1950] in his classic text *A History of Experimental Psychology,* suggests that the Dutch astronomer Bessel and his work on developing the "personal equation" provided a key turning point. Bessel recognized that individual's responses to the same stimuli differed. By calculating the difference between two observers on a task, it was possible to correct the scores of one person relative to another by either adding or subtracting this difference. This insight, Edwin Boring suggested, was an important milestone in encouraging the study of individual differences in psychology and education.

A variety of individual differences have been examined since Bessel began his studies. Some were not particularly scientific, for example, the study of bumps on one's head, handwriting analyses, and palm reading. Others such as reaction times to stimuli with variations in intelligence and personality characteristics, have a strong empirical base. Among the types of personality characteristics studied were those called "learning styles."

Learning styles are personal dispositions that influence a student's ability to acquire information, to interact with peers and the teacher, and to otherwise participate in a learning experiences. *Included among such qualities are our motives, perceptual skills, modes of processing information, and a variety of preferences for sensory stimulation, gathering information, social relationships, and the qualities of the physical environment.* Students vary on all of the latter dimensions and each affects their satisfaction with particular teaching styles and their ability to acquire the knowledge and skills in a course.

A considerable amount of empirical data has been gathered on the major approaches to learning style. *What such models suggest about teaching and learning processes ought to be a part of our conceptual base.* Anyone interested in using a model, or parts of different models, can choose among more than two dozen models [cf., Claxton & Smith, 1984; Grasha, 1983; 1990a; Johnson, 1992; Keefe, 1984] for discussions of various approaches. *My bias is toward selecting and using models of learning style that have clear ties to formulations of teaching style.* This makes it easier to examine the interplay among teacher and student styles in the classroom. An introduction to this latter issue was provided in the context of the discussion of the use of Carl Jung's personality types to describe teaching style in Chapter 1. Additional details on how to accomplish an integration of teaching and learning styles is provided in the discussion of the model in Chapters 4-6.

For now, let us simplify things and focus our attention only on the styles of learners and a model that provides a contrast to that of psychological type discussed in Chapter 1. This model was developed by Sheryl Hruska-Riechmann and I in the early 70's. For over two decades the Grasha-Riechmann Student Learning Style Scales [GRSLSS] have been used to identify the preferences learners have for interacting with peers and the instructor in classroom settings [Grasha, 1972; 1990a; Riechmann & Grasha, 1974; Hruska-Riechmann & Grasha, 1984]. The social learning styles identified in this model are the Competitive, Collaborative, Avoidant, Participant, Dependent and Independent. A description of each style and the preferences of students who are represented by each learning style are presented in Table 3-5.

It is important to remember that the styles describe a blend of characteristics that apply to all students. Some learners are simply stronger on some dimensions than others. These styles can become a part of our teaching philosophy in the following ways.

- *They provide a conceptual rationale for using team projects, small group discussions and independent study options, computer- assisted instruction and other methods.* The latter processes, for example, cater to the independent and collaborative styles in students. Other methods encourage different styles and thus provide a rationale for selecting specific instructional processes.

- *They become instructional goals we may wish to pursue.* Many teachers focus on their content goals for a class. Another way to approach the issue of course design is to ask "what learning styles do I want to encourage." Knowing that many students are comfortable in their dependent modes of learning, a teacher might want them to practice collaborative and independent styles of learning. Not only does such stretching help to build their competency with different styles, it teaches valuable skills that may transfer to other settings including jobs. Practicing a diverse set of learning styles in the classroom can produce additional benefits down the road.

- *They provide a rationale for using a variety of approaches to instruction.* It is difficult to teach to every combination of learning style. Yet by providing variety in the methods used within and/or across class sessions, a teacher can at least partially meet the divergent styles of learners in a class.

Answer the following questions in the privacy of your thoughts. What styles currently underlie the way you teach in one or more of your courses? What styles would you like to encourage in the future? What could you do to provide more variety in your teaching and subsequently meet a wider variety of learning needs in your students?

Table 3-5
The Grasha-Riechmann Student Learning Styles

Competitive

Students who learn material in order to perform better than others in the class. Believe they must compete with other students in a course for the rewards that are offered. Like to be the center of attention and to receive recognition for their accomplishments in class.

General Classroom Preferences

> Become a group leader in discussions ...Teacher-centered instructional procedures...Singled out in class for doing a good job...Class activities where they can do better than others.

Collaborative

Typical of students who feel they can learn by sharing ideas and talents. They cooperate with the teacher and like to work with others.

General Classroom Preferences

> Lectures with small group discussions...Small seminars...Student-designed aspects of courses...Group projects.

Avoidant

Not enthusiastic about learning content and attending class. Do not participate with students and teachers in the classroom. They are uninterested and overwhelmed by what goes on in class.

General Classroom Preferences

> Generally turned off by most classroom activities... Would prefer no tests...Pass-fail grading systems...Does not like enthusiastic teachers...Does not want to be called on in class.

Participant

Good citizens in class. Enjoy going to class and take part in as much of the course activities as possible. Typically eager to do as much of the required and optional course requirements as they can.

General Classroom Preferences

> Lectures with discussion...Opportunities to discuss material...Class reading assignments...Teachers who can analyze and synthesize information well.

Dependent

Show little intellectual curiosity and who learn only what is required. View teacher and peers as sources of structure and support and look to authority figures for specific guidelines on what to do.

General Classroom Preferences

> Outlines or notes on the board...Clear deadlines and instructions for assignments...Teacher-centered classroom methods...As little ambiguity as possible in all aspects of course.

Independent

Students who like to think for themselves and are confident in their learning abilities. Prefer to learn the content that they feel is important and would prefer to work alone on course projects than with other students.

General Classroom Preferences

> Independent study...Self-paced instruction...Assignments that give students a chance to think independently...Projects that students can design...Student-centered rather than teacher-centered course designs.

Views of Human Nature

Personal assumptions about learning, our definitions of teaching, and formal theories of teaching and learning yield many beliefs about how we should teach. There is, however, another set of beliefs that affect our teaching styles. These are the views or assumptions that we make about human nature. Psychologist Lawrence Wrightsman [1992], for example, has devoted 30 years of his professional career to identifying those views that people most rely upon when evaluating others. Based upon analyses of historical and philosophical works, interviews with people, and the outcomes of surveys, he has identified eight pervasive assumptions. They are listed in Table 3-6 as polar opposites.

Table 3-6
Views of Human Nature

Based on a 30-year research program, Psychologist Lawrence Wrightsman has identified a number of assumptions about human nature that consistently appear in the beliefs of people. Of course, once they become a part of our belief system, they often appear in our everyday actions. Those that are consistent across a variety of situations are presented below in the form of eight bipolar dimensions.

Trustworthy	Untrustworthy
Rational	Irrational
Willpower	Lack of Willpower
Altruistic	Selfish
Independent	Conforming
Complex	Simple
Similar	Different
Stable	Unstable

The assumptions listed above appear in the behaviors of students and faculty in the college classroom. *One way is that they affect the selection of instructional processes.* For example, some teachers employ multiple forms of an exam and have a test heavily proctored. This suggests that students cannot be trusted to do their own work. On the other hand, some instructors allow students to select and work on independent projects. This practice is consistent with humanistic principles of learning and also suggests that people can be trusted to learn without a teacher standing over them.

Basic assumptions about human nature also appear in the way students evaluate and judge college faculty. In one study, student ratings of teachers were obtained on overall teaching ability, the clarity of classroom presentations, and the emotional climate between teacher and students. Students who held more positive views of human nature [e.g., trustworthy, rational, stable, altruistic] gave more favorable evaluations than students who held negative views about human nature [e.g., untrustworthy, not rational, unstable, selfish]. In addition, students who viewed others as dissimilar were able to identify differences in the teaching styles among instructors better than did those who assumed people were similar [Wrightsman, 1992].

Self-Reflection Activity 3-6
Views about Human Nature and Your Teaching

To assess how assumptions about human nature identified by Lawrence Wrightsman affect your teaching, respond to the following questions. The responses of a participant in a recent workshop I conducted are included as an example.

1.] What are 4-5 instructional processes you frequently employ in your courses.
   For Example:
      I have assignments that everyone in class has to complete.
      My assignments always have clear deadlines and late penalties.

Your Response:

   Instructional Process # 1

   Instructional Process # 2

   Instructional Process # 3

   Instructional Process # 4

   Instructional Process # 5

Self-Reflection Activity 3-6 [Continued]

2.] Which one or more of the views about human nature listed in Table 3-4 are associated with each of your instructional processes?

For Example:

Common assignments

They probably relate to the fact that I see the instructional needs of students as similar and that people would be willing to conform to the same requirements.

Deadlines

This relates to my belief that some students lack the willpower to complete assignments on time unless there are firm deadlines and penalties for being late.

Your Response:

Instructional Process # 1:

Instructional Process # 2:

Instructional Process # 3:

Instructional Process # 4:

Instructional Process # 5:

3.] What alternatives do you see to the views of human nature that underlie your teaching? Please explain.

For Example:

None. I wish that students could do things without deadlines and penalties. Even if I changed, I'd still have the same group of students and I'm not sure that they would change because of me.

Your Response:

Guiding Metaphors for Teaching

As noted in Chapter 1 of this book, a metaphor is one of the devices we may use to define ourselves as teachers. A number of attitudes, values, beliefs, and assumptions about teaching and learning are embedded within our metaphors. *In effect, our metaphor for teaching represents an integration of all of the elements of a conceptual base for teaching shown in Figure 3-1.* Thus, teachers who see themselves as a *midwife, Yoda, matador,* the *Roman orator Cicero, Captain of the Starship Enterprise*, or a *blacksmith pounding an anvil,* likely have different beliefs about the teaching-learning process.

Consider the examples of Yoda and the *matador.* The responses of workshop participants who developed each metaphor are described below to illustrate how each element in Figure 3-1 is associated with them.

• *Yoda*

Personal assumptions: Teaching and learning best occur in the context of an apprentice relationship where the learner is initially dependent upon an older and wiser person for guidance and direction. As the learner matures, direct contact with the master is not needed but the lessons learned are held in memory to be referred to and employed as needed.

Definition of teaching: For me, teaching is the transfer of knowledge and information from a more experienced person to one who is searching for a more effective and enlightened way to think and act. It occurs in a 1:1 relationship and relies on the use of problems, dilemmas, thoughtful parables, stories, and anecdotes, and modeling to stimulate effective thoughts and action.

Formal principles: As a mentor in this mode of teaching, I operate more in line with cognitive and humanistic principles of learning. For example, from a humanistic point of view, Yoda models effective actions and provides support, and encouragement to help the learner develop a positive self-image. Support, encouragement, and a positive self-concept have been shown in research studies to be associated with high levels of academic achievement. From a cognitive perspective, Yoda often presents the learner with problems to solve and dilemmas that challenge his or her ability to think creatively and critically about issues. While Yoda provides guidance, learners also are left to figure out many things for themselves.

View of human nature: An initial assumption I make is that people are conforming and lack willpower to do things. Yoda's teaching style helps them to become more independent and to develop the willpower to succeed.

• *Matador*

Personal Assumptions: Learning is a difficult enterprise and occurs in a competitive atmosphere. Students learn best when directly challenged by the teacher to think and act in particular ways. Sometimes harsh tactics are needed to promote learning. A learner is not literally killed by the teacher [i.e., as a bull is by the matador]. Rather, the goal of teaching is to replace old habits and ways of thinking with new ones the teacher sees as more effective.

Definition of teaching: I see teaching as a struggle to get learners to acquire information and to act in ways that one wants. Students can be expected to resist efforts to teach them and need to be drawn into an engagement with the teacher. The teacher's goal is to show them who is in charge and to get them to learn things the teacher knows is valuable for them. It is important that the teacher emerge as the victor in this struggle.

Formal principles: My matador style of teaching is based on behavioral principles that emphasize the need for learners to have their behavior shaped in progressively small steps by a teacher. Students need detailed prompts and instructions from the teacher in order to learn. The student is motivated to do well by the use of punishment for not doing what is asked. [i.e., bad grades and evaluations] Eventually such things motivate them to do well because they become aversive stimuli that people try to avoid by thinking and acting in appropriate ways.

Views of human nature: People are basically untrustworthy, they lack willpower to do what is right for themselves, and sometimes want to be too independent for their own good. Teachers need to watch them, to prompt them to do the right things, and to get them to conform to ways of thinking and behaving that in the long run will do them some good.

Our *guiding metaphor* summarizes in a distinct and highly memorable word, phrase, or image our personal model of the teaching-learning process. *This model includes a variety of attitudes, values, beliefs, and assumptions about teaching and learning and thus serves to guide and direct our actions as teachers.* This personal model subsequently plays a role in all of our decisions about how and what to teach. In this regard, metaphors for teaching and learning are like those in other areas of endeavor. They are more than figures of speech. Because they represent our attitudes and values, they subsequently influence the patterns of thought and actions we employ in all aspects of our lives [Lakoff & Johnson, 1980].

Susan Sontag [1989], for example, notes that the "guiding metaphor" for the practice of medicine over the past 100 years has been the battlefield metaphor. A disease is caused by bacteria and viruses that attack the body. We mount defenses against them and also have weapons in the form of drugs and other medical treatments to fight these "invaders."

Thus, we talk about the war on cancer, or the battle against AIDS. Such metaphors shape the way we think about something. As a result, our immediate response to a new disease entity is to find a way to "fight it." While this strategy may payoff, Susan Sontag notes that it limits our perspective. People sometimes become locked into a guiding metaphor. As a consequence, for example, they may fail to consider or appreciate prevention or alternative modes of healing as ways to counter disease.

In much the same way, someone who perceives themselves as Yoda or as a matador doing battle with students is unlikely to appreciate other ways of examining the teaching-learning process. Yet, according to Willard Frick [1987], our growth and development depends upon challenging our existing metaphors for who we are and considering alternatives. In effect, we must decide whether or not the metaphor that describes us is something we want to continue using. Or, perhaps it needs to be modified or changed in order for us to become more effective. He labels this a "symbolic growth process."

Experiences of a faculty member teaching at a catholic college provide a good illustration of the latter point.

> In the church there are three kinds of masses. The old Latin mass was very formal with a priest standing on an altar speaking in a foreign tongue. The English mass has the priest facing the congregation more often, English is spoken, and there is some ritualized interaction among the participants and the priest. In contrast, the folk mass is a joyous celebration with the priest and congregation on the same level, often in a circle, with everyone participating in the service. Metaphorically, I saw classrooms as one of these three forms of the mass. My own classes were nothing less than a folk mass in my mind. That is, until I started to ask students to evaluate my style as a teacher. It then became very clear that I was somewhere between the old Latin mass and the new English mass. They failed to see the joyous celebration of learning that I did. I was not happy with this insight but it led me to explore alternatives to my teaching style. The folk mass now becomes a goal that I strive towards achieving as I modify what I am doing in class.

As with other elements in our conceptual base, it is important to become aware of them. Otherwise they operate implicitly in what we think and how we behave. By bringing the elements into conscious awareness, we can better understand the roles they play in our lives. Then we can decide whether such views are sufficient or whether they must be modified or changed. *The key here is that we make an informed choice about how to conceptualize our roles as teachers.*

With our guiding metaphors, this can be done by first unpacking the attitudes, values, and assumptions that underlie them. We then ask ourselves, "what changes, if any, do I need to make in the guiding metaphor that represents my personal model of the teaching-learning process. Self-Reflection Activity 3-7 is designed to help you achieve the latter goal.

Self-Reflection Activity 3-7
Exploring Our Guiding Metaphor for Teaching

1.] What is your guiding metaphor for teaching? List it in the space provided. If you have not already done so, complete Self-Reflection Activity 1-3 in Chapter 1 of this book. It contains a process to help you identify the metaphor that defines you as a teacher.

"My guiding metaphor is....."

For the questions that follow, refer to the examples of Yoda and the matador for ideas about how to approach answering them.

2.] What personal assumptions about teaching and learning are implicit or explicit in your guiding metaphor?

3.] What definition of teaching is suggested by your guiding metaphor?

4.] What formal principles of teaching and learning underlie your metaphor?

5.] What beliefs about human nature in Table 3-6 are embedded in the guiding metaphor that you developed?

Self-Reflection Activity 3-7 [Continued]

6.] How compatible are your teaching methods with your guiding metaphor? Use the format below and the examples provided as a guide to assist you with completing this part of the task.

My guiding metaphor is ..... *[e.g., Yoda]*

Your response:

Students are ..... *[e.g., Disciples of a wise teacher]*

Your response:

The classroom is..... *[e.g., A forum for important dialogue]*

Your response:

Pedagogy is directed towards..... *[e.g., Expanding awareness]*
                                 [e.g., Identifying one's strengths]
Your response:

My teaching methods are..... *[e.g., Socratic dialogue on cases]*
                            [e.g., 1:1 consultations on projects]
Your response

My teaching style is..... *[e.g., Facilitative, encouraging, other directed]*

Your response:

My teaching style encourages students to become..... *[e.g., Independent]*
                                                    [Responsible]
Your response:

Self-Reflection Activity 3-7 [Continued]

7.] What aspects of your teaching processes are incompatible with the guiding metaphor that you have chosen?

8.] Based on your analysis of your guiding metaphor, how would your metaphor have to change? [Review the process in Table 3-7 for ideas for how to answer the latter question. Use either your "ideal metaphor" or the "bridge metaphor" to respond to this question].

9.] What implications does this new metaphor have for the specific instructional processes that you would employ?

Table 3-7
Modifying Personal Metaphors for Teaching

Current Guiding Metaphor for Teaching

-A class is like one big happy family.

Ideal Metaphor
Having thought about the analysis of your current guiding metaphor, what would be an *ideal metaphor?* That is, one that would capture all of the modifications and changes you believe are needed in your teaching? Try not to censor the possible response[s] that occur to you. Be open and creative about new possibilities for your role as a teacher.
For Example:
-A class is like a spaceship crew exploring new worlds in the universe.

Comparisons of Features
Compare the characteristics of the current *guiding metaphor* to the *ideal metaphor* to see how they differ and where they overlap.

Big Happy Family	Spaceship Crew
Small	Small
Close-Knit	Close-Knit
Focused inward	Focused inward
Traditional group	Nontraditional group
Not in motion	In motion
Low risk taking	High risk taking
Not adventurous	Overly adventurous

Identify a Bridge Metaphor
Sometimes our "ideal metaphor" appears unrealistic or too far removed from where we currently are as a teacher. Thus, something more reasonable is needed. This bridge metaphor would share as many of the common features as possible. The bridge metaphor also would reconcile the different features of our current and ideal metaphors [e.g., suggesting something that is between not being adventurous and being overly adventurous; low risk taking and high risk taking].
For Example:
-Airline crew flying a plane to New York City.
-Cruise ship crew taking passengers to Bermuda.
-Canoe trip with tour guides on a navigable stream or river.

Epilogue

Themes and Variations

This chapter argued that without an explicit philosophy of teaching, our teaching styles are intellectually hollow. Like scholarship, our teaching should be based upon a conceptual base that provides a roadmap to guide and direct our thoughts and behaviors. To do this, however, the *disembodied method bias* that pervades the selection of instructional processes must be overcome. That is, teaching methods and approaches are often adopted without first exploring the theoretical and conceptual base we would want to use in the classroom. Instead, all too often, people "teach as they were taught" or they "teach the course the way it was taught the last time."

Our styles as teachers should follow from a multidimensional philosophy of teaching. This would include such things as: our personal assumptions about instructional processes and learning; a definition of teaching, formal principles of teaching and learning from the research literature; our views of human nature; and our personal model of for the process of teaching as illustrated by our guiding metaphor. *Each element alone or in combination would serve to provide a conceptual structure for how we can and should teach.* Because many of the ideas contained in these elements of a teaching philosophy are part of our culture, they already exist as part of our styles as instructors. The problem is that they are not well developed and most of us are not consciously aware of them.

Our teaching is much better off if we take the time to consciously explore the conceptual components of our styles as teachers. *Then, we can make an informed choice about what aspects of our conceptual base we want to keep and what aspects we want to change or modify.* Our philosophy of teaching then becomes something that results from conscious deliberation and is not something we "fell into" because our methods just happened to reflect certain intellectual issues.

Furthermore, taking time to consciously explore the elements of our conceptual base would make the selection of teaching processes more than a personal whim. It also would force us to consider issues besides "what content should I teach" when designing a course. Becoming aware of our conceptual base would help us challenge our personal beliefs abut effective instructional processes. We might realize that some of what we do lacks a conceptual justification or is at odds with our philosophy of teaching. Overall, paying attention to our theoretical base would help us overcome the drift towards "mindless" ways of designing courses. That is, to fall into the trap of allowing our course designs to be routine and predictable.

The frame of reference for the material in this chapter was that of the teacher. While it is important for faculty to identify a philosophy of teaching and to act upon it, an important element in developing that philosophy has not been mentioned. *This is the conceptual base that underlies students' views about the teaching-learning process.* When their views about teaching and learning are compatible with ours, then the process runs very smoothly. Thus, if the *Captain of the Starship Enterprise* describes our styles as teachers, and students see themselves as *crewmembers,* there is a shared view of the classroom. On the other hand, if students perceive themselves as "lost in space," then they are likely to experience a certain amount of tension and frustration with our teaching style.

A Fly in the Ointment: Students Typically Fail to Share Our Vision

The outcome of an extensive research program suggests that discrepancies between faculty and student perceptions of the teaching-learning process are more the rule than the exception [cf., Grasha, 1990b; Grasha, 1990c; Grasha, 1994; McConnell, Bill, Dember, & Grasha, 1993]. For example, Howard Pollio's [1986] research presented in Chapter 1 showed that metaphors of *containers, journey-guides, and master-disciples* were popular with teachers. Also, my work shows that other faculty voices prevail. Common images include the teacher as *midwife, gardener, lion tamer, entertainer,* and *choreographer,* and others. A peaceful coexistence among faculty and students would exist if students perceived themselves as *containers to be filled, babes at birth, flowers and vegetables to be tended to, lions to be tamed, an audience for entertainers,* and *dancers to be choreographed.* Unfortunately, this does not appear to be the case.

Table 3-8 reports the results of a study in which a random sample of 351 student metaphors were taken from a database of over 2000 metaphors. [Grasha, 1993]. The students in this sample represented all disciplines and grade levels. *It is clear that the viewpoints of students about the classroom as expressed in their metaphors do not match those of faculty.* To begin with, their metaphors suggest much more adversity than challenge in courses. While they take journeys, they tend to be individual journeys. Rather than seeing themselves as containers into which nutritious substances are poured, they perceive themselves as being crammed or stuffed into containers and time periods. Only a very small minority of students [2%] depict themselves as disciples to a master.

One conclusion from this data is that faculty models of teaching and learning are moving east while those of their students are moving west. The good news is that if two people travel far enough on the globe in opposite directions from the same starting place--they will eventually meet. Such meetings between students and faculty to discuss their mutual philosophies of teaching and learning are rare in higher education. In over two decades of facilitating several hundred workshops and seminars about teaching-learning issues, only three had students and faculty discussing teaching and learning issues.

Table 3-8
Categories of Student Metaphors for Teaching and Learning

Category	Examples
Adversity / Challenges [26%] Facing Adversity/Challenge [61%] Overwhelmed by Them [22%] Overcoming Them [17%]	Swimming through mud. Running a race where others have a 3 minute headstart. Reaching summit of a mountain.
Journeys [11%] Individual Journeys [85%] Guided Journeys [15%]	Solitary canoe trip in wilderness. Riding an endless assembly line. Gentle hand guiding children.
Family / Group / Teamwork [11%]	A happy family working together. A baseball team. An archeological dig.
Personal Excitement / *Having a Good Time [8%]*	Partying all night. Enjoying the holiday season.
Containers [7%]	Packing a parachute. Getting an hour show in 1/2 hour.
Passive Participant / *Uneventful Experience [7%]*	Watching grass grow. Following directions of a recipe.
Lost / Alone / Caught in *a Foreign Land [7%]*	Driving alone in a desert at night. Finding self in a foreign land where you do not know the language.
Adventure / Discovery / *Exploration [6%]*	Riding starship to explore universe. Taking a trip to a new country.
Superior Performance / *Accomplishment [5%]*	Bird takes first flight and soars. Running marathon in 5 minutes.

Emotional Roller Coaster [3%]	Riding up and down on a coaster
	Coaster ride that is sometimes fun
	  but at other times makes you sick
	  to your stomach.

Master-Disciple [2%]	Sitting down with a wise person
	  who opens your mind to the
	  wonders of the world.

Miscellaneous [7%]	Doing dog tricks to get a bone. Looking down a long dark tunnel with a light at the end.

The Cost of Keeping Students Out of the Equation

Teaching is a hierarchical enterprise. Usually faculty plan course requirements, decide what content to teach and how it will be taught. In theory, we operate with the best interests of students in mind. *In reality, we plan and make course related decisions based upon our assumptions about what represents the best interests of students.* Sometimes our assumptions are accurate and at times they are not. Yet, students are seldom involved in our deliberations about what and how to teach.

There are two costs to this oversight. One is that our philosophies of teaching largely develop based upon how we see things. At worst they are myopic and at best they are incomplete. As my research with metaphor illustrates, faculty conceptions of teaching and learning are often discrepant. The second cost is that some students find their needs as learners not being met. Tension and frustration occur and this undoubtedly is reflected in the personal models or metaphors they use to describe the teaching-learning process.

In effect, a closer examination of student metaphors suggests that the majority view the emotional climate of the classroom as largely negative. A sense of pessimism about the teaching-learning process prevails. This was demonstrated in a series of studies our research team conducted on the content of faculty and student metaphors [cf., Grasha, 1990a; Grasha, 1994; McConnell, Bill, Dember, & Grasha, 1993]. Trained judges evaluated more than five hundred metaphors for the presence of optimistic and pessimistic themes. Among faculty, the prevailing theme was one of optimism. The classroom was viewed as a pleasant arena where useful and exciting things happened. Their metaphors suggested they were happy, success oriented, focused on challenges and opportunity, and oriented towards development and exploration.

The metaphors of students across disciplines and grade levels were much more pessimistic. They reflected apprehension toward the future, unhappiness, a fear of failure, anxiety, cynicism, and a focus on problems. These outcomes were surprising and one concern was that perhaps we were dealing with a group of cynics. Further inquiry suggested this was not the case. When given the Dember Optimism-Pessimism personality test, they scored higher on optimism than pessimism. Also, when their metaphors for other areas of their lives were examined, they were much more optimistic in describing relationships, jobs, graduating from college, and family life. Their metaphors for what it was like to attend class or to take exams were largely pessimistic in content. The data relevant to this latter point is shown in Figure 3-5.

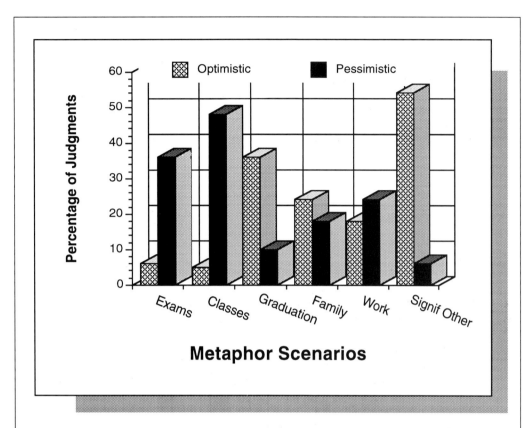

Figure 3-5: Percentage of student metaphors for classes, exams, graduation, family, work, and their significant others judged to be optimistic and pessimistic.

The fact that students view classroom experiences in a pessimistic manner is extremely important. One reason is that data clearly shows that learning occurs much more effectively in the context of a positive emotional climate. Another is that the more pessimistic students become, the less willing they are to ask questions in class and to interact with the instructor and other students. In addition, they are less likely to see classroom issues as challenges, opportunities to learn something, or as problems to be solved. They also are more anxious about their performance and less willing to take responsibility for their learning. In effect, pessimism lowers motivation, distances students from faculty and promotes behaviors that may not help with success in school.

There are several things that we can do to promote a more optimistic outlook:

- *Examine the aspects of your teaching style that promotes a pessimistic outlook in students.* In our research program, college students rated the extent to which a list of metaphors, optimistic and pessimistic in content, applied to specific classes. We then correlated the metaphor ratings to those used to evaluate their teacher's behaviors. Those things teachers do to promote an optimistic and pessimistic outlook are shown in Table 3-9. Eliminating behaviors associated with pessimism helps to create a positive emotional climate.

Table 3-9 Teacher Behaviors Associated with Optimism and Pessimism	
Optimism	Pessimism
• Shows a genuine interest in students • Knows if students are understanding the material presented • Skillful in observing student reactions • Displays an enjoyment of teaching • Stimulates intellectual curiosity • Presents material in an interesting manner • Encourages classroom discussions • Invites criticism of instructor's ideas • Displays self-confidence	• Does not give reasons for criticism • Does not appear to know if class is understanding material • Not skillful at observing student reactions to material • Assignments difficult to complete • Fails to present material in an interesting manner • Does not encourage classroom discussion • Does not explain material clearly • Displays lack of genuine interest in student • Does not respect students • Is not well-prepared for class

• *Consider creating a NEST.* In our research program, we often ask students what metaphors would describe a class if changes were made and they visited the class at a future date. We also ask them to specify what classroom processes would be associated with this new metaphor. [cf., Grasha, 1990a; Grasha, 1990c; Grasha, 1993]. When a thematic analysis of their responses is performed, the metaphor of a **NEST** emerges as shown in Table 3-10.

• *Obtain information from your students on the metaphors they use to describe your class.* Table 3-11 describes a processes for obtaining information about your students' metaphors. In my experience this process yields a number of fascinating insights into how students perceive our teaching. Sharing a summary of the responses to the WIF process with the class, what you learned and what you plan to do based upon this information demonstrates that you took the activity seriously.

• *Develop a personal model for teaching that integrates or bridges your metaphors of teaching and learning with those of your students.* Table 3-7 illustrated how such bridging metaphors can be developed. Reducing such discrepancies and then acting upon the insights provided helps to creates less tension in the classroom.

Table 3-10
Creating a NEST in the Classroom

Nurture

Students want to feel that teachers care about them. Little things like learning their names, taking the extra time to explain things, and making attempts to interact with them inside and outside of class on course-related issues. Being available to meet with students who need help and making suggestions for how they can do better are appreciated. Students tell us such things convey to them that the "teacher really cares about me."

Empower

Students report they want to feel as if they have some input and choice in how a class is run and the assignments that they do. Allowing choices for selecting class projects, who they will work with on course- related activities, flexibility in meeting deadlines, and asking them for ideas for how to improve the learning experience are viewed as empowering.

Structure

Included here are such things as: teachers giving a detailed syllabus; clear instructions for what is expected on assignments and exams; clear evaluation processes; and class sessions that are well-organized and focused on topics.

Teamwork

Students tell us they want to feel "a part of something." They do not want to be an anonymous face in the crowd. Courses should emphasize people working together on common projects, small group activities and discussions, and other things that bring students and faculty together. Metaphors such as an "archeological dig," "baseball, basketball, soccer teams," and a "happy family" describe the nature and quality of the teamwork they desire.

• *Ask students to respond in writing to the question, "What are 2-3 aspects of this class that interfere with your developing a positive outlook on the course?"* Responses to this question often yield useful information. Contrary to what some faculty think, students are often very insightful about classroom processes they like and dislike. Their perceptions should not be used to think of ideas to enhance the quality of the experience for teachers and students.

Table 3-11
The WIF Process for Students to Generate Guiding Metaphors

WIF Process [Words-Images-Feelings]: Think about this course for a moment. *In the space provided below, list several words, images, and feelings that you would use to describe this course.* Be as honest and objective as you can.

Words: (e.g., traditional, cutting edge, pedestrian, innovative, etc.)

Images: (e.g., carnival, funeral, peaceful glen, inattentive audience, etc.)

Feelings: (e.g., anxious, happy, excited, frustrated, etc.)

1.] Summarize what you have written above into a *guiding metaphor.* That is, an integrated/summary metaphor that includes many of the themes inherent in the words, images, and feelings that you have about the course. For example, this class was like *parents taking actions to insure that their children have what they need to get ahead in life, working a difficult puzzle and not being able to find a solution, or a ship visiting different ports of call where everyone on board gains from the experience.* List your *guiding metaphor* in the space provided below.

2.] What are the teaching techniques that support your *guiding metaphor?* For example, "the difficult puzzle" metaphor reflects the difficult assignments the teacher gives us and how impatient he gets when we can't get the answer. *List the elements of the class that support your guiding metaphor in the space below.*

Table 3-11 [Continued **]**

3.] If you were to make adjustments in this class, what *words, images, and feelings* that you listed on the last page would you like to see deleted from those that currently describe this class?

   Deleted Words:

   Deleted Images:

   Deleted Feelings:

4.] What additional *words, images, and feelings* would you like to use to describe this course in the future? Use your hopes, dreams, and desires for your classes to respond to this question.

   Additional Words:

   Additional Images:

   Additional Feelings:

5.] How would the deletions and additions you made modify and/or change your *guiding metaphor?* What would it now become?

6.] What are the implications for how the instructor should teach and the role of the student in class in the modifications and changes you made to your guiding metaphor?

4. An Integrated Model of Teaching and Learning Style

In seeking knowledge, the first step is silence, the second
listening, the third remembering, the fourth practicing, and the
fifth--teaching others.

- Ibn Gabirol

Before adopting any approach to modifying or enhancing our teaching, it is important that we come to some decisions about "Who I am as a teacher" and "What do I want to become?". In the first three chapters, I argued that to deal with such issues we must first engage in processes of self-reflection. The goals of such analyses include: defining our current styles as teachers, examining their strengths and weaknesses; identifying the role our personal values play in teaching; and understanding factors that facilitate and hinder personal change. I also argued that any variations in our teaching should be tied to an underlying conceptual base. Thus, our teaching, like our scholarship, is guided by philosophical issues, theories and models, conceptual concerns, the outcomes of the work of other scholars in the area, as well as our own interpretations of such things. *When grounded in an underlying philosophy of teaching, instructional processes are guided less by past habits, pressures to try the latest trends, or tendencies to conform to what everyone else is doing.* The content of the first three chapters explored ways that we could come to terms with such issues.

In the remaining chapters of this book I will develop an integrated model for using information about teaching and learning styles. The model evolved from my work over the past two decades using the Grasha-Riechmann Student Learning Style Scales and more recent explorations on teaching style. As William Reinsmith noted in his model of archetypal forms in Chapter 1, teaching involves both *presence* and *encounter.* The stylistic patterns in such transactions are critical not only to understand what is happening in the classroom but to help us see what could be occurring. Information about the styles of teachers and learners must become an essential ingredient in our conceptual base for teaching.

In presenting my model, I am by no means trying to short-circuit the need for self-reflection, analysis, and exploring a conceptual base for one's teaching. It would be tempting to say, look no further, all that you need is in this and the remaining chapters. After all, exploring the model will involve self-reflection and analysis and formal principles of teaching and learning that underlie it will be articulated. Furthermore, how to use those principles to select a variety of instructional processes will be presented. Learning about and using the integrated model includes all of the things that I have argued in the first three chapters that were important for teachers to do. *The key phrase here, however, is that the model outlines "one way to accomplish such goals, but it is not the only way."*

The model of teaching and learning style presented in this chapter should not be followed blindly as a recipe for success in teaching. While it has a great deal of empirical support and practical experience to back up its recommendations, it must be placed in context with other ideas and approaches to instruction. *Our selection of instructional processes always must be based upon an informed choice after considering other alternatives.* The process of seeking information about various approaches to teaching is extremely important. Without such inquiry, we effectively have few choices and must rely on past habits.

The Need for an Integrated Model of Teaching and Learning Style

Models in any field emerge for a variety of reasons. New information may fail to fit the tenants of older models, it may not work well in practice, or people simply want something better. Of the three reasons provided, Richard Lahey [1994] argued that our desire for something new is often overlooked or discounted as one of the reasons for seeking new models and theories. Lahey noted that older models of a phenomenon are often replaced because people eventually grow tired of them. Their proponents become weary of fighting a mounting wave of adversity [which is not always based upon data that refutes the model], or the proponents move on to other areas of interest. A critical mass forms for a better way and the process of model building moves forward a notch.

One example in the field of teaching is the demise of interest in behavioral models of instruction [cf., the description of theoretical models of teaching and learning in pages 118-125 of Chapter 3]. *Self-paced instruction, Keller Plans, behavioral objectives* for learning, and intriguing methods to reward student achievement have taken a back seat to the *cognitive revolution* in teaching. Encouraging critical and creative thinking, teaching students to solve problems and to make decisions, developing writing skills to encourage reflection, analysis, and communication, and helping students become self-directed, self-initiated learners are now much more in vogue.

Behavioral approaches have been de-emphasized in spite of evidence that supports the effectiveness of manipulating environmental stimuli to *prompt, trigger, encourage,* and to *reward* desirable behavior in the classroom. In fact, behavioral principles continue to be used in educational settings as anyone who employs earning points and grades to motivate students can attest. It is, however, no longer as popular as it once was. The responses to the questionnaire on theoretical positions in Chapter 3 [cf., Figure 3-4] clearly demonstrated that college faculty endorsed cognitive and humanistic views to a much larger extent in their teaching. Those who argued for a strong behavioral component in educational practice had their day and many moved on. Some, in the spirit of *if you can't beat them--join them,* decided to merge their ideas with those found in the cognitive revolution. The result is a hybrid model called *cognitive-behaviorism.*

In line with the themes raised above, I did not set out to develop an integrated model of teaching and learning styles because there were fatal flaws in other approaches. Other ways of conceptualizing teaching and learning style have empirical support as well as practitioners who use them successfully. I certainly was not exploring an alternate model to create a revolution. My reasons were very modest. I was simply dissatisfied with certain aspects of current conceptions of teaching and learning style and wanted to suggest a remedy. My areas of dissatisfaction included:

- *Most contemporary approaches tended to emphasize either the styles of teachers or those of learners.* Most of the models of teaching style described in Chapter 1 share this quality as did my early work with the *Grasha-Riechmann Student Learning Style Scales* [cf., Table 3-5]. While useful in their own right, it became clear to me that they only offered a one-sided point of view. The relationship between the styles of teachers and students needed to be explored.

- *For those models that accounted for the styles of both teachers and students, they were largely descriptive and mildly prescriptive* [cf., the discussion of the model based on Carl Jung's theory of personality described in Chapter 1]. Such approaches, for example, did not specify how various styles of teaching could be adopted or modified or the conditions under which it was appropriate to employ a given style. Associations between the educational practices of individuals with particular styles were simply noted. And in some cases, people were not seen as having a great deal of flexibility in varying their styles. Jung, for example, argued that our dominant preferences for qualities such as introversion or extroversion were inborn. Thus, one did not wake up one morning and decide to change a dominant preference.

Because the dominant preference was pervasive, those subordinate to it could be tinkered with and enhanced, but they always remained in the background. Thus, someone who preferred to gather new information and to explore the world through their senses, possessed a less developed sense of intuitive thinking. Intuition may occasionally emerge on an activity and surprise that person, but usually was subordinate to the sensing preference. Under such conditions, teachers had to rely on their dominate preferences and seek ways to accommodate differences between their styles and those of their students.

Accommodating differences in style is an important part of teaching to diversity. A reliance on this strategy, however, does not allow for periodically creating beneficial mismatches in style.

- *I wanted a model that also provided for stretching the styles of students and faculty.* If managed well, I knew that informed and well-chosen mismatches in style could provide opportunities for both parties to grow. Matching student and teacher styles up to a point provides a certain amount of satisfaction for both parties. Unfortunately, when carried to an extreme, matching styles can lead to boredom and satisfaction with the status quo.

• *I wanted an approach that was clearly grounded in the classroom.* Some contemporary approaches such as those based on the Myers-Briggs Type Inventory, Group Embedded Figures Test and the Kolb Learning Style Inventory use a general assessment of personality that is then related to the classroom. I wanted to assess style using a more direct link. That is, both the formal measures of teacher and student styles, and the characteristics that emerged from them, needed to be grounded in classroom experiences.

There were two reasons for this requirement. One was technical and related to the reliability and validity of devices to measure style. I knew from other research I was doing that situation specific tests generally were more reliable and valid than those with a general frame of reference [cf., VanSchoyk & Grasha, 1981; Grasha, 1983]. The other reason was that grounding the measuring devices in instructional processes would make it easier to link the qualities of teachers and students. This could facilitate recommendations for instructional practices. This latter point was one of the forces that led to the development of the Grasha-Riechmann Student Learning Style Scales. It also became part of the rationale for my developing the Teaching Style Inventory described later in this chapter.

With the above issues in mind, I began in 1988 a program of research designed to develop an integrated model of teaching and learning style. *My goals were to describe the stylistic qualities of teachers and students, to show how they related to each other, and to offer suggestions for how this information could be used to enhance the nature and quality of classroom experiences.* A less detailed version of this model emphasizing the teaching style component was published in a special section on teaching style in the journal *College Teaching* [Grasha, 1994]. Outside of workshop and conference presentations, this is the first time the complete model has appeared in print. This chapter outlines the major features of the model while the final four chapters of this book highlight specific examples of ways to apply the modeling the college classroom.

The Elements of the Integrated Model: Teaching Style

While I had a considerable amount of experience working with the independent-dependent; collaborative-competitive; and participant-avoidant student styles, they were only one part of the equation. To develop an integrative model, I needed to conceptualize the styles of teachers in ways that would be compatible with this approach to learning style. Thus, my initial task was to develop a system that would define and identify the styles of college faculty.

I initially turned to analyzing my experiences, held numerous discussions with colleagues and participants in workshops, interviewed people, attended classes, and began reviewing the literature on teaching. While there was a diversity of opinion on the issue, a working definition of teaching style soon emerged. *I began to see it as a pattern of needs, beliefs, and behaviors that faculty displayed in their classroom.*

It also became clear that the styles of faculty were multidimensional and affected how they presented information, interacted with students, managed classroom tasks, supervised course work, socialized students to the field, and mentored students. [A detailed examination of how such elements occur in various approaches to style was described in Chapter 1.]

Overall, such efforts produced a diverse and rich source of material about how and why people taught in particular ways. I then turned my attention to determining what qualities of faculty were pervasive across a variety of disciplines and classroom environments. A thematic analysis of the information I had gathered from all of the sources mentioned above suggested that five teaching styles were pervasive in the college classroom. They were the styles of Expert, Formal Authority, Personal Model, Facilitator, and Delegator. Table 4-1 describes each one of them along with the advantages and disadvantages they created for teachers.

It would be fair to say that I did not discover the five styles as much as I catalogued what was already there. Together, the styles appear to be prevalent aspects of faculty *presence* in the classroom. They are not isolated qualities that affect only a few teachers. And because they interact in predictable ways with the learning styles of students, they also help us to understand the nature of teacher-student *encounters*.

Like Colors on an Artist's Palette

While it might appear tempting to place teachers into one of five boxes, my initial observations suggested that such attempts at parsimony were premature. Instead, it quickly became apparent that everyone who teaches possesses each of the five teaching styles to varying degrees. In effect, each individual style was like a different color on an artist's palette. Like those colors, they could be blended together. In all, four combinations of styles were present in an analysis of how college teachers conducted their classes. These four clusters or blends of teaching styles are listed in Table 4-2.

The clusters were obtained from a thematic analysis of my observations of teachers in the classroom, interviews with college faculty, and the responses of several hundred workshop participants who related the five styles to the instructional processes they employed in the classroom. The order of each style in the cluster [e.g., Personal Model/Formal Authority/Expert] reflects the perceived importance of that style in the blend.

College teachers also use some styles more often than others. Thus, the organization of each cluster in Table 4-2 reflects the fact that certain blends of styles are dominant while others play more of a secondary role. The primary or dominant styles are like the foreground in a painting. They are easily seen and central to understanding the artist's vision. The other qualities are similar to the background in a painting and support and add texture to what is figural.

When teachers lecture, for example, one sees the expert and formal authority side of them much more easily than the modeling, facilitative, or delegative parts of their styles. The latter lie in the background and often contribute to

Table 4-1
Five Teaching Styles

Expert
Possesses knowledge and expertise that students need. Strives to maintain status as an expert among students by displaying detailed knowledge and by challenging students to enhance their competence. Concerned with transmitting information and insuring that students are well prepared.

Advantage: The information, knowledge, and skills such individuals possess.
Disadvantage: If overused, the display of knowledge can be intimidating to less experienced students. May not always show the underlying thought processes that produced answers.

Formal Authority
Possesses status among students because of knowledge and role as a faculty member. Concerned with providing positive and negative feedback, establishing learning goals, expectations, and rules of conduct for students. Concerned with the correct, acceptable, and standard ways to do things and with providing students with the structure they need to learn.

Advantage: The focus on clear expectations and acceptable ways of doing things.
Disadvantage: A strong investment in this style can lead to rigid, standardized, and less flexible ways of managing students and their concerns.

Personal Model
Believes in "teaching by personal example" and establishes a prototype for how to think and behave. Oversees, guides, and directs by showing how to do things, and encouraging students to observe and then to emulate the instructor's approach.

Advantage: An emphasis on *direct observation* and *following a role model*.
Disadvantage: Some teachers may believe their approach is *the best way* leading some students to feel inadequate if they cannot live up to such expectations and standards.

Facilitator
Emphasizes the personal nature of teacher-student interactions. Guides and directs students by asking questions, exploring options, suggesting alternatives, and encouraging them to develop criteria to make informed choices. Overall goal is to develop in students the capacity for independent action, initiative, and responsibility. Works with students on projects in a consultative fashion and tries to provide as much support and encouragement as possible.

Advantage: The personal flexibility, the focus on students' needs and goals, and the willingness to explore options and alternative courses of action.
Disadvantage: Style is often time consuming and is sometimes employed when a more direct approach is needed. Can make students uncomfortable if it is not employed in a positive and affirming manner.

Delegator
Concerned with developing students' capacity to function in an autonomous fashion. Students work independently on projects or as part of autonomous teams. The teacher is available at the request of students as a resource person.

Advantage: Helps students to perceive themselves as independent learners.
Disadvantage: May misread student's readiness for independent work. Some students may become anxious when given autonomy.

Table 4-2
Four Clusters of Teaching Styles

Cluster 1
[38%]*

Primary Teaching Styles: Expert/Formal Authority
Secondary Teaching Styles: Personal Model/Facilitator/Delegator

Cluster 2
[22%]

Primary Teaching Styles: Personal Model/Expert/Formal Authority
Secondary Teaching Styles: Facilitator/Delegator

Cluster 3
[17%]

*Primary Teaching Styles:*Facilitator/Personal Model/Expert
*Secondary Teaching Styles:*Formal Authority/Delegator

Cluster 4
[15%]

Primary Teaching Styles: Delegator/Facilitator/Expert
Secondary Teaching Styles: Formal Authority/Personal Model

* The percentage of faculty whose primary styles fell within each
of the clusters [Grasha, 1994].

the nuances in someone's approach to lecturing. Some lecturers use personal examples of how the material affected them or demonstrate how to use particular skills. Others employ Socratic questioning strategies or simply ask, "What do you think?" In the latter cases, parts of the personal model, facilitator, and delegator styles begin to appear.

Teaching styles are more than interesting qualities people possess. They also serve an important function in the college classroom. Once again, consider the metaphor of an artist creating a painting. Colors on a canvas are blended and organized to make a statement or to create a mood. In much the same way, each of the four clusters of teaching styles depicted in Table 4-2 makes a statement about "Who I am as a person." They also help to create a particular mood or emotional climate in class.

For example, an emphasis on the Expert/Formal Authority blend sends a message to students that "I'm in charge here." It also creates a neutral or "cool" emotional climate. As normally practiced, lectures are vehicles for transmitting information where students become relatively passive participants. In this atmosphere, the expression of emotions is usually held in check except for those rare instances a lively debate occurs.

In contrast, an emphasis on the Delegator/Facilitator/Expert blend creates a different picture. It sends a message to students that "I'm here to consult with you on the projects and issues you are exploring." The nature and quality of the interactions are different. Teachers and students work together, share information, and the boundaries between teacher and student are not as formal. The emotional climate is relatively warmer. Also, there are more opportunities for participants to openly express how they feel about tasks and, perhaps, about each other.

Constraints on the Expression of Teaching Style

An artist's imagination, her propensity for taking risks, the subject matter, and the colors available on the palette place limits on artistic expression. In much the same way, several factors appear to confine the expression of the five teaching styles described in this chapter.

When asked the question *"What influences your teaching style?"* 560 college teachers in various workshops and seminars I conducted frequently listed the following items:

- Course was required or not required or the class was available only for majors or was open for non-majors.
- Size of the class
- The subject matter [e.g., hard sciences versus humanities]
- Grade Level of the students [e.g., first-year, seniors, graduate]
- How much they liked the class
- Time pressure
- Need to prepare students for standardized exams
- Information about alternate ways to teach
- Willingness to take risks
- Not wanting to deviate from department and college norms for teaching

Participants reported that the Expert/Formal Authority approach to teaching was popular when classes were large, required in the major, the students were mostly freshmen and sophomores, there was time pressure to cover a large amount of material, or they had to prepare their students for taking standardized exams in their fields. They also indicated that the Expert/Formal Authority blend was preferred because it provided an acceptable way to "go through the motions" of teaching courses they disliked. In addition, it was popular because it helped them to easily meet the expectations of colleagues for "how I should teach."

In contrast, participants using a Delegator/Facilitator/Expert blend of styles reported they were more willing to take risks. They also stated they were more likely to employ such styles in upper- level undergraduate and graduate courses.

Instructional Strategies Associated with Each Cluster of Teaching Styles

Classroom observations suggested that faculty falling within each of the clusters in Table 4-2 were more prone to use particular teaching methods. My initial list of these instructional processes were shared with participants in my workshops and seminars. I was interested in whether others concurred with my observations and if their experiences suggested that instructional methods other than those I had identified fit each of the four clusters. The participants agreed with my initial scheme and provided additional items for my list. Table 4-3 illustrates the outcome of this effort. Detailed descriptions of the instructional processes shown and suggestions for using them effectively are presented in Chapters 5 and 6.

The Distribution of Teaching Style in the Classroom

Having identified the five styles of teaching, I turned my attention to understanding how they were distributed across grade levels, rank and gender of instructors, and various academic disciplines. To accomplish this latter goal, the I developed the Teaching Styles Inventory. It contains 40 items that assess attitudes and behaviors associated with each of the five styles. Participants in these studies were asked to select two classes they taught that they believed were different. They then rated the extent to which forty items associated with each of the five styles applied to those two courses. This procedure allowed me to obtain profiles of the five styles for everyone who took the inventory and to relate the scores to grade level, rank, gender, and academic discipline.

Overall, the Teaching Style Inventory was administered to 381 faculty representing 125 public and private colleges and universities in the United States. Two hundred and seventy-five were participants in national and regional workshops I conducted. The remaining 106 teachers were selected from random samples conducted within two large universities. Information on 762 classrooms across 10 groups of disciplines was obtained in this study.

The outcomes of this investigation are presented beginning on page 165. Before reading about them, you might want to assess the degree to which each teaching style appears in your classroom. Completing Self-Reflection Activity 4-1 will allow you to do this. In the process, you also will become familiar with the source of the information that was used to depict how teaching styles were distributed in the college classroom.

Table 4-3
Teaching Methods Associated With Each
Teaching Style Cluster

Cluster 1	Cluster 2
Primary Styles Expert/Formal Authority *Secondary Styles* Personal Model/Facilitator/Delegator	*Primary Styles* Personal Model/Expert/Formal Authority *Secondary Styles* Facilitator/Delegator

• Exams/Grades Emphasized
• Guest Speakers/Guest Interviews
• Lectures
• Mini-Lectures + Triggers
• Teacher-Centered Questioning
• Teacher-Centered Discussions
• Term Papers
• Tutorials
• Technology-Based Presentations
	• Role Modeling by Illustration
	  - Discussing Alternate Approaches
	  - Sharing Thought Processes
	    Involved in Obtaining Answers
	  - Sharing Personal Experiences
	• Role Modeling by Direct Action
	  - Demonstrating Ways of
	    Thinking/Doing Things
	  - Having Students Emulate Teacher
	• Coaching/Guiding Students

Cluster 3	Cluster 4
Primary Styles Facilitator/Personal Model/Expert *Secondary Styles* Formal Authority/Delegator	*Primary Styles* Delegator/Facilitator/Expert *Secondary Styles* Formal Authority/Personal Model

• Case Studies
• Cognitive Map Discussion
• Critical Thinking Discussion
• Fishbowl Discussion
• Guided Readings
• Key Statement Discussions
• Kineposium
• Laboratory Projects
• Problem Based Learning
  - Group Inquiry
  - Guided Design
  - Problem Based Tutorials
• Role Plays/Simulations
• Roundtable Discussion
• Student Teacher of the Day
	• Contract Teaching
	• Class Symposium
	• Debate Formats
	• Helping Trios
	• Independent Study/Research
	• Jigsaw Groups
	• Laundry List Discussions
	• Modular Instruction
	• Panel Discussion
	• Learning Pairs
	• Position Papers
	• Practicum
	• Round Robin Interviews
	• Self Discovery Activities
	• Small Group Work Teams
	• Student Journals

Self-Reflection Activity 4-1
Taking and Analyzing the Teaching Style Inventory

In order to respond to this activity, first complete the *Teaching Styles Inventory* beginning on page 160. It is designed to assess aspects of your attitudes and behaviors about teaching. There are no correct answers to each item. Thus, try to be as honest and objective as you can when responding.

Recording Your Responses to the Teaching Styles Inventory

1,] *Compute your average score on each of the styles using the scoring key provided on page 164. Use your average scores on each style to rank order their occurrence in each of the two classes you rated.* Use a rank of 1 for the teaching style with the highest average score and a 5 for the one with the lowest score. Rank order the others accordingly. If you had a tie score on two styles, assign both the same rank. Place the ranks you obtained for each style on the appropriate lines below.

	Course #1	*Course #2*
Expert	____ [ ]	____ [ ]
Formal Authority	____ [ ]	____ [ ]
Personal Model	____ [ ]	____ [ ]
Facilitator	____ [ ]	____ [ ]
Delegator	____ [ ]	____ [ ]

2.] *Use the norms for the test in the scoring key on page 164 to determine whether each score was low, moderate, or high.* Place a **L** to indicate low score, **M** for moderate, and **H** for a high score in each of the brackets shown above.

A Few Moments of Private Reflection

1.] *Examine the rank ordering of each style and the magnitude of the scores for each class.* In what ways are your teaching styles similar and different in each course?

2.] *If the occurrence of the styles are similar in each class, is this appropriate?* That is, given the nature of the content, the level of each course, the types of students, and your personal beliefs about education--should your style of teaching in each class be the same?

3.] *Did you answer no to the last question?* If so, what teaching style[s] ought to be emphasized that currently are not prominent in how you teach?

4.] *Was the distributions of teaching styles for each course different?* If it was, how did the content, the level of each class, the types of students, and your beliefs about education influence the styles you used?

5.] *What additional factors affected the teaching styles you used?*

6.] *Compare your scores to the information reported on a national sample of faculty on pages 165-168.* This data shows how teaching styles vary with a teacher's rank, course level, gender, and academic discipline. In what ways are your styles similar and different from the national sample?

Teaching Styles Inventory: Version 3.0

Copyright © 1991, 1994 by Anthony F. Grasha, Ph.D.

To complete the *Teaching Styles Inventory* you will need to use two of the undergraduate or graduate courses you currently teach or that you have taught within the past 6-9 months. Select any combination of two undergraduate or graduate courses that are different from each other in some way. They may differ because one is more or less challenging to teach, the content is different, the level of the students varies, the amount of work required of you and your students is dissimilar, your interest in teaching each varies, or perhaps they are perceived differently in other ways. Pick two courses and then focus on several aspects of the course by completing the items listed below.

Brief Title of Course 1

Primary Level of This Course 1
Freshmen _____ Sophomore ____ Junior ____ Senior ____
Beginning graduate level course _____ Advanced graduate level course _____

Is this course required for undergraduate majors and/or a graduate degree:
Yes _____ No _____

What is the average enrollment in the course? _____

How many times have you taught this class? _____

On a rating scale of [1 2 3 4 5 6 7] where a *1* indicates *I do not enjoy teaching this course* and a *7* indicates *I really enjoy teaching this course,* rate the extent to which you like teaching this class? _____

Brief Title of Course 2

Primary Level of Course 2
Freshmen _____ Sophomore ____ Junior ____ Senior ____
Beginning graduate level course _____ Advanced graduate level course _____

Is this course required for undergraduate majors and/or a graduate degree:
Yes _____ No _____

How many times have you taught this class? _____

On a rating scale of [1 2 3 4 5 6 7] where a *1* indicates *I do not enjoy teaching this course* and a *7* indicates *I really enjoy teaching this course,* rate the extent to which you like teaching this class? _____

Briefly list 2-3 reasons why you see the two courses listed above as different from each other.

Teaching Styles Inventory: Version 3.0

Page 2

Respond to each of the items below in terms of how they apply to each of the two courses you listed on the first page of this questionnaire. Try to answer as honestly and as objectively as you can. Resist the temptation to respond as you believe you "should or ought to think or behave" or in terms of what you believe is the "expected or proper thing to do." Use the following rating scale when responding to each item:

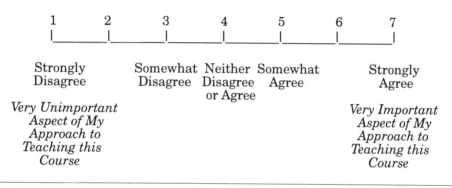

| 1 | 2 | 3 | 4 | 5 | 6 | 7 |

Strongly Disagree   Somewhat Disagree   Neither Disagree or Agree   Somewhat Agree   Strongly Agree

Very Unimportant Aspect of My Approach to Teaching this Course   *Very Important Aspect of My Approach to Teaching this Course*

Course #1   Course # 2

01.] Facts, concepts, and principles are the most important things that students should acquire. ____ ____

02.] I set high standards for students in this class. ____ ____

03.] What I say and do models appropriate ways for students to think about issues in the content. ____ ____

04.] My teaching goals and methods address a variety of student learning styles. ____ ____

05.] Students typically work on course projects alone with little supervision from me. ____ ____

06.] Sharing my knowledge and expertise with students is very important to me. ____ ____

07.] I give students negative feedback when their performance is unsatisfactory. ____ ____

08.] Students are encouraged to emulate the example I provide. ____ ____

09.] I spend time consulting with students on how to improve their work on individual and/or group projects. ____ ____

10.] Activities in this class encourage students to develop their own ideas about content issues. ____ ____

11.] What I have to say about a topic is important for students to acquire a broader perspective on the issues in that area. ____ ____

12.] Students would describe my standards and expectations as somewhat strict and rigid. ____ ____

Teaching Styles Inventory: Version 3.0   Page 3
Copyright © 1991, 1994 by Anthony F. Grasha, Ph.D.

Use the following rating scale when responding to each item:

1	2	3	4	5	6	7
	___	___	___	___	___	___	

Strongly   Somewhat Neither Somewhat   Strongly
Disagree   Disagree Disagree Agree   Agree
    or Agree

Very Unimportant   *Very Important*
Aspect of My   *Aspect of My*
Approach to   *Approach to*
Teaching this   *Teaching this*
Course   *Course*

                                         Course #1   Course # 2

13.] I typically show students how and what
to do in order to master course content.   _____   _____

14.] Small group discussions are employed to
help students develop their ability to
think critically.   _____   _____

15.] Students design one or more self-directed
learning experiences.   _____   _____

16.] I want students to leave this course well
prepared for further work in this area.   _____   _____

17.] It is my responsibility to define what students
must learn and how they should learn it.   _____   _____

18.] Examples from my personal experiences often
are used to illustrate points about the material.   _____   _____

19.] I guide students' work on course projects by
asking questions, exploring options, and
suggesting alternative ways to do things.   _____   _____

20.] Developing the ability of students to think and
work independently is an important goal.   _____   _____

21.] Lecturing is a significant part of how I
teach each of the class sessions.   _____   _____

22.] I provide very clear guidelines for how I want
tasks completed in this course.   _____   _____

23.] I often show students how they can use
various principles and concepts.   _____   _____

24.] Course activities encourage students to take
initiative and responsibility for their learning.   _____   _____

25.] Students take responsibility for teaching part
of the class sessions.   _____   _____

26.] My expertise is typically used to resolve
disagreements about content issues.   _____   _____

Teaching Styles Inventory: Version 3.0
Copyright © 1991, 1994 by Anthony F. Grasha, Ph.D.

Page 4

Use the following rating scale when responding to each item:

```
    1         2         3         4         5         6         7
    |_____|_____|_____|_____|_____|_____|
```

Strongly
Disagree

Somewhat   Neither   Somewhat
Disagree   Disagree   Agree
           or Agree

Strongly
Agree

Very Unimportant
Aspect of My
Approach to
Teaching this
Course

Very Important
Aspect of My
Approach to
Teaching this
Course

Course #1   Course # 2

27.] This course has very specific goals and objectives that I want to accomplish. _____ _____

28.] Students receive frequent verbal and/or written comments on their performance. _____ _____

29.] I solicit student advice about how and what to teach in this course. _____ _____

30.] Students set their own pace for completing independent and/or group projects. _____ _____

31.] Students might describe me as a "storehouse of knowledge" who dispenses the facts, principles, and concepts they need. _____ _____

32.] My expectations for what I want students to do in this class are clearly stated in the syllabus. _____ _____

33.] Eventually, many students begin to think like me about course content. _____ _____

34.] Students can make choices among activities in order to complete course requirements. _____ _____

35.] My approach to teaching is similar to a manager of a work group who delegates tasks and responsibilities to subordinates. _____ _____

36.] There is more material in this course than I have time available to cover it. _____ _____

37.] My standards and expectations help students develop the discipline they need to learn. _____ _____

38.] Students might describe me as a "coach" who works closely with someone to correct problems in how they think and behave. _____ _____

39.] I give students a lot of personal support and encouragement to do well in this course. _____ _____

40.] I assume the role of a resource person who is available to students whenever they need help. _____ _____

* Use the scoring key on the next page to obtain your scores on each teaching style.

Teaching Styles Inventory: Version 3.0   Page 5
Scoring Key

1.] *Copy the ratings you assigned to each item in the spaces provided below.*

	Course	*Course*	*Course*	*Course*	*Course*
	#1 #2	#1 #2	#1 #2	#1 #2	#1 #2
01.]	__ __	02.] __ __	03.] __ __	04.] __ __	05.] __ __
06.]	__ __	07.] __ __	08.] __ __	09.] __ __	10.] __ __
11.]	__ __	12.] __ __	13.] __ __	14.] __ __	15.] __ __
16.]	__ __	17.] __ __	18.] __ __	19.] __ __	20.] __ __
21.]	__ __	22.] __ __	23.] __ __	24.] __ __	25.] __ __
26.]	__ __	27.] __ __	28.] __ __	29.] __ __	30.] __ __
31.]	__ __	32.] __ __	33.] __ __	34.] __ __	35.] __ __
36.]	__ __	37.] __ __	38.] __ __	39.] __ __	40.] __ __

2.] *Sum the ratings for each column and place the total in the spaces below.*

___ ___   ___ ___   ___ ___   ___ ___   ___ ___

3.] *Divide each column score above by 8 to obtain the average numerical rating you assigned to the items associated with each teaching style.* Place your average rating to the nearest decimal point in the spaces below.

___ ___   ___ ___   ___ ___   ___ ___   ___ ___

Expert   Formal   Personal   Facilitator   Delegator
              Authority   Model

4.] *The teaching styles that correspond to each pair of columns are shown above.*

5.] *Range of low, moderate, and high scores for each style based on the test norms.*

	Low Scores	*Moderate*	*High Scores*
Expert	[1.0-3.2]	[3.3-4.8]	[4.9-7.0]
Formal Authority	[1.0-4.0]	[4.1-5.4]	[5.5-7.0]
Personal Model	[1.0-4.3]	[4.4-5.7]	[5.8-7.0]
Facilitator	[1.0-3.7]	[3.8-5.3]	[5.4-7.0]
Delegator	[1.0-2.6]	[2.7-4.2]	[4.3-7.0]

Teaching Style and Academic Rank

The average scores on the inventory for each academic rank are shown in Figure 4-1. The higher the average score, the more participants perceived that teaching style as being displayed in their classes. When faculty rank is considered, the only changes in teaching style that were statistically reliable [i.e., not likely due to chance] were those associated with the Expert and Formal Authority styles. Faculty holding the rank of professor tended to employ the latter two styles more often than did other teachers.

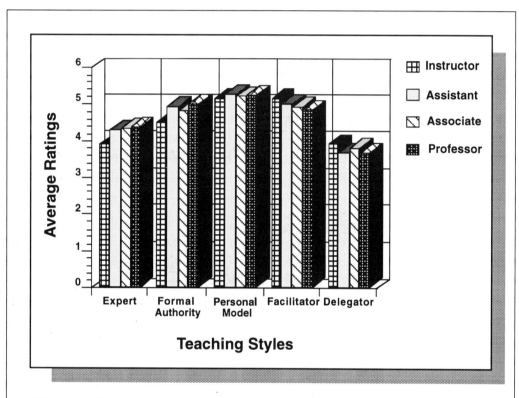

Figure 4-1: The distributions of the five teaching styles for the academic ranks of instructor, assistant professor, associate professor and full professor. [n= 23 Instructors; 193 Assist. Prof.; 258 Assoc. Prof; 286 Professors]

Teaching Styles and Course Level

Changes in each style for different course levels are shown in Figure 4-2. The higher the rating on each style, the more it was perceived as an important part of a class. Note that the Personal Model style changed very little with the level of courses. The other styles, however, were used differently in upper-level versus lower-level classes. Participants were less likely to assume the Expert and Formal Authority styles with their advanced undergraduate and graduate courses. In contrast, they were more likely to use the Facilitator and Delegator styles in more advanced courses. If upper-level classes attract better prepared student, then the faculty adjusted their styles for the capability levels of their students.

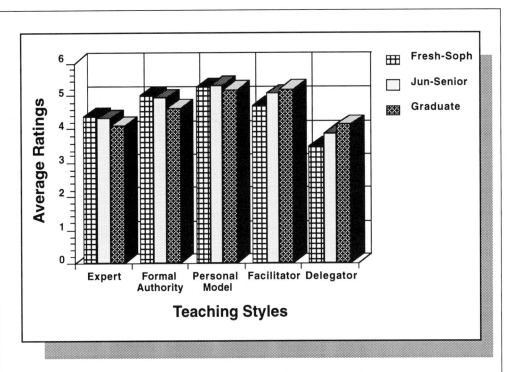

Figure 4-2: The distributions of the five teaching styles for Freshmen-Sophomore [n= 365]; Junior-Senior [n=260]; and Graduate level courses. [n=130].

Teaching Style and Gender

Differences in teaching styles between men and women faculty were noted and these data are shown in Figure 4-3 on the next page. Compared to their male counterparts, women reported somewhat lower scores on the Expert and Formal Authority scales of the Teaching Styles Inventory and somewhat higher scores on the Facilitator and Delegator styles. These differences were statistically reliable [i.e., not likely due to chance]. Such findings are consistent with information showing that women in authority positions are more likely to downplay their expertise and authority and are more likely to be more democratic [i.e., collaborative and participative] in dealing with those under them [Eagly and Johnson, 1990; Eagly and Karau, 1991]. These qualities are very much a part of the facilitative and delegative styles of teaching.

Teaching Style and Academic Discipline

Variations in teaching style occurred among the ten groups of academic disciplines represented in the national sample. This information is shown in Table 4-4. The average scores for each teaching style suggest that the Expert style was used more frequently by faculty teaching in the areas of mathematics/computer science and arts/music/theater. It was employed less often by those in the humanities and education areas. The Formal Authority style appeared to a higher degree in foreign language and business administration classrooms whereas education, humanities, and the theater

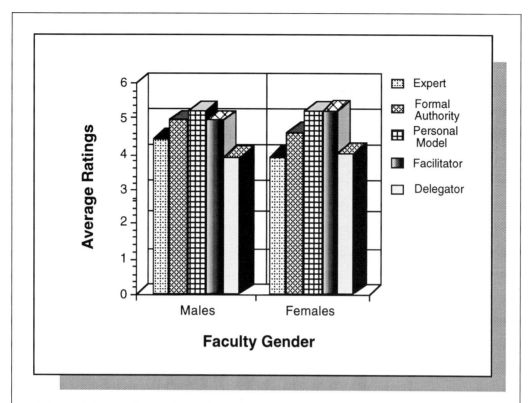

Figure 4-3: The distributions of the five teaching styles in courses taught by male faculty members [n=385] and female faculty members [n=375].

disciplines reported using the Personal Model style more often than did faculty elsewhere. Finally, the Facilitator and Delegator teaching styles occurred to a lesser extent in the classrooms of mathematics/computer science teachers than in other academic areas. The latter styles were observed more often among individuals teaching in education and in the arts/music/theater areas.

The Elements of the Integrated Model: Learning Style

Before describing how the styles of teachers and learners interact and ways to effectively manage the diversity of style in the classroom, a little background on the learning styles in this integrated model is needed. My interests in learning styles began early in my career following a number of informal observations of the ways students approached classroom tasks [Grasha, 1972]. What initially intrigued me were variations in the preferences people had for working with peers and the teacher in the classroom. In collaboration with Sheryl Hruska-Riechmann, an inventory designed to identify and categorize such preferences was developed [cf., Hruska-Riechmann & Grasha, 1982; Grasha, 1985; Grasha, 1990a]. This inventory, the *Grasha-Riechmann Student Learning Style Scales [GRSLSS],* has been widely used in higher education and other educational settings internationally for more than two decades.

Table 4-4
Mean Teaching Style Scores
for Ten Discipline Groups

Discipline	Expert	Formal Authority	Personal Model	Facilitator	Delegator
1 Arts/Music/Theater	4.68[2,10]	5.14[10]	5.73[2-10]	5.27[8,9]	3.99[9]
2 Humanities	3.92[1,5,9]	4.73[3,7]	5.16[1]	5,12[9]	3.77[9]
3 Foreign Languages	4.22	5.43[2,5,6,10]	5.29[1]	5.01[9]	3.82[9]
4 Social Science	4.32	5.01[10]	5.23[1]	5.00[9]	3.76[9]
5 Applied Studies	4.61[2,10]	4.92[3]	5.22[1]	5.00[9]	3.72[9]
6 Applied Sciences	4.29	4.70[3,7]	5.29[1]	4.96[9]	3.82[9]
7 Business Admin.	4.41	5.22[2,6,10]	5.21[1]	4.79[9]	3.86[9]
8 Physical/Biological Sciences	4.47	5.02[10]	5.18[1]	4.60[9]	3.53[10]
9 Math/Computer Science	4.66[2,10]	5.11[10]	5.23[1]	4.28[1-8,10]	3.29[1-7,10]
10 Education	3.93[1,5,9]	4.51[1-4,7,8,9]	5.32[1]	5.41[7,8,9]	4.10[8,9]

Notes:

The number of classrooms in each discipline group that were represented in the data shown above were as follows: #1 [34]; #2 [130]; #3 [24]; #4 [96]; #5 [100] #6 [92]; #7 [56]; #8 [95]; #9 [72]; #10 [62]

The Newman-Keuls test was used to determine whether the variations in mean ratings between pairs of discipline groups were statistically reliable (i.e., not likely to be due to chance). For each teaching style, the academic disciplines that showed statistically reliable variations in their mean ratings are represented by the superscript notations (all p's $< .05$). For example, for the Arts/Music/Theater group, the notation 4.68[2,10] appears for the Expert teaching style. This signifies that the Arts/Music/Theater group's ratings on the Expert style were significantly different from discipline group # 2 (Humanities) and # 10 (Education).

Table 4-5
Advantages and Disadvantages of Learning Styles

Competitive
Students who learn material in order to perform better than others in the class. Believe they must compete with other students in a course for the rewards that are offered. Like to be the center of attention and to receive recognition for their accomplishments in class.
Advantages: Motivates students to keep up and to set goals for learning.
Disadvantages: May turn less competitive people off and style makes it more difficult for people to appreciate and to learn collaborative skills.

Collaborative
Typical of students who feel they can learn by sharing ideas and talents. They cooperate with teachers and like to work with others.
Advantages: Develop skills for working in groups and teams.
Disadvantages: Not as well prepared for handling competitive people. Depend too much on others and not always able to work as well alone.

Avoidant
Not enthusiastic about learning content and attending class. Do not participate with students and teachers in the classroom. They are uninterested and overwhelmed by what goes on in class.
Advantages: Able to avoid the tension and anxiety of taking serious steps to change their lives. Has time to do enjoyable but less productive tasks.
Disadvantage: Performance drops and negative feedback acts as another reminder of their failings. Keeps them from setting productive goals.

Participant
Good citizens in class. Enjoy going to class and take part in as much of the course activities as possible. Typically eager to do as much of the required and optional course requirements as they can.
Advantages: Gets the most out of every classroom experience.
Disadvantage: May do too much or put others' needs ahead of their own.

Dependent
Show little intellectual curiosity and who learn only what is required. View teacher and peers as sources of structure and support and look to authority figures for specific guidelines on what to do.
Advantages: Helps them to manage their anxiety and obtain clear directions.
Disadvantages: Difficult to develop skills for exhibiting autonomy and self-direction as a learner. Does not learn how to deal with uncertainty.

Independent
Students who like to think for themselves and are confident in their learning abilities. Prefer to learn the content that they feel is important and would prefer to work alone on course projects than with other students.
Advantages: Develop skills as self-initiated, self-directed learners.
Disadvantages: May become somewhat deficient in collaborative skills. Might fail to consult with others or to ask for help when it is needed.

The styles of Competitive, Collaborative, Avoidant, Participant, Dependent, and Independent in the Grasha-Riechmann model were briefly introduced in Chapter 3 to illustrate the role of learning style in a conceptual base for teaching [cf., pages 126-128 and Table 3-5]. A brief description of each style is repeated in Table 4-5 for convenience and easy reference. In addition, several advantages and disadvantages of each style that my experience with this scheme identified are presented in this table.

The Characteristics of The Grasha-Riechmann Styles in the Classroom

Like the five teaching styles, the learning styles are best thought of as a blend or profile that resides within every student. Some students possess more of one style than another and it is typically the dominant qualities that are most easily seen in class. As the information in Table 4-5 illustrated, each style also has advantages and disadvantages for students and one should not see any one characteristic as necessarily good or bad. Competition, dependence, and even avoidance has a place in our lives as does collaboration, independence, and participation. The issue is whether the display of a particular style leads to positive or negative outcomes for us. *Thus, a reliance on any one of the six styles or the rigid application of any one of them can produce problems for people.* Ideally, there would a comfortable balance among the six styles. More often, however, certain qualities are more pronounced than others.

Our best stance as teachers is to acknowledge that students are different and ensure that our instructional processes take such diversity into account. To do this well, we need to know more about the learning styles of our students. Several points are worth mentioning based on the outcome of work over the past twenty years using the Grasha-Riechmann Student Learning Style Scales [GRSLSS]. They are:

- *The original formulation of the six dimensions suggested that they were bipolar or represented three pairs of dichotomies* [i.e., Competitive-Collaborative; Avoidant-Participant; Dependent-Independent]. This was a working assumption during the early development of the GRSLSS and *it quickly became apparent that the Competitive-Collaborative and Dependent-Independent dimensions were not the opposites of each other.* If they were, we would expect that correlation coefficients of the scores on each pair of scales would be highly negative. [A correlation coefficient is a statistical test used to determine whether two measures are related]. For the latter two dimensions, the correlations in large samples of students are generally in the range of[$r = -.22$ to $-.33$]. This suggests a relatively weak bipolar relationship between them. In contrast, the Avoidant-Participant dimensions represent a dichotomy. The correlation coefficients for scores on these two scales typically fall in the range of [$r = -.69$ to $-.75$].

• *While learners generally prefer certain styles, this preference can and often does change depending upon how the teacher structures the class.* Thus in lecture oriented courses, it is not unusual to find associations between the dependent and competitive styles occurring. In courses that emphasize group processes and a student centered orientation, the collaborative and participatory styles are much more in evidence. Similar changes have been noted with the other dimensions. Such shifts have been a consistent pattern beginning with the early work with the styles [cf., Grasha, 1972].

It also appears that for such shifts in style to occur, teachers must extensively use teaching methods compatible with certain styles. Occasional use of such classroom processes does not appear to alter the learning styles students report using.

The ability of classroom procedures to affect the learning styles that students display is important. *It suggests that we do not have to view students preferences for how they like to learn as immutable.* This may seem strange to those readers used to viewing personality characteristics as traits that people possess. Traits have the quality of being durable and as remaining unchanged across situations. There is, however, another view of personality. That is to view personality characteristics as "states" that people can display depending upon environmental circumstances. While arguments in the literature tend to treat the personality "trait" and "state" distinction in either/or terms, it does not have to be conceptualized this way. Everyone, for example, has a certain degree of manifest or background anxiety within them. It is always with us to varying degrees. Yet, some situations trigger higher levels of anxiety than others. Some students who are less anxious during class may become more anxious during an exam. The situation changes and so does the degree to which a given personality characteristic is displayed.

As personal dispositions, the six Grasha-Riechmann learning styles behave in the same manner. They can be viewed as personal preferences that occur across different situations. Yet, these preferences typically are not rigid and inflexible. *They can be changed and modified depending upon the classroom procedures used.* After all, no one was born an avoidant, competitive, collaborative, or dependent learner. These are acquired characteristics shaped by a student's past experiences in educational settings. The fact that they can be further reinforced or even modified by the consistent application of educational practices should not be surprising.

This change in personal qualities through situational influences also is compatible with the work of Walter Mischel [1984]. He has studied a variety of personality traits and has shown them to be influenced by situational factors. Thus, Mischel rejects a strict "trait" interpretation of personal dispositions. *A major conclusion from his work is that the more ambiguous the situation, the more personal dispositions guide and direct our actions. On the other hand, the more structured the situation, the less dominant personal dispositions become.* In the latter case, the physical and psychological aspects of situations provide guidelines for how individuals should behave. Thus, a situation might support someone's personal dispositions or force individuals to rely upon less dominant qualities to meet the demands placed upon them. The important point is that personal qualities alone do not dictate someone's actions. They interact with and are influenced by aspects of our environment.

• Because the Grasha-Riechmann learning styles, like other personality characteristics, are susceptible to situational influence, teachers have three options for dealing with them.

1.] *Instructional processes can be designed to accommodate particular styles.* In a classic study using the Grasha-Riechmann styles, John Andrews [1981] reported that students with a strong Collaborative style reported more benefits from participating in a peer-centered chemistry discussion section. In contrast, students with a strong preference for the Competitive style reported benefits from instructor-centered classes and not from participation in a peer-centered section. Andrews noted that students with strong "personal" styles [Collaborative, Participant, Dependent] found review sessions, study questions, and learning from other students most beneficial. Those with more "impersonal" styles [Independent, Avoidant, Competitive] found the text, handouts, and lectures to be most beneficial.

2.] *Instructional processes can be designed to provide creative mismatches in the styles students possess.* Here the intent is to create classroom environments where students have a chance to experience the less dominant qualities of their learning styles. Thus collaborative learning might be used to encourage students with a weaker Collaborative and Participatory style to develop skills working in teams. Highly structured independent study assignments might be employed to encourage the development of independence or to get the more reticent avoidant students to participate.

3.] *A variety of instructional processes can be used so that students are exposed to methods that accommodate as well as provide "creative mismatches" with their preferred learning styles.* While this is a variation on the adage "variety is the spice of life," it also provides a middle ground between the latter two strategies. Students are exposed both to familiar and unfamiliar ways of learning and may find it less tension arousing to adapt to such demands.

One way to match, mismatch, or provide variety is to ask how particular course goals can be achieved by encouraging different learning styles. The idea is to develop options for how you might teach. One way to do this is to focus on three styles in the Grasha-Riechmann model such as the Dependent, Independent, and Collaborative styles. In workshop settings I often ask college teachers to pick 8-10 goals for a course [e.g., content, skill, attitudinal] and to ask three questions for each goal.

For example, in my introductory psychology class I want students to understand the distinction between short-term and long-term memory processes. The three questions and how I answered them are:

> • *How can I teach to achieve this goal in a Dependent manner?*
> *Answer:* I can give a lecture on each perspective on human memory.

> • *How can I teach to achieve this goal in an Independent manner?*
> *Answer:* I can provide students with instructions to visit the library and to look up the a discussion of each memory process. They would have to write a short paper on this assignment.

> • *How can I teach to achieve this goal in a collaborative manner?*
> *Answer:* I can give each member of a pair of students a different assignment. One must become an "expert" on short-term memory while the other learns about long-term memory. They bring the information they acquired to class and teach each other. A write-up of what each discovered is turned in as proof of having completed the assignment.

This process generates options for how our goals can be lined up with particular learning styles. *As a result, the interrelationship of learning and teaching styles surfaces.* To achieve the latter goals, a teacher must be willing to adopt several different styles. To teach to a Dependent learning style involves using an Expert/Formal Authority style described in Table 4-1. The suggestion noted above for teaching to learners with an Independent style asks a teacher to assume more of a Delegator role. Students with a Collaborative style can be accommodated when a teacher adopts a Facilitator style of teaching. The bottom line is that I now have three options for teaching to any one of my course goals. I can consistently focus on one option or vary those I choose to adopt within or across class sessions.

Which of the latter options I choose should in part be based on information about the preferred learning styles of my students. Our research program employs the *General Class Form* and *Specific Class Form* of the *Grasha-Riechmann Student Learning Style Scales [GRSLSS]*. Copies of both instruments appear at the end of this chapter. The *General Class Form* of the *GRSLSS* asks students to rate how various attitudes and behaviors apply to all of their classes. It is used at the beginning of a course to assess the learning styles of students or to evaluate the presence of various styles in a department or college. The *Specific Class Form* becomes an outcome measure to assess the impact of instructional practices on the learning styles of students. It is particularly helpful when someone wishes to encourage particular styles or to inhibit the display of others.

The Distribution of Learning Style in the Classroom

Over the past two decades, several thousand students have taken the *GRSLSS* in a variety of colleges, universities, and classroom settings. To illustrate the distribution of the styles among college students, how the data are used to examine specific student populations, the results two recent studies are depicted in Figures 4-4 and 4-5

Shown in Figure 4-4 are the learning styles of 150 students entering their first year of medical study compared to the norms for a national sample of 1000 students [Montauk & Grasha, 1992]. Participants were tested during the orientation week of medical school and generally after two-three months of completing their undergraduate degrees. The *General Class Form* of the *GRSLSS* was used and students were asked to focus their responses on courses they had taken during their last term as seniors.

Beginning medical students were studied in order to examine the distribution of learning styles in a population of highly selected, well motivated, and academically proficient students. A secondary interest was to determine whether stereotypes of premeds as highly dependent and competitive "grade grubbers" was accurate. An analysis of the distribution of learning styles showed that their perceptions of their learning styles as seniors generally followed the shape of the distribution of style in our national sample. In line with the national norms, the students displayed relatively higher scores on the independent, collaborative, dependent, and participant styles and relatively lower scores on the avoidant and competitive styles.

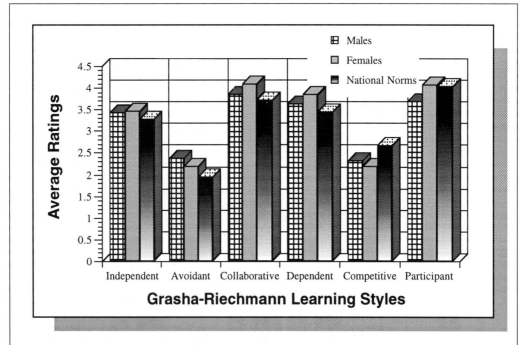

Figure 4-4: Learning styles of a recent sample of 150 male and female students in the entering class of a major medical school compared to the national norms for the GRSLSS.

Statistical analyses revealed that the entering class of medical students saw themselves as somewhat more avoidant, collaborative, and dependent than students in the national sample. The elevation in the avoidant style could be due to senior year burnout. While they were somewhat more dependent than those students in the norm group, the medial students were significantly less competitive. On the latter dimension they did not fit the stereotype of the competitive "grade-grubber." The scores on the GRSLSS also revealed that the women were more collaborative than the men.

Figure 4-5 depicts the distribution of the learning styles of a random sample of 1678 students 84 faculty members at a small Midwestern university. Both the students and the faculty took the general form of the GRSLSS. The faculty responded to the test as they thought they would have as undergraduate students.

Our interest in this study was to determine how much the learning styles of students resembled those of the faculty members who taught them. In Chapter 2, several issues in initiating changes in one's teaching were discussed. Included was the observation that some faculty members teach to a projected image of themselves. If this were true, one might expect that the learning styles of students in an institution would resemble the preferences of the faculty members. *In effect, professors would adopt teaching styles that reproduced the learning styles they were most comfortable with as students.*

The correspondence of the data for faculty and student learning styles shown in Figure 4-5 provided some support for the compatibility in the learning

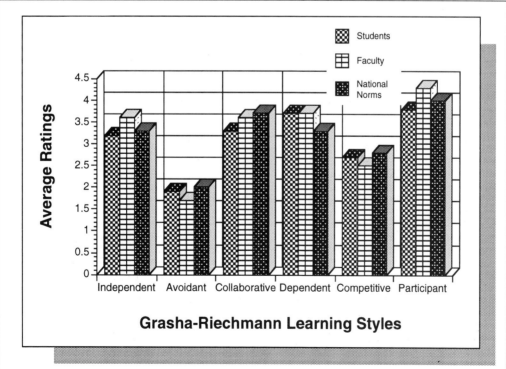

Figure 4-5: Learning styles of a random sample of 1678 students and 84 faculty members at a small Midwesterner university.

styles of teachers and students. The overall shape of the two distributions of style were similar but there were some differences in the magnitude of several styles. The independent, collaborative, and participant learning styles, for example, were higher among the faculty members than they were for the students. Yet, the similarity in the prevalence of the six styles among faculty and students suggests that *the learning styles of faculty play at least a small part in the modes of instruction they choose to employ.*

Relationship of Learning Style to Other Variables

Other data on the Grasha-Riechmann styles has consistently shown the following relationships of learning style to other variables.

- *Academic Major:* There are no significant differences in the profiles of students majoring in a variety of academic disciplines.

- *Graduate and Undergraduate Students:* The learning style profiles are surprisingly similar for undergraduate and graduate students. One of the consistent complaints from graduate students I have heard over the years is the similarity in instructional processes between their graduate and undergraduate courses.

- *Type of Institution:* Two-year college students tend to adopt more dependent, competitive, and participant styles than do students in four-year institutions. This is particularly true of students in two-year technical programs.

- *Sex:* With the exception of women having somewhat higher scores on the collaborative style, consistent sex differences in learning style have not been observed in our undergraduate samples in the liberal arts majors. Among physical education majors, however, males adopt more competitive, avoidant, and independent roles to a higher degree than females. Women were much more participatory and slightly more dependent in their styles [Kraft, 1976]. This latter finding is similar to the higher dependent and participatory scores found in a sample of nursing students [Swartz, 1976]. The data discussed earlier in this chapter from the senior premed majors and presented in Figure 4-4 also reflects several sex differences,

- *Age:* Students over 25 years of age tend to be more independent and participatory in their learning styles. Those under 25 display higher levels of avoidance and competitiveness and lower levels of participation in the classroom.

- *Grades:* Students with an Avoidant style tend to get lower grades while those with a Participant style higher grades. Since these two dimensions of style relate to the degree of involvement in classroom processes, this finding is not surprising. We have found no consistent association between grades and the other learning styles.

• *Learning Style, Instructional Preferences and Teaching Style:* An overview of the general classroom preferences were presented in Chapter 3 in Table 3-5. More recent work with the Teaching Style Inventory and the classroom processes associated with them reveals that particular teaching styles encourage students to adopt various learning styles. A summary of this relationship based on the consistent themes found in classroom observations, interviews with faculty, and content analyses of the learning style demands of various methods appears in Table 4-6.

Table 4-6
The Relationship of Learning
and Teaching Styles

The primary blends of learning styles that are associated with and compatible with each of the four clusters of teaching styles. The teaching styles shown help to reinforce and to develop the learning styes of students within that cluster. Teaching and learning styles are listed in the order of their importance for a particular combination of styles.

Cluster 1

Primary Teaching Styles: Expert/Formal Authority
Primary Learning Styles: Dependent/Participant/Competitive

Cluster 2

Primary Teaching Styles: Personal Model/Expert/Formal Authority
Primary Learning Styles: Participant/Dependent/Collaborative

Cluster 3

Primary Teaching Styles: Facilitator/Personal Model/Expert
Primary Learning Styles: Collaborative/Participant/Independent

Cluster 4

Primary Teaching Styles: Delegator/Facilitator/Expert
Primary Learning Styles: Independent/Collaborative/Participant

The Elements of the Integrated Model:
Using and Modifying Our Teaching Styles

Having identified five teaching styles, important blends of those styles, and specific teaching strategies and learning styles associated with each cluster, I began to investigate the following two questions:

- What do teachers need to do to effectively employ the four clusters of styles?

- If someone wanted to modify their style of teaching, what factors would they have to consider?

In order to answer these questions, I turned to the literature on college teaching but surprisingly did not find it helpful. Once again I was reminded that descriptions of the personal qualities of college faculty were abundant. Very little, however, was written about how to adopt or even modify particular styles. I had encountered a roadblock that I was able to bypass only after reading the work of Paul Hersey and Ken Blanchard [1992]. While they wrote about the factors that influenced leadership styles in business and industry, their observations appeared relevant to the college classroom. Their work suggested that the classroom teacher could be viewed as a leader and/or a manager of classroom resources. Hersey and Blanchard argued that the capability of people, the interest managers had in controlling tasks, and their concerns for building interpersonal relationships were important determinants of leadership style.

I also recognized that any application of the latter concepts to the classroom would be deficient unless information about the learning styles of students were added to the equation. There were three reasons for this:

- *There were obvious connections between the teaching styles that faculty employed and the learning styles that students developed.* The empirical basis for this conclusion was outlined in the last section of this chapter. To focus on one and ignore the other factor would fail to deal with the dual issues of "presence" and "encounter" in the teaching-learning process.

- *A sensitivity to the styles of students would enhance the chances of instructional practices succeeding.* One would not knowingly begin a course using the teaching styles of Clusters 3 or 4, for example, if the students were largely dependent and competitive. While this would create a "creative mismatch" between the instructional methods and preferred learning styles, it would represent too much of a discrepancy. The attempt likely would not be very satisfying to the teacher or the students. Similarly, a focus on Cluster 1 teaching styles and instructional processes would not be advised for students who were largely independent or collaborative in orientation. Thus, the styles of the students would affect how quickly certain teaching styles could be adopted and which ones were likely to be successful.

• *Conflicts between teachers and students often reflect an incompatibility in teaching and learning style.* Teachers with an Expert/Formal Authority style may find tension in the relationship with their more Collaborative and Independent learners. Similarly, Students with Dependent and Competitive styles may find teachers with a Facilitator and Delegator emphasis difficult to get along with. A knowledge of such stylistic differences could help faculty to plan ways of teaching that minimize such tensions [e.g., Using a variety of instructional approaches versus relying on given style] or that allow them to be dealt with constructively [e.g., Using the Facilitator style to have students recommend instructional processes for class].

Such things convinced me that a sensitivity to learning style was a dominant issue in choosing among styles of teaching. The other factors in the Hersey-Blanchard model played important but supporting roles and each is listed in Table 4-7.

Effectively Employing Various Styles of Teaching

What do teachers need to take into account in order to adopt and effectively employ the four clusters of teaching style?

The four factors described in Table 4-7 must be taken into account. Each must be present to a different degree within the four clusters in the model described earlier in Tables 4-2 and 4-3. How each of the four factors in Table 4-7 appear in each cluster is described below. A summary of the degree to which each is needed is depicted in Table 4-8.

• Cluster 1

Here the Expert and Formal Authority blend is dominant. My observations suggested that these styles worked best with students who were less capable with the content and who possessed more Dependent, Participant, and Competitive learning styles. Cluster 1 teaching also was effective when teachers were willing to control classroom tasks. While it might be nice to do, it did not appear necessary in most circumstances for a teacher to devote time to building relationships with students. Nor did they have to be overly concerned with encouraging students to build relationships with each other. One need only observe how this teaching style is played out in large classes to appreciate the latter point.

• Cluster 2

The combination of the Personal Model, Expert, and Formal Authority teaching styles are prominent. Students need to possess more knowledge than they would in a lecture class because they will frequently have to show what they know. The coaching of various skills and problem solving abilities characteristic of such teaching leaves students with few opportunities to hide their ignorance. It also helps if students possess Participant, Dependent, and Collaborative learning

Table 4-7
Factors Associated With Selecting
A Teaching Style

Teacher's Sensitivity to Learning Styles of Students

Sensitivity determined by teacher's:

- Willingness to integrate information about learning
  style into a philosophy of teaching

- Ability to use information about Competitive-Collaborative;
  Avoidant-Participant; and Dependent-Independent styles
  to match teaching and learning styles; to encourage a
  "creative mismatch" between such styles; or to design
  variety into the teaching and learning processes used

Capability of Students to Handle Course Demands

Capability determined by student's:

- Knowledge of course content
- Ability to take initiative/responsibility to obtain information
- Ability to work with other students effectively
- Emotional maturity to handle constructive criticism and feedback
- Motivation to perform well

Need for Teacher to Directly Control Classroom Tasks

Control maintained by how instructor:

- Organizes course and defines what must be learned
- Specifies performance levels for students
- Maintains control over classroom processes
- Closely monitors student progress

Willingness of Teacher to Build/Maintain Relationships

Interest in relationships indicated by how much teacher:

- Encourages two-way communication
- Listens carefully to students
- Assists with resolving conflicts
- Provides positive feedback and encouragement
- Stresses good interpersonal communication skills
- Consciously concerned with building rapport
- Shows students how to work together

styles or are flexible enough to develop them. Such styles work nicely in learning environments where coaching and following the examples of role models are prominent. Teachers must have some interest in influencing how learners use the knowledge and skills that are taught. They also must work to develop relationships. Research shows that effective models are typically people who are liked and well-respected [Bandura, 1986].

• Cluster 3

The blend of Facilitator, Personal Model, and Expert in this cluster provides a good match to students who have more Collaborative, Participant, and Independent styles as learners. In addition to possessing or being willing to acquire appropriate content, students also need to be willing to take initiative and to accept responsibility for meeting the demands of various learning tasks. Teachers must exercise some control over the processes used in order to facilitate learning. But they should be less interested in controlling the specific details of the content students acquire. Some of what students will learn about the material in this mode of teaching cannot be programmed in advance. Similarly, there should be more interest in developing and practicing other skills [e.g., ability to work with others] and a broader range of content related skills [e.g., critical and creative thinking]. Developing and maintaining a professionally friendly and warm relationship with students is helpful.

• Cluster 4

This combination of the Delegator, Facilitator, and Expert modes of teaching works best when students have appropriate levels of knowledge and possess Independent, Collaborative, and Participant learning styles. Their capabilities also must include a willingness to take initiative and to accept more responsibility for their own learning. To use the highly student-centered teaching methods of Cluster 4 or the independent study processes means that teachers must be willing to give up direct control over how learners engage various tasks and their outcomes. An independent study or collaborative project, for example, would be less interesting if the teacher planned every detail and the outcomes were highly predictable. Teachers must be willing to "empower" students and to develop rapport with them. The instructor must be viewed as approachable in order to consult effectively with students and to act as a resource person. Good working relationships among students, however, has to be something they largely work on themselves in the context of their tasks.

Table 4-8
A Summary of the Model's Requirements
for Teaching in Each Cluster

Cluster 1

General Classroom Methods
Traditional teacher-centered presentations and discussion techniques.

Degree of Sensitivity to Learning Styles that Teacher Needs
[Low] As normally practiced, differences among students do not have to be considered. Students can be treated alike although the methods used can be enhanced if allowances for learning styles were made.

Capability of Students to Handle Course Demands
[Low-Moderate] Students typically do not need to display what they know during class periods nor do they have to take much initiative or responsibility for obtaining information. Need the emotional maturity to sit quietly in class and the motivation to periodically ask or to answer questions. Additional knowledge and participation required in advanced courses.

Control of Classroom Tasks
[Moderate-High] Works best with teachers who are willing to control the content presented, the flow of information, and how class time is spent.

Willingness of Teacher to Build/Maintain Relationships
[Low] Classroom tasks do not normally demand that teachers develop relationships with students or help students to do so with classmates.

Cluster 2

General Classroom Methods

Role modeling and coaching/guiding students on developing and applying skills and knowledge.

Degree of Sensitivity to Learning Styles that Teacher Needs
[Moderate-High] Must know how to teach students who possess different styles and be able to encourage Participant, Dependent and Collaborative learning styles

Capability of Students to Handle Course Demands
[Moderate] Needs adequate knowledge and skill , must take initiative and accept responsibility for obtaining what they need to learn. Needs emotional maturity to handle feedback and must have the motivation to improve.

Control of Classroom Tasks
[Moderate] Important for teacher to periodically empower learners to show what they can do.

Willingness of Teacher to Build/Maintain Relationships:
[Moderate-High] Effective models are liked and respected by students.

Table 4-8 [Continued]

Cluster 3

General Classroom Methods
Collaborative learning and other student-centered learning processes consistently emphasized in a course.

Degree of Sensitivity to Learning Styles that Teacher Needs
[Moderate-High] Teacher often consults with students, processes the outcomes of group work, and suggests alternative approaches to handling issues. Collaborative, Participant, and Independent styles work best and teacher must be able to encourage their expression.

Capability of Students to Handle Course Demands
[Moderate] Need adequate levels of knowledge, initiative, and a willingness to accept responsibility for learning. Students must have enough emotional maturity and motivation to work with others on tasks.

Control of Classroom Tasks
[Low-Moderate] Teacher to gets tasks going and then turns the processes of running them over to students. Even when the teacher is more center stage [e.g., when processing a group task or case study], emphasis is on listening to student ideas, facilitating a discussion, and clarifying ideas.

Willingness of Teacher to Build/Maintain Relationships
[Moderate-High] Good relationships facilitate the teacher's role as a consultant and make students more willing to share their ideas.

Cluster 4

General Classroom Methods
Emphasis on independent learning activities for groups and individuals.

Degree of Sensitivity to Learning Style that Teacher Needs
[Moderate-High] Teacher acts as a consultant and resource person for students. Must know how to emphasize and to help students adopt Independent, Collaborative, and Participant styles.

Capability of Students to Handle Course Demands
[High] Students need proficient levels of knowledge and skill, and must take initiative and accept responsibility for their learning. Need emotional maturity to work alone and with others and the motivation to succeed when asked to work independently.

Control of Classroom Tasks
[Low] Important for teacher to move into the background and serve as a consultant and resource person.

Willingness of Teacher to Build/Maintain Relationships
[Low-Moderate] Students must manage their own interpersonal processes in groups. Good communication needed when consulting with students.

Modifying Teaching Styles

If someone wanted to modify their style of teaching, what factors would they have to consider?

In my experience with the model, the issue of modifying or enhancing one's teaching style is often approached with an eye towards adopting particular methods. Thus, some people either want to give up, for example, a teacher-centered approach and move in a student-centered direction. *Effectively, they want to switch from Cluster 1 to some other cluster in the model.* Or, some teachers don't want to totally give up how they teach. *They only want to import methods from other clusters to add variety to what they are already doing.*

Both are legitimate ways to think about modifications in one's style as a teacher. In this model, various blends of teaching styles occur when particular instructional processes are used. Thus, wanting to adopt a particular method [e.g., Role Plays, Learning Pairs, Guided Readings] is equivalent to wanting to adopt a certain blend of the five teaching styles. Whether people state the type of teacher they want to become directly [i.e., by specifying a particular blend of teaching styles] or indirectly [i.e., by focusing on particular methods they wish to adopt], there are three questions that must be answered.

1.] *Am I ready to change and how committed am I to following through on my plans?*

It would be helpful if the issues raised in Chapter 2 on changing teaching style were dealt with first. As noted in that chapter, the compatibility of proposed modifications with your values, beliefs that hinder change, where the pressure to take action is coming from, and where in the cycle of change you reside will affect the outcome of such efforts. Otherwise, one runs the risk of engaging the task in a halfhearted manner or in making superficial variations in style that are soon discarded.

2.] *Are my proposed changes compatible with my philosophy of teaching?*

Two conditions must be met. *One is that you have come to terms with the elements of a conceptual base described in Chapter 3.* The current model of teaching and learning style should not be the only component of your conceptual base. How it fits into your overall philosophy of teaching must be clear to you.

The second condition is that you are willing to creatively experiment with the factors shown in Table 4-7 to produce a desired outcome. This model provides general guidelines for change and not a detailed recipe. A willingness to "tinker" with the model and to customize it to your circumstances is needed.

3.] *Can I objectively assess where my students and I stand on each of the four factors in the model?*

Experience with the model suggests that teachers should possess certain levels of sensitivity to the learning styles of students, the capability of their students to handle course demands, their own needs to directly control classroom tasks, and their willingness to build and maintain relationships with students. Otherwise the teaching strategies in this model are unlikely to be adopted successfully. The minimum conditions needed were summarized in Table 4-8 on pages 182 and 183.

There are several things that can help you to assess where your students and you currently stand on each factor. *Use Self-Reflection Activity 4-2 beginning on the next page to take a preliminary pass at how this can be done in the context of using the model.*

Inevitably, when I present the model in a workshop or seminar someone asks; "Why do I need to think about all of this to teach?" "Why can't I just go out and do it!" Or they ask, "This seems to be a bit complicated. Isn't there an easier way?"

Such questions appear in one form or another in almost any area of personal change with which I am familiar. If I could paraphrase a bit, in my experience the person is really saying, "I want some simple answers." No one likes to think that change is complicated. We may recognize that it probably is, but deep down inside we hope that it isn't. This may be one reason people are attracted to speakers, books, videotapes, and computer programs that promise "instant relief," "quick cures," or "immediate benefits." They just can't wait.

Reflecting, thinking and analyzing, experimenting, discussing, regrouping, and reassessing are critical to any change process. Without them, there is seldom any chance of anything of significance emerging in our lives. Looking for quick solutions or less effortful ways to do it are unlikely to serve our students, our institutions, or ourselves very well. The model in this chapter provides one structure around which the reflection and planning, so critical to success in teaching, can occur. Experience suggests that working through the details is likely to prove beneficial.

Self-Reflection Activity 4-2
Using the Model to Select a Style of Teaching

Introduction

This activity describes one way to use the model to plan changes in your style as a teacher. It is designed to help you personalize the four factors identified in Tables 4-7 and 4-8 that affect our selection of teaching styles and corresponding classroom processes. *Variations on the process described here for using the model are discussed in the Epilogue section of this chapter.*

It is important to assess where you or your students stand on the factors associated with adopting particular styles of teaching for two reasons. *One is that this assessment can help you to alter an approach to teaching one of your courses.* Thus, you can evaluate whether your current style provides a good match to your attitudes and values and the characteristics of your students. Secondly, *the data obtained can help you decide what conditions would have to apply for you to successfully experiment with a style of teaching you currently do not use.* Thus, you will become aware of the minimum conditions that must apply before you attempt any innovations.

Ideally, the information required by the model should be available before teaching a course. We do not, however, live in an ideal world. Normally what can be done is the following:

a.] *The assessment of the student related factors [i.e., Learning style, capability] can take place during the first week of class.* Modifications compatible with this assessment can be brought on line gradually throughout the term. The lessons learned from this experience can then be applied to the next group of students taking the course.

b.] *The assessment can take place during the first week of class and with modifications in instructional practices introduced after the midterm or during the second term of a two quarter or semester class.* Some people also have used an initial class list obtained after the registration period to contact and obtain information on students before the course begins.

c.] *This assessment can be obtained from a sample of students taking courses in a department* to obtain a profile of how students generally fit several factors in the model.

Please complete each part of this activity. Your responses will help you to determine where you and your students currently stand with regard to each of the four factors presented in Table 4-7 and 4-8. This activity also will show you what additional information you need in order to make an informed judgment about changes in your style of teaching.

As you work through this activity, use as a frame of reference a specific course that [a] you want to change how it is taught, [b] you want to evaluate whether your current style is appropriate for that course, or [c] you have never taught the course before and you want to explore options for teaching.

Self-Reflection Activity 4-2 [Continued]

Sensitivity to the Learning Styles of Students

1.] Is information about the Grasha-Riechmann learning styles something that currently is [or could be] a part of your philosophy of teaching?

[Yes]_____ [No] _____ [Maybe]_____

If *no*, what is a major reservation you have about using information about the learning styles of your students.

2.] If you answered *yes* or *maybe* to the question above, how much interest do you have in adopting teaching processes that would encourage appropriate combinations of Competitive-Collaborative; Avoidant-Participant; and Dependent-Independent Styles?

a.] Which one of the following three responses best applies to you?

[Low interest] _____ [Moderate interest] _____ [High Interest] _____

b.] How do you explain your level of interest? What contributes to it?

3.] Do you have information about the Grasha-Riechmann Learning Styles of the students taking the class that you want to evaluate?

[Yes] _____ [No] _____

a.] Does your department or college have information that you might be able to use?

[Yes] _____ [No]_____

b.] If *no*, use the *General Class Form* of the *GRSLSS* at the end of this chapter to obtain student perceptions of their styles as learners. The *Specific Class Form* of the *GRSLSS* can be employed at the end of the term to help you evaluate whether your interventions had measurable effects on the learning styles of students.

c.] If you gave the GRSLSS to a group of students, use the norms for the test shown on the scoring key to create a profile for your students. List the average score on each of the learning styles in the space provided below.

Independent _____ Avoidant _____ Collaborative _____

Dependent _____ Participant _____ Competitive _____

Self-Reflection Activity 4-2 [Continued]

4.] Which learning styles tend to be most preferred among your students? Which are least preferred? Use the magnitude of the scores and the norms for High, Moderate, and Low scores to help you decide. Having done this, which two learning styles are your most preferred and which two are your least preferred?

   a.] *Two Most Preferred Styles:*

   b.] *Two Least Preferred Styles:*

5.] Which one of the following represents a goal you want to pursue in adopting a particular style of teaching?

   ___ I want to match or accommodate the most preferred learning styles of my students?

   ___ I am interested in *stretching students* so they get an opportunity to develop their least preferred styles?

   ___ I would like to add variety to my teaching so that I can periodically accommodate preferred styles as well as *stretch students* to periodically use their   least preferred styles as learners.

   a.] Give a brief reason for your selection of a goal in the space below.

6.] What Cluster [s] in Table 4-3 and 4-7 would you have to teach in order to achieve the goal you selected above?

7.] Are the other factors in the model present to the degree needed for you to teach in the Cluster[s] you want? *Complete the remainder of this analysis to find out.*

Determining The Capability of Students to Handle The Demands of Courses

Knowledge of Course Content

8.] Use of the front side of a 4 x 6 index card during the initial class session to obtain information about other courses students have taken as well as about job and life experiences. These are important indicators of the knowledge they are likely to possess entering a class.

Another indicator is asking them what skills, information, and interests they could contribute to the course. Finding ways to use such things can make a class a much richer experience for all concerned. Some teachers obtain their class lists after the registration period and contact as many students as they can before the course begins to obtain such information.

Self-Reflection Activity 4-2 [Continued]

Ability to Take Initiative / Responsibility

9.] Use the *top half of the back side of the 4 x 6 index card* to ask students to list the projects they have initiated and/or worked on independently in their courses during the last three academic terms.

10.] What conclusions about the overall abilities of the class to take initiative responsibility can you draw from the experiences they report about working independently in other courses? How would you rate the class?

      [Low] _____ [Moderate] _____ [High]_____

   a.] If you have them available, the magnitude of the scores of students [i.e., Low, Moderate, High] on the Independent learning style of the *GRSLSS* also provides useful information about student capability.

   b.] Do both measures of initiative and responsibility agree?

   c.] Are there individual students in class who appear to have a higher level of capability in this area than the other members of the class? If so, could you use them as peer tutors or could they be given additional projects to pursue in order to maintain their interest in the course? Could such students help you teach certain parts of the course where their knowledge could be used with activities and demonstrations?

Ability to Work with Other Students Effectively

11.] On the bottom half of the 4 x 6 card, have students list the collaborative and group projects they have engaged in other courses. Ask them to indicate what they liked most and least about working in groups.

   a.] If you have the Collaborative learning style scale scores of students on the *GRSLSS,* use the magnitude of those scores as an indicator of how well they work with other students. The more collaborative they view themselves, the more likely it is that they can work effectively with other students.

   b.] What is your overall impression of the group's ability to work effectively with other students?

      [Low] _____ [Moderate] _____ [High] _____

Emotional Maturity

12.] Use information from teaching similar students in the past and/or initial experiences with current students on their ability to work on class activities with other students in a positive manner. Such things also can help us see whether students are able to accept constructive criticism and feedback. Also, whether they have had successful experiences working on group projects in the past can be obtained from their responses on the 4 x 6 index cards. Based on this information, rate their emotional maturity.

      [Low] _____ [Moderate] _____ [High] _____

Self-Reflection Activity 4-2 [Continued]

Motivation to Perform Well

13.] Use he overall GPA of students offers clues to students' academic motivation. Asking them for this information anonymously during an initial class session provides a general idea of the motivation level of students. More often than not, however, one needs to see how well a class engages the content and instructional processes to evaluate where students stand on this particular item.

Overall Assessment of Capability

14.] Review the capability factors mentioned thus far and answer the following questions.

a.] Do you have enough information on the capability factors to determine whether students possess or are likely to possess low, moderate, or a high degree of capability?

[Yes] ____ [No] ____

b.] If "yes," what is your overall assessment?

[Low] ____ [Moderate] ____ [High] ____

c.] If "no," what must you do in order to obtain the information?

Need for Teacher to Directly Control Classroom Tasks

15.] Examine the Formal Authority score you obtained on the *Teaching Styles Inventory* in *Self-Reflection Activity 4-1* earlier in this chapter. This teaching style is concerned with correct, acceptable, and standard ways of doing things as well as with providing the structure necessary for students to learn. If you have not already done so, you might want to complete the instrument at this time.

a.] Within what range did your score reside?

[Low] ____ [Moderate] ____ [High] ____

b.] Do you currently use the teaching processes in Clusters 3 and 4 of the integrated model shown in Table 4-3?

[Yes] ____ [No] ____

c.] If you answered *Yes,* are you comfortable using them as well as satisfied with them?

If you scored in the high range on the *Teaching Styles Inventory,* and answered no to either one of the last two questions, then you likely have a relatively high need to control classroom tasks. *Some flexibility on this dimension would be needed to use student-centered instructional processes.*

Self-Reflection Activity 4-2 [Continued]

Willingness of Teacher to Build/Maintain Relationships

16.] Examine your score on the Facilitator teaching style on the *Teaching Styles Inventory*. Teachers using this style must be concerned with their relationships with students. Good rapport also is a necessity in order for them to encourage students as well as to consult with them.

    a.] Within what range did your score on the Facilitator style reside?

        [Low] _____ [Moderate] _____ [High] _____

    b.]] In addition, the frequency with which critical communication skills are used in interactions with students is another indicator of a teacher's willingness to build and maintain relationships. Use the rating scale below to help you decide.

        On a 1-7 rating scale where 1= infrequently and 7= frequently, how often when working with students do you:

            - Encourage two-way communication with students. _____
            - Listen carefully to what students have to say. _____
            - Help students resolve conflicts on course projects. _____
            - Provide positive feedback and encouragement. _____
            - Use good interpersonal communication skills. _____
            - Encourage students to use good communication skills. _____
            - Work hard to build rapport with students. _____
            - Ask students for feedback on how well I work with them. _____
            - Meet with students to discuss their concerns about the class and course related activities. _____
            - Help students identify the strengths and weaknesses of their interactions on course activities. _____
            - Suggest ways students can work more effectively together. _____
            - Encourage students to give each other constructive criticism as well as positive feedback when working together.

    c.] *Sum your ratings to each of the items above:* Total _____

        [Low Score: 12-36] [Moderate Score 37-65] [High Score 66+]

17.] Using the information above, how would you assess your current willingness to build and maintain relationships with students?

        [Low] _____ [Moderate] _____ [High] _____

18.] While your current actions may not suggest you devote time to this issue, perhaps you want to in the future. If so, what areas or communication and relationship building do you need to work on?

Self-Reflection Activity 4-2 [Continued]

Putting It All Together

19.] Review your analysis of each of the four factors associated with selecting a teaching style. Use your responses to summarize your overall assessment of the degree to which each factor is present. Place your response in the space provided below.

- Sensitivity to Learning Styles of Students

   [Low] _____   [Moderate] _____   [High] _____

- Overall Capability of Students to Handle Course Demands: Knowledge/Initiative/Work with Others/Maturity/Motivation

   [Low] _____   [Moderate] _____   [High] _____

- Need for Teacher to Directly Control Classroom Tasks

   [Low] _____   [Moderate] _____   [High] _____

- Willingness of Teacher to Build/Maintain Relationships

   [Low] _____   [Moderate] _____   [High] _____

20.] Are Each of the factors above at sufficient levels to teach in the Cluster [s] you had identified earlier in this activity? Review Table 4-8 to see the minimum requirements.

   [Yes] _____   [No] _____

If yes, you could proceed with the changes you have considered making. If no, think about what you must do to change. Sometimes, this means acquiring information that you might need in order to proceed [e.g., more details on learning styles; information on specific teaching strategies, working on group dynamics skills [cf., the discussion in Chapter 7].

On the other hand, you might want to examine issues of student capability, teacher control over task, and willingness to build relationships in more detail. For example, such factors can be seen as qualities that are static. That is, people either have sufficient levels of them or they do not. Or, they can be viewed as dynamic and changeable. For example, you might need to take time to discuss the pros and cons of how people work together on classroom tasks and make suggestions to help build relationships. Or, you might need to help students develop various capabilities as part of your course design. Or, perhaps you must recognize that control over tasks can occur in a variety of ways. The issue is not always *giving up control* but *redirecting it. The Epilogue to this chapter discusses the latter issues in more detail.*

Finally, you may want to explore other ways to engage the integrated model. As noted on page 186, the processes described in this activity suggest ways to employ the model by examining all of its elements. Other strategies to engage the model can be found in the Epilogue to this chapter.

Epilogue

Themes and Variations

The integrated model of teaching and learning style was developed to show how the stylistic qualities of teachers and students could be used to enhance the nature and quality of the classroom experience. A thematic analysis of how people teach, information in the research literature, and interviews with faculty revealed five styles. They were the Expert, Formal Authority, Personal Model, Facilitator, and Delegator. All teachers possess each of he five teaching styles to varying degrees. In effect, each style is like a different color on an artist's palette that can be combined to produce different blends of teaching styles.

These teaching styles are only one half of the equation for understanding the dynamics of the classroom. A complete picture must account for the instructor's *presence* as well as the nature and quality of the *encounter* with students. An important variable that influences such interactions are the learning styles of students. The integrated model uses the Grasha-Riechmann learning styles of Competitive-Collaborative; Avoidant-Participant; and Dependent-Independent. Students possess different blends of these styles and certain combinations are compatible with particular clusters of teaching style. Also, each of the four clusters of teaching style tend to reinforce and develop various combinations of learning styles as noted below.

The four primary blends of teaching styles, the general classroom processes associated with each, and the learning styles they reinforce and develop are shown below. Each blend of teaching and learning style is listed in the order of its importance for that cluster.

- Expert/Formal Authority:
    Traditional teacher-centered classroom processes
    Encourages Dependent, Participant, Competitive styles.

- Personal Model/Expert/Formal Authority:
    Personal modeling; Guiding and coaching
    Encourages Participant, Dependent, Collaborative styles.

- Facilitator/Personal Model/Expert:
    Collaborative and other student-centered
      learning processes
    Encourages Collaborative, Participant, Independent styles.

- Delegator/Facilitator/Expert:
    Independent group and individual learning activities.
    Encourages Independent, Collaborative, Participant styles.

The integrated model assumes that four factors play a role in whether the four blends of teaching styles can be employed successfully. They include:

- Sensitivity of teachers to the learning styles of students.
- Capability of students to handle course demands.
- Degree to which teachers want to control classroom tasks.
- Willingness of teachers to build and maintain relationships with and among students.

The degree to which each factor must be present varies among the four clusters of teaching styles. For example, to use the traditional teaching methods associated with the Expert/Formal authority blend, for example, a high degree of sensitivity to the styles of students is generally not needed. It also works best with students who are not highly capable and with teachers who want to control classroom tasks. Building and maintaining relationships with students, however, would be nice, but it is not absolutely needed to use this style.

On the other hand, just the opposite conditions would be needed to use the Delegator/Facilitator/Expert blend. Here, a sensitivity to style helps teachers to personalize their interventions with students. In addition, students need a high degree of capability to function independently, the teacher needs to control less and empower students to work independently, and instructors must maintain at least a minimal degree of interest in building and maintaining relationships. In this cluster students spend time working in groups on their own or individually. They must take more responsibility for maintaining the relationships they have with peers and with the instructor.

The chances of teaching successfully with a particular blend of styles increases when the minimal levels of each of the four factors described above are present [cf., Table 4-8]. Similarly, to modify or enhance one's style of teaching by choosing instructional processes that encourage particular blends of teaching styles also requires minimal levels of each factor.

Options for Engaging the Integrated Model

Self-Reflection Activity 4-2 introduced one way to use the model. The activity suggested ways to assess and employ all of the elements in the model. Such suggestions relied upon having access to a relatively large amount of information about students and the teacher. While ways to obtain it were presented, it may not always be feasible in every situation to gather such data. Consequently, several alternate ways to engage the model are described below. To use them, do the following:

- List the major instructional goals you want to achieve.
- Ask the question, *How can I teach in different ways to achieve my goals?* Six ways to answer this question are described here.

  a.] *Focus on the Independent, Dependent, and Collaborative learning styles.* Think of how to teach each content goal using each of the learning styles. *For example,* for each goal, develop ways to use an independent study activity [e.g., completing a study guide; writing a position paper], a teacher-centered activity [e.g., listening to a lecture on the content; using a computer program to teach content points], or a group project [e.g., a collaborative learning activity such as a jigsaw group]. Within and/or across different class sessions, choose among the options identified above.

b.] *Select one of the four blends of learning styles in the model that interests you.* This will place you in one of the four clusters in the model. Use the teaching methods in that cluster as a basis for trying to achieve your goals [cf., Tables 4-6 and 4-3] Those methods will encourage students to employ the blends of learning styles that interest you. Depending upon the preferences of your students, this strategy may match and/or provide a "creative mismatch" with the styles of your students.

c.] *Select more than one blend of learning styles that appear across the four clusters of styles in the model.* Use the teaching methods from that cluster to help you achieve your instructional goals.

d.] *Use the Grasha-Riechmann Learning Style Scales [General Form] to identify the most and least preferred styles of your students.* Consider matching instructional processes to the most preferred styles, creating a "creative mismatch" by focusing on developing the least preferred styles of students, or varying instructional processes so that within and/or across class sessions students with different styles experience teaching processes they prefer.

e.] *Use the Teaching Styles Inventory to obtain a profile of your most and least preferred teaching styles.* Use that information to enter each of the four clusters in the model to find additional ways to achieve your content goals. Focus on how you can match your preferred teaching styles and/or that allow you to "stretch" your current styles and gradually employ teaching processes you normally have not used.

f.] *Select teaching strategies in each of the four clusters of the model that interest you.* Match the teaching strategies to each of your content goals. Avoid the temptation to see anyone teaching process as a *master key* that will allow you to achieve all of your goals. Typically a variety of instructional processes must be employed to meet the content goals we have. Unfortunately, some people fail to recognize this latter point and overuse a single set of teaching methods.

There are several points about the six strategies mentioned above that must be made. *One is that each allows a marriage among content goals, teaching and learning styles, and classroom methods to occur.* These elements are interrelated regardless of how you choose to enter the four clusters in the model [cf. Tables 4-6 and 4-3]. Making a choice about any one of them is equivalent to choosing the others. *Instructional goals, teaching processes, as well as teaching and learning styles cannot be divorced from each other.*

New Perspectives on Teacher Control, Student Capability, and Relationship Building

I have found that of the four factors described in Table 4-7, the latter two are the most difficult for many people. They are important elements in the resistance to enhancing and modifying one's instruction. This is particularly true of making the large leaps from the teacher-centered methods of Clusters 1 and 2 to the student-centered processes described in Clusters 3 and 4. [cf., Table 4-3]. One of the attractions of the Expert/Formal Authority style, for example, is the control it provides over a classroom environment. It is not easy to take a less central role and to empower students. I have had colleagues tell me, "I could never show a videotape, use vignettes from a CD-ROM, or hold a small group discussion in my classes. Such things would take valuable time away from what I have to offer." Or, as another said, "I would consider it an insult for someone to ask me to teach that independent study section of introductory psychology. It assumes I have nothing to give the students and they can learn everything they need on their own!"

I also knew that some faculty members were uncomfortable with nontraditional teaching methods for other reasons. A frequent comment from workshop participants was, "I tried group projects once and they did not work. Very few read the assignment beforehand and all the students did was socialize." Or, "I put people in small groups but only a few worked on the task." "I'm not sure they even know how to work as part of a team." In effect, they either did not trust the capability of students to benefit from alternate approaches or they perceived [in some cases correctly] that the students were deficient in the skills needed. *The problem was that the propensity of students to change or to acquire the needed skills were discounted. Furthermore, some teachers seemingly were at a loss for how to handle the problem or unwilling to devote time and energy to developing such skills.* As one person told me, "I have no choice but to continue teaching like I always have." Such problems lead to a certain amount of inevitable frustration with Cluster 3 and 4 teaching processes.

Developing Additional Perspectives on Control

Concerns about losing control over what happens in class, being taken advantage of by students, or having my role diminished are understandable. What most teachers do not recognize is that *the underlying elements of control and authority found in the popular lecture-discussion method are identical to those required by all classroom procedures.*

The elements of control in the lecture-discussion method are:

• The authority of the teacher is respected.
• Time on task is strictly managed.
• Outcomes of the time on task are specified.
• Teachers and students have clear roles.
• Participants are held accountable for acquiring the material.

The elements of control described above can be transferred to other situations. In such cases, control is not *given up*. Rather, it is *redirected* toward a broader set of goals and objectives such as developing critical thinking, teamwork, or the capacity to work independently. Consider how this can be done in a Cluster 3 teaching method such as small group discussions.

- *Permission is not needed.* Students normally will respect the teacher's authority to have them break into small groups. The role of teacher contains a number of sources of power and authority. They include expertise, authority of the title, the ability to reward and punish students, and respect for the teacher [Raven, 1992]. All of these are strong inducements for students to comply with a teacher's directives. What students need are clear directions about the task, the outcomes to be achieved, and how they are expected to behave.

- *Tell students what to expect from their time together.* Tell them the purpose behind the small group format and what you hope to accomplish. You might want them to define concepts, integrate issues from the text, apply principles and concepts, or simply to have someone else listen to their ideas.

- *The time on task, however, must be strictly managed.* Announce an agenda for the session and indicate how much time will be spent discussing issues.

- *Assign participants clear roles to play.* People interact better in any setting when their roles are clearly defined. In a small group discussion, several roles are possible. They include; a recorder of the groups' deliberations, a time keeper, a discussion monitor who checks to insure that everyone gets a chance to speak, or if appropriate, a devil's advocate.

- *Hold participants accountable for acquiring the information.* The outcomes of the small group discussions should be shared with the whole class. The instructor may comment or ask individual members of the class to clarify certain points. The remarks of the teacher and participants can be used to develop exam questions about the issues discussed. Or, students might write a short reaction paper or list 2-3 new ideas the small group discussion raised.

Developing Additional Perspectives on Student Capability and Relationship Building

Capability can be perceived as static-- a quality that students may or may not possess. The disadvantage of this attitude is that one must wait for a group of "mature students" to show up before trying alternative teaching strategies. On the other hand, capability can be viewed as dynamic and as a quality teachers can develop over time. Thus, variations in teaching styles beyond the Expert/Formal Authority modes can be used to foster progressive improvements in students. By adopting more facilitative and delegative modes of teaching, students can learn to take initiative, assume responsibility, develop their knowledge and skills, and modify their styles as learners.

John Hersey and his colleagues conducted a study to illustrate how such changes occur [Hersey, Blanchard, and Caracushansky, 1992]. Students were randomly assigned to two sections of the same business course One group was taught using teacher-centered methods for two semesters. Thus, the Expert/Formal Authority blend of teaching styles prevailed. In the second group, however, attempts were made to gradually increase the capability level of students in the areas of taking initiative and responsibility for their learning. The second group started out with the lecture-discussion method but was gradually introduced to more student-centered teaching approaches. Thus, methods compatible with the Facilitative and Delegative styles were progressively employed. The results were remarkable. Compared to those students experiencing a steady diet of the lecture-discussion method, those exposed to more student-centered teaching processes showed significant gains in content achievement, were more satisfied with the course, they had higher levels of enthusiasm and morale, and were less tardy and absent from class

In a similar manner, students may not possess the skills needed to work together. Some remain silent or do not contribute to the group. A few may try to dominate discussions or create conflicts with other group members. The result is that the group fails to function well and the teacher becomes frustrated. The underlying problem is a lack of skill in how to work together. Thus, the teaching methods in Clusters 3 and 4 of Table 4-3 sometimes demand that faculty spend time teaching students how to work together.

One of the best ways to accomplish the latter goal is to require that groups process their interactions. Periodically, at the end of a collaborative activity, 10-15 minutes might be set aside and participants are asked to respond briefly in writing to the following three questions:

- What helped your group's ability to work well today?
- What hindered your group's ability to work well today?
- What is something you could have said or done to have improved the group's ability to work together?

In this example, students are instructed to focus on specific behaviors and not to blame others or to put classmates down when responding to these questions. The written comments are then shared and discussed in the groups. The instructor unobtrusively listens in on the conversations and afterwards collects the written responses in order to identify the themes within them.

Issues the groups identified are then periodically summarized and presented in future class sessions. The teacher may comment on ways to overcome some of the issues identified and/or ask students to suggest things they would do or perhaps to describe actions already taken to manage such concerns.

Such discussions should focus on the concept that "the group as a human system has a problem." This perspective helps students focus on how everyone contributes to effective and ineffective group performance. A point I like to make is that "everything you say or do and everything you fail to say and do contributes to how well a group works together." I also suggest that while it is sometimes easier to look outward to find someone to blame, it is best that we first look into a mirror.

The major point is that students don't learn to work well in groups unless they are given time and encouraged to process in a supportive manner how they work together. This takes up class time that some teachers unfortunately are unwilling to spend. Yet, it is time devoted to examining the pros and cons of working together that ultimately helps students learn how to interact and work with others.

Of course, it is often the individuals who fail to spend time on developing effective working relationships that complain the most about students' lack of ability to participate in group work. Barbara Walvoord [1990] in her book *Thinking and Writing in College* noted that one of the most enduring lessons she learned when working with faculty on teaching issues is that they *get what they ask for.* The problem she finds is that faculty members make too many assumptions about what students should be capable of doing. In some cases, such assumptions are based more on wishful thinking than a clear assessment of student capability. Or, teachers are unwilling to take the time to do things that would obviously enhance the level of performance. In either case, the result is the same. A less than satisfactory outcome occurs.

Satisfaction with Styles of Teaching: Teacher and Student Perspectives May Differ

In our research program, teachers were asked to rate how satisfied they were with the courses they taught. A 1-7 point rating scale was employed where a 1= *not very satisfied* and a 7 = *very satisfied.* The best predictors of teacher ratings were then determined. This analysis showed that faculty members who used a Facilitative and Personal Model teaching style were more satisfied with their courses. Teacher satisfaction also was related to the academic rank of participants. Full professors were more satisfied with their classes than were instructors and assistant professors.

Such findings, however, did not correspond to the results of a recent study by Julie Sand [1994]. She asked students to evaluate the teaching styles of their instructors. Student perceptions of teaching styles were then related to several aspects of the classroom environment. Teachers with a Facilitator style were rated highly for contributing to students' learning. On a less positive note, the use of the Facilitator style also was rated by students as a major contributor to instructor-student conflict, frustration with teaching methods, and the failure of a course to meet student needs. Her findings indicated that students and faculty differ on what contributes to satisfaction within the classroom. Using a facilitative or student-centered form of instruction may contribute to tension and anxiety among students comfortable with more traditional methods.

My experience suggest that until such processes become the norm in higher education, some precautions would seem appropriate. Unless students and teachers clearly possess the knowledge, skills, and capabilities to immediately use such methods, it often helps to do the following:

- *Introduce new strategies gradually* into a course.

- *Follow the philosophy that less is more.* Concentrate on doing a couple of new things well rather than trying to integrate too many new approaches into a course all at once.

- *Provide a clear rationale* for why you want to use particular teaching strategies. Thus knowing how various instructional processes fit into your philosophy of teaching and learning gives you a clear set of criteria to justify their use.

- *Give students explicit instructions* about what is required of them.

- *Monitor the reactions of class members* to your instructional processes and initiate timely interventions to reduce the impact of any negative reactions. For example, meeting with students to discuss issues or modifying aspects of the course that are producing problems is often helpful.

- *Solicit ideas from students* for how particular approaches can be used more effectively.

- *Use the information gathered about how well new strategies are working out* as an "opportunity to learn how to improve your ability to use them better" and not as an "excuse to give up." Trying new teaching methods is not unlike trying out any new skill for the first time. Mistakes occur, there are momentary setbacks, and fine tuning is often needed.

- *Get a colleague to join you in trying something new or to agree to act as a consultant* as you undertake an innovation. Arrange to meet with him or her on a regular basis to discuss your plans and your execution of them.

Grasha-Riechmann
Student Learning Style Scales
General Class Form

The following questionnaire has been designed to help you clarify your attitudes and feelings toward the courses you have taken thus far in college. There are no right or wrong answers to each question. However, as you answer each question, form your answers with regard to your general attitudes and feelings towards all of your courses.

Respond to the items listed below by using the following rating scale. Follow the instructions of the person administering this questionnaire and put your answers either on a separate sheet of paper or on a computer scored answer sheet that is provided.

Use a rating of 1 if you *strongly disagree* with the statement.
Use a rating of 2 if you *moderately disagree* with the statement.
Use a rating of 3 if you are *undecided.*
Use a rating of 4 if you *moderately agree* with the statement.
Use a rating of 5 if you *strongly agree* with the statement.

01. I prefer to work by myself on assignments in my courses.
02. I often daydream during class.
03. Working with other students on class activities is something I enjoy doing.
04. I like it whenever teachers clearly state what is required and expected.
05. To do well, it is necessary to compete with other students for the teacher's attention.
06. I do whatever is asked of me to learn the content in my classes.
07. My ideas about the content often are as good as those in the textbook.
08. Classroom activities are usually boring.
09. I enjoy discussing my ideas about course content with other students.
10. I rely on my teachers to tell me what is important for me to learn.
11. It is necessary to compete with other students to get a good grade.
12. Class sessions typically are worth attending.
13. I study what is important to me and not always what the instructor says is important.
14. I very seldom am excited about material covered in a course.
15. I enjoy hearing what other students think about issues raised in class.
16. I only do what I am absolutely required to do in my courses.
17. In class, I must compete with other students to get my ideas across.
18. I get more out of going to class than staying at home.
19. I learn a lot of the content in my classes on my own.
20. I don't want to attend most of my classes.
21. Students should be encouraged to share more of their ideas with each other.
22. I complete assignments exactly the way my teachers tell me to do them.
23. Students have to be aggressive to do well in courses.
24. It is my responsibility to get as much as I can out of a course.
25. I feel very confident about my ability to learn on my own.
26. Paying attention during class sessions is difficult for me to do.

• *Please continue questionnaire on the next page.*

Grasha-Riechmann
Student Learning Style Scales
General Class Form

Rating Scale

Use a rating of 1 if you *strongly disagree* with the statement
Use a rating of 2 if you *moderately disagree* with the statement.
Use a rating of 3 if you are *undecided*.
Use a rating of 4 if you *moderately agree* with the statement.
Use a rating of 5 if you *strongly agree* with the statement.

27. I like to study for tests with other students.
28. I do not like making choices about what to study or how to do assignments.
29. I like to solve problems or answer questions before anybody else can.
30. Classroom activities are interesting.
31. I like to develop my own ideas about course content.
32. I have given up trying to learn anything from going to class.
33. Class sessions make me feel like part of a team where people help each other learn.
34. Students should be more closely supervised by teachers on course projects.
35. To get ahead in class, it is necessary to step on the toes of other students.
36. I try to participate as much as I can in all aspects of a course.
37. I have my own ideas about how classes should be run.
38. I study just hard enough to get by.
39. An important part of taking courses is learning to get along with other people.
40. My notes contain almost everything the teacher said in class.
41. Being one of the best students in my classes is very important to me.
42. I do all course assignments well whether or not I think they are interesting.
43. If I like a topic, I try to find out more about it on my own.
44. I typically cram for exams.
45. Learning the material was a cooperative effort between students and teachers.
46. I prefer class sessions that are highly organized.
47. To stand out in my classes, I complete assignments better than other students.
48. I typically complete course assignments before their deadlines.
49. I like classes where I can work at my own pace.
50. I would prefer that teachers ignore me in class.
51. I am willing to help other students out when they do not understand something.
52. Students should be told exactly what material is to be covered on exams.
53. I like to know how well other students are doing on exams and course assignments.
54. I complete required assignments as well as those that are optional.
55. When I don't understand something, I first try to figure it out for myself.
56. During class sessions, I tend to socialize with people sitting next to me.
57. I enjoy participating in small group activities during class.
58. I like it when teachers are well organized for a session.
59. I want my teachers to give me more recognition for the good work I do.
60. In my classes, I often sit toward the front of the room.

===

Grasha-Riechmann
Student Learning Style Scales
Scoring Key General and Specific Class Forms

1.] *Copy your responses from the sheet of paper with your ratings on it to the space provided below for each item.*

Learning Style Test Items

01. ___	02. ___	03. ___	04. ___	05. ___	06. ___
07. ___	08. ___	09. ___	10. ___	11. ___	12. ___
13. ___	14. ___	15. ___	16. ___	17. ___	18. ___
19. ___	20. ___	21. ___	22. ___	23. ___	24. ___
25. ___	26. ___	27. ___	28. ___	29. ___	30. ___
31. ___	32. ___	33. ___	34. ___	35. ___	36. ___
37. ___	38. ___	39. ___	40. ___	41. ___	42. ___
43. ___	44. ___	45. ___	46. ___	47. ___	48. ___
49. ___	50. ___	51. ___	52. ___	53. ___	54. ___
55. ___	56. ___	57. ___	58. ___	59. ___	60. ___

2.] *Sum your ratings for each column and place them in the spaces below.*

_____   _____   _____   _____   _____   _____

3.] *Divide your total score for each column by 10 and place your answer in the spaces below.*

_____   _____   _____   _____   _____   _____

Independent   Avoidant   Collaborative   Dependent   Competitive   Participant

4.] *The names of each learning style associated with each column are shown above.*

5.] *Check whether your score represents a relatively Low, Moderate, or High score based on the norms for each learning style scale shown below.*

	Low	Moderate	High
Independent	[1.0-2.7]	[2.8-3.8]	[3.9-5.0]
Avoidant	[1.0-1.8]	[1.9-3.1]	[3.2-5.0]
Collaborative	[1.0-2.7]	[2.8-3.4]	[3.5-5.0]
Dependent	[1.0-2.9]	[3.0-4.0]	[4.1-5.0]
Competitive	[1.0-1.7]	[1.8-2.8]	[2.9-5.0]
Participant	[1.0-3.0]	[3.1-4.1]	[4.2-5.0]

Grasha-Riechmann
Student Learning Style Scales
Specific Class Form

The following questionnaire has been designed to help you clarify your attitudes and feelings toward this class. There are no right or wrong answers to each question. However, as you answer each question, form your answers with regard to your attitudes and feelings toward this particular class.

Respond to the items listed below by using the following rating scale. Follow the instructions of the person administering this questionnaire and put your answers either on a separate sheet of paper or on a computer scored answer sheet that is provided.

> Use a rating of 1 if you *strongly disagree* with the statement.
> Use a rating of 2 if you *moderately disagree* with the statement.
> Use a rating of 3 if you are *undecided*.
> Use a rating of 4 if you *moderately agree* with the statement.
> Use a rating of 5 if you *strongly agree* with the statement.

01. I preferred to work by myself on assignments in class.
02. I often daydreamed during class sessions.
03. Working with other students on class activities was something I enjoyed doing.
04. I liked it whenever the teacher clearly stated what was required and expected.
05. To do well, it was necessary to compete with other students for the teacher's attention.
06. I did whatever was asked of me to learn the content in this class.
07. My ideas about the content often were as good as those in the textbook.
08. Classroom activities usually were boring.
09. I enjoyed discussing my ideas about course content with other students.
10. I relied on my teacher to tell me what was important for me to learn.
11. It was necessary to compete with other students to get a good grade.
12. Class sessions typically were worth attending..
13. I studied what was important to me and not always what the teacher said was important.
14. I very seldom was excited about the material covered in class.
15. I enjoyed hearing what other students thought about issues raised in class.
16. I only did what I was absolutely required to do in this course.
17. In class, I had to compete with other students to get my ideas across.
18. I got more out of going to class than staying at home.
19. I learned a lot of the content on my own in this course.
20. I didn't want to attend most of the class sessions.
21. Students should have been encouraged to share more of their ideas with each other.
22. I completed assignments exactly the way my instructor told me to do them.
23. Students had to be aggressive to do well in this course.
24. It was my responsibility to get as much as I could out of this course.
25. I felt very confident about my ability to learn on my own.
26. Paying attention during class sessions was difficult for me to do.

• Please continue questionnaire on the next page.

Grasha-Riechmann
Student Learning Style Scales
Specific Class Form

Page 2

Rating Scale

Use a rating of 1 if you *strongly disagree* with the statement
Use a rating of 2 if you *moderately disagree* with the statement.
Use a rating of 3 if you are *undecided.*
Use a rating of 4 if you *moderately agree* with the statement.
Use a rating of 5 if you *strongly agree* with the statement.

27. I studied for tests with other students.
28. I did not like making choices about what to study or how to do assignments.
29. I tried to solve problems or answer questions before anybody else in class could.
30. Classroom activities were interesting.
31. I tried to develop my own ideas about course content.
32. I gave up trying to learn anything from going to class.
33. This class made me feel like part of a team where people helped each other learn.
34. Students needed to be more closely supervised on course projects.
35. To get ahead in this class, it was necessary to step on the toes of other students.
36. I tried to participate as much as I could in all aspects of the course.
37. I had my own ideas about how this class should be run.
38. I studied just hard enough to get by.
39. An important part of taking this course was learning to get along with other people.
40. My notes contained almost everything the teacher said in class.
41. Being one of the best students in class was very important to me.
42. I did all course assignments well whether or not I thought they were interesting.
43. If I liked a topic, I tried to find out more about it on my own.
44. I typically crammed for exams.
45. Learning the material was a cooperative effort between students and the teacher.
46. I wanted class sessions to be highly organized.
47. To stand out in this course, I completed assignments better than other students.
48. I typically completed course assignments before their deadline.
49. I was able to work at my own pace in this class.
50. I wanted the teacher to ignore me in class.
51. I was willing to help other students out when they did not understand something.
52. Students should have been told exactly what material was to be covered on exams.
53. I wanted to know how well other students were doing on exams and assignments.
54. I completed required assignments as well as those that were optional.
55. When I didn't understand something, I first tried to figure it out for myself.
56. During class, I tended to socialize with people sitting next to me.
57. I enjoyed participating in small group activities during class.
58. I liked it when the teacher was well organized for a session.
59. I wanted the teacher to give me more recognition for the good work I was doing.
60. In this class, I often sat toward the front of the room.

5. Teaching and Learning Styles in the Management of Five Basic Instructional Concerns

> The path to improved performance in teaching does not lie in excusing one's shortcomings as beyond influence.
>
> - Milton Hildebrand

Five Fundamental Instructional Concerns

The integrated model described in Chapter 4 deals with more than understanding the interdependency among the elements of teaching styles, learning styles, and instructional processes. The connections among these elements help us to achieve several objectives. *One is the need to integrate formal principles of teaching and learning into our conceptual base for teaching.* Thus, our selection of instructional processes become grounded in intellectual concerns rather than past habits, an attraction to popular methods, or assumptions about how colleagues and students expect us to teach. *The model also helps us to achieve our goals as teachers by specifying different ways to achieve them.* If I want students to learn terminology, acquire skills, apply principles, evaluate issues, or to do anything else, the model suggests a variety of ways to accomplish such goals.

Finally, the model is a device for managing several basic issues connected with the academic performance of students in the classroom. Regardless of how they choose to teach, college faculty implicitly or explicitly must deal with five basic instructional concerns. Each is listed below in the form of a critical question that must be addressed.

- How can I help students acquire and retain information?

- What can I do to enhance the ability of students to concentrate during class?

- How can I encourage students to think critically?

- What will help me to motivate my students?

- How can I help them to become self-directed learners?

Let us examine each question and the implications it has for teaching within the integrated model. This will link the teaching and learning style elements of the model to issues faculty must address in helping students to learn.

1.] How can I help students acquire and retain information?

For the past couple of years, I have been involved in a project examining the efficacy of various instructional processes on student outcomes. Figure 5-1 shows the combined results of several studies on the retention of facts and concepts. Students retook their final exam after varying amounts of time. Their average test scores are shown in two ways. One is the percentage of correct responses on the final exam after different periods of time [i.e., Number correct on exam/Total number of items on exam]. *This figure compares students to the standard of how many items they could have gotten correct.*

The second method for assessing retention expresses what is retained as a percentage of how much was originally learned. Thus, if students on average scored 73% on the final exam, this becomes the baseline against which the amount forgotten is calculated [i.e., Number correct on exam/ Number correct on final exam]. *This method allows us to gauge how much of the information they initially knew was subsequently forgotten.* It shows the loss of whatever information they initially acquired over time.

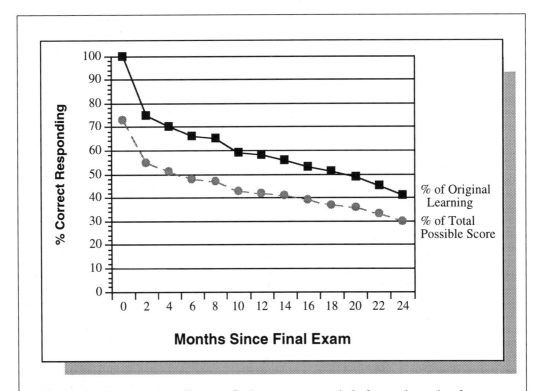

Figure 5-1: Correct responding on a final exam over a period of several months after completing the course. The data shown is a composite based upon several studies that have examined this issue.

One way to interpret the information in Figure 5-1 is that the retention of course content is not particularly impressive. Both methods of calculating test scores show that four months after the course, students have forgotten 30%-50% of the information. A year later, they have forgotten 40%-60% of the information on the final exam. Along similar lines, other research shows that immediately after a class session, students' scores on a multiple choice test average 60% and they can recall on short answer questions about 50% of the content [Scerbo, Dember, Warm, and Grasha, 1992].

It would be tempting to say, "Ain't it awful!" Yet, things are not as bleak as they may initially seem. *Forgetting is a problem but it also is a natural process that is sometimes adaptive.* After all, it is impossible to keep at our fingertips everything learned in classes or anywhere else. Our information processing system would be overwhelmed trying to do so. Thus facts, figures, and concepts not immediately needed are put aside to attend to more pressing demands.

Implications for Teaching

Forgetting often represents two things. One is a failure to acquire the information. The second is a failure to retrieve information. Research suggests that teachers can help students to acquire and retrieve information better by using active learning processes. Teachers encourage active learning when they do take the actions in the checklist in Self-Reflection Activity 5-1. [cf., Bonwell and Eison, 1991; Davis, 1993; Grasha, 1995a; 1995b].

The suggestions for improving retention contained in the activity can be woven into almost any teaching situation. It might not be possible to use all of them during one class session. Across class sessions, however, each of them eventually could be integrated into a course. Teaching methods associated with the four clusters in the integrated model [cf., Table 4-3] provide a variety of teaching formats into which the items in the checklist can be embedded. The important point is that if we want students to retrieve what they have learned, there are clearly things that will help.

Furthermore, what we have forgotten is not the critical issue. *What is more important is to find the information we need in the future and/or to relearn it.* Relearning is generally easier after original learning and there is a savings in the time needed to do it, that is, provided the information needed was available at a later time period. Availability demands that students search for specific concepts to use and/or to transfer what they know to new situations. Instructional processes should emphasize such things in the following ways:

- *Teach with the transfer of information in mind.* Show students through examples and demonstrations how concepts fit a diverse set of situations.

- *Have students work on cases, problems, questions, applications, and other activities where they have to find and/or select the information that applies.* Try to select things that illustrate the diversity of situations where the course content applies and where students have to search for and select among alternative ideas.

Self-Reflection Activity 5-1
A Retention Checklist

The following teacher behaviors have been shown to enhance the ability of students to learn and retain information. Check each one and indicate the frequency with which you use it on a 1-7 rating scale. *For those given ratings of 1, 2, and 3, what could you do to increase their use in the classroom?*

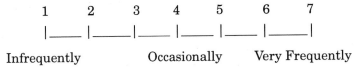

1   2   3   4   5   6   7

|___|___|___|___|___|___|

Infrequently   Occasionally   Very Frequently

_____ Provide an overview of the material to be covered through questions, an outline, a story, an activity, or other organizing devices.

_____ Use small group discussions and activities.

_____ Ask questions frequently. Have students respond after allowing them time to think about or write an answer.

_____ Have a well organized class session.

_____ Repeat important points in several different ways.

_____ Less is more—typically emphasize about 4-7 points per class session.

_____ Use concrete examples to illustrate critical information.

_____ Allow students time to formulate and ask questions.

_____ Provide time to write about, discuss, and practice concepts in class through discussion groups and activities.

_____ Use vivid imagery to highlight points and to stimulate the imaginations of students.

_____ Show how facts, concepts, and principles apply in different contexts and ask students to do the same.

_____ Encourage students to organize the information in ways that are personally meaningful to them but also appropriate for my discipline.

_____ Use outlines, concept maps, lists of terms organized in categories and other devices to help students understand how course information is organized and how ideas are interconnected.

_____ Provide activities and assignments in and out of class that increase the amount of time students spend on course related tasks.

_____ Use a short quiz on the material before a class begins and just before it ends. This helps students to focus on important points.

- *Emphasize the general principles that organize specific facts and concepts in a field of study.* Knowing, for example, that one characteristic of fruits is they have seeds makes it easier to later identify specific examples of fruits. Similarly, understanding that anxiety has multiple causes prevents someone from stopping their search after they have uncovered a single cause. Research suggests that general principles are retained better than specific facts. In addition, general principles are like a magnet and attract other facts and concepts associated to them within our cognitive system. This makes it subsequently easier to relearn and/or retrieve this information.

This goal cannot be accomplished simply by lecturing to them. Students need practice in identifying instances of general concepts that organize a field of study. What they discover through their own effort and can apply to other situations is retained longer. This is not to say that "telling" is unimportant. The issue here is one of balance. *Telling* and *doing* are both parts of the educational enterprise. Most contemporary writers and researchers in this area suggest that students doing something active in class needs to become part of the foreground.

Implications for the Integrated Model of Teaching and Learning Style

As will become clear later on in this chapter and in Chapter 6, the teaching processes in this model encourage active learning. They do so in two ways. *Some like peer teaching processes, role plays, and project teams are student-centered.* Little happens unless students participate in the process. *Others like teacher centered discussions and lectures create active learning episodes within them.* Although they are teacher-centered, the suggestions for using them will emphasize ways of involving students. The model takes seriously data from the literature that such processes help students to learn and to retain information. One consequence of active learning is that it likely makes the process of relearning a lot easier. Less time to reacquire the facts and concepts should be needed.

The use of teaching strategies to prepare students to relearn information at a later period of time is not often discussed in the literature. Instead, the focus is on helping them to perform well while they are in the course. Most teachers hope that the learning will transfer. But, we typically are not present when students have to demonstrate what we taught them later on in their lives. In the integrated model, this translates into developing our students' capacities to work independently and to collaborate and consult with others. Activities and projects that encourage Independent and Collaborative learning styles would appear to be important for achieving the latter goal.

Teaching students in an active manner is best achieved by using our expertise in combination with blends of the Personal Model, Facilitator, and Delegator styles. Such styles involve students in their learning and reinforce Participant, Collaborative, and Independent styles of learning. An emphasis on the teaching processes in Clusters 3, and 4 of the model would appear most appropriate for achieving this goal. However, one must also consider that interspersing active learning activities into more traditional approaches to instruction is also desirable. Taking time to encourage active learning can pay dividends well after a course is completed.

2.] What can I do to enhance the ability of students to concentrate during class?

Whatever the classroom task, often it is difficult for students to devote 100% of their attention to it. This is particularly true of presentations but it also applies to discussion methods, independent study, observations of demonstrations, self-discovery activities, and other tasks. Technically this is labeled a *vigilance decrement.* In everyday terms it means that people have predictable lapses in attention. When asked to keep records of their ability to concentrate, students often report an initial increase in attention followed by a dramatic drop. The findings from one such study are illustrated below in Figure 5-2.

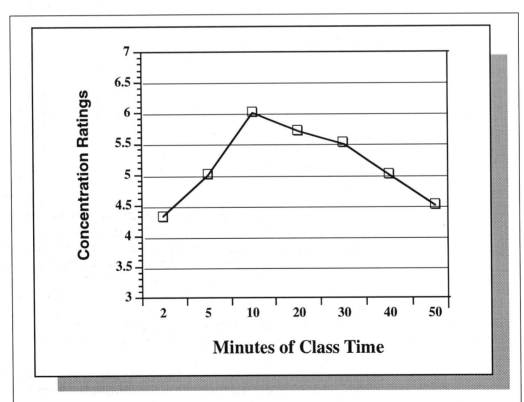

Figure 5-2: Students were periodically reminded their concentration on a classroom presentation. They used a 1-7 rating scale where a 1= Not Concentrating Very Well and a 7 = Concentrating Very Well. [Based on Stuart and Rutherford, 1978].

As their attention wanes, students also are unable to remember the last thing the instructor said. I have conducted numerous demonstrations of this phenomenon in my classes. I will stop class after several random intervals of time, and ask students to "write down the last thing you are thinking about." They typically report thinking about an upcoming date, a weekend activity, what they will have for lunch or dinner, an amusing event in their lives, a current event, the way the instructor and other students are dressed, and a sexual fantasy. With their minds preoccupied, it is not surprising that the amount of information teachers believe is omitted from their notes.

The attention decrement is so powerful that it occurs whether the instructor emphasizes what is important or not. The data from a study by Mark Scerbo and his colleagues in Figure 5-3 illustrates this latter point.

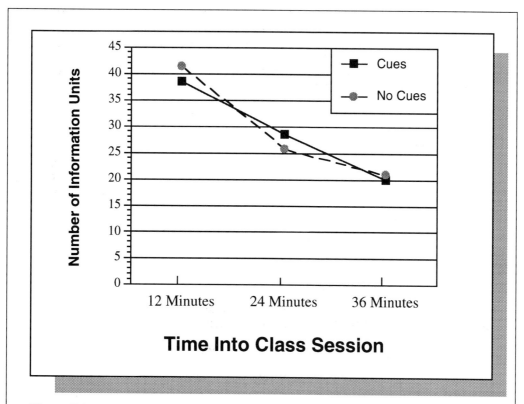

Figure 5-3: The number of content points recorded during a lecture. Important points were either highlighted verbally or in writing during the lecture [Cued] or students had to decide what were important points to record [No cues]. [Based on data in Scerbo, et al., 1992].

Implications for Teaching

The data on how well students pay attention need to be taken seriously. Most teachers spend a considerable amount of time and effort preparing lectures or otherwise designing a class session. No one wants to be in a position of *talking to themselves.* Thus, consider how the ideas in Self-Reflection Activity 5-2 can be applied to your courses.

Self-Reflection Activity 5-2
An Attention Checklist

The following represent teacher behaviors that have been shown to enhance the ability of students to pay attention in class. Check each one and indicate the frequency with which you use it on a 1-7 rating scale. *For those given ratings of 1, 2, and 3, what could you do to increase their use in the classroom?*

```
      1      2      3      4      5      6      7
      |____ |_____|_____ |_____ |_____ |_____|

   Infrequently        Occasionally      Very Frequently
```

_____ *I try to increase uncertainty and remain unpredictable.* New activities, different ways of presenting content, and an occasional surprise are a regular part of my classes.

_____ *Movement is created in class.* I move around the room and place students into different configurations [e.g. small groups, horseshoe, fishbowl] for presentations and discussions.

_____ *The physical characteristics of information are varied.* I use different colors and sizes of lettering when using overheads and the board. Also I use visual aids that vary in their physical and spacial properties when teaching [i.e., size, shape, color, arranged in different ways].

_____ *During class, students are periodically asked to record questions and comments they have on material covered in a session.* This helps them to focus their attention on issues they consider important.

_____ *The occurrence of unimportant information is minimized.* I don't go off on tangents or introduce topics that pull the attention of students away from the major focus of the session.

_____ *Steps are taken to eliminate environmental noise.* This includes students talking, window shades flapping, hallway chatter, inappropriate room temperatures, trash, notes on the board from the last class, and other things that become distractions.

_____ *I try to eliminate as much semantic and emotional noise as possible.* I avoid using terms that students don't understand, overly complex sentence structures, and try not to present information too quickly for students to follow. I recognize that difficult content, the words I use, or other comments may frustrate and/or offend some students.

_____ *Information is related to student needs.* I understand that people pay more attention when information relates to their needs. This can include needs for information to take a test, to work, to be able to understand current events, or appreciate in more detail their environment. Thus, I ask myself, "How can I make this information touch their lives?"

Self-Reflection Activity 5-2 [Continued]

Use the following rating scale.

```
      1      2      3      4      5      6      7
     |____|_____|_____|_____|_____|_____|
    Infrequently      Occasionally      Very Frequently
```

_____ *I try to create redundancy in my presentations.* Important ideas in class are emphasized several times and in a slightly different way. This includes creating redundancy by emphasizing things in different mediums. Examples of this latter issue include verbal presentation followed by a short activity or case study that highlights the points that were just made. Or, videotapes, short clips from films or computer demonstrations are used to reinforce various principles and concepts presented in class.

_____ *Students are given feedback on how accurately they are paying attention.* I do one or more of several things to achieve this goal. I ask questions and typically give students time to think about or write a short answer to the question. I also call on people and correct any misunderstandings or gaps in their knowledge about the information.

_____ Sometimes I give a short 3-4 item multiple choice or short answer quiz to help students determine if they are focusing on the important principles and concepts in a session.

_____ *Emphasize activity and involvement in class.* Keep a class focused on answering questions, discussing issues, solving problems and actively thinking about issues and doing tasks.

_____ *The pace of a class session is varied.* I change from teacher-centered to student-centered instructional processes on a regular basis during a session. Also, I try to vary the pace with which different instructional processes are conducted. Some might be longer or shorter than others, My activity level and that of the students varies, and the rate at which I present information changes.

_____ *Take short breaks.* Provide a 1-2 minute stretch break every 30 minutes and a 10-15 minute break if a class period exceeds ninety minutes. Breaks provide a change of pace and help to counter fatigue

_____ *Try to reduce attentional workload.* Attention tends to wane when mental workload becomes uncomfortable. *Thus, I try to keep my class sessions from becoming crammed with facts.* This only increases mental effort and increases the chances of fatigue setting in.

_____ *I watch that my class sessions do not become boring or dry.* Under such conditions, students tend to fill the time with other thoughts. They daydream, think of other things they have to do, or mentally work on personal problems or other issues. Such thoughts increases mental effort and their frustration levels which takes them away from the task at hand.

Implications for the Integrated Model of
Teaching and Learning Style

One way to hold the attention of students is to *vary the instructional methods employed.* This introduces an element of unpredictability and novelty into the classroom. Both are necessary for helping students to sustain attention during class. Variety can be added by employing a number of the instructional processes in the four clusters of the integrated model [cf., Table 4-3 in Chapter 4]. This can be done within and/or across class sessions. It is important that such attempts occur in conjunction with applying elements in the integrated model. This means that classroom methods are selected after considering the learning styles you hope to encourage in pursuing your instructional goals, the capability of students to handle course demands, and your needs to control classroom tasks and to build relationships.

3.] How can I encourage students to think critically?

The term *critical thinking* has numerous definitions in the literature. Philosophers often emphasize inductive and deductive reasoning and formal logic while psychologists and educators stress a broad range of "thinking skills." According to psychologists Diane Halpern [1989], the term *critical thinking* has three characteristics:

- *Critical thinking has a purpose:* It involves deliberate conscious thought and reflection directed towards accomplishing some goal. This includes solving problems, making decisions, applying information to our lives, or otherwise probing beneath the surface of issues and events to understand them better. Purposeful thought processes separates critical thinking from routine and largely automatic cognitive processes involved in brushing our teeth, driving the usual route to school or work or from the thinking involved in daydreams or night dreams.

- *Critical thinking is reasoned:* It is emphasizes our ability to examine all of the information relevant to an issue or problem and then to form an accurate conclusion.

- *Critical thinking evaluates in a constructive manner more than one side of an issue as well as the positive and negative attributes of a situation.*

Students typically do not do engage in critical thinking with the proficiency many instructors want. It is not that they cannot think critically [i.e., in the sense that Diane Halpern defines the term], but they lack the necessary practice and experience to do so. *In fact, some of our classroom practices may discourage the development of critical thinking.*

One way to examine the latter problem is to use ideas from the work of William Perry [1970;1981] and Mary Belenky and her colleagues [1986].

Both researchers used in-depth interviews of college students and others to identify patterns among individuals in their level of intellectual development. William Perry's interviews were conducted on a predominately male sample while Mary Belenky and her colleagues interviewed 135 women. Participants in both studies were questioned about their views of learning and education, significant events in their lives, how they handled moral issues, as well as other concerns. The themes associated with how people understood important issues in their lives were then identified.

While some differences were noted between the samples, there were many similarities across both studies. Both researchers found patterns in how people thought that differed in their complexity. A summary of three such patterns of thinking common to both studies and their implications for critical thinking are identified in Table 5-1. Perry labels such modes of thinking *positions* while Belenky refers to them as *ways of knowing.*

Both Perry and Belenky viewed these patterns of thought as different levels of intellectual development. They were not, however, fixed stages that someone entered and then abruptly left. *Rather, people had preferences for certain modes of thinking that varied with their age and experiences, life circumstances, and to a lesser extent their gender.* In effect, as we mature, our capacity to employ more complex ways of understanding the world [e.g., relativism/procedural knowledge] increased. Yet retreating to less complex modes of thinking was not uncommon and often served as a form of self-protection. Therefore, someone might be able to use a broad relativist point of view when discussing the merits of a piece of poetry. When faced with time pressures to complete a task, this same person might ask their boss or teacher to "tell me exactly what I should think about and do here."

Implications for Teaching

There are several implications for how we teach in the two models. To discuss them, let us examine in more detail the characteristics of each pattern of thinking and how college teachers can cope with the issues they present.

Dualism/Received Knowledge
Seeking The "Right" Point Of View

The *dualism/received knowledge* modes of thinking emphasize *black-white, correct-incorrect*, or *right-wrong* ways of making judgments and forming opinions. It also stresses that authorities are right and their views deserve special considerations. Joanne Kurfiss [1988] points out that such thoughts are encouraged by instructional practices in educational settings. For example, the use of true-false and multiple choice exams and textbooks that present subject matter as consisting of a large number of correct or incorrect facts and concepts promote dualistic thinking. Classroom procedures with few opportunities for students to challenge a teacher's ideas or those in the text also contribute. Such conditions may prompt students to develop the idea that the teacher or some authority is always right and not to ask too many questions.

Table 5-1
Patterns in How People Think

Identified by Perry/ Belenky	Description of Three Modes of Thinking and Their Implication for Critical Thinking
Dualism / Received Knowledge	Belief that information is either correct or incorrect, right or wrong, and that there are fixed ways of looking at the world. Reliance on authorities to determine how and what to think. *Implication: for Critical Thinking:* Leads to difficulty thinking independently, generating alternative perspectives, and being able to analyze information.
Multiplism / Subjective Knowledge	Ability to see that uncertainties, doubts, and unknowns exist and these in turn naturally lead to multiple points of view. Have difficulty, however, developing reasons why some opinions would be better than others. Tendency to turn inward and not to not rely as much on external authorities for answers. Men view having opinions as every person's right, while woman simply acknowledge that differences in opinion can be expected and are valuable. *Implication for Critical Thinking:* Leads to considering alternative points of view but without an ability to formulate and employ criteria for deciding consistently among them.
Relativism / Procedural Knowledge	Recognition that points of view differ in quality and that good ones are supported by evidence and other criteria. Thus, discipline, legal, moral, religious and other criteria are used to determine which opinions can be accepted, rejected, or that need additional analysis. Men tend to rely more on objective external criteria while women tend to blend both external criteria and internal criteria such as their personal values and beliefs. *Implication for Critical Thinking:* Leads to independent thinking, analyzing information and using appropriate criteria to draw conclusions.

Multiplism/Subjective Knowledge
Developing Multiple Points of View

This mode of thinking develops when people begin to see that the world is not tied up in neat little packages and that authorities do not always have correct answers. This happens through exposure to multiple interpretations and diverse opinions on issues and having the views of authorities challenged. Essentially students begin to see the limitations of dualistic thinking in the context of coming to terms with complex issues.

While students begin to see that multiple viewpoints exist, *they typically lack the capacity to decide what points of view are better than others.* Kurfiss finds fault for this problem with many of our educational practices. Students often are not asked to critically examine opposing points of view. Nor are they asked to specify which ones were more acceptable than others. Diverse perspectives are simply left to stand as if the recognition of alternatives was sufficient. Or, classroom processes are not used that would allow everyone to grapple with the complexity of an issue. Often a question is asked and those few students able or willing to respond get to deal with the issue.

Research shows that a majority of college students and other adults rely on the dualism/received knowledge and multiplism/subjective knowledge approaches to analyzing and understanding issues [Belenky et. al., 1986; King, Kitchener, and Wood, 1985]. Such individuals want authorities to provide *correct or right* answers and prefer to focus on expedient or simplistic explanations to complicated issues. They are concerned with *getting the facts* from what others say or from what they read. When asked to think for themselves about issues for which there is no clear answer, they may resist or become frustrated with not being able to form an acceptable response.

Relativism/Procedural Knowledge
Using Criteria to Evaluate Multiple Points Of View

With this style of processing information, people see the need to probe beneath the surface of issues. They examine and evaluate ideas, positions, and alternatives against discipline and other applicable criteria. For example, a question such as, "Is it proper for one human being to kill another?" is seen as having several answers. An individual employing a relativistic mode would not simply respond *yes* or *no*. The answer would depend upon the context and the criteria used to develop a response. Thus, someone might say; "If a person is on a battlefield, then killing would be justified because your basic survival needs are threatened. However, if someone calls you a jerk, killing that person is not allowed because it is too violent a solution to a minor provocation. It also violates legal and moral principles that guide our actions." Eventually, people develop a personal commitment to relativism. It becomes less of *let's see, what criteria can help me decide.* Instead, the criteria become integrated with a person's values and outlook on life. The distinction between what are discipline related and other criteria and someone's personal values becomes an artificial distinction. Criteria for evaluating issues and making decisions are integrated into someone's personal makeup. Thus the question, "What is the poet saying?" may not elicit a preferred mode of literary interpretation. Instead, someone may respond by stating, "What the poet is saying to me is......."

In spite of its usefulness for thinking broadly about more complicated issues, *relativism/procedural knowledge as a mode of thinking is employed less often and is relatively uncommon even among college seniors and older adults* [Baxter-Magolda,1992; Kurfiss, 1988; Ryan, 1988]. To develop this capacity, students need practice *thinking for themselves*. Teachers must provide opportunities for students to analyze ideas and positions, debate points of view, write position papers, have ideas challenged, and to justify their position on issues. Opportunities for doing such things are not always taken advantage of or made available to students. Thus, is not surprising that this is the least developed mode of thinking.

Complete the checklist in Self-Reflection Activity 5-3 to determine how your teaching encourages critical thinking. Working on such issues on classroom tasks can help students to begin the process of thinking differently about course related and other issues in their lives. It typically takes more than classroom tasks for more advanced ways of thinking to become pervasive parts of our lives. Students must be willing to risk using higher level modes of thinking outside the classroom. It also helps if they receive encouragement to do so in other areas of their lives and take advantage of such opportunities. Developing the capacity to think in a relativist manner is a complicated process. Robert Kloss [1994] notes the classroom is a natural place to begin "nudging students" away form dualistic thinking patterns. It may also be one of the few places some students have to obtain such experiences.

Implications for the Integrated Model of Teaching and Learning Style

Overall, the development of critical thinking is unlikely to occur through any one instructional process. It must become an instructional goal and the teaching and learning styles most likely to encourage it should be engaged. Marsha Magolda Baxter [1992] states that instructional processes that encourage students to find their own voice should be emphasized. This is virtually impossible to accomplish in classrooms where the instructor does all or most of the talking. In the integrated model, this can be accomplished by emphasizing the teaching processes in Clusters 3 and 4 of the model. Here, the Facilitator and Delegator teaching styles are dominant and Collaborative, Participant, and Independent learning styles are encouraged. Such blends are quite helpful for achieving critical thinking goals.

Self-Reflection Activity 5-3
A Critical Thinking Skills Checklist

The following represent teacher behaviors that have been shown to enhance the ability of students to think critically in class. The items are based on behaviors that would help students to overcome dualistic modes of thinking and engage in more complex ways of thinking. Check each one and indicate the frequency with which you use it on a 1-7 rating scale. *For those given ratings of 1, 2, and 3, what could you do to increase their use in the classroom?*

```
  1     2     3     4     5     6     7
  |____|____|____|____|____|____|
```

Infrequently   Occasionally   Very Frequently

_____ I discuss alternative ways of interpreting and understanding issues.

_____ Concrete examples are used to show students that changing one's mind for cause is legitimate and is sometimes helpful.

_____ Classroom activities examine alternate points of view.

_____ Tests emphasize essay questions that ask students to integrate diverse points of view.

_____ Students are required to explain their reasons for rejecting a point made in class.

_____ When students cite authorities, I probe for ways those authorities might be challenged.

_____ Students are asked to think of more than one interpretation of an observation they have about course content.

_____ Students are asked to analyze cases and problems that have several solutions and must apply and cite discipline related criteria to find a solution.

_____ Discussion questions ask students to think of several responses to an issue and then to cite the evidence they used to form a response.

_____ Students are asked to analyze issues to determine what assumptions are being made and to determine which ones are more credible than others.

_____ Activities are used in class that force students to grapple with complex issues and to form their own conclusions about them.

_____ Students are given demonstrations of how to get beneath the surface meaning of a conclusion and then asked to practice this skill.

4.] What will help me to motivate my students?

Various theories of teaching and learning suggest a framework for motivating students. *Behavioral models of teaching, for example, encourage instructors to reward desirable behavior.* Thus grades, earning points, opportunities for teacher and peer recognition become ways to increase motivation. On the other hand, *humanistic writers assume that everyone is motivated to self-actualize and achieve their potential in life.* For their part, teachers help students to reach their potential when they provide a supportive environment. This helps them to take risks as learners, to share ideas, and to make choices about what to learn and how to do it. *The cognitive approach to learning also assumes that learners are naturally motivated to seek new information and skills.* This happens best when students face challenging problems and are asked to make decisions. College teachers should use activities that tap into this information seeking and problem solving interest in order to produce constructive outcomes in students.

Implications for Teaching

Besides the general approaches suggested by various theories, the literature also contains specific ideas for motivating students that cross theoretical lines. Some were developed from the experiences of practitioners while others can be found in the outcomes of research studies where students were asked what motivated them to learn and pay attention in class.

Peter Beidler [1993], for example, suggests that teachers have to discover "what kind of pony their students want." Or, at least that is how he managed to motivate his daughter to do well in school. She wanted a pony and he agreed to purchase one provided she met certain conditions. Several lines of research suggest other approaches [i.e., not involving the purchase of favorite pets or toys] [cf., Lowman [1994; 1995; McDaniel, 1985]. They are contained in the checklist found in Self-Reflection Activity 5-4.

And what do students have to say about all of this? Actually, quite a lot. The results of a survey of 700 students on what affected their level of motivation are shown in Table 5-2 [Sass, 1989]. It is clear from this list that students find specific things that teachers do helpful. Several items reinforce the idea that what is motivating to students also plays a role in their ability to acquire and retain information and to pay attention in class.. For example, several points in Table 5-2 also were factors identified in the checklists found in Self-Reflection Activity 5-1 as aids to the acquisition and retention of content [e.g., well prepared and organized teacher, hands-on activities and discussion, course material is made real, concrete, and understandable]. Similarly the items in Table 5-2 on providing variety and making information relevant also were noted earlier in Self-Reflection Activity 5-2 as important for enhancing student concentration in class. *Thus, several of the factors students find motivating also are those that have been shown to aid retention and their ability to pay attention in class.*

Self-Reflection Activity 5-4
Motivation Checklist

The following represent teacher behaviors that have been shown to enhance the ability to motivate students in class. Check each one and indicate the frequency with which you use it on a 1-7 rating scale. *For those given ratings of 1, 2, and 3, what could you do to increase their use in the classroom?*

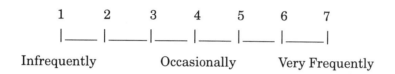

    1   2   3   4   5   6   7
    |___ |____|____ |____ |____ |____|

    Infrequently   Occasionally   Very Frequently

_____ Take the time and effort in class and at other periods of time to help students to clarify and understand course content.

_____ Encourage students to do well and offer an environment where this is possible. This include providing tasks where all students are able to succeed.

_____ Challenge students to do their best by providing assignments that are fair, that demand time and effort but are not impossible to complete

_____ I'm patient with students and understand that what is easy for me to understand is often not easy for them.

_____ Display empathy with learners and the factors that facilitate and hinder their ability to learn

_____ Possess a sensitivity to students' difficulties acquiring information and suggest corrective actions

_____ Able to take steps to enhance a student's sense of competence through feedback, recognition, and appropriate rewards

_____ Try to insure that every student has several success experiences.

_____ Provide students with stimulating activities and/or problems to solve that capture their interest and curiosity.

_____ Avoid using threats, punishment, and repercussions when trying to get students to perform better.

_____ Provide the support, encouragement, and resources students need to be successful on classroom tasks and projects.

_____ Emphasize ways that students' efforts and abilities were responsible for the successful things they accomplished.

_____ I help them see that a poor performance can be a temporary occurrence and coach them on specific actions to take in order to rebound.

Table 5-2
Elements of the Classroom Identified by Students as Motivating

- Enthusiasm of the teacher.

- Studying course material that is perceived as personally relevant and important.

- Having a well prepared and organized teacher.

- Assignments and course material is challenging but "doable."

- Students are actively engaged in classroom learning through hands-on activities and discussions.

- Variety and novelty are present in the assignments and classroom learning techniques.

- Students feel they have good rapport with their instructors and that teachers are approachable.

- Course material is made real, concrete, and understandable through the use of appropriate examples.

* Based on information contained in [Saas, 1989]

Implications for the Integrated Model of Teaching and Learning Style

Several items in Table 5-2 have direct applications for the integrated model. For example, students reported that being *actively engaged in classroom learning,* and having *variety and novelty present in assignments* were important. They also noted that teachers who build relationships and establish *good rapport* and who are *approachable* increased their levels of motivation. Such factors are most noticeably present in Clusters 3 and 4 of the model where the Facilitator and Delegator styles of teaching are emphasized. Yet, such qualities can become an integral part of the teaching processes in Clusters 1 and 2. To do so, teachers must be willing to experiment with variations on the traditional ways that the Expert, Formal Authority, and Personal Model styles are expressed. Suggestions for how to do this are described in the discussion of the instructional processes in Clusters 1 and 2 in the next section of this chapter.

5.] How can I help my students to become self-directed learners?

The major concern here is to get students to take initiative and responsibility for their learning. Most teachers yearn for this quality and some have argued that "the ultimate goal of the educational system is to shift to the individual the burden of pursuing his own education" [Gardner, 1989, p. 1]. In a recent book on this issue, Todd Davis and Patricia Hillman Murrell [1993] argue that a college education is a worthwhile commodity and that students must be held answerable and accountable for their actions or inactions in the classroom. To do so, teachers must have clear expectations that students invest physical and psychological energy in their learning. *Quality time on task* appears to be a necessary precondition for student initiative and responsibility for their learning to develop.

It is also clear that approaches to instruction that encourage self-directed learning will have to become much more prevalent. Students must learn to appreciate that learning on their own is an important educational outcome. They will need more than an occasional classroom activity, guided reading, or independent study to reinforce this idea. Because the majority of our students have a dualistic and multiplistic orientation to thinking, they need a diverse set of experiences that encourage them to "think and learn for themselves."

Unfortunately, students sometimes resist becoming self-directed learners. In my experience, those with dualistic leanings, for example, are more likely to discount this goal. They *see the teacher as largely responsible for their successes and failures as learners.* The recent remarks of a colleague illustrated this point when she said, "Several students reported on my course evaluations that they had to learn too many things on their own. While I perceived this as something positive, they obviously did not." On my course evaluations in my introductory class, students sometimes respond with "more notes" to the question "What would you like to have had more of in this class?"

Finally, faculty attitudes about the capabilities of their students need to be adjusted. On many occasions I hear college faculty berate the "passive-dependent nature" of students. This is spoken as if such qualities are etched in concrete and could never change. The work on teaching and learning styles discussed in Chapter 4 clearly shows that the classroom environment can encourage students to modify their styles as learners. This is not always easy nor does it occur fast enough for some faculty members. With patience, encouragement and student-centered classroom activities, people can learn how to take more initiative and responsibility for their learning.

There are two questions about self-directed learning that are important here.

- Why are students passive-dependent?

- Are they capable of taking more initiative and responsibility for their learning?

One cause of a passive-dependent learning style are educational processes that place students in a reactive rather than proactive mode. The traditional lecture-discussion method is one example. Another is the *lock step* nature of most requirements for a major and the relative lack of independent study options for students in large universities. One also can blame an authority structure in our society that tells students to *do as I say* and that authorities know what is best for you. It is easy for many students to feel *one-down* under such circumstances and to prefer the *passive-dependent* option. They see it as adaptive and because it protects them from the tension that would occur if they challenged the prevailing authority structure.

Clearly students are capable of taking more initiative and responsibility for their learning. Our work with the Grasha-Riechmann Learning Styles has shown that many have or can acquire the ability to function as independent, participant, and collaborative learners. Also, in examining styles of learning outside the classroom, students routinely engage in self-directed learning experiences including such things as learning to cook, fixing flat tires, to using computer programs [Grasha, 1990a; 1990b]. The *Naturalistic Learning Style Checklist* is used to determine task and personal dispositions associated with such independent learning projects. The data from one study is shown in Table 5-3. Note how often college students report that such efforts are planned by themselves, motivated by enhancing personal growth, rewarded by self-satisfaction, and that there is a considerable amount of personal initiative involved in the learning processes employed.

Implications for Teaching

To encourage self-directed learning and to develop the skills to do so means that teachers should consider the ideas contained in Self-Reflection Activity 5-5. The suggestions are based on several sources of research and application [cf., Bandura, 1986; Grasha, 1990a; 1995; Watson and Tharp, 1993; Weiner, 1986]

Implications for the Integrated Model of Teaching and Learning Style

The capability of students to take initiative and responsibility is one of the factors in choosing instructional methods in the model [cf. Table 4-7 in Chapter 4]. This is particularly true of the instructional processes in Clusters 3 and 4 in the model. To encourage students to become self-directed learners, college teaches must be willing to step into the background to allow for the free expression and development of self-directed tendencies.

The modes of instruction that work best here are the Facilitator and Delegator styles. Here, teachers can function as consultants and resource persons to students. To use these styles effectively, good interpersonal rapport with students is needed. Thus, working on relationships becomes important for teachers who want to show people how to become self-directed learners. It also is important for teachers to perceive students' capabilities to take initiative

Table 5-3
Summary of Naturalistic Styles Checklist Data

Category	Top-Ranked Items	Number of Times Item Chosen
Type of Learning	• Gained new knowledge/insight • Learned new skills/knowledge • Worked on attitude change • Emotional change	188 133 83 58
Hours Spent	• Between 26 and 99 • More than 100 • Between 8 and 25	61 59 29
Learning Processes Employed	• Learned by doing • Observed a model • Asked a friend • Practiced physical skills	150 104 95 94
Learning Related to	• Leisure/Social Life • Personal growth • Work	137 130 59
Motivated by	• Enhancing personal growth • Curiosity/interest/novelty • Desire to be successful • Problem to solve	200 194 96 76
Planned by	• Self • Instructor/resource person • Friend/Family member • Written instructions	131 71 68 33
Rewarded by	• Self-satisfaction • Recognition by others • Grade/degree/credit • Promotion/status	169 90 52 30
Cognitive Processes Used	• Thinking logically/rationally • Analyzing information • Using rules to guide thinking • Forming principles	107 99 89 80

Self-Reflection Activity 5-5
A Checklist for Encouraging Self-Directed Learning

The following teacher behaviors have been shown to enhance the ability of students to become self-directed learners. Check each one and indicate the frequency with which you use it on a 1-7 rating scale. *For those given ratings of 1, 2, and 3, what could you do to increase their use in the classroom?*

```
    1       2       3     4     5     6     7
    |____|____|____|____|____|____|
 Infrequently        Occasionally    Very Frequently
```

_____ *Tasks for students to pursue independently* are a part of my classes.

_____ *Tasks are structured so that students can experience "small wins"* along the way to larger successes.

_____ *I work on developing good relationships with students.* This helps them to accept feedback on how to work effectively in an independent manner and to use me as a consultant and resource person.

_____ *I help students to see that their successes are due to their effort and ability.* This generates pride in accomplishment, is motivating, and is likely to keep them on tasks where the development of self-directed skills are important.

_____ *When a task is not going well, I help students gain a broader perspective on the reasons why.* They need to see that situational factors, bad luck, and forces outside of their control sometimes play a role. An objective perspective helps to counter any unnecessary tendencies for self-blame, exaggeration, negative thinking,

_____ *I progressively increase the amount of initiative and responsibility* I require of students on classroom tasks.

_____ *Students can pick and choose tasks and activities to work on.*

_____ *Students are encouraged to try new activities* instead of safe and secure ways of doing things.

_____ *I redirect the control I normally have over classroom tasks to empower students to learn on their own.* Research suggests that this increases the strength of beliefs in self-efficacy or agency that students need to improve performance.

_____ *Students are given or shown examples of people* who have accomplished things in a self-directed manner and how they did it.

_____ *I remind students of the resources that are available to help them work on course related issues now as well as after they graduate.*

and responsibility as something that can be developed. *In particular, it is helpful to apply the adage that in order to develop responsibility, people must be given something responsible to do.* Presumably, this would not occur in a *sink or swim* manner, and students would be supported in their efforts. Students probably need more opportunities to work independently as well as to choose among tasks that interest them. It is a challenge for teachers interested in developing such skills to provide such things. Teachers might consider asking students to suggest the types of options that would work for them. Thus both the opportunities and the choices can be developed collaboratively.

Epilogue

Themes and Variations

Regardless of how they teach, college faculty must be concerned with helping students to do the following:

- Acquire and retain information
- Concentrate and attend to course material
- Think critically
- Become motivated learners
- Become self-directed learners who take initiative and responsibility for their learning

The integrated model is a device for helping teachers to manage the concerns listed above. It does so in several ways.

Active learning processes are stressed in the integrated model. Not only does an active mode of learning enable our students to achieve the latter goals, it also provides a foundation for relearning information in less time in the future. Teaching methods in the model that encourage Independent and Collaborative learning styles are particularly important for accomplishing the latter goals. They play a critical role showing students how to work alone in order to obtain needed information and if necessary to work alongside and with others.

Similarly, exposing students to the combinations of teaching styles in the model helps them to acquire information in different ways. The variety and novelty inherent in doing this encourages students to pay attention and it motivates them. Teaching with a variety of styles also helps students to see content in different contexts which increases the chances that the knowledge will later transfer to new situations. The exposure to diverse teaching styles helps students to think much more deeply and critically about the issues they face. And, when they encounter the Facilitator and Delegator styles of teaching, an added benefit is that their capability for becoming self-directed learners is enhanced.

OSCAR and the Five Instructional Concerns

Specific actions faculty can take to enhance their ability to manage issues with attention, critical thinking, retention, motivation, and helping students become self-directed learners were presented in the chapter. Several checklists were used to summarize those points. It is possible, however, to identify five principles of learning that help us to integrate several of the major concepts contained in those checklists into our teaching. I use the acronym OSCAR to summarize these concepts. They are:

> **O**rganization and structure: While there are many dimensions to organizing and structuring a class [e.g., syllabi, organization of a session, using outlines of critical points], a critical one is helping students to organize the way they think. Thus, the use of prequestions to help students focus on important points during a session or questions that promote critical thinking can be very helpful. Similarly, asking students to develop outlines, flow charts, diagrams, or cognitive maps [cf., Chapter 8] helps them to organize and structure the information. Such things have been shown to enhance the ability of students to learn by directing their attention to important issues, relating new concepts to those they already know about, and helping students to develop new perspectives on course material.

> **S**timulate imagination: Our memory systems tend to encode information in both verbal and imagery based memory codes. The more concrete the information, the more likely that both codes will be well-developed. Conceptual and theoretical content, however, tends to emphasize the verbal memory code. When both are present, our memory is improved because there is a backup memory code if one is not available. Thus, it is important to stimulate students' imaginations when teaching. This includes using metaphors, evoking mental images of concepts, and using vivid examples to illustrate points.

> **C**oncrete examples emphasized: Pictures, three-dimensional models, demonstrations, laboratory exercises, active participation activities, and anything that students can see, hear, touch, and otherwise experience enhances learning. One reason is they take abstract concepts and bring them to life for students. They also stimulate different sensory modalities and thus they increase the type of information that can be used to encode the concepts. In effect, concrete examples make course content memorable and captures the attention of students.

> **A**pplications developed: People are interested not only in *what is* but in *what can this become*. Thus, placing information into a broader frame of reference helps to accomplish the latter goal.

Showing students the applications of content or helping them to develop applications for themselves is very helpful. When a concept can be applied, it no longer is an abstract entity but one that has utility and subsequently something that captures students attention and becomes memorable. The process of having students develop applications is motivating, helps them to think critically, and encourages self-directed learning.

Repetition and redundancy: These are important concepts for enhancing a student's ability to retain information. The repetition, however, should occur in several ways. One is that teachers need to provide it in the context of a class session. Not only is saying something more than once important, but doing so in different contexts should be stressed. Besides giving them such examples, having students experience concepts in a variety of contexts is useful. When teaching principles of persuasion, for example, I typically have students identify them in television commercials, in everyday conversations, and in a variety of printed materials. In this way, students get to see for themselves how concepts occur in more than one situation. Furthermore, it is helpful to have students develop different contexts in which course concepts are likely to occur. Thus they not only create the examples but the repetition of the information is encouraged.

Principles of OSCAR are embedded in several of the suggestions in the five checklists presented in this chapter. To employ them effectively, we must use various blends of the teaching styles in the integrated model. And if done well, all of us might end up as OSCAR winning teachers.

6. Managing the Expert, Formal Authority, Personal Model Styles

> Outstanding teachers exhibit great artistry in the ways in which they conduct their classes. However, careful analyses of their teaching usually reveal that their artistry rests upon a foundation provided by their mastery of some identifiable teaching skills....
>
> - Bette and Glenn Erickson

Instructional Processes and the Integrated Model

This chapter and Chapters 7 and 8 will examine the specific details of how to employ the instructional processes associated with each cluster of the integrated model. A review of each cluster is shown in Table 6-1. Several aspects of the integrated model are repeated below to reinforce the assumptions underlying it.

- *The teaching methods in the model are associated with particular blends of teaching styles.*

- *Whether particular combinations of teaching styles and corresponding classroom methods can be used effectively depends upon four factors.* They include: Our sensitivity to the learning styles of our students; Student capabilities to handle course demands; Our needs to control classroom tasks, and our willingness to build and/or maintain relationships with and among students.

- *Teaching styles, learning styles, and classroom processes are interdependent.* Selecting any one has direct implications for the appearance of the other two. For example, if one decides to use a traditional lecture-discussion method, the Expert and Formal Authority blend of teaching styles are evoked and such instruction is likely to reinforce and develop a blend of the Dependent, Participant, and Competitive styles of learning. Similarly, the use of independent research projects works best with a Delegator, Facilitator, and Expert blend of teaching styles and will encourage Independent, Collaborative, and Participant learning styles.

- *One approach for selecting instructional methods is to first examine our instructional goals and the learning styles of students we wish to encourage.* Thus, our goals could be taught in ways that match the preferred styles of students or that provide a *creative mismatch* with those preferred styles.

The remainder of this chapter will explore the teaching styles and methods found in Clusters 1 and 2. The discussion will focus upon using them to encourage active learning.

Table 6-1
Teaching Methods Associated With Each
Cluster of Teaching and Learning Styles

Cluster 1	Cluster 2
Primary Teaching Styles Expert/Formal Authority *Primary Learning Styles* Dependent/Participant/Competitive	*Primary Teaching Styles* Personal Model/Expert/Formal Authority *Primary Learning Styles* Participant/Dependent/Competitive

• Exams/Grades Emphasized
• Guest Speakers/Guest Interviews
• Lectures
• Mini-Lectures + Triggers
• Teacher-Centered Questioning
• Teacher-Centered Discussions
• Term Papers
• Tutorials
• Technology-Based Presentations
	• Role Modeling by Illustration
	  - Discussing Alternate Approaches
	  - Sharing Thought Processes
	    Involved in Obtaining Answers
	  - Sharing Personal Experiences
	• Role Modeling by Direct Action
	  - Demonstrating Ways of
	    Thinking/Doing Things
	  - Having Students Emulate Teacher
	• Coaching/Guiding Students

Cluster 3	Cluster 4
Primary Teaching Styles Facilitator/Personal Model/Expert *Primary Learning Styles* Collaborative/Participant/Independent	*Primary Teaching Styles* Delegator/Facilitator/Expert *Primary Learning Styles* Independent/Collaborative/Participant

• Case Studies
• Cognitive Map Discussion
• Critical Thinking Discussion
• Fishbowl Discussion
• Guided Readings
• Key Statement Discussions
• Kineposium
• Laboratory Projects
• Problem Based Learning
  - Group Inquiry
  - Guided Design
  - Problem Based Tutorials
• Role Plays/Simulations
• Roundtable Discussion
• Student Teacher of the Day
	• Contract Teaching
	• Class Symposium
	• Debate Formats
	• Helping Trios
	• Independent Study/Research
	• Jigsaw Groups
	• Laundry List Discussions
	• Modular Instruction
	• Panel Discussion
	• Learning Pairs
	• Position Papers
	• Practicum
	• Round Robin Interviews
	• Self Discovery Activities
	• Small Group Work Teams
	• Student Journals

The Teaching Methods of Cluster 1

Exams/Grades

Faculty teaching in each of the four clusters use grades to evaluate students. I find that teachers with Expert/Formal Authority styles perceive them as very important. Those with a Facilitator, Delegator, and Personal Model approach tend to view grades as a necessary evil. Nevertheless, they *bite the bullet* and somehow manage to find a way to assign them. To their credit, faculty with the latter styles also use other evaluation schemes. Written and oral feedback, for example, is typically employed to provide feedback on specific strengths and weaknesses of students' work. Furthermore, faculty teaching in Clusters 3 and 4 are more likely to allow qualitative criteria to influence their grades [e.g., impressions of the quality of a student's work, the effort given to the course, participation in class and on projects.] Those with an Expert/Formal Authority style may include the latter criteria in grading schemes but typically they assign points or a letter grades to these activities.

In my experience, faculty teaching in Clusters 3 and 4 are more likely to engage in self-evaluations as well as assessing the work of classmates. For example, one of my colleagues, Len Lansky, teaches in a Facilitator and Delegator mode. He uses a *baseball team* metaphor to have students evaluate each other on group tasks. At various periods during the term, students rate each other as members of the *first team, second team* or *scrubs.* They must give specific reasons for their evaluations and these are discussed within the work teams. The goal is to provide team members with information they can use to enhance the quality of their work.

Obviously, such a scheme is not for everyone, I only mention it to illustrate an important point. *Evaluative processes in Cluster 1 teaching are likely to rely almost exclusively on traditional forms of evaluation based upon quantitative information [e.g., points, letter grades].* Those in Clusters 2, 3, and 4 are much more likely to include other forms of evaluative processes to assess the outcomes of the independent and collaborative tasks used. A variety of ideas for doing such things were outlined in Table 3-2 of Chapter 3.

In spite of some deviations from accepted practices, exams and term papers are the most frequently employed methods of assessing student performance. When given 100 points to distribute among eleven sources of data for assigning grades, Jim Eison reported that 65% of the points were assigned to objective exams, essay exams, and term papers [Eison, 1980]. Problem sets, term projects, class discussing, laboratory performance and reports, and attendance were used but they were not as popular as the latter three processes.

My recent experiences with college faculty in workshops, studying their syllabi, and observing people teach suggest that not much has changed since Eison's study. Those teaching in each of the four clusters use exams and papers to evaluate students. The difference is one of emphasis. Objective and essay exams are particularly popular with faculty using the Expert/Formal Authority styles. Such evaluation processes are employed less often instructors by operating in Cluster 4. There, position papers, a write-up of a project and faculty impressions of the quality of the products produced are used to evaluate the work of students.

Improving the Effectiveness of Exams

There are several actions faculty adopting an Expert/Formal Authority teaching style can take to enhance such examination and grading processes.

Define the Content You Want to Measure

Classroom exams are notorious for being developed *on the fly* and emphasizing factual knowledge rather than critical thinking. Most teachers construct an exam by looking at the last one they gave and/or by focusing on the content they would like students to reproduce. Yet, course content is not a unitary construct. It comes in a variety of forms. These include such things as basic facts, general concepts, attitudes and values toward issues, skills, principles, assumptions, theoretical perspectives, and models of phenomenon in a field. This information can be listed, applied to problems within a discipline, or used as part of critical and creative thinking processes.

The various forms of content can be formed into several objectives that can be pursued in our teaching. Four objectives related to learning and applying information that I have found helpful include:

[a.] Basic Knowledge and Understanding
[b.] Applications of Course Content
[c.] Thinking Critically
[d.] Problem Solving and Decision Making

These four were selected after an analysis of the literature on course objectives I conducted for a recent project. *The goal of this analysis was to reduce the multitude of objectives in the literature into those that required different types of cognitive processing.* Displaying basic knowledge and understanding, for example, demands a different kind of cognitive processing than would applying information, thinking critically, and solving problems and making decisions.

For example:

• *Demonstrating basic knowledge and understanding* relies on the students ability to search for information in long-term memory and to pull together networks of associations as well as categories and patterns of relationships among related content items.

- *Applications of course content assimilates* relevant information and/or skills in order to achieve some utilitarian goal. Typically this involves search processes in long-term memory that yield a finite set of concepts, principles, and/or skills that can be used in some appropriate manner on a task.

- *Critical thinking typically uses knowledge schemas* [Packets or combinations of facts, figures, data, as well as various categories, and patterns of related information] to do the following: Analyze situations; Identify assumptions; Bring diverse pieces of information together; Form valid interpretations and conclusions; and Evaluate the adequacy of information and evidence in order to support a position.

- *Problem solving and decision making relies upon our capacity* to carefully analyze and define problems, to bring information together to generate alternative solutions, and to use criteria in order to select appropriate solutions or to make decisions.

Teachers often want students to demonstrate the capacity to meet several of the objectives listed above. Each is described in more detail in Table 6-2.

The descriptors in this table can become part of essay, short answer, and objective questions. One advantage of designing exams using such objectives is that the students capacity to do more than memorize facts can be assessed.

Relate Course Objectives to Exam Items

This is best done by taking care to plan your course from the beginning with the following sequence in mind.

Course Objectives —— Exam Objectives —— Exam Items

Thus, if application or problem solving and decision making items were used on the exam, they should also become a part of how the content was taught. Students must know the general learning outcomes you expect. For example, "In this course you will be asked to apply the theories covered to case studies."; " The principles and concepts taught will be used to help you make decisions about public policy." Or, you should give students a study guide that lists major concepts to be covered and indicates the learning outcomes you expect. For example, "Einstein's theory: Show how it predicts the nature of the gravitational forces among objects in the universe." The important point is to keep your students informed about your course and exam objectives. *Exams should not ask them to engage in thinking processes or to demonstrate abilities they were not asked to employ in class.*

Develop a Blueprint for Your Exams

A good way to check whether your course objectives and exams are consistent is to develop an exam blueprint. Like a blueprint for a construction project,

---

Table 6-2
Course Objectives and Exam Items

Basic Knowledge and Understanding
The ability to identify and recall content and to organize and select facts.

Exam questions within this category would ask students to:
Categorize, Convert, Compare, Contrast, Define, Describe the significance of...,
Differentiate, Explain, Generalize, Give examples of..., Identify, Interpret the
meaning of..., List, Name, Organize, Outline, Repeat, Summarize the major
points in ...

Applications
The ability to use various facts, ideas, concepts, and principles to discuss and/or
produce a specific outcome.

Exam questions within this category would ask students to:
Apply, Demonstrate, Design, Develop, Illustrate how, Model, Modify,
Reconstruct, Schedule, Use information to estimate or predict what will happen
when..., and Prepare a [chart, outline, program] using the content.

Critical Thinking
The ability to analyze situations, synthesize information, identify assumptions,
form valid interpretations and conclusions, and evaluate the adequacy of
evidence to support positions.

Exam questions within this category would ask students to:
Analyze, Appraise, Assess the validity of ..., Conclude, Critique, Deduce,
Develop support for..., Evaluate the evidence for..., Examine the other side
of..., Identify assumptions, Identify the arguments made by..., Infer, Integrate,
Interpret, Justify, Paraphrase ..., Prioritize, Rate the appropriateness of...,,
Synthesize

Problem Solving and Decision Making
The ability to analyze and define problems, generate alternative solutions, and
use criteria in order to select appropriate solutions or to make decisions.

Exam questions within this category would ask students to:
Brainstorm ideas for, Choose, Compute, Define the problem in..., Develop
alternative solutions for ...., Develop an appropriate representation of the
elements in the problem of..., Identify the critical elements in the problem of
..., Identify relevant criteria for selecting... Plan, Solve, Use criteria in order to
select... Use appropriate heuristics/formal rules to...

an exam blueprint specifies how course objectives can be evaluated for particular concepts. An example of a blueprint is shown in Table 6-3. As you can see, particular content issues can be related to a single or multiple objectives. Once you know, for example, that you want students to understand as well as apply concepts in a theory, you can then write the exam questions to achieve these goals. An added benefit is that the blue print provides a record of the types of questions you write. This helps you to check how well exam items are distributed across your content objectives.

To Enhance Critical Thinking use Alternative Forms of Testing

Several ideas for accomplishing this goal include:

- *A Library search.* Students are given questions related to the course content but are required to use at least two sources in addition to the text and lectures to develop an answer. They are encouraged to use reference materials in the library to do this.

- *Student-generated exam questions.* Students write exam items, and the instructor selects certain ones to be used on an in-class or take-home exam. Sometimes formulating a good question takes as much skill and knowledge as answering it. In addition, the ability of students to think critically as they answer questions can be enhanced if the teacher gives them feedback on their questions.

- *Experiential tests.* Students are given several concepts from class and told to observe or participate in some experience in which the concepts will be used. This might involve visiting a courtroom, a business organization, or a manufacturing plant. Students write reports on how the concepts played a role in such situations.

- *Open-ended exam format.* This type of exam gives students a chance to respond to very open-ended questions. In the process, they are encouraged to use their own ideas as well as those from the course. The questions should be fun items and not the standard compare and contrast or "summarize the major issues in..." types of questions. One of my favorite open-ended exams appears in Table 6-4.

Assigning Grades

Many faculty and students perceive grades as a valuable and important aspect of the educational process. Grades help teachers to motivate students, to reward them for their accomplishments, and they provide at least general feedback on a student's progress. Students tend to rate them as serving important functions in their education and as motivating them [Polezynski and Shirland, 1977].

Table 6-3
Elements of a Test Blueprint for a Hypothetical Course

Objectives & Questions

Course Content	Knowledge/ Understanding	Applications	Critical Thinking	Problem Solving/ Decision Making
Id, Ego, Superego	Define each term		What are the assumptions about the mind that each term signifies?	Think of a sociopath. What part is dominant? Weakest?
Oxygen		Describe its molecular structure.		Appraise the role it plays in aging.
Friction		Predict what will happen when oil is applied to a rough surface.		Develop two alternative solutions for reducing friction in a car engine.
American Revolution	List the major events leading up to the *shot heard around the world.*		Prioritize events in terms of their importance for starting the war and cite evidence to justify your ideas.	
Shakespeare	What are three characteristics of his style of writing.		Critique the conclusions of some scholars that he did not write his works.	Identify criteria that would be needed in order to decide whether Shakespeare wrote Hamlet.

Table 6-4
An Open Ended Exam

Facts, Insights, Values, Uncertainties, and Contradictions

1.] FACTS are an inescapable part of a_____ course, but they are not its chief reason for being. We have been exposed to many facts this term; it is good to have them in our possession, and they may even be useful. Select a fact from the term's work which seems to have some utility, and discuss it briefly. *If you mastered no useful facts during the term, skip this question.*

2.] INSIGHTS are more central to a study of_____than are facts, though of necessity they are often based on facts. Sometimes an insight is entirely our own; sometimes it is an author's, and we take it over because it has meaning for us. Whichever it is, its function is to illuminate a part of us. If you have had such an insight this term, describe it in context and explain its chief benefits. *If you have had no insights during the term, skip this question.*

3.] VALUES are said by many to lie at the heart of humane learning and to be the chief concern of _____. Through_____we expand our consciousness by grappling with the values of others, and come thereby to have a better understanding of our own values. Select a value or value-set of your own which has been tested or probed by the term's reading, and describe the circumstances. *If none of your personal values were involved in the work of the term, skip this question.*

4.] UNCERTAINTIES lie at the heart of the most profound human questions, and such questions cannot therefore be answered by rote or by formula; each of us must, according to his temperament and desire, find his own path out of the dark wood. Select a problem from the term's work which you consider to be of significant importance, recall briefly for your reader how the question was handled by the term's authors (whichever ones dealt with it), and discuss the ambiguities and paradoxes which prevent its satisfactory and complete resolution for you personally. *If nothing struck you as ambiguous or paradoxical during the term, skip this question.*

5.] CONTRADICTIONS occur in every field. Facts may not agree, people say they value one thing but act differently, theories and models of phenomenon work well under some circumstances but not other, and shifts from normal functioning to chaos and back occur on a regular basis. *What contradictions did you notice in the facts, models, theories, issues, actions, or other aspects of the concepts covered this term? If you did notice any contradictions in the course material, skip this question.*

On the other hand, grading has its controversial elements. There are a number of flaws in traditional grading schemes. The emphasis on grades leads to a *grade orientation* among the majority of college students [Janzow and Eison, 1990]. A set of attitudes and behaviors develops where the pursuit of course grades becomes a sufficient reason for being in college. *Grade oriented students* believe that without regularly scheduled exams, they would not learn or remember as much. They also believe that written assignments and projects that are not graded are a waste of time. Grade oriented students also try to fake paying attention when their thoughts are not focused on the lecture. Such attitudes are probably reinforced by faculty since the majority of college faculty believe that grades must be stressed in educational settings.

Other research suggests that there is not much of a correlation between grades and future success in life and they are often used as a means of maintaining power and control over students [Milton, Eison, and Pollio, 1986]. This leads to perceiving students as adversaries who must be kept in line. These authors also show that college faculty sometimes use rather idiosyncratic systems for assigning grades that have little basis in good evaluation techniques. One faculty member I know gives five exams. To get an "A" in the course, the student must obtain an "A" on each of the five exams. One "B" and the students is assigned a B+ for the term. "You have to be perfect in my course to get an "A" he proudly proclaims. Others use twelve or more categories to place people [e.g., A+, A, A-, etc.]. It is, however, psychometrically difficult to obtain this level of precision with a high degree of accuracy using points on exams. Fewer categories would be better. Furthermore, grades tend to give students very little useful information about their performance in a course. Specific strengths and weaknesses are ignored by grading.

Finally, grades are so important in educational systems that they are sometimes treated as a precious commodity that shifts in value. Some institutions, for example, now worry about grade inflation or the tendency for faculty to be lenient when assigning grades. As one administrator told me, "Grades don't mean what they used to mean. Good ones are too easy to get these days. Faculty just don't have the same standards for excellence they used to have." Some colleges are rather smug about their attempts to maintain grading standards. "A grade of *C* here would be a *B* anywhere else," the president of a prestigious liberal arts college recently told me. "We've got grade inflation under control I was assured. Yet the grading policies at that school were interesting. If students earned a *D* or *F* in a course, they were assigned a grade of *non-entry* which is no grade at all. Also, it did not count against the student's GPA. The intent was to encourage students to try difficult courses without penalty. The result was that the campus GPA was inflated and somehow no one recognized that this was in effect is an example of grade inflation.

Enhancing the Process of Grading

Grading Systems Should be Objective, Reliable, Flexible, and Encourage the Mastery of Content

- *Objectivity* refers to letting students know the criteria upon which the grade is based [e.g., exam scores, analyses of cases, term papers, attendance, etc.]. Such criteria should be listed in a syllabus along with the expected standards of performance needed to obtain them.

- *Reliability* is achieved when instructors have specific and unambiguous data on students and when both teachers and students understand what the data mean.

- *Flexibility* reflects the fact that student ability varies across classes and one's exams are not always equally difficult. Thus, trying to match last year's grade distribution with this year's students is not a good idea. Similarly an easy and difficult exam should not count the same towards a final grade. Also, it would be better to error on the side of leniency and to give students the benefit of the doubt when assigning grades. Students who miss a cutoff by a 1-3 points could be given the higher grade and improvement over the term might be a factor in grading. The use of extra-credit assignments is another way to add flexibility to a grading scheme as is curving the distributions for each test or the term. Of course, such things need to be spelled out in advance when a grading policy is announced and applied fairly to all students.

- *Mastery of content* and not getting as many points as you can must be emphasized on an exam.

One way to accomplish the mastery of content goal is to use a take-two testing process suggested by Alfred Toma and Ronald Heady [1996]. This involves administering the same test twice. It is initially administered in the normal manner and the format of the test is immaterial. The students are told that they will have an opportunity to change their answers during a second application of the same test. They are encouraged to discuss the test with classmates during the interim. The teacher grades the test by only marking wrong answers without making comments, providing correct answers, or even specifying the exact nature of the mistakes.

During the second administration of the test [preferably during the second class session] students are given time to correct their original responses using new answer sheets. Typically, the second administration takes about one-half of the time than the first one. *The teacher grades the second test and computes an average test grade based upon the average of the two tests.*

Another way to enhance student mastery of the content is to specify some minimum criterion level that they have to achieve on every test. This could be a score of 70 or 80% or a letter grade of at least a *C*. Students are then permitted to retake the exam until they obtain the minimum level of competency. Some teachers give students the score they obtained that met or exceeded the minimum standard on retesting. Others, only give the minimum score even if the retest score was higher.

To encourage mastery of the content, the objectives for the class are typically spelled out in detail. Students are given study guides that contain key terms and questions they will be held responsible for being able to answer. Another variation is to give students a copy of the midterm or final exam on the first day of class. They are allowed to keep it and to use the questions to organize the course material. In a similar manner, some instructors give students a list of 6-8 essay questions and tell them that the exam will cover half of the questions. Mastery approaches reduce student uncertainty about exams, make them less anxious, and help to guide and direct students through the material.

Avoid Grading Schemes Based on the Assumption of a Normal Distribution of Student Ability

Here teachers try to assign as many *A's* as they do *F's* and more *C's* than they do any other grade. While student abilities are normally distributed in a large population, it is not necessarily true of those in a given class. When admission criteria are used, students academic skills and abilities are not normally distributed. Thus, to distribute grades this way is unreasonable.

Remain Open to Other Possibilities for Assigning Grades

Several that faculty in workshop settings have reported helpful include:

- *Contract Grading:* Here students and the instructor discuss the types of activities and the quality of work expected for obtaining a particular grade. The teacher also indicates what he or she will do to help students fulfill the contract. This agreement is put in writing and each party is expected to live up to it.

  An alternative is for the teacher to offer a number of ways students can earn points towards a final grade. Thus, exams are assigned *x* number of points, as are short papers, research projects, helping to run a class session, and other activities. The activities and the number of points they receive are spelled out in the syllabus. This allows students to pick and choose among course activities that they want to pursue. This system also helps to promote the development of self-directed learning skills discussed earlier.

- *Student Assigned Grades:* Students are asked to assign themselves a grade. However, they must justify in detail the reasons for this grade against criteria that apply to the course. This might include performance on exams, course projects, time spent on course activities, amount of reading completed, and participation and attention in class.

A variation is to have students do this and the instructor reads it after tentatively deciding what grade to assign. The students may have convincing arguments that they should receive higher or lower grades than the teacher has contemplated giving. My experience is that when given specific criteria to write about, most students take the task seriously and often give themselves a lower grade than I would.

• *Grades Plus Descriptive Feedback:* Letter grades provide general feedback. Some instructors write a note, send an E-mail message, or provide a audio or video cassette with a detailed rationale for the assigned grade. This helps students to make corrections on their performance in the future. Larry Cross [1993] and his colleagues suggest that such descriptive feedback in addition to a student self-evaluation would be a very powerful way for students and faculty to jointly participate in the evaluation process. It also would take the emphasis away from a terminal marker of performance [i.e., a grade] and provides students with informative feedback.

Guest Speakers/Guest Interviews

This can be a very exciting way of introducing students to important themes, issues, and controversies in the field. It is also an underutilized approach to teaching. In my experience, some faculty think that a guest speaker must come from outside the college or university to be effective. This is not necessarily the case. Colleagues within your department, in related fields, and administrators are often good sources for speakers. People in academic leadership positions often have strong backgrounds in disciplines and their specialty interests typically fit the context of a particular course. Administrators and other staff members also have a better feel for the student body, classroom facilities, and the atmosphere on a campus.

When properly used, a guest speaker can provide the novelty needed to capture students' attention. Their elaborations on issues often provide a different context for the content of the class. The latter factor plays an important role in helping students to acquire and retain information. In informal surveys I have conducted, students report that the chance to hear another person speak is a factor in their motivation to attend class.

Enhancing the Use of Guest Speakers/Interviews

Prepare the Guest

Take the time to give your guest background on the course, your goals as a teacher, information about the students, and what you hope to accomplish by having them speak.

Suggest Several Points You Would Like to Hear the Guest Make

I typically ask my guests if they would be comfortable raising a couple of issues in their visit. Also, since I encourage active learning processes in my classes, I also ask them to involve students and give them examples of activities I have used. In this way, if the guest is giving a presentation, it fits the types of processes that students are accustomed to experiencing. If students are used to being actively involved in class, a long dry presentation is unlikely to be greeted with enthusiasm.

Interview a Guest Speaker

There are several ways to do this. One is to pretend that you are the host of a television talk show and to interview them. When I use interviews, I find that interviews allow me to ask questions that help students get into the background of a topic. Interviews also allow me to guarantee that my guest will comment on aspects of the topic that I would like the class to hear my guest's opinions on. The interview creates an informal atmosphere and is a process students have seldom seen in the classroom.

When interviewing a guest, I typically do so for about half of the class period. I then give students a couple of minutes to think of a question or comment they have. The remainder of the class time is spent with the students asking questions and commenting.

Have the Students Interview a Guest Speaker

Two or three students become an interview panel. They research the topic the guest will discuss and one of them conducts a short background interview before the guest speaker appears in class. The interview panel takes information from their research and the background interview and develops a set of questions. The instructor reviews the questions, modifies them if necessary, and suggests additional questions. After a brief introduction by the teacher, the students conduct the interview. Fifteen-twenty minutes should be saved at the end of the class period for the instructor and other students to ask questions.

When using an interview process, pay attention to the physical layout of the room. Place chairs in a circle in small classes or use a horseshoe arrangement or *theater in the round* in larger classes. Make sure that the guest and interviewer [s] are comfortably seated where everyone can see and hear. In an auditorium, also use a microphone so that everyone can be heard. The latter might sound like an obvious suggestion but I find that a number of people resist using electronic devices to amplify their voices.

Lectures

In recent years, proponents of active and collaborative learning have criticized the lecture because it is overused and reinforces a passive-dependent mode of learning. In its most traditional form, 70% of the time is spent with the teacher sharing information in a one-way communication pattern. Student questions and comments are usually welcomed, and an occasional discussion occurs between the students and instructor. This is very much a teacher-centered instructional process that provides a good active learning experience for the teacher.

Enhancing the Quality of Lectures

Use Conceptual Prequestions, Stories, Metaphors, and Other Organizational Devices

These advanced organizers direct students' attention to important concepts, principles, and issues. They also provide an anchoring structure to which new information is attached, and they stimulate students' memories for information learned in the past that is related to a current topic. The result is that the acquisition and retention of information are facilitated.

Conceptual prequestions ask students to focus on important issues in a lecture. They are posted on the blackboard, an overhead transparency, or in an outline of the session given to students. Examples include, "What problems did the early colonists in America face that were largely absent from their lives in England?" What are three principles that help us to understand a chain reaction in a nuclear explosion?" "How is modern poetry similar to and different from that of the 17th and 18th century?" "What geographical term best describes southern Mala?"

Anywhere from 3-5 prequestions are normally used to help students focus on important aspects of the presentation. John Richards and Christine McCormick [1988] reported that such questions were very effective in helping students to recall information 24 hours after a presentation. Students who took notes and listened to a lecture without prequestions *remembered only 11% more than those who just listened and did not take notes. However, students who took notes and were given conceptual prequestions could recall 52% more information.*

In a comparison of teacher generated cognitive maps [e.g., flow charts, schematics], outlines of the presentation, and lists of key terms, Judith Lambiotte and Donald Dansereau [1992] reported that each device was an effective aid to retention. The effects of each varied, however, with the amount of prior knowledge students possessed. Two days after a presentation, instructor generated lists of key terms were associated with 52.8 critical items recalled. Maps and outlines led students with prior knowledge to recall only 20.5 critical items of information. The cognitive maps and outlines the teacher generated probably interfered with the way these students had organized the information. *On the other hand, each of the three organizational devices were almost equally effective for helping students with little prior knowledge recall information.* The number of critical content items recalled was 46.3 for cognitive maps, 44.6 for outlines, and 58.5 for lists of key terms.

Organize Presentations and Clarify Important Terms, Concepts, and Principles

The organization and clarity of information are important for students to follow a presentation. Students also find teachers effective who do such things well [cf., the discussion in Chapter 1 on the specific behaviors associated with teaching style]. Students also note that an organized presentation and class session helps them to acquire and to retain information, to pay attention, and to maintain their motivation to learn. While this seems an obvious point, a frequent complaint I hear from students is that a presentation is "hard to follow." In observing college teachers, some engage in a *stream of consciousness* in their presentations that makes it difficult to follow them. Or, they use language and terms that a number of students do not understand. The result is that participants become frustrated and fail to benefit from the presentation.

Ruth Day [1988] reports that teachers who use a *tree outline* to organize presentations have students who are more satisfied with the session and who remember more of it. *A tree outline was much more effective than a list of key terms or a topical outline.* One reason is that faculty are more likely to remind their students of the major elements in the presentation. This helps them to obtain an overall picture of where the presentation is going and where it has been. This is because instructors must come back to each fork in the tree and summarize what was just said before going on to the next branch.

Stimulate the Imaginations of Students

People encode information using a verbal and an imagery code. Images tend are more vivid than verbal codes and thus lead to better recall. Thus, anything that helps to increase the mental imagery associated with information is likely to lead to better learning and retention. Not only does such information have an imagery code, but it also possesses a verbal code. Two memory codes are better than one particularly if the second is based on mental imagery.

There are several ways to do this. The use of concrete examples and an emphasis on the applications of information makes it less conceptual and theoretical. Providing practical exercises, demonstrations of phenomena, metaphors, analogies, stories, acronyms, mnemonic devices, anecdotes, well-constructed charts, pictures, pieces of art, and videos also help. To use such things effectively, try to frequently intersperse them into a lecture.

One illustration of this latter point is a study by Gerald Evans [1984]. In his lectures, he used metaphors containing concrete examples of statistical ideas from fields outside Business Administration. He was interested in how such metaphors would help students to acquire the corresponding statistical concepts in the field of business. He compared the test performance of students in a section employing such metaphors to those in a section where they were not used. The lectures were preceded by a pretest and a post-test was given immediately afterwards. Students who had metaphors as a regular part of the lectures had a 82% gain in the information acquired. Those in the control group only showed a 42% gain in learning.

Another popular method of converting verbal information into an imaginal form is the use of keywords. Thus, in learning vocabulary or terms in any field, people listen to a sound in the word and construct a concrete image connecting that sound to an image of what the word means. *Der tisch* in German means *table*. The sound in *tish* sounds like *tissue*. The image becomes a table with a slit in the middle with tissue coming out of it. *Angiosperms* in Botany means *flowering plants*. A key sound in *angiosperms* is *angel*. An image of an angel holding a bouquet of flowering plants is then formed. Students who use keywords typically recall 65-85% more information than those who do not. They also remember the words and their meaning for longer periods of time [cf., Atkinson, 1975; Roberts, 1985; Rosenheck et al., 1989]. Teachers can encourage the use of keywords for studying. Also, they can be used in class as part of a lecture to help students remember the meaning of important terms and concepts.

Use the Retention, Attention, Critical Thinking, and Motivation Checklists in Self-Reflection Activities 5-1 to 5-4 in Chapter 5 to Help Plan a Presentation

They include ideas that research shows enhances students' abilities to learn, to pay attention, to think critically, and to remain motivated during lectures and other class formats. The ideas in those checklists are grounded in the scholarly literature on good instructional practices.

Obtain Regular Feedback from Students

Audience feedback is important for improving lectures. A teacher rating form like the one in Chapter 1 can be helpful. Also, taking time several during the term to have students complete the following four items also yields useful information.

- On a rating scale from 1 to 7 [where a 1= the worst presentation I have been to and a 7= the best presentation I have attended], what rating would you give the presentation during this session?

- Give two or three concrete examples of behaviors the instructor engaged in that led you to give the session the rating you did.

- Give one or two concrete suggestions for things the instructor could have done that would have enabled you to give this session a rating of 7.

- What is one behavior you could have engaged in that would have made this a better session for you.

Note that the questions ask students to fixate on specific behaviors and not aspects of the teacher's personality. Also, the last question helps them to examine their responsibility for the success of a session. When using this format recently, a student criticized me for not calling on her. On the last question she wrote, "I could have raised my hand more often in class to get your attention."

Mini-Lectures + Trigger Stimuli

An alternate approach is to use two or more shorter lectures during a session. Each is followed by "trigger stimuli." These are questions, demonstrations, examples of points, and activities designed to involve students with the material. Once the "trigger stimulus" is processed, the next mini-lecture occurs.

Suggestions for planning and executing a mini-presentation include:

- *Keeping it to about ten or twelve minutes in length.*

- *Preceding the mini-presentation with a brief thirty second overview of what will be covered.* Conceptual prequestions could be used here as well other advanced organizers.

- *Allowing no more than two or three key teaching points to be made during the presentation.*

- *Avoiding a natural tendency to stray from the topic.* Thus, keep what you have to say relatively clear, simple, and focused on the issue at hand.

- *Stressing concrete vivid examples of key points and their applications.* This stimulates the imagination and interest of listeners. Visual aids should be used.

- *Varying your rate of speech, inflection patterns, and tone of voice.*

- *Giving a brief sixty to ninety second summary or wrap-up* at the end of the presentation.

After the presentation, trigger stimuli are used to engage the students in the material. Examples of trigger stimuli appear in Table 6-5.

Teacher-Centered Questioning

The teacher's reactions to course content and application activities are given as questions for the class at large to answer. When asking such questions, it is important to do two things. One is to wait for students to respond because research shows most teachers answer their own questions within 1.5 seconds of asking them. Silently counting to 10 helps as does standing still and not talking until someone in class decides to respond. Student responses can be increased by asking everyone to write a brief answer to the question for a couple of minutes. Then students are asked to share their responses.

Table 6-5
Examples of Trigger Stimuli

Trigger stimuli should relate to the content covered and provoke students to discuss the content by relating it to the "trigger stimulus." Thus, a teacher might use the stimulus and ask: "Based on what I have just said, "What does this mean?" "In addition to the points I made, what additional ideas about the topic does this raise?" "What words, images, feelings come to mind from what you have just seen or heard? What do your reactions suggest about the issue under discussion?" *The following are ideas for trigger stimuli to use after a mini-lecture:*

- Reading a powerful passage in a fiction or nonfiction book
- Title of a book or article
- Short scenes from movies or television shows
- An outrageous statement by the instructor
- A potentially outrageous statement by a public figure
- Personal narratives
- A vivid picture depicting some event or incident
- A few lines of vivid poetry
- Headlines from a newspaper story
- Reading a paragraph from a newspaper story
- A metaphor
- Playing a popular song or reading the words from it
- Passages from a speech by an expert in the field
- Reading a short conclusion from a scholarly article
- Cartoon from a newspaper or magazine
- Laboratory demonstration of concepts
- Role play
- Depicting a scene from a play
- Chart or graph that illustrates a major problem
- Short case study
- Debates
- A joke
- A strongly worded question
- A historical dilemma in the field
- Quotes from historical figures about a current issue
- Controversial solution to a problem
- Problems that illustrates information in the mini-lecture
- A mystery associated with the material presented
  [e.g., exceptions, unknowns]
- A paradox suggested by the content
- Incident in the life of a prominent person in the field
- Humorous anecdote
- The beginning of a statement that students must complete
- A compelling personal dilemma that the instructor or students faced
- Contradictions in data or information that must be resolved
- A classic case or research study

Secondly, pose questions in ways that are likely to generate a response. Research by John Andrews [1980] shows that some questions are better than others in generating a high number of responses or student statements. Listed in Table 6-6 are the types of questions that are asked by teachers in the classroom along with the average number of student statements [i.e., NSS] that type of question normally evokes. NSS reflects the average number of different statements students typically make to that category of question. It represents the "discussion power" of the question.

Note that the questions associated with more discussion are broad but have a clearly defined point or direction contained within them. Also, the more narrow questions [e.g., Analytic convergent, lower level divergent, and quiz show questions] lead to fewer student responses. *However, teachers tend to ask them more often than they do other types of questions.* Finally, the list above can be used as a checklist to assess the discussion value of potential questions before class. Some teachers do this by developing a list of questions before class and categorizing them beforehand.

J.T. Dillon [1990] suggests several other ways to get students to respond besides asking a direct question. He notes that teachers sometimes might be better off asking fewer questions and allowing their students to talk more. *Several ideas he suggests include:*

- *Make a declarative or factual statement, pause, and wait for a student to elaborate. Example:* "The allies had a terrible choice to make. They had to choose between a conventional attack on Japan or dropping the atomic bomb on Hiroshima."

- *Make a reflective statement.* "Mark, you seem to feel that B.F. Skinner was wrong in suggesting that free will is a myth."

- *Describe your own state of mind.* "I'm not sure what the two of you meant. Just a minute ago you suggested that people are born innately good but now you are saying just the opposite."

- *Redirect a students's question.* "I'm not sure what I think about that. I'd like to hear what some of you have to say about it. Where do you stand on the issue that Carol made?"

- *Invite students to elaborate on a statement.* "Phyliss, you said that the "big bang" theory of the origins of the universe did not make sense to you. I'd like to hear your reasons for what you said."

- *Play the devil's advocate.* Say something controversial about an issue or in response to something a student said. "Couples would be much better off signing a premarital agreement including the terms of any divorce that might occur. This would get them to focus on important issues before they got married."

Table 6-6
Types of Classroom Questions and Their Ability to Encourage Discussion

Playground Questions [NSS = 5.08]

Do other animals experience stress, anxiety, love, loneliness, and other emotions in the same ways that human beings do?
Can we make any generalizations about the play from the opening line?

Brainstorm Questions [NSS = 4.88]

What possibilities are there for refuge in *A Farewell to Arms*?
What factors would have kept modern humans and Neanderthals from mating even though they lived in the same place and time?

Focal Questions [NSS = 4.29]

What should a teacher do? Reward every instance of desirable behaviors or only give a reward every once in awhile for correct behaviors?
Where is the *Wild Boy* better off? In the forest where he started or in civilization being socialized?

Multiple Consistent Question [NSS = 3.69]

Does Kafka like religion? Was he favorably disposed to the development of Christianity? After reading, should we praise Christianity?
In what ways did Freud and Jung disagree on the nature of the unconscious mind? Whose views about the unconscious seem to be more popular today? Does popularity of a theory necessarily mean that it is correct?

General Invitation Question [NSS = 2.66]

Are there any comments on the reading I assigned in Chapter 10?
What reactions did you have to the movie?

Shotgun Question [NSS = 2.50]

What principles of physics and chemistry are involved in a nuclear explosion?
What physical characteristics do sharks and dolphins have in common?

Analytic Convergent Question [NSS = 1.95]

What concepts in the text help us understand why people fall in love?
What were the reasons the American Revolution succeeded?

Lower Level Divergent Question [NSS = 1.92]

What are the names of some other generals during the Civil War?
What are the names of the other planets in the solar system?

Quiz Show Question [NSS = 1.45]

What is the definition of a shyness used in the textbook?
What are the parts of a neuron?

* NSS represents the number of student statements each question evokes. In addition, the higher this index, the more other students respond to what any given person says. [Based on information reported in Andrews, 1980]

Teacher-Centered Discussions

In a lecture oriented course, a common practice is for the teacher to engage the class as a whole in a discussion. It might evolve out of using the suggestions for questioning and getting student responses mentioned in the last section. Or, a student might raise a point in response to something the teacher said or that appeared in the text or an outside reading. While trying to hold a discussion with the entire group is difficult to manage, there are things that teachers can do to make them more effective. They are described in Self-Reflection Activity 6-1.

Term Papers

Although not strictly limited to individuals teaching in Cluster 1, they are a prominent part of the syllabi for courses emphasizing an Expert/Formal Authority style. Some of my students use the phrase, *two tests and a term paper* to describe the general requirements of such classes. Term papers deal with topics that teachers assign or that students select from a list of possible issues. They can provide a good learning experience for students if handled in a competent manner.

In a study of writing assignments across disciplines, Barbara Walvoord [1990] found that the majority of college faculty do not handle such assignments well. *In effect she states that most college faculty, "get what they ask for."* Part of the problem is that some teachers make unreasonable assumptions about the capabilities of students. Walvoord reports that faculty often assumed that the students were professionals in training. That is, they were miniature representations of the faculty member. *Of course, most instructors recognized that students needed to develop their skills, but the assumption was that the differences were one of degree and not of kind.* One consequence was that writing assignments were not supervised well. A topic was assigned, students were expected to know how to write the paper, and a letter grade and comments were dutifully placed on the finished product. Such things did little to influence the development of writing skills.

Of course these same faculty members were surprised when students did not perform up to the their expectations. There were two problems with the term papers and other written assignments that were submitted. Some students did not know how to use discipline related evidence to develop and support ideas. They used conventional wisdom or aspects of their everyday experiences to make sweeping generalizations. Others were text processors who put ideas together from references. However, a sense of thematic development, organization and transition among the elements of the paper were missing. Not only did their writing projects not hang together well, but students were largely unaware that a problem existed.

Self-Reflection Activity 6-1
A List of Suggestions for Enhancing
Teacher Centered Discussions

The following represent teacher behaviors that have been shown to enhance teacher centered discussions. *Place a check next to those that you believe would help you to lead more effective discussions with your classes.* For each item checked, think of a way that you could begin to use it immediately.

_____ *If students raise an issue, make sure that the issue is clear and that everyone has heard it.* Simply restate the issue raised and/or ask someone in class to do so.

_____ *Suggest a time limit for the discussion* by saying, "Let's spend five minutes on this issue and see what we can make of it." Extend the time only if it looks as if interest is high. If necessary, offer to meet with students who want to continue discussing an issue outside class.

_____ *Write on the board or an overhead a list of the major themes that are emerging from the discussion.* This makes the information a public record and helps people to follow what is said. Before ending the discussion ,the teacher might summarize any meta themes in what was said by referring back to the list of themes.

_____ *Display enthusiasm, responsiveness, and a genuine interest* in what is said. Enthusiasm is contagious.

_____ *If a misunderstanding occurs when two people speak on an issue, first make sure that you clarify what each is trying to say* before offering ideas and suggestions for resolving the disagreement. Consider asking other students what they might suggest as a solution.

_____ *Discourage students who try to monopolize conversations* by avoiding eye contact with them, asking others what they think, or by asking how others react to what was said.

_____ *Discourage class members from being judgmental or attacking* the person who is making a point. Have them critique the idea and not the personality of the individual stating an opinion.

_____ *Watch any tendencies on your part to be judgmental, to use punishing remarks, sarcasm, inappropriate humor, or to monopolize the discussion.*

_____ *Avoid the use of terminal statements permitting no disagreement with you.* "For example, try not to say, "That's fine, let's move on." Or, "I'd like you to think of it this way."

_____ *If the discussion turns heated, overly controversial, and is getting out of control [i.e., people are speaking without listening to what is said], stop the discussion.* Ask class members to write a brief response. Have them pair up with a partner to discuss each other's point of view. Then let individuals respond but place a time limit on responding [e.g., 30-60 seconds].

Enhancing the Quality of Writing Assignments

Based upon her study, Walvoord suggests several things that can enhance the quality of writing assignments and make them a better learning experience for students. They include:

Less is More

It is better to assign fewer papers and to have students work on those in more detail than to try to do too many. Most students do not have well developed writing skills and requirements to write papers overwhelm them. Similarly, assigning a shorter, focused term paper would be better than having them try to complete a broader and longer writing assignment.

Require Outlines and Drafts

The outline can be topical, a tree outline, or presented in another form [e.g., as a concept map, diagram]. While the outline might mimic the organization of the paper, it is not necessary that it does so in all respects. Most writers find that an outline is a beginning. It represents a place to start from and is not a blueprint to follow rigidly. Yet, the outline should contain enough information to help you detect whether students are focusing on important ideas in the topic. A first draft helps to determine if the elements that were identified in the outline are organized and structured in a readable manner.

Give Specific Feedback

Avoid saying that's *good, nice job, good organization,* and other global statements. Look for specific things to say that illustrate the good and bad points about the paper. Ask yourself, "Could the student use this comment to improve some aspect of this paper."

Have One or More Model Assignments Available for Students to Consult

Good models are papers written by people who have taken the course in the past. An alternative, is to select samples of what people are turning in, block out their names, and photocopy it so that others in class can see how some students are managing the task.

Tutorials

As normally practiced, the teacher meets with students individually or in small groups for a seminar. The topics chosen for study are either assigned by the teacher or jointly agreed upon by the instructor and students. The amount of faculty opinion and guidance and the amount of faculty-student interaction varies, depending upon the needs of the particular faculty member and students involved. Usually, the Expert/Formal Authority style is very much a part of the teaching style employed. The instructor typically shares ideas but also spends time helping students to sharpen their thinking on an issue. Students are usually required to complete an integrative writing or research project as part of the tutorial.

problem will work if your class is about to try the same thing. As noted in Chapter 1, most students possess an extraverted and sensing cognitive style. Such individuals appreciate "here and now" examples much more than they do those that are "there and then."

I have found it helpful to have an informal panel of undergraduate majors who screen anecdotes and examples of points for me. Those that receive "two thumbs up" are retained and the others are dropped by the wayside. The students in my informal panel also suggest ideas to illustrate issues I will raise in class.

Modeling by Direct Example

In class, a laboratory setting, or when supervising a student, the teacher engages in the thought processes and/or skills the student is expected to learn. The teacher shows students how to do something. This might be how to solve a problem, set up a laboratory experiment, or how to finger the strings on a violin. Another common way teachers model by direct example is to "think aloud" for students while solving a problem or performing some skill. In effect, the steps needed to solve the problem or to use the skill is performed while the teacher labels and talks about what he or she is doing. I sometimes call the latter process the "television chef" mode of teaching. This refers to how chefs show how to cook something on television. They show but they also talk the viewer through the important things they are doing.

Much of the learning that occurs through direct example arises through observation and through private reflection about the model's actions. Some of what is learned also can be very deliberate and subject to interventions by the teacher. One area is when demonstrations of various ways to apply the content, to complete tasks, or to use skills and techniques are provided.

Enhancing the Effectiveness of Role Modeling

Students Must Possess the Necessary Prior Knowledge and Experience

While almost anyone can gain something from watching almost anything, learning is maximized when students are properly prepared for observing. Thus, readings, presentations, and other experiences that describe what will be modeled improve the chances of retaining what is observed.

Motivation, Enhancing Attention and Retention, and Testing Learning Must Occur

These are critical components of role modeling that enhance its effectiveness [Bandura, 1986]. Table 6-7 outlines the components of each of these factors.

Table 6-7
Critical Components Of Role Modeling

Motivation
When observing a model, motivation is strengthened when there is a *clear and immediate need* for applying the content or using a skill, the *benefits* are clearly stated, and words of *encouragement* are offered.

Attention
Increases if an overview of what the teacher will do and the reasons why particular steps will be employed is given. This does not need to be overly detailed but it establishes a perceptual set for what the student needs to watch. Thus an overview of what the student will see and a few statements such as, "Pay particular attention to.... or, When I begin to, please notice...." will focus the learners attention on relevant issues and skills.

Retention
Enhanced when the teacher insures that skills and tasks to be modeled are well *organized*. This includes having all materials, equipment, and any other personnel available. *Teachers help retention when they label important parts of what they do, call attention to relevant discriminations, and summarize their previous steps before beginning something new.* Whenever possible, good role models organize their actions so that the least difficult aspects are shown first before the more difficult parts.

Testing
Observations of a model should be followed whenever possible by allowing students to perform *what was observed. Such practice works best when it occurs as soon as possible after watching the model.*

Observations of a Model Should be Active and Not Passive

Teachers should encourage students to take notes and to ask questions. However, because questions are disruptive and break the flow during a demonstration of a task, solving a problem, showing a procedure or skill, questions are best handled afterwards.

If the role model appears on film or videotape, periodically stopping the film or tape to highlight important parts of what was done and /or what will come next also assists with retaining what was observed.

Do Not Delay Feedback

Learning is maximized when the delay between doing something and receiving feedback is held to a minimum. It is important to remember that acquiring skills involves using external feedback (i.e., information and guidance from the individual teaching the skill) and internal feedback (i.e., self-instruction, proprioceptive cues, attention to environmental information). In particular the ability to benefit from internal feedback is severely hampered with such delays. Remembering the *feel* for doing any task lessens with time. It can, however, be relearned with additional practice.

Thus, when students are asked to model anything, it is important that the teacher observe what they did and provide feedback as soon afterwards as possible. Sometimes, students need feedback while a task is unfolding or during their attempts to use a particular skill. In such circumstances, a coaching/guiding mode of instruction is appropriate.

Coaching/Guiding Students

Examples of opportunities for coaching occur when students work a math problem on the board, they role play principles of good communication, or have to diagram on the board the steps taken to solve a formal logic problem. In the laboratory, coaching/guiding might occur when students try to use an unfamiliar piece of laboratory equipment, try new procedures for doing an experiment, or they struggle with following standard procedures for completing an experiment. In one on one supervision, coaching might occur when a faculty member works alongside of a student nurse when she sets up an IV or gives an injection. Or, the teacher helps a violinist place his or her fingers in the proper location along the frets of the instrument.

Teachers should adopt a coaching mode of instruction to help correct deficiencies in students' skills [e.g., laboratory, artistic, sports, discipline specific skills] as well as with their ability to complete certain types of tasks [e.g., working problems, writing papers, interpreting charts and data tables, carrying out a research project, analyzing data]. If time or circumstances do not allow this to occur, students can verbally reconstruct what they plan to do. The teacher can then ask questions to check their understanding.

And whenever possible, the old adage" see one, do one, and teach one" should be applied to testing the learning that occurred from observing others. Thus, students who have benefited from observing a model and/or coaching can teach a peer how to do what they have learned. "To teach is to learn twice" and thus students are engaged in an active learning activity when helping peers to learn.

Several components of effective coaching are summarized in Table 6-8.

Table 6-8
A Summary of the Elements of Effective Coaching

Preview the Task or Skill
Ask the learner to verbally review the sequence and specific elements in the skill or task they want to learn.

Establish Mutual Expectations
Coaching works best if both parties understand what aspects of the task or skill need examined and where specific help is needed. Have the learner state what specific elements he or she would like to have assistance with learning. Specific target behaviors are identified that will help focus the instructor's attention on particular deficiencies. The teacher should, however, feel free to suggest other areas to examine and to make further comments if needed.

Observe Students Performing
Depending on the type of task, the skill to be used, and the competency of the student, you may want to be physically present or to observe through a television monitor or two-way mirror what is being done.

Become an Encouraging Person
Say positive things about what the person is doing and remind him or her that additional practice will make them more proficient.

Give Appropriate Feedback
Feedback is best when provided after a task or skill is completed. It should focus on the specific behaviors observed. Avoid generalities such as *nice job* or *you missed a couple of things early on.* Be specific about the components of the *nice job* and exactly what was missed *early on.* Furthermore, emphasize both the strengths and weaknesses of what was observed. Be sure to ask students what additional things they might want you to comment on. Try not to be evaluative when providing feedback. Focus on the person's behavior and not their personality. Finally, ask students to recount what they learned from their performance and what they need to do next time in order to improve.

Help the Student Develop a Checklist
A list of important principles and behaviors needed to perform a skill should be developed. A checklist is important because it provides guidance for the future and it allows students to develop as self-directed learners when they are just beginning to use what they learned.

Specify Next Steps
The coaching session concludes with a discussion of areas that need additional work. Whenever possible, a time and place should be set aside for a future meeting. The agenda includes additional problems that may arise and the outcomes of the student's subsequent attempts to master a task or develop particular skills.

Epilogue

Themes and Variations

Issues involved in teaching in Cluster 1 [i.e., with the Expert/Formal Authority styles] and Cluster 2 [i.e., with the Personal Model/Expert/Formal Authority blend of styles] were discussed. Cluster 1 is associated with more traditional teaching methods such as lectures, mini-lectures, teacher centered questioning and discussions, term papers, an emphasis on exams, grades, term papers, and technology based presentations. While emphasizing traditional approaches to teaching, suggestions were made for creating opportunities for active learning to occur in the context of such traditional instructional formats. Similarly, suggestions were presented in this chapter for enhancing the role modeling and the coaching/guiding modes of instruction in Cluster 2.

The important point is that the barriers to active learning and student involvement are not intrinsic to particular teaching processes. In my experience, the barriers lie elsewhere. In the context of the integrated model, *one barrier to active learning is the preferences some faculty have for maintaining a traditional status hierarchy between teachers and students.* Thus, the teacher is unwilling to give up or redirect control over classroom tasks and tends to use instructional processes that cater to a Dependent learning style. I sense that sometimes there is a certain amount of comfort in such dynamics for both students and faculty alike.

Another barrier to student involvement is that teachers are not always willing to admit that students can learn in alternate ways. They misread or discount their students' capacity to take more initiative and responsibility. Or, they don't see them progressing much beyond the blend of Dependent, Avoidant, and somewhat Competitive styles. Thus, faculty play it safe and provide a *no hassle or at least low hassle* approach to teaching content. As the discussion in the chapter showed, students can function in other modes of learning. They certainly do so outside of the classroom. The challenge is to devise strategies for teaching, including modifications of traditional modes, to bring out such capabilities. Ways of teaching within the integrated model provide ways to break the chains of tradition.

Finally, the interest of faculty in helping students acquiring foundational or core knowledge is pervasive. [Rockwood, 1994;1995]. Teacher-centered and teacher-directed learning processes target the acquisition of foundational knowledge through a foundational resource, the authority of the teacher. Students need this content to function in a discipline and college faculty control both the processes for obtaining it and the product students produce. This product is either right or wrong with the standard for judgment residing in the teacher. *A majority of faculty teach as if the hierarchy and authority needed for teaching foundational knowledge only can come from traditional methods.* As one professor said, "Using small groups and active learning activities take time away from getting students the content they need."

Yet, there are other options. One is to integrate into traditional methods several of the methods discussed in this chapter such as questioning strategies and mini-lectures with trigger stimuli. Not only do they help with the process of teaching foundational knowledge, but they pay dividends in terms of student retention, attention to task, motivation, and developing critical thinking capacities. Another option is to use the cooperative learning strategies in Cluster 3 to teach foundational knowledge [cf.,Rockwood, 1995]. The instructor maintains control over the process and the content covered. But, instruction occurs both through group interaction as well as the faculty member's comments, questions, and points of clarification.

Finally, knowledge may also reside in the outcome of a group's deliberation. This is sometimes referred to as collaborative learning. Here, there is a recognition that knowledge is a social construct and learning a social process, [Bruffee, 1993]. Learning from this perspective is much more of an ongoing process than a particular outcome that is produced by someone at a given point in time. *Students are not just receivers of knowledge orchestrated by an outside authority but they also produce it through group interaction.* The methods of Cluster 4 in the integrated model begin to move students in this direction.

The discussion in Chapters 7 and 8 provide specific links between the integrated model of teaching and learning style and the cooperative learning processes of Cluster 3 and the more collaborative learning processes of Cluster 4. In the process, specific suggestions for ways to engage students in each type of learning process are presented. The attempt is not to suggest that the two forms of learning are mutually exclusive. Rather, the presentation highlights elements common to each approach, how they differ, and ways for faculty members to make an orderly transition between the two types of learning.

In the final analysis, we are not talking about two fundamentally different types of learning. Rather, the differences between cooperative and collaborative learning reflect the nature of the encounter between students and teachers in particular whether or not the instructor's presence is a dominant part of the interaction. Both types of learning also demand that teachers have good interpersonal skills and that they understand group dynamics. Variations begin to occur in Cluster 4 where teachers behave more like consultants and resource people to students. This means that faculty members must use more of the facilitative and delegative side of themselves. In the process, students begin to have the independent and collaborative sides of themselves strengthened.

7. Developing Consultant, Resource Person, Active Listening, and Group Process Skills

> It is attention to the particulars that brings any craft or art to a high degree of development.
>
> - Kenneth Eble

Important Skills for Teaching in Clusters 3 and 4

The teaching processes described for Clusters 3 and 4 described in Table 4-3 and 6-1 highlight the Facilitator and Delegator styles of teaching. Consequently, the instructional methods become more student-centered than those in Cluster 1 and they emphasize small group learning processes as well as opportunities for independent work and study. To teach effectively in Clusters 3 and 4, teachers will need to do three things.

- Organize class sessions and course activities and tasks around a variety of student-centered instructional processes.

- Consult with students individually or in small groups as they prepare to participate in classroom activities and tasks [e.g., getting material together for a debate, developing questions for a learning pairs' activity].

- Work with students who are engaged in independent study processes such as research projects, position papers, guided readings.

Thus, the skills instructors need to operate effectively in Clusters 3 and 4 go beyond those needed for a presentation or to lead a traditional classroom discussion. Instructors also will have to use their skills as consultants, resource persons, and active listeners. And when small group leaning processes are used, teachers also will need to understand how groups function and how to make them function more effectively. Consequently, a working knowledge of group process skills also is needed in order to teach effectively in Clusters 3 and 4.

The ideas that follow in this chapter can be helpful in developing and employing the skills mentioned above. The critical components of each skill are identified and suggestions for effectively using them are made. As with any set of skills, they must be practiced in order to be effective. In particular, examining the strengths and weaknesses of our attempts to do so should become a regular part of our working with students in the facilitative and delegative modes of teaching.

Consultant

The teaching methods of Cluster 3 and 4 create opportunities for students to work autonomously in small groups or independently on course activities and projects. Normally students will develop questions about their work, problems in completing assignments will occur, and they will need additional guidance. Thus, the teacher will need to meet individually or with small groups of students to discuss such concerns and to consult with them on appropriate courses of action.

As consultants, teachers may provide specific advice and directions in response to student questions or concerns about classroom tasks, activities, and projects. It is also important, however, to sometimes put aside tendencies to give explicit directions in the interests of developing self-directed learners.

Good consultants know how to balance the directive and nondirective aspects of the role. Of the two, becoming more nondirective in working with students is the most difficult thing for faculty to do. This derives from the anxiety inherent in breaking old patterns of teacher-student interactions, impatience, or from situational constraints. Too often, when confronted by a student's question or problem, a natural and overlearned tendency to express what one thinks emerges. This tendency is magnified when instructors and/or students are pressed for time, when difficult questions and problems must be handled, or when emotional issues are involved.

Teachers should consider the following guidelines when assuming a consultative role:

- *Allow students to speak freely about a question or problem and to identify what they perceive as the major components of the issue before interjecting ideas.* Of course it is permissible to listen and to request elaboration or the use of clarifying questions when a student presents a question or problem. Students often feel at ease if a faculty member acknowledges that there are several ways to view most situations and that sometimes there is no simple solution.

- *Listen and take the time to get inside the frame of reference of the student.* Explore why they are concerned or confused about some issue. Ask questions and summarize your understanding of how they see things to show that you are aware of their point of view. Ask students to correct any misunderstanding you may have. Only then, can advice be given or options suggested with some assurance that it is heard and accepted.

- *Whenever possible, ask students how they might answer the question or solve the problem if you were not available.* Explore what options they would consider and how they might tackle the problem if left alone. Reinforce those things they would do that you believe would be helpful. Gently explain why some answers or approaches might be ill advised. The goal is to help students develop their capacity to think for themselves.

- *Suggest options and give information so that students can make an informed choice.* Choosing from options encourages the development of independent thinking and allows in some cases for students to develop creative alternatives to issues. It also motivates them to pursue a particular course of action since they now have a vested interest in the outcome.

Resource Person

This is most effective when a faculty member does not possess the information or skill needed and/or where exploring other resources would enhance the knowledge base of a student. Sometimes students need to know that various journals, books, reference materials, computer databases, and other types of information are available. They also may benefit from meeting with others knowledgeable about the issue they wish to explore. Such referrals also teach students what resources are available for them to consult in the future. This latter point becomes important for helping them develop skills in relearning what they once knew.

Teachers can help students gain as much as possible from a resource person by doing the following things:

- *Define the specific reasons* for the student consulting a particular resource. Let them know what you believe they can discover.

  Examples:
  The Citation Index will help you to identify where this researcher has been cited in the literature.

  Professor Davis did his dissertation on William Faulkner's work and he can recommend readings that will help you.

- *Suggest specific issues to resolve through the consultation or the information the student should obtain.*

  Examples:
  You will be able to determine not only where the researcher has been cited but which articles she has written that have been used by others in the area.

  Professor Davis can suggest authors who have studied Faulkner's ability to deal with the impact of unexpected events in peoples' lives.

- *State how the resource will help in solving the immediate problem as well as expanding the student's base of knowledge.*

  Examples:
  The Citation Index will give you the list of articles the author has written on this topic that others considered important. The reference sections of those articles also will contain citations to other authors in the area.

  I'm sure that Professor Davis will have ideas to help you develop your paper. I'm also sure that you will gain a broader understanding of Faulkner from the readings he suggests.

- *Provide a vehicle for students to use the information* once acquired. Three possibilities include a follow-up session with the instructor, a written document, or providing a forum for the information to be shared with other students are three possibilities.

- *Remind the student that prior preparation enhances the benefits* to be obtained from the resource. For example, when another expert is contacted, a student should be reminded to outline mentally or in writing what is or is not understood, to have a specific set of questions in mind, and to take written notes of what was said.

- *Insure that people you send students to have no objection to meeting with them.* A courtesy call in advance is often helpful and in my experience appreciated. Try not to overuse any one person as a resource. I have also found it helpful to tell colleagues and others that they can refer students and others to me if they need a resource person for a particular topic.

Active Listening

When consulting with students or acting as a resource person, listening to what they are saying is an important skill. Unfortunately, two things get in the way of using this skill effectively. *In the rush to be helpful, some faculty begin to formulate a response as students are talking about a problem or issue with a project.* At times, students experience anxiety, stress, and tension when trying to complete course activities. This is particularly true when the course design deviates from traditional practices. *Because no one likes to admit that their course design could cause discomfort, a tendency to ignore or discount such feelings occurs.* It would be better for building relationships with students to acknowledge the emotional issues inherent in what students are saying. Assume that what they are saying is true and then talk to them about what the underlying issues are all about.

Active listening helps us to focus our attention on what is said and to understand not only the content but any emotional components as well.

Sometimes the process is described as *listening with our third ear.* Recently a student told a colleague that "I'm not sure I can complete this research project." My friend's response was to offer advice immediately on what the other students were doing to insure a successful outcome. It would have been better for him to have acknowledged the student's frustration and anxiety first and to ask what was making her anxious before trying to give advice. As it turned out, her mother was very ill and she was preoccupied with her mother's health and thus unable to concentrate on projects at school. She knew what to do but was simply unable to concentrate on the task at hand.

There are five skills that are helpful here. They are summarizing and validating information, paraphrasing, reflecting feelings, and asking questions that foster clarity and understanding. Let us examine each in more detail.

Summarizing

The teacher condenses what was said in the same words the student uses to describe a problem they are having with a project. It is particularly useful when a great deal of information was provided. The *focus in summarizing is on the content of the conversation.*

> *Example:*
> Let's see if I understand the points you have just made about your research for your paper on Easter Island. Captain James Cook's brief visit in 1774, as well as the work of others, suggested that the inhabitants of Easter Island were unaware that other people existed. No trace of the islanders having any outside contacts has been found and they had canoes that were very frail. The problem you identified is that people claimed their ancestors visited a reef 260 miles away but the inhabitants did not have boats that were capable of making the trip.

Validation

Sometimes a student suggests that several ways of dealing with a problem or issue are possible. Under such conditions, it helps not only to summarize but to validate what was said. Validating means that you can see things from other points of view. Validating does not mean that you agree with the other perspectives, it only shows that you understand what they are. *Of course, validating is not employed if blatantly incorrect solutions or points of view are offered by a student.*

> *Example:*
> I can see from the references you cite that algae can grow and multiply in the pack ice in Antarctica. I find that interesting because if it's correct it suggests that pack ice might be part of a complex ecosystem.

Paraphrasing

This is a way of checking with another person to insure that the underlying thoughts and feelings are understood as they were intended. *When teachers paraphrase effectively, the ideas and feelings of students are put into their own words.* Paraphrasing involves listening to a deeper level than does summarizing and is especially useful when emotional concerns must be acknowledged. Thus, the accuracy of content and the emotional tone of what was said can be immediately checked.

Example:
Student: I'm totally bent out of shape trying to get this project completed. Sometimes I feel like I'm spinning my wheels. I take two steps forward and one backwards almost everyday. There has got to be a better way to do things.

Faculty member: You sound frustrated and disappointed that you are not making progress on this project and you don't know how to proceed.

Reflection of Feelings

Here, a teacher periodically verbalizes the student's feelings when positive or negative emotions are present in a conversation. Remember that by "reflecting another person's feelings" and avoiding getting "hooked" by negative feelings, a teacher can clear the air so that productive conversations continue. One way to accomplish the latter goal is to reflect feelings and then move the conversation forward by asking a question or suggesting a next step. The key is to keep the conversation focused on the task.

Examples:
Student: "This article is really good. It shows that molecules called cadherins seem to work like a zipper in holding adjoining cells together."

Teacher: "You sound pleased with the information. How are you planning to integrate it in your presentation?

Student: "The twenty minutes you gave me to present in class is really starting to bother me."

Teacher: "You sound frustrated. What do you see as the problem?"

Asking Questions to Foster Understanding

It is often difficult to follow everything someone is saying or to understand it completely the fist time. Periodically stop and ask a question if you are not following the conversation. Sometimes it also helps to probe for more information with a question. I find that people who share information often

Table 7-2
Processing How Students Work in Groups

One of the easiest aspects of group process to observe is what people say and do contributes that contributes to group functioning. Answer the following questions, and then share your responses with other members of your group. Complete *each question using the most recent time your group met as a frame of reference.*

Group Task Functions

These behaviors enable your group to confront and work through the problems, decisions, and issues before them.

- Who attempted to clarify the purpose of the task? How was this done?
- Who asked for or made suggestions on the best way to proceed? What did they say and how did others respond?
- Who gave or asked for facts, ideas, opinions, feelings, or alternatives? Give examples to support your observations.

  Who initiated a discussion or suggested alternative ways the group could accomplish its task or stay on target? What did they say or do that was particularly helpful?
- Who attempted to summarize what was said? How often did this occur and when during the group's meeting did this happen?

Group Maintenance Functions

Some behaviors help to promote effective working relationships and help your group to communicate well and to deal with interpersonal issues.

- Who helped others get into the discussion? How did they do this?
- Who attempted to reconcile disagreements or to look for common elements in conflicts? What did they say or do?
- Who commented on how the group was working together and tried to get people to examine the effectiveness of what they were doing? What did they say or do?
- How did the group test for a consensus of opinion? Was everyone involved or did only a few people participate?
- Who tried to get people to compromise or to mesh two or more ideas that were on the table?
- How were the feelings of individuals in the group acknowledged? Who did this and how did they do it?
- How were individual contributions to the group's discussion acknowledged?
- Did anyone say they appreciated the ideas or contributions of other members of the group? What was said?

* Continued on next page

Table 7-2 [Continued]

Communication and Interpersonal Skills

Examines other aspects of the interpersonal communication and interaction styles of group members that contribute to group functioning.

- Who seemed to talk the most and for how long did they talk? Was this helpful to the discussion or the work the group was doing, or did it leave some people out?
- Did people interrupt one another frequently?
- Did certain individuals carry on conversations with one another and ignore other members of the group?
- Do certain people do more than their fair share of the work in the group? If yes, why does this seem to be happening?
- What style of communication was used [e.g., assertions, questions, tone of voice, gestures, demands, probing, inquisitive, opinions, statements of fact, other].
- How did the style of communication facilitate and hinder the ability of the group to discuss issues and/or to work together on a task?
- What could you or members of your group do to work better together the next time you meet?

* Information in this table is based upon information presented in Grasha [1987a]; Toppins [1989]; and Mouton and Blake [1986]

Have Students Process How They Work Together

If the students are working or discussing issues in small groups, have them periodically set twenty to thirty minutes aside to talk about what they liked and disliked about a discussion or work session. This is particularly helpful to a group that will continue to interact over time. Talking about "how we worked together inside and outside class" may identify areas where improvements can be made. The form shown in Table 7-2 can be used by the group to facilitate such discussions

The items in Table 7-2 are first completed in writing by each member of the group. Then their reactions are discussed. The first two to three times this procedure is tried, one of the groups might do this in a fishbowl setting with the instructor leading the discussion. The target group and the instructor sit so that other members of the class can observe. This helps to break the ice, models the task, and allows people to ask questions about the process.

While the groups process their answers, the instructor should rotate between groups, sit on the outside, and listen. Rather than intervene if the group needs help, students should be encouraged to work out the problem for themselves.

The teacher would record the general issues that emerged in how people worked together.. At an appropriate time during that session or in the next one. The factors that hinder and facilitate group work could be posted on the board. For those issues that get in the way, the class suggests solutions and the teacher also offers advice.

Become Sensitive to Student Needs for Inclusion, Control, and Affection.

In the classroom, inclusion needs appear in a student's preferences for interacting and associating with others. The need to influence the ideas, opinions, and actions of other members of the class suggests the need for control. Affection needs reflect a person's desires to be appreciated and recognized by other members of the class [Schutz, 1982]. Satisfying these needs is very important for how groups work together.

Course designs that emphasize opportunities for students to interact, state their opinions, comment on one another's ideas, and participate in planning course activities stand the best chance of meeting such needs. The design alone, however, will not necessarily allow students to have such needs satisfied. They will have to take some initiative along these lines in order to avoid feeling frustrated or dissatisfied with what is happening in class. To *insure a successful outcome in meeting such needs for themselves and others, students should be reminded to do the following [Grasha, 1987a]:*

- *Inclusion*
  Speak up and make sure that your ideas are known to the group. Try to draw others into a discussion particularly those individuals who are shy, silent, or withdrawn.

- *Control*
  Request responsibility for carrying out group decisions. Suggest that other people become involved in implementing group ideas and decisions. Consider rotating the responsibility for leading a discussion or running a meeting. Make sure that an agenda for a meeting on a group project reflects the needs of everyone present.

- *Affection*
  Let people know that you appreciate their ideas. Support ideas that you consider attractive instead of sitting back and waiting for others to do so. Ask others if they appreciate your efforts in the group. This might be done humorously, but the message is, "We need to show our appreciation for each other more."

Give Students a Checklist for How to Organize Their Team Meetings

A copy of a checklist for organizing team meetings appears in Table 7-3. The items in the checklist have been shown to lead to productive meetings of work groups [cf., Grasha, 1987a] Students should review it before meeting to insure that important issues in organizing and running a meeting are taken into account. Another use of this checklist is to use it to process how well the group worked together. Each item would be examined by the group to identify things that need to be attended to before the group meets again.

Remind Students of Common Pitfalls in Group Work

James Davis [1993] suggests that the tendency for the following four issues to arise must be kept in mind. Each issue and several of my experiences with them are discussed below. As you read, think about how you have encountered each issue in your experiences with classroom groups.

1.] *Individuals do not always work as hard in groups as they do by themselves.* This is called *social loafing* and is prevalent when it is not possible to distinguish the individual's contribution to the group output. Thus, it is important for groups to insure that everyone participates in a discussion and that everyone has a clearly defined role and task to complete on group projects.

2.] *Groups sometimes can be unwieldy, inefficient, and slow.* Groups tend to deal with three meta issues when working on a task. They include the quality of the decisions or output, the acceptance of any decisions among members of the group, and the time it takes to complete a task. Thus, when a discussion group rushes to finish a task, the quality and acceptance is likely to be low. Similarly, when groups strive for high quality decisions and maximum acceptance, it takes more time.

Most teachers want a quality product in which everyone participated. Many students because of their lack of experience working in groups and other pressures can't wait to complete a task. Thus, teachers need to make sure that students stay on task, that haphazard or incomplete work is not acceptable, and that students are reminded that quality work takes time.

3.] *Groups are susceptible to "groupthink."* This is a tendency to push members to think alike, to ignore or discount alternative points of view, to believe that they are invulnerable to making a bad decision, to put down or chastise those who criticize the "will of the majority," to look at others in stereotypic ways,

Table 7-3
A Checklist of Helpful Behaviors for Classroom Work Groups

Goals

Make sure that your group's meeting has clear and specific goals. Do you want to share information, solve problems, make decisions, or gather additional information or additional facts on an issue. One or more of these goals could form the basis for a meeting.

Translate the goals into a set of specific agenda items. Set your agenda with the latter goals in mind and coordinate each goal with a specific agenda item [*Discuss* additional information needed to complete the task. *Decide* who is going to get that information.

Establish priorities for your agenda: A common problem with most meeting is that try to accomplish too much. With an agenda— less is more. Keep it short and rank order the items in terms of their importance for the group.

Establish time limits for each item on the agenda: Increase them only if group members agree.

Norms

Begin on time and end on time. People tend to feel as if the work of the group was accomplished efficiently when this is done.

Socialize before or after a meeting but not during it. Set time aside before or afterwards to meet what is an important need that people have.

Follow your agenda. Keep people from sidetracking the agenda by agreeing to discuss it if time remains at the end of the meeting or as part of your next one.

Have any decisions bound to key actors, deadlines, and next steps. Do not let decisions hang as if they will magically be implemented. Make sure everyone knows who is responsible, a time frame for implementing is established, and next steps are specified.

Put an evaluation of the time you spent together on the agenda. Take a few minutes at the end of your meeting to discuss what made it go well and what hindered discussions. Or, make such a discussion the agenda for your next group meeting.

• Continued on next page

Table 7-3 [Continued]

Working Together
All members of the group should take initiative and responsibility to: *Insure that someone will keep track of the time* spent on each agenda item. *Have someone appointed to record important points.* This is often best done on newsprint, a blackboard, or overhead where everyone can see what was said. *Make it clear who is in charge of running the meeting* and who is responsible for leading the discussion of each agenda item. *Speak for yourself.* Tell people what you think and feel and avoid saying "we think or feel, or everyone thinks." *Take responsibility to ask questions, to clarify what is said, and to periodically summarize issues* and points that have been raised. *Request facts, seek relevant information, and ask for suggestions or ideas* to keep a conversation moving along. *Explore differences* and try to find a mutually agreeable solution. *Make sure as many people as possible* have a chance to speak. *Recognize the contributions that people are making* to the group's work. *Express individual and group feelings.* Members emotional feelings regarding issues and each other influence discussions. They must be expressed to clear the air and to promote further dialogue.

* Based on information in Grasha [1987a]

and to ignore or discount criticism of the group's work or the product it produces. Essentially groups come to believe: "There is only one way to do things—our way." "You are either with us or against us." "We can do no wrong here."

Groupthink has been implicated in a variety of blunders including the Bay of Pigs invasion and the space-shuttle Challenger disaster. Yet, it also affects groups working on almost any task where there is pressure to finish a task in a relatively short amount of time. *Some of the normal checks and balances groups use to monitor their activities are put aside in the interests of being efficient.* All groups need to be reminded of this phenomenon and the problems it can create.

4.] *Groups are susceptible to the risky-shift phenomenon.*
Sometimes, groups tend to gamble more than individual
members would if each were making the decision alone.
Thus, a group might be more willing to bet on a "long-shot"
in a horse race than would individual members. One of the
underlying causes is a diffusion of responsibility. It is not clear
who is in charge of the outcome so no one is.

The "risky-shift" occurs because it is much more difficult
to blame any one member for what the group accomplishes.
To counteract this tendency, students working on projects
should have specific roles and responsibilities. Thus, when
some aspect of the group's task is clearly someone's
responsibility, individuals become accountable for what
they do as well as for the group's product.

In my experience, the "risky-shift" occurs in classroom
groups when they take an extreme position on an issue, try
to do more with a project than they have time available, or
propose a course project that is potentially dangerous. In a
social psychology research methods class, I once had a
research team propose to stage a mock gun battle in
downtown Cincinnati complete with blanks and ketchup.
They wanted to see how bystanders reacted. Having some
authority such as the teacher comment on the wisdom of
their choices also inhibits the "risky-shift" in class. Thus,
the work of students in groups must be closely monitored
to counter this tendency and the other issues mentioned in
this section.

Reminding students that the four problems mentioned above
occur and negative influence they might have on the group's
work is important. To sensitize students to them, it is helpful
to ask groups to periodically focus the processing of how
they worked together on each of these issues. Thus, the agenda
for examining their work includes the extent to which each
tendency was present or absent.

Epilogue

Themes and Variations

The teaching processes of Clusters 3 and 4 in the integrated model emphasize elements of independent and collaborative learning. To use such processes effectively, teachers must be able to listen carefully to what students are saying. Both the content and the emotional tone of their messages must be acknowledged. Thus, a capacity for active listening is needed. Furthermore, to encourage students to develop as self-directed learners, faculty members must assume the roles of consultants and resource persons. And because collaborative activities are an important part of teaching with the Facilitator and Delegator styles, a working knowledge of group process skills is needed. Taking the time to familiarize oneself with and to develop all of the skills mentioned above is a prerequisite for teaching in Clusters 3 and 4.

In my experience, the lack of familiarity with the skills covered in this chapter are a major source of dissatisfaction among faculty wanting to use the teaching processes in Clusters 3 and 4. Paradoxically, I have not found instructors lining up to acquire such skills. As one person recently told me, "I just can't seem to do group work well in class. For some reason it does not come together for me." When I then suggested that he learn to become more proficient in using several group process skills he replied, "I suppose that would help but I'm not sure I want to spend the time doing that."

I suspect that there is still a large amounts of skepticism about using collaborative and cooperative learning processes. An emphasis on *getting the content out* dominates many discussions on alternative methodologies and some are not convinced that the use of groups will allow sufficient content to be taught. This is part of the unwillingness to learn how to do such things well.

One suggestion I have made for those who are initially skeptical and resistant is to try an experiment. *Commit to an appropriate Cluster 3 or 4 strategy for only one class session and assess what happens.* Ask students for feedback and suggestions for how to make it work better in the future if it were ever used again. To think of this as an experiment takes the pressure off of trying to integrate something into an entire course. That may come later if the experiment works out. For the moment, the task is to simply have a little taste of a group task with no commitment to doing more.

For those who are convinced, however, the teaching methods of Clusters 3 and 4 cannot be engaged unless sufficient attention is given to the issues raised in this chapter. The teaching strategies are not simply devices for assigning students tasks to work on with others. The interpersonal as well as the group dynamics issues of doing so cannot be ignored. To think otherwise is to invite frustration and disappointment when using such methods.

8. Managing the Facilitator and Delegator Styles of Teaching

> I have tried to indicate that if we are to have citizens who can live constructively in this kaleidoscopically changing world, we can only have them if we are willing for them to become self-starting, self-initiating learners.
>
> - Carl Rogers

Teaching in Clusters 3 and 4

The teaching processes for Clusters 3 and 4 of the integrated model highlight the Facilitator and Delegator styles of teaching [cf., Table 6-1 in Chapter 6]. These teaching styles and corresponding processes of instruction encourage and reinforce collaborative, independent, and participant learning styles. The demands placed upon students will be different than most of them are used to experiencing in classes taught in a more traditional manner. This will present a challenge to some learners while others are likely to become anxious. This latter group will find that the ground-rules for learning have changed and may not know how to deal with the situation. *Thus, they will need additional support and encouragement from the teacher.*

When students first encounter the instructional processes of Clusters 3 and 4, they often need time to discuss their concerns about new ways of learning and they often need encouragement and support from they teacher. Perhaps the most important thing they need is to feel successful learning in this way. *Thus, it is also helpful if instructors structure early activities so that everyone can have several success experiences.* For example, a less complicated case study might be used or a relatively easy small group task assigned. *Finally, clear directions and instructions must be provided in writing for such tasks.* Students who are anxious about new ways of learning need the structure that written directions can provide.

The Teaching Methods of Cluster 3

Case Studies

Roland Christensen and Abby Hansen [1987] describe cases as detailed story-like accounts of incidents designed to raise important issues about the content of an area. Generally speaking, cases can be any systematic account of something that is worth studying in more detail. The case material in effect becomes a "trigger" for helping students to analyze and synthesize information, apply concepts and principles in a course, solve problems and make decisions, and generally to identify and examine broader implications of the content. The characteristics of materials that make for a good case study appear in Table 8-1.

Table 8-1
Types and Attributes of Materials
Employed in Case Studies

Examples of Case Materials

- Films or videotapes on a topic
- A business plan
- Description of a marketing problem a company faced and solved
- Current research study
- Classic research study
- Narrative description of some problem or concern
- A nonfiction account of a historical or other important event
- Magazine or newspaper article
- Book dealing with a topic relevant to a course
- Instructor designed story or narrative of an issue
- Minutes of a regulatory body
- Description of a mystery or puzzle in a field.
- A story about discovery and invention in a discipline
- Television show
- Advertisement on television, radio, newspaper, or magazine
- Popular movie
- Clinical case study
- Narrative description of how a new process or procedure in a discipline was invented, developed or used.
- A series of photographs or works of art on a particular topic

Characteristics of Good Case Materials

- Engage the interest and imaginations of students
- Contain examples of and the use of content students must acquire
- Provide interesting examples of principles and concepts
- Do not have simple answers and thus are more complicated than they appear on the surface. Good case materials often contain engaging unknowns, paradoxes, and other complications.
- Can be analyzed to produce a deeper understanding of issues
- Allow for some degree of resolution of the issues raised in the case through analysis, synthesis, and the discussion of alternative paths to obtain a resolution.
- Are at an appropriate level of complexity and difficulty for the students.
- Can be partitioned into themes, parts, or issues that can be individually and jointly analyzed
- Allow engaging questions to be written about the content to help guide and direct the students attention to important issues
- Are amenable to discussion in small and large groups
- Sustain the interest of students [and the instructor] for one or more class periods

There are a number of processes used in class that help to make cases more effective [cf., Christensen and Hanson, 1987; Hutchings, 1993; Welty 1989].

- *State the general goals you want the case to accomplish and communicate these to students.* Perhaps you want them to identify certain principles and concepts in the case, apply information or skills, evaluate the implications of various concepts, or solve a problem or make a decision. *Students should be informed in advance what you hope to accomplish.*

- *Allow participants adequate time to read the case and to develop a response to your questions.* This can be done in class or outside of class if the case is very detailed and complicated. If time is available and the group is large, give them an opportunity to discuss with peers their responses before presenting them to you.

- *Require students to do a written preliminary analysis insures that people have read the case and supporting materials [i.e., textbook assignments, outside readings, other materials] and have thought about the issues involved.* In effect, students are prepared to participate. Students can take information from the class session [s] dealing with the case and do a rewrite of their analysis. The rewrite asks them to clarify points, to correct errors, and to respond to several follow-up questions that extend the analysis. When I use cases, both the initial and the final write-up of the case is graded. Typically I will assign 50 points to a case and give them up to 25 points for each part.

- *Place the responsibility for responding on the students.* Use the strategies for asking questions discussed in this and the last chapter to keep students focused on the issues. Use questions as a device to help students organize their thoughts about particular issues and to guide and direct the discussion in class.

  Always acknowledge the good points that participants make. If some response was not adequate, ask other students how they see the issue. If you respond, be careful not to put people down for their ideas. Remember that there is value in incorrect answers and misconceptions. They can help to take a discussion off in a new and productive direction.

- *Keep any content points you make short, specific, and to the point.* A case analysis should not be a springboard to launch a lecture. On the other hand, doing a few short 5 or 10 minute mini-lectures as part of the processing of a case is sometimes desirable and helpful.

- *Always provide a summary of key issues raised and any resolutions of issues that were obtained* as part of a wrap-up at the end of a session.

Cognitive Map Discussion

Cognitive mapping is based on the premise that information that is organized in a personal but appropriate scheme for an academic discipline will be learned and retained better. The cognitive maps [i.e., sometimes called concept maps, mind maps, knowledge maps] that students design to represent course material can include tree diagrams, flow charts, graphs, as well as any two or three dimensional representations of the concepts covered in the text, class sessions, outside readings, or some activity. They can be used not only to generate discussion but as a study skill to help students prepare for exams.

There are two things that must be done before students can develop a cognitive map. *They first need a list of key terms, concepts, events, and principles, or ideas from the sources described above.* Students might develop the list and/ or the instructor might suggest terms, concepts, and principles that should be included. The number of terms, concepts, events, or principles ought to be broad enough to cover the major issues under study.

Next, students integrate and organize the items into a scheme that helps them to understand the connections among discrete parts of the information. Thus, their map should suggest categories for organizing concepts. The connections among ideas within a category and across categories should be clearly evident in the map. Such connections illustrate the way concepts are associated as well as the interrelationships and interactions among the diverse elements in a course. This can be done in a somewhat informal manner as illustrated in Figures 8-1 and 8-2. Or, the connections among elements in the map can be given descriptive labels as shown in Figure 8-3.

Discussing Cognitive Maps in Class

- *Students bring their cognitive schemes to class and are asked to form small groups of three.* Each member of the group is given approximately five minutes to present the way they mapped the material.

- *Next the teacher asks group members to challenge each other and to see how complete their maps are.* This is initially done by having the students in each group select 2-3 concepts they had on their maps that were not included on the schemes their partners developed. In turn, they question each other on how each concept could be included. The goal here is not simply to have each student say, "How would this item fit into your map?" Rather, the goal is to have group members help each other clarify how concepts might fit into the different perspectives represented in the map.

- *A second round of challenges has the instructor select issues and concepts related to the material the teacher believes is important.* The students in each group then discuss how that information currently is or could be included in their cognitive maps. Again, the goal is to have group members help each other find ways to integrate course concepts.

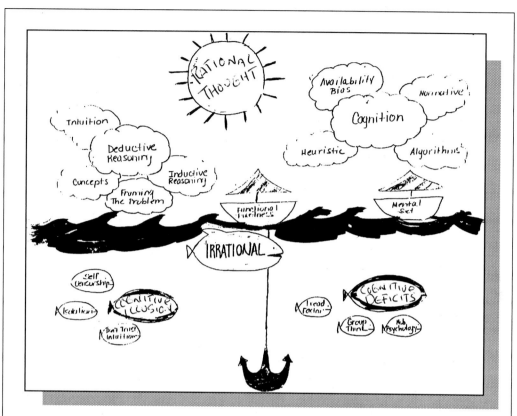

Figure 8-1: A map of problem solving and decision making issues.

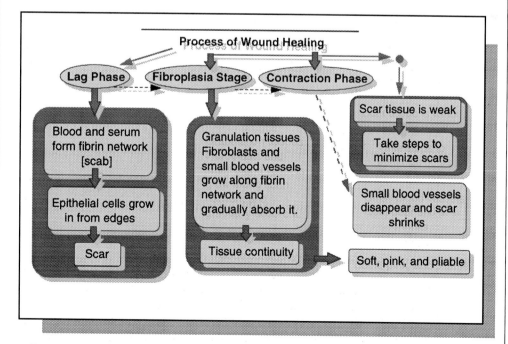

Figure 8-2: A cognitive map of concepts and principles related to wound healing.

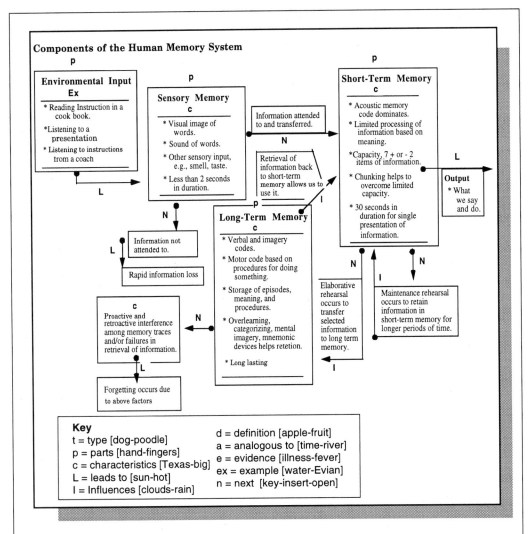

Figure 8-3: This student's map of our memory system used a procedure where each component is labeled to indicate the type of relationship that exists among the various elements. The key shown illustrates several relationships that can appear in a map.

- *A variation is to have the instructor pose a discussion question or a problem* and to have the groups try to answer it using the information in their cognitive maps or schemes.

- *While students discus their maps, the teacher monitors what is said and develops ideas for important concepts and principles that may be left out of some of the maps.* Students are instructed to take the feedback they received in the small group discussions and from the instructor and to modify their cognitive schemes.

- *The final maps are typically assigned a point value towards the final grade in the course.*

Critical Thinking Discussion

As noted in the discussion in Chapter 5, the development of critical thinking skills is an important issue in higher education. Several general suggestions for how to integrate critical thinking into our teaching were described in Self-Reflection Activity 5-3 in Chapter 5. What follows are three discussion processes that can be used to encourage critical thinking. One is based on the work of David Perkins and the second on Craig Nelson's work using the William Perry and Mary Belenky schemes for critical thinking. The third approach is two Mini-Methods for Critical Thinking that help students gain a broader perspective on issues.

Knowledge as Design

David Perkins (1986; 1987) argues that we tend to treat terms, concepts, and principles as if they existed in a vacuum, that is, divorced of a context or frame of reference. Students, for example, may be asked to learn definitions of terms or to read about facts, concepts and principles in textbooks. Some do so without exploring the larger frame of reference in which the idea is embedded. Thus a textbook presents terms such as *short-term memory*, *thermodynamics*, or *Alzheimer's disease* and a definition is conveniently provided and readily accepted by students.

Such intellectual laziness is very common. As a way out of this dilemma, David Perkins argues that any piece of knowledge, or for that matter any object or event, should be viewed as a *design, that is, as a structure that is devised to accomplish a particular purpose.* Most of us are more comfortable thinking of a car, jet plane, or a tall building as representing a design. That is, the structure or form of such objects allows certain functions to occur (e.g., a car provides transportation, a building provides office space). Ordinarily, terms, facts, concepts, principles, and math formulas are not thought of as representing a design. When they are, a comprehensive understanding of almost anything is possible.

Listed below are five questions that David Perkins suggests we ask to understand what something means. An example of how a student in one of my classes used them appears in Table 8-2.

1.] What is its purpose [s]?
   [What is this term, concept, or principle designed to accomplish?]

2.] How is it structured and organized?
   [What are its components and how do they relate to each other?]

3.] What is an example or model case of it?

4.] What statements and reasons are used to explain and/or evaluate it?

5.] How can we tell if it has achieved its purpose?

Table 8-2
Using the David Perkins' Process

The example below is a response from a student in one of my classes.

Concept: Mindlessness.

What is its purpose?
Allows us to respond to questions, requests, and demands in a routine manner or to engage in tasks without devoting a great deal of conscious attention to our response.

How is it structured and organized?
Mindless thinking occurs when we become trapped by categories, we assume a single perspective when looking at things, and when engaged in relatively routine activities.

What is an example or model case?
I picked the wrong handouts for class from a pile of papers and passed them out to students before I caught the error.

What statements and reasons are used to explain and/or evaluate it ?
Mindlessness is accompanied by low levels of self-awareness and awareness of what other people are doing. May produce problems for people by making them look silly. Also, may lead someone who makes mistakes to feel they have less control over their lives.

How do we know it has achieved its purpose?
Has achieved its purpose when we can respond to several routine requests without thinking about them or can do one task while simultaneously engaging in another.

There are several ways David Perkins' ideas can be integrated into a classroom session:

Option 1

- Have students select 5-8 terms from the textbook and/or class session that they do not understand very well. They are asked to answer the four questions for each term and to bring their written responses to class. Students are placed in small groups of two peers and they exchange their responses.

- Each person reviews what their partner wrote and indicates what was not clear or suggests another way a given question could be answered. Such comments are written in the margins of the papers.

- People rewrite their responses taking into account what their partner said and all of the material is turned into the teacher for credit.

- Option 1 is particularly helpful as part of a review of the material before an exam.

Option 2

- During a class session, periodically take time to answer each question when a particularly intriguing or difficult term or principle occurs. The class as a whole can participate while the teacher writes on the board or overhead. Or, small reaction groups can be formed to do a preliminary analysis of the term. Responses are then shared with the class.

- Listen carefully to how students answer each question so you can help them clarify what they mean and to model more appropriate ways of responding to each question.

The Perkins' process also gets students to think about the broader implications of terms, concepts, and principles. After all, students do nor normally think of terms such as *cancer, Alzheimer's disease, quarks, birds, bacteria, or helium* as having a purpose nor do they usually explain how such things have achieved their purposes. My experience with this process is that students are initially puzzled and find it an odd way of trying to look at something. After they get into it, they soon realize that it forces them to examine issues at a much deeper level.

Criterion-Based Discussions

Craig Nelson [1989;1991] suggests a process that helps to develop the capacity of students to develop what William Perry labels a relativist mode of thinking [cf., Table 5-1 in Chapter 5] An important part of learning to think in this manner is to use criteria to support a point of view. To accomplish this goal, he suggests that teachers do the following:

- On a regular basis [e.g., once every two weeks] students answer the questions shown in Table 8-3 as an outside of class activity.

- In class, students meet in small groups of 3-5 people and then share their responses to the questions.

- The students' approach to each question is then handled as part of a general class discussion. The teacher comments, probes for more information, and tries to help clarify issues.

- Students may be asked to redo their initial workup based on comments they heard in class. Both their original responses and the revised versions are turned in for credit.

Table 8-3
Classroom Critical Thinking Questions

Students do a common reading and come prepared with written answers to the following questions:

1.] What are 3-5 major points/arguments the author is making. List them in a couple of sentences.

2.] What are 2-3 criteria that our discipline uses when evaluating whether information is accurate or inaccurate?

3.] Can you think of any other criteria that might be used?

4.] Apply the criteria you listed above to each of the major points/ arguments you identified in the article. Make one of the following decisions about each major point/ argument and give a reason for your response. The decisions are: Accept, Reject, Withhold Judgment.

5.] What additional information would you need in order to convince you to either accept or reject any argument or point that you withheld judgment on?

6.] What would you have to do to obtain the information you need?

* Questions based in part on those suggested by Craig Nelson, Department of Biology, Indiana University.

My experience with the questions above and the classroom process for using them is that they generally take several sessions before students become comfortable with them. It typically takes two or three sessions before their responses dramatically improve. Of course, this represents a new way of thinking about issues and consequently it will take time for them to develop an acceptable level of proficiency with the process.

I also find it helpful to do the initial work on the first assignment in class. Students are placed in small groups to answer the questions and we talk about their responses. This gives students a better idea of what is expected and how to approach the problem. At the end of the session, I give them a complete and competently written response to this initial assignment so they also have a model of a good response.

Finally, it helps to explain to students why such activities are used in class. Some students look at almost anything that requires extra mental effort as *busy work*. Thus, I find a suggestion of Nelson's helpful. He teaches his students the basics of the William Perry/Mary Belenky scheme discussed in Chapter 5. This provides a roadmap for them to follow as they begin to learn new ways of thinking. It also puts activities for encouraging critical thinking into a conceptual base with which students can identify.

Mini-Methods for Critical Thinking

The two mini-methods for encouraging critical thinking described here are designed to provide a structure for leading students through the analysis and synthesis of issues in course content. They help students to understand how one knows something to be accurate as well how to draw conclusions based information that is given. Those presented here are variations on suggestions found in Neustadt and May [1986] and Lee [1992].

Mini-Method:
Time Line Plus

- Take some event and then ask students *"What is the story here?"* The event should clearly have a temporal sequence of incidents associated with it. Charles Lee used this process to help his class develop the story associated with the storming of the Bastille on July 14, 1789. Lee had a list of events associated with the fourteenth and fifteenth of July, 1789.

- *Next a time line is constructed.* As events are produced, lines are used to connect them temporally. Not all lines should be horizontal but rather they should branch here and there to show the interrelation among the events. In effect a flow chart of events and how they branch and connect to others is constructed.

- An alternative is first to list the events and then draw the time line.

- This strategy can be completed with the entire class. Or, small groups of students might be asked to construct such a time line. Their time lines are then shared and a composite time line is developed based on those from the smaller groups.

I have used this process to have students construct a time line of important events in their lives. They are asked to select those things that are memorable in their lives from their earliest recollections to the present. Participants are encouraged to show connections between such events or to speculate how earlier events might have influenced later ones. They then take concepts related to child, adolescent, and adult development and indicate which ones applied to each node in their time line.

A colleague teaching principles of meteorology had students in his class use it to trace the development of a tropical depression that eventually became hurricane Hugo. Elements of the weather and characteristics of the storm at critical points in time became the *events* that were plotted by students. Students had to explain what various configurations meant and how they contributed to the development of the storm.

When properly used, students gain a better understanding of the temporal relationship among factors in an event. Developing the time line also helps them to see the interdependencies among the elements.

Mini-Method:
Known-Unclear-Presumed Information Discussion

This strategy helps students to clarify what they know about an issue before more formal reading and discussion occurs.

- *Students divide a sheet of paper into three vertical columns,* labelling the left one *Known,* the middle one *Unclear,* and the right one *Presumed.*

- *They are shown a trigger stimulus and asked to fill in each column.* In one of my classes, I gave them a picture of four members of the *Guardian Angels* walking down the steps into a subway station in New York City. This is a civilian group that was organized to patrol subway stations and neighborhoods to deter crime. The picture depicted four minority group members of the Guardian Angels with *firm and stern* expressions on their faces. The individuals shown also wore the uniforms of the Guardian Angels.

  Initially students filled their *unclear column* with questions such as: "Who are these people?" "Why are they entering a subway as a group?" The *presumed column* was filled with statements such as "probably a gang looking for a victim," or "members of a militia."

- *Students then discuss their reactions in small groups with major ideas and issues identified shared with the entire class afterwards.* A group sheet is then constructed. About 5 minutes is allocated for the individual task and 8-10 minutes for the group task. Typical reactions from spokespersons of the classroom groups are posted on the board or overhead.

- *An optional mini-lecture is given to clarify points of misunderstanding or to provide a helpful elaboration on an issue.* In my class, a ten minute mini-lecture was given on the *Guardian Angels* to indicate what they have done to try and curb crime in New York City.

- *Students use information from the small and large group discussions as well as the mini-lecture to answer the questions* they initially had and to correct any misunderstandings.

- *The small groups reconvene and are then given questions designed to help them broaden their perspective and to think critically about the topic under consideration* [i.e., in this case the types of social control mechanisms societies have for keeping crime at bay]. With this topic, two questions were used: [a.] Should citizens form paramilitary groups to help deter crime? List the potential advantages and disadvantages of doing this. [b.] If such groups help to constrain criminals, what limits should be placed on their actions and how should they be regulated?

In my class, the small groups were assigned one of the two questions and were asked to develop a response within 15 minutes. A recorder was chosen to identify and catalogue the major themes in the discussion. In the time that remains in the class period, the teacher has a chance to clarify issues and to ask other reflective questions to get people in class to think about the issues involved.

Colleagues in other disciplines have used the following as *trigger stimuli.*

- Picture of George Washington Crossing the Delaware River.
- Picture of the Mai Lai massacre in Vietnam.
- Picture of Atomic bomb explosion over Hiroshima with a caption reading $E=MC^2$.
- Slaves being sold at auction.
- A short film of a suspension bridge vibrating and falling apart.
- Slide of an early painting by Picasso.
- Demonstration of a model racing car propelled by CO_2 moving across the floor.
- Results of a controversial political poll.
- An unfinished piece of poetry.
- Sexist advertisement for a brand of Gin.

Fishbowl Discussion

Select a topic for discussion. Sources of discussion topics include issues raised by the text, outside readings, a news story where course concepts could be applied, or issues that were raised in class.

- *Form an outer and inner group.* The inner group is best kept to 5 - 7 students and sits within an inner circle with other members of the class placing themselves around the inner group.

- *Have the inner group discuss the issue for eight to twelve minutes.* At the end of this period, members of the outer group are allowed to comment on the ideas presented or to ask questions to clarify what was said.

- *A variation is to leave one or two empty chairs within the inner group.* Outer group members are informed that if they have something to contribute, they should feel free to enter the inner group. Similarly those in the inner group can leave the group whenever they have nothing else to contribute.

Guided Readings

Guided readings contain many of the elements of a tutorial described later in this section. The content is dictated by what is read. Thus the general suggestions for running a tutorial apply here as well. There are, however, a number of variations in using guided readings that can provide a unique experience for students and teachers alike. *They include:*

- *Select a topic for the guided reading that you know virtually nothing about.* Find one or more students who are willing to read a book and/or several articles in this area and discuss the content with you. Here, the teacher becomes much more of a learner and the students get to see how a professional struggles trying to learn new material.

- *Select a topic that one or more students know more about than you do.* Have them select the readings and meet with them to discuss concepts and ideas. It is not unusual, for example, to have students who possess computer and other technological skills that are applicable to a discipline. They can help a teacher learn how to make translations. I have learned a lot about computer graphics, using the Internet and Worldwide Web, statistical packages for the mainframe, and designing a CD-ROM tutorial from students with such skills.

In addition, with layoffs in companies and people making mid-life career changes, students with job related skills in a variety of areas are on our campuses. A guided reading in an area can give them a chance to share what they know in the context of discussing a particular book or article. In such cases, the teacher often benefits more than the student. A colleague who taught advertising had two students who worked in the field join him in reading articles that dealt with the emerging area of advertising products on the Internet. He was not particularly computer literate but became more aware of what could be done by the end of the seminar.

- *Run a journal club.* Here the teacher and students read one scholarly article every week or two. The students take turns leading a discussion on an article each week. The instructor asks questions to help students clarify points and to examine the broader implications of issues. Student led discussions of the scholarly articles are much more effective if they are asked to highlight certain issues when they read them [e.g., research design, biases, unwarranted conclusions, evidence to support interpretations, etc.]. By varying the issues covered each week, variety and novelty is introduced into the sessions. Faculty members not only suggest issues but refer the students to sources where they can acquire needed background information on particular issues.

I find it helpful if the instructor provides a list of potential articles with a brief description of the content. At the initial meeting, students express their preferences for the readings they would find interesting. Those articles selected to be read are determined by the faculty member after taking the students preferences into account.

Key Statement Discussions

Students' reactions to exercises and application assignments are written up and turned in at the end of a class period. Their comments may include something new they observed, problems they had in applying a principle, difficulties completing an activity, or themes that appeared in the readings or class sessions that were not clear. Teachers take these comments and form a list of *key statements* [Grasha, 1995e].

A *key statement* has two parts. *Each one contains a "fact or observation about an issue or event students suggested followed by a critical thinking question.* In effect, key *statements* capture issues students raised but transform them into broader themes that have the potential for elaboration during a discussion. Essentially the instructor sorts the reactions students raised and brings about 4-6 with the highest potential for discussion back to the next class period.

Examples of key statements from several disciplines appear below:

a.] In the play *Rosencrantz and Gilderstern are Dead*, Playwright Tom Stoppard has the two characters play a game of asking each other questions. What does it suggest about the way that teachers and students ask questions in the classroom?

b.] Clouds do more than just deliver rain and snow. They also help control the flow of energy around our planet. What principles and concepts in meteorology explain how this occurs?

c.] For over 50,000 years, Neanderthals and modern humans lived side by side in the same geographical area. And for all those millennia, the two apparently had nothing to do with each other. What would keep two groups of early humans from mating and interbreeding for such a long period of time?

d.] Superconductors have the ability to conduct electricity without resistance and to do so for long periods of time after the source of electricity is removed. In one case, for as long as four years after the batteries were removed. How does this phenomenon fit with know principles of electrical flow? How does it differ from such principles?

e.] When a crowd of people watches someone who needs help [e.g., fixing a flat tire, getting someone who is bothering him or her to stop, becoming ill], that person is less likely to receive help than if fewer people are present. Why does this happen? Under what circumstances do you think it is more likely to occur? Under what circumstances do you believe it is less likely to occur?

There are several parts to setting up a discussion of *key statements.*

- *The items are listed on an overhead or a blackboard and comprise an agenda of potential discussion topics for that session.* Or, if the list is extensive enough, the topics can form an agenda of discussion issues that can be spread out over several class sessions. The key statements are then prioritized by having the class vote on each item. Those that receive the top 2-3 votes are used as discussion topics.

- *Small groups are formed.* The groups are asked to do one of the following. One is to have each group talk about the same topic for 10-20 minutes. A recorder in each group takes notes. Afterwards, the recorders share the viewpoints that were expressed in each group and other class members ask questions or offer additional points of view. Instructors also respond to issues the groups raised or add additional points of their own.

- *Time limits should be placed on each part of this process* [i.e., prioritizing items, small group discussion, recorder reports, and student and instructor comments.] Each element makes this process work and running out of time breaks the continuity of the process. It is difficult to restart a discussion in the next class period when interest and energy in a topic has dissipated.

- *An alternative is to place the class into smaller groups (three to five people) and each group receives a different key statement,* This works best if the number of key statements are held to two or three. Each small group then discusses the issue and the recorder shares the outcome with the class. The recorders from each group with a similar topic report and then the discussion is opened up to other students and the teacher to comment. Afterwards, the next topic is addressed.

- *Strict time limits should be enforced.* The goal is to have each of the higher priority items discussed and not to spend all of the class period on any one item. This version of the process generally works best in a 90 minute class session.

Kineposium

This is an excellent task for brainstorming ideas as well as getting as many people to comment on an ideas as possible. As the name implies, it is a *moving symposium* [Grasha, 1995e.

- Students are divided into several small groups (four to six members). One individual is assigned as a recorder and all of the groups discuss a common topic.

- Students meet in their small groups for 5-7 minutes to discuss the issue. At the end of this period everyone except the recorder moves clockwise to another group. The recorder then summarizes what the previous group had said and then leads a discussion with the new people to further clarify the issue.

- Changing groups about three or four times is generally sufficient to adequately discuss the information. The recorders then summarize the discussions that occurred in their groups. During this time period, it is helpful to ask each recorder only to present ideas that were not mentioned by the others.

- As the recorders speak, the instructor notes on the board or on an overhead the major themes that emerged from the discussion. Afterward, the teacher can comment, clarify points, or raise additional issues for students to think about.

Laboratory Projects

Laboratory experiences are an excellent device for teaching important discipline skills as well as critical thinking abilities. Every discipline has protocols for running laboratory activities and thus I don't want to concentrate on how to run labs here. Rather, their use as self-directed learning activities in the context of teaching a class is emphasized in this section. To the extent that students follow instructions in a laboratory manual, and use the lab instructor as a consultant, they are engaged in self-directed learning. An important issue is whether this is enough.

Ideally, students should see the relation of their discipline to other areas of human endeavor and recognize it as an interesting intellectual challenge. Unfortunately, they often view it as completing discrete steps along the way to completing a course or obtaining a degree. Traditional laboratory courses, however, reinforce this point of view. The laboratory assignments become another series of discrete steps to follow and facts to acquire. The sense of exploration and discovery in a discipline and the relationship of scholarly activity to real world concerns is often missing in such traditional approaches to laboratory instruction.

To counter this tendency Janice and Peter Conrad [1993] use student designed laboratory projects to get students involved in a discipline. In their basic Botany course, they have undergraduate students learn how to gather and evaluate information from primary literature sources, to design and evaluate experiments and to present results. Their goal is to connect laboratory events with what happens in class and to issues in the real world. The process they employ can be generalized to other disciplines.

Student designed laboratory projects contained several elements. As you read a description of those components the Conrads used on the next page, think about extensions of their ideas to your discipline.

- *In the early part of the term, students worked on designing extensions of laboratory projects the teacher initially provided.* They worked in teams of three to four people on these laboratory projects. In this case they did an exercise to assay the elongation growth of cells. The groups reviewed articles from the literature on cell growth and then designed experiments to confirm and extend the research findings.

  The task and readings were selected by the teacher. The extension to design other experiments were outcomes of small group discussions. This process began to introduce students to thinking for themselves and extending the results of one experiment to other issues.

- *Learners were encouraged to plan and carry out the experiments they designed on plant growth during the early part of the term.* They also were allowed to work on laboratory research projects at times other than designated lab time. Students met at least briefly during lab time to discuss protocols and progress on their projects. In this way those in other groups could see what was happening. Some of the questions small groups investigated included; What is the effect of acidity on growth? Will silver ions inhibit ethylene, a natural growth regulator? Do added growth regulators enhance growth?

- *Halfway through the term, students were given an open-ended assignment.* In this case, they were asked to design an original experiment using potato plants. The type of experiment they designed was left up to the discretion of each of the groups. Now they had to participate in science by observing, forming a hypothesis, and designing an experiment to test their hypothesis rather than following a laboratory protocol. They also had to seek out and read literature that was relevant to their problem.

  The students could now build on what they learned from the semi-structured nature of the project from the first half of the term. In effect, the instructors set them free during the second part of the course. The groups were now independent research teams. Some of the research questions they developed included: Is total darkness better than 16 hours of light and 8 hours of darkness? Do cytokimins stimulate growth?

The authors reported that overall students were excited about the way the laboratory experience was conducted. Most groups functioned as teams and became highly motivated, productive, and supportive of each other. Some did not and this was probably due to the instructors not paying sufficient attention to important group process issues raised earlier in this chapter. Furthermore, initially some students were anxious about having to work in groups and to *think scientifically* for themselves. The use of small groups helped those students to overcome such tendencies.

Problem Based Learning

Such approaches use case studies, problems, real world issues, and other devices to encourage inquiry on the part of students. There are a number of approaches that fit this approach. Those presented here include Group Inquiry, Guided Design, and Problem Based Tutorials.

Group Inquiry

John Clarke [1988] employs a model for group inquiry that emphasizes group discussion. His instructional strategy has five phases that can be completed in a one hour and twenty minute class session or divided over two 50 minute sessions. A variation of his model that I have found useful across disciplines is described below. The example from an American History course were suggested by Clarke and help to illustrate the basic features of the model.

Phase 1: Orientation to a Major Issue

a.] List in a prominent location the major concern that will be addressed by the group inquiry process. *Example:* Today's class will explore the foundations for the United States of America's form of government.

b.] Rephrase the overall problem into a question students can discuss. *Example:* What were the intellectual foundations of our form of government implied by the Declaration of Independence?

c.] *Activity:* Ask students to develop initial answers to the question. They can discuss their initial thoughts in small groups [10 minutes]. Obtain opinions from members of each of the groups and list important terms, principles, or concepts that are emerging from the discussion on the board or overhead [5-8 minutes].

Phase 2: Creating Tension around Ideas

a.] *Develop a thought provoking question based on the ideas that students initially generated.* This question should allow the instructor to subsequently challenge students to think about the issue at a deeper level. Example: Do you think *laws of nature, God's law,* or the *opinions of mankind* were most influential in the move towards independence?

b.] *Activity:* Have students discuss this question in their small group [10-12 minutes]. Poll the groups and obtain a summary of their responses. List important ideas on an overhead or the board [5-8 minutes].

c.] *Summarizing Learning:* Ask everyone to write a brief summary of what they have learned thus far. This is an opportunity for personal reflection. Suggest a question to guide them. *Example:* Why do you now think Jefferson wrote the Declaration of Independence? Afterwards, 2-3 volunteers are asked to share what they have learned [5 minutes].

Phase 3: Verification of Facts

a.] *Activity:* Ask students to search the text and/or their notes for factual evidence that helps clarify the concepts or problem and/or that supports their point in their summary. They should draw up a list of facts that support what has been said. Also, have them note facts that do not fit well or that contradict something that has been said in class [10-12 minutes]. *Example: Facts* that support the issue that life, liberty, and the pursuit of happiness were major issues on the minds of people of the time are listed. Other complaints that people may have had as the basis for independence are listed.

b.] *Sharing Facts:* Ask the groups to share what they think the strongest and the weakest evidence was in their analysis of the available facts. This can be done within the small groups and/or later shared with the entire class.

Phase 4: Seeking Causal Relationships/Extending the Analysis

a.] *Activity 1:* Describe in writing an issue related to the topic that focuses on the unknown, an apparent contradiction, paradox or imbedded dilemma. *Example:* Can you think of instances in which life, liberty, and the pursuit of happiness are mutually exclusive?

b.] *Activity 2:* Create a short demonstration of the problem as it actually appears or could appear in a real setting. Short films, newspaper articles, personal experiences, self-reflection activity, photos, or lab demonstrations can be used. *Example: What* would happen if Alaska published a Declaration of Independence tomorrow, proclaiming liberty?

c.] Each activity could be discussed or one of them chosen. In either case, have students discuss the issue in small groups [8-10 minutes]. Obtain the opinions from spokespersons in each of the groups [5 minutes]. Highlight on a transparency or on the board the major points that students are making.

Phase 5: Interpretation and Analysis

a.] *Activity:* Ask students to take the information they have acquired in their personal reflections, the large and small group discussions, and to suggest a solution to the original problem. Have them evaluate ways their initial point of view has changed and/ or has been affirmed by the discussion in class [8-10 minutes]. Their responses should be in writing.

b.] Afterwards, Have selected students share their ideas either in small groups or with the class at large [5-8 minutes].

Instructor's Role

The instructor's role in the group inquiry process is important. Clarke notes that the initial problem and likely follow-up questions must be developed in advance. A teacher must anticipate possible responses of students in order to do this. With practice, such things will emerge in class but it does not hurt to be somewhat prepared.

Also, he suggests that it is important for instructors to facilitate the process but to delegate the responsibility for the discussion to members of the class. Teacher comments should be relegated to asking for clarification and to correct misunderstandings about the process. They also should be oriented towards keeping creative tension in the discussion and to keeping students focused on the issues. Several things that help this process.

- Use the written record of comments kept on the overhead or the board to tie student contributions together, to point out differences, or to wrap up the discussion.

- Convert student statements to questions and ask for other opinions.

- Deflect questions of interpretation to other members of the group.

- Ask students to provide examples of what they mean.

- Ask questions that require inference, prediction, analogy, or a synthesis of divergent ideas.

- If the class looks blank, reframe the last student response as a new question or assertion.

Finally, at the end of the discussion, the instructor can add additional ideas or points of view that help students see things they may have missed in their deliberations.

Guided Design

This approach explores solutions to open-ended problems by having students work through the problem solving process described in Table 8-4 [Wales and Nardi, 1982]. The guided design process can be used as a supplement to other instructional methods or as the primary design for an entire course. In the latter case, the content is taught through a series of problems that students try to solve. The teacher functions in the background as a consultant and resource person as well as a mentor and model for students. When used as the primary focus of a course design, the course emphasizes independent study through the use of technology based auto-tutorial presentations [e.g., audio, video, computer tutorials], textbook and outside reading assignments, and other programmed instructional materials. Competency based testing is used and grades are determined based upon test scores and the problem solving projects.

Table 8-4
Steps in the Guided Design Process

1.] State the problem and establish a goal that will be pursued in resolving it.

2.] Gather information relevant to defining the problem and understanding the elements associated with it.

3.] Generate possible solutions.

4.] List possible constraints on what can be accomplished as well as factors that may facilitate getting a solution accepted.

5.] Chose an initial or possible solution using criteria that an acceptable solution must meet. The criteria can include tangible and monetary costs and benefits, intangible and personal or psychological costs and benefits, the likely acceptance of the solution by others, as well as discipline or other standard criteria normally applied to such problems.

6.] Analyze the important factors that must be considered in the development of a detailed solution. What has to be done, who does it, when should it happen, and where would the solution be used are possible things to explore here.

7.] Create a detailed solution.

8.] Evaluate the final solution against the relevant criteria used earlier to insure that it meets at least those requirements and others that now appear to be necessary.

9.] Recommend a course of action, and if appropriate, suggest ways to monitory and evaluate the solution when it is adopted.

When employed as a supplement to other teaching processes, the problem solving format shown in Table 8-4 can be employed to help students develop their problem solving and critical thinking skills. Several things are helpful.

- *Have each stage completed in turn.* Depending upon the topic, each stage can be completed in class or additional work can be completed outside of class.

- *Students should keep a problem based journal to record their reactions to each stage of this problem solving process.* In class, they share their responses with members of a small discussion group. A recorder in each small group keeps a record of the ideas that are generated through each stage of the process.
- *A spokesperson from each group reports* back to the entire class at the completion of each stage.

- *The teacher writes a sample of important responses on the board* or on an overhead so that a public record of what was said is maintained.

- *The instructor moderates this process, asks questions, and suggests ideas to keep the process moving along.* The primary responsibility, however, for developing ideas and solving the problem must rest with the students. The instructor may act as a consultant or resource person to help students discover ways to obtain a solution.

Depending upon the scope of the problem selected, the process can be completed in one session or over several class sessions. A sample of problems that faculty in workshops have reported using this process with include:

a.] How would you design a shelter for human beings on the surface of the moon?

b.] What investment strategy would maximize long-term income for a 35 year old married male? A 35 year old unmarried female?

c.] How would you design a nuclear weapon so it did not produce harmful radiation?

d.] What was the major cause of the American Civil War?

e.] Instead of dropping an Atomic Bomb on Japan, what other strategy likely would have ended World War II?

f.] How can the dispensing errors that pharmacists make in a community pharmacy be reduced?

g.] What is the best way to stop the sale of illegal drugs?

h.] What is an the best alternative for the federal government to raise money if the current income tax were repealed?

Problem Based Tutorials

In some professional fields such as nursing, medicine, pharmacy, psychology, engineering and others, a tutorial can be taught using problems as the organizing device. As one example, Richard Eisenstaedt [1990] and his colleagues developed a problem based tutorial and offered it to 32 students in lieu of the traditional lecture based hematology-transfusion medicine module of a Pathophysiology course. *The course had the following elements:*

- *The curriculum focused on clinical vignettes* chosen to encompass the major objectives of the traditional course.

- *Students worked in small work teams of three to five students on each vignette.* They had to decide what issues in the cases they needed additional information about, where to obtain it, and who on the team was responsible for getting it.

- *Information the work teams needed could be obtained from multiple sources.* Students used the readings in a bibliography they were given, the medical school library, and through consultations with the instructors.

- *Students in each team met periodically to compare notes and to discuss differential diagnoses and potential treatment plans for each scenario.* Each team met about three times a week for 1-2 hours with additional time allocated for independent study.

Participants reported they were very satisfied with this approach to learning clinical content. When their scores on the module exam were compared to those on a follow-up exam two years later, retention was quite good. Students in the problem based tutorial remembered 97% of the information compared to 85% for those taught in a more traditional lecture course.

Role-Plays/Simulations

Role-playing and simulating events in class can illustrate situations where principles from a discipline are employed. Furthermore, role plays and simulations may help students gain insights about how to employ particular ideas. Students might role play situations to illustrate or to apply concepts and to have their use of that material critiqued. Finally, the instructor might develop role playing situations to illustrate particular concepts or to give students practice applying them in class. Based on an analysis of the literature [cf., Fuhrmann & Grasha, 1983; Grasha, 1995e], suggestions for setting up instructor and student designed role plays, using commercially available role plays and simulations, as well as general procedures for making such teaching strategies effective are described in the following paragraphs.

Role Playing Student Designed Situations

- *When role playing a personal situation, ask the student to take the role of the director of a play.* That student then picks from classmates someone to play their role and those of other parties in the situation. The director and cast have ten to fifteen minutes to develop the play. It is important that everyone be clear about who was present, where the event occurred, what was said and done and the outcomes that occurred.

- *Generate personal scenarios by having small groups of people describe a situation to each other where course concepts were or could have been used.* Each group selects the best one and the person suggesting it assigns roles and directs the other members in how to participate.

- *As many of the scenarios that fit the time allocated in class are performed in front of the entire class.* An option is to break the class into two or three subgroups and to have more than one role play going on at the same time. It would be important for the instructor or one or more students to summarize afterwards the major points presented by the role plays for the entire group.

- *Another strategy for generating personal involvement is for students to play their own role.* They then select other members in their small group or from the class to play the other members of the situation. Again the students have ten minutes to prepare the scenario.

Examples of the types of issues that can be examined with the first two options are listed below. They were suggested by people in my workshops who have used personal issues and concerns students had as the basis for role plays in class.

- A personal problem or conflict among people.
- A meeting where a decision had to be made.
- Applying principles of communication on the job.
- A conversation with a difficult person.
- Interviewing for a job.
- Explaining how the stock market operates to six graders.
- Counseling a client.
- Interviewing a client.
- Selling a product to a customer.
- Describing a mathematical solution to novices.
- Describing the principles of physics involved in an car crash to a newspaper reporter.
- Selling a product on the telephone.
- Interpreting the results of a political poll to a TV reporter.
- Trying to teach a friend how to play a difficult piano piece.

Role Playing Teacher Designed Scenarios

- *The teacher develops situations and roles.* Students receive an overview on how to role play or they receive very specific directions. For example, participants might use certain concepts from the text in their actions, to exaggerate certain behaviors, or to be as helpful as they can in resolving the problem.

- Role descriptions and guidelines are typed on 2 x 4 index cards for the students to employ. Or, if students need to have more detailed knowledge to participate, assignments for the session can be given out during an earlier class period so students can prepare.

Several teacher designed scenarios participants in my workshops have used include:

- Scenarios taken from current news events that illustrate course principles.
- The distribution of nutrients in a cell [Students play parts of the cell and the nutrients involved]
- A chemical reaction [Students role play the elements in the reaction]
- Closing a sales presentation to a client.
- A meeting with a client to discuss a design for a bridge.
- Meeting with an potential group of investors to discuss building a space station on the moon.
- A simulated crime scene with students gathering evidence.
- An actual meeting between two or more historical figures.
- A fantasy meeting between two or more historical figures [e.g. Sigmund Freud and Stalin; Harry Truman and the Emperor of Japan; Socrates and Carl Chessman; Richard Nixon and Ghandi].
- A critical scene from a book the class is reading.
- The rotation of planets around the sun in our solar system.
- An interview with a historical figure [Works well but the person playing the historical character needs time to prepare.]
- Taking a medical history.
- Presenting an advertising campaign plan to a client.
- Presenting the design of a new machine to a patent attorney.
- Ordering a meal in a restaurant using a foreign language.
- Describing economic principles that influence inflation on a television talk show.
- An interview between a chemist and a newspaper reporter wanting Information on the chemistry of *acid rain* or the *ozone hole* in the atmosphere.
- A mock trial.
- Product development meeting for developing a new brand of soap [or some other product].

Using Commercially Available Role Plays/Simulations

There are a number of simulations that are prepackaged for creating interactions in the classroom. The content includes such things as: resolving conflicts, mock jury trials, the operation of a management team dealing with a problem, the constraints on people living in the inner city, running a city government, developing a marketing campaign, developing and presenting a proposal for a building project, and many others. The best sources of such information in my experience are the educational and professional affairs people in the national organizations of a discipline. Next in line are the curriculum resource people often found in schools and departments of education or in the media services centers on campus.

General Procedures in Role-Playing

Role-playing works well when it is focused on clearly defined issues. It is also helpful to have specific instructions in order to set the stage for what students will do and what those observing are going to see. This means setting the stage so that they know what is going to happen. Specific information and materials are given to the actors to help them develop their roles. Always give them 5-10 minutes in class to review the materials and to think about how they will play their roles. Or, if the scenario involves developing the role to a deeper level, time to prepare outside of class should be allowed.

Remind participants that they should not read a script. While there may be general directions for how to behave and certain things to say, how such things are said should be left up to the discretion of the role player. The role player is expected to accept certain facts and to adopt these as his or her own. The resulting attitudes and feelings are displayed and perhaps changed as the events in the scenario unfold.

When questions not covered by the instructions are raised, participants should feel free to makeup facts or experiences that are appropriate to the circumstances. The player should not, however, make up facts that are inconsistent with the role. To maintain continuity and a sense of realism, the role player should not consult the role description once the role-playing begins.

Regardless of the type scenario used, it is important to have the members of the class who observe become active participants in the session. Class members can be assigned to critique the situation, to focus on how course ideas appeared in the interactions or to suggest ways to handle the situation differently. They also might watch a particular individual in the role play to observe and to later comment on how that person played his or her role. In the latter case the role play might be reenacted with the student responsible for observing one of the role players stepping into the action. It is important to allow those playing roles the opportunity to discuss any comments they have or to respond to comments made by other members of the class.

Afterwards, the instructor should summarize what was said, offer his or her observations, and if appropriate, model how something could have been said or done. Important content points should be highlighted and clarified. If there is still a lack of clarity about what happened or what points were illustrated, an *instant replay* can be done. Here, the original cast or a new cast of players are asked to redo the situation but they must take into account information in student and teacher comments about the first attempt.

Roundtable Discussion

Questions and topics are given to students in class to consider. Everyone is allowed 10-15 minutes to write a personal reaction to the issue. Having done this, they then share their reactions in a roundtable discussion format. Small groups of 4 to 5 students meet to share their responses to the questions.

Afterwards, students are asked to comment on the following questions:

- What are one or two new ideas I acquired from this discussion?
- What concepts, principles, and issues covered in this activity
  do I need to learn more about?

A recorder in each group should take notes on common responses to the discussion topic as well as how group members responded to the latter two questions. Recorders should be asked to share their "most powerful examples" of responses to these issues and the two follow-up questions.

Instructors can summarize the major points that develop, suggest other ways to look at the issue, share personal experiences and reactions, and clarify any misconceptions, and as well as provide additional material to supplement student responses.

Student Teacher of the Day

The instructor designs a schedule for the course with a list of topics that students will be responsible for teaching for five to seven class periods during the term. Students are assigned to small groups of five to seven peers who will have a designated member as the teacher for each of the topics. On a given day, each student teacher of the day could teach his or her group the same topic or several different subjects might be taught that day in different groups [Grasha, 1972].

The student teacher is responsible for developing a presentation for a small group as well as questions and/or an activity or demonstration to get people involved. During a class session, each teacher of the day will have about two-thirds of the session to meet with his or her group.

Factors that help the teacher of the day model work effectively:

- *Student teachers need time to prepare.* Thus, the assignment of
  topics should be made early in the term. It is also helpful for
  the instructor to meet with the student teachers a week or so

before the session. At that meeting, expectations are developed and the course instructor makes suggestions about how to teach the topic. It is also useful to remind the student teachers not to read a presentation, to have a handout outlining what they want to cover, and to use discussion questions and visual aids. Usually the course instructor and the student teacher write exam items on the topics that were covered that day.

- *During the class session, the instructor for the class can sit outside of the groups to check on what is going on and after the discussions solicits questions and comments about the content.* Also, asking the student teachers if there are any questions they were unable to handle can be used to solicit opinions from the class. Or, the instructor might comment on issues that were raised or that need further explanation. Finally, the student teachers should be asked to report on a couple of points about the topic, or the comments that members of their group made, that they thought were particularly useful.

- *To insure that quality instruction takes place, a teacher must closely monitor the work of the student teachers.* They should receive feedback on their performance and given tips on how they could have improved the quality of their presentation. Feedback can come from comments from the instructor or from a short evaluation by participants in the small groups given at the end of a session. Asking group members to list one or two specific things they liked and disliked about the session and to make one suggestion for improvement provide useful information to the student teacher of the day. The course instructor should periodically summarize the feedback provided and share suggestions for improvement with the class.

An alternate way to run the Teacher of the Day Model is for the course instructor to designate the type of instructional processes that will be used in particular groups. Thus, the student teachers of the day prepare their sessions around the instructional process they are assigned. Each group might use the same process or several can be rotated among different groups.

- *True-False Test:* The student in charge develops an 8-10 item true-false test on content points. *All of the items are false.* After administering the test to his or her group, the student goes through each item and indicates why it was false and responds to the questions and comments of peers.

- *Poster Session:* The content of the presentation occurs in a poster session format. Students in the group read the poster material and ask questions about the content. The student teacher of the day also has questions prepared for group members of a factual as well as open-ended nature. Then, the members of various groups move to other posters that are on display and the process is repeated.

- *Demonstration:* Student teachers of the day do a demonstration of a course related phenomenon or concept. These are shown in each small group. Participants ask questions and the student teacher of the day also questions participants to check on their understanding of what occurred. If time remains, the groups rotate to see another demonstration if more than one was used.

- *Newspaper/Magazine Items:* Two or three short newspaper or magazine articles illustrating points covered in the text are copied. Students in each of the groups read each article and then write a comment and a question about the content. The comments and questions are shared in the small groups with everyone including the teacher of the day responding to the items.

The Teaching Methods of Cluster 4

Contract Teaching

This is an excellent way to provide a structure for students as they learn to become self-directed learners. Contracts or agreements formalize expectations for what students and the teachers must do in a class. There are a number of ways to set up such contracts. The two described here are based on concepts from Humanistic and Behavioral orientations to instruction.

Humanistic Orientation

In two classic works on teaching, Carl Rogers [1969; 1975] recommends an open-ended form of contracting that provides students with security and encourages responsibility for their learning. The process he recommends involves a one on one negotiation between the teacher and each of the students in class. It has the following components:

- *Students develop ideas for independent study activities. This* can include outside readings, papers, research projects, field trips, internships, leading discussions in class, attending workshops, or any other activity that is clearly relevant to the course.

- *Students meet individually for 20-30 minutes with the instructor to discuss their ideas.* Their teacher may suggest variations or alternatives to think about.

- *The criteria that will be used to evaluate student projects are discussed.* The grade that students would like to obtain also is discussed and the amount of self-directed study the student does is keyed to a particular grade.

- *The teacher and student reach an agreement.* This agreement includes what will be accomplished, the level of competence that must be demonstrated, when assignments are due, and how they will be evaluated. The role and responsibilities of the faculty member also are a part of the agreement. Typically, this means the teacher will serve as a consultant and resource person and will be available at certain times to meet with students.

- *This agreement is put in writing.* It can be modified, however, but both the instructor and student must agree to any changes.

Typically such agreements involve the self-study components of a course. Yet they sometimes include provisions that students will attend class and participate in course activities. Furthermore, some of the independent study assignments students agree to do often involve helping out with particular class sessions [e.g., being a teacher of the day, leading a small group discussion, doing a demonstration, engaging in a debate or panel discussion].

One advantage from Rogers' point of view is that once an agreement is reached, students have less uncertainty about how their performance will be assessed. This removes a great deal of fear and apprehension from class. It makes learners feel that discussions about issues are possible and that the instructor is concerned with their development. In addition, it gives them permission to engage in self-directed learning activities with the expectations for their performance known in advance.

An example of a completed contract I negotiated using the process outlined above is shown in Table 8-5. It takes about 30-45 minutes of discussion to develop an agreement with students. The majority are typically prepared when the arrive for the meetings. For those that are not, I generally restate what is needed for us to obtain an agreement and they are asked to do additional homework.

Students sometimes want to change the agreement once the term is underway. Normally this is not a problem provided that the changes will not interfere with running the class [e.g., when they have agreed to be a Teacher of the Day on a particular date.] The process is new to most of them and thus one can expect they will not be as committed to some things they initially agreed to do. Also, as the course gets underway, additional ideas for what they might do begin to emerge. It is helpful, however, to have a date beyond which changes will not be allowed. For me, I tell students that substantive changes in the agreement cannot be made after the fourth week of class.

Table 8-5
A Negotiated Course Agreement

Course: Research Methods in Social Psychology
Student: Tanya D. /*Teacher*: Tony Grasha
Date: January 10, 1995

Activity 1: Tanya will do two Teacher of the Day sessions this term for a small group of 6-8 students. The topic for session 1 will be *Biases in Social Research.* The topic for session 2 will be *The flaws in a classic research study on obedience to authority.* Each session will run approximately 30-40 minutes.

Deadlines: Class sessions on February 4 and February 25
Key tasks for Tanya:

   1.] Provide an outline of information to be covered in each session
       and a description of the active learning processes to Tony. This
          will be completed no later than ten days in advance of each session.
   2.] Meet with Tony to discuss the outline and the conduct of each
       small group session no later than seven days in advance.
   3.] Redo the outline and plan for the session and have it back to Tony
       no later than three days in advance of the session.
   4.] Develop 2-3 questions that students will use to evaluate the session

Instructor Responsibility:

   1.] To meet with Tanya at the times specified above to consult with
       her on her presentations.
   2.] To meet after each session she runs to discuss her evaluations and to
       think of ways to enhance what she does in the future.

Activity 2
Description: Tanya will read *Women's Ways of Knowing* as a self-study. She will write a ten page double spaced critical review of the research methodology used in the book and its implications for research in social psychology.

Deadline: A critical analysis of the book will be due March 6, 1995.
Key tasks for Tanya:

   1.] Write a first draft of a critique for Tony and one other member of the
       class to read no later than February 18th.
   2.] Meet with Tony to discuss the draft
   3.] Meet with a peer to discuss the draft
   4.] Rewrite the paper using comments from Tony and classmate.

Instructor Responsibility:

   1.] To read Tanya's draft and to provide comments.
   2.] To answer questions at Tanya's request about issues she is facing .

Evaluation: The Teacher of the Day activity will not be graded Instead, Tanya will receive constructive feedback on how well she taught the sessions and Tony's perceptions of how well she understood the concepts involved. The book critique will be graded on a High Pass, Pass, and Fail system. If the grade is not passing, Tanya will be given the opportunity to rewrite the paper.

Behavioral Orientation

The process described above works well in smaller classes [e.g., 10-20 students]. In larger courses, contracting can be accomplished using a point system for activities. The amount of work needed to obtain a particular grade is specified and students have options for what they can do. An example of such a contract appears in Table 8-6. Students decide what grade they want and how much of the class activity they want to do.

For this process to work, the following elements should be present:

- *Students should perceive that their actions will have a payoff in the contract.* Thus, as a student completes any given activity, he or she immediately knows the amount of the reward that can be achieved.

- *Students should know exactly what is expected for a particular grade, and that appropriate actions will lead to positive reinforcement.* Furthermore, as students complete various tasks, they can easily determine how much credit toward a particular grade they have earned.

- *Reinforce frequently with small amounts.* Grade requirements should be broken into smaller units, with each unit becoming something the student gets reinforced with for completing. Thus a student should not have to complete five activities before getting 20 points. The points for each activity are assigned when it is completed.

- *A contract must reward accomplishment rather than obedience.* Thus the contract should state, "If you accomplish *x*, then you will receive *y* amounts of reinforcement." It should not say, "If you do what I tell you to do, you will be rewarded with ......"

- *Use criteria of quality as well as quantity.* There are several ways to do this. One is to establish criteria for each activity--that is, it must conform to certain standards. These may be neatness, well formulated ideas, or, with exams-- a criterion of 90 percent of the items completed.

- *If the size of the class permits, consider negotiating with students the terms of the contract.* Negotiation gives students a chance to include additional activities that are likely to meet his or her learning needs.

- *Have students sign the contract.* This ensures that they have read the terms, that they understand what is expected, and that it helps to develop commitment to the course.

Table 8-6
A Behavioral Contract

Exam Performance	Points Earned
90-100 items correct	50 points
80-89 items correct	40 points
70-79 items correct	30 points
0-69 items correct	20 points

Activities	Points Earned
- Design a research project	15 points
- Implement a research project	40 points
- Write a book report on as many outside reading books as you want	20 points each book
- Run a class session on a topic of your choice related to course content	20 points
- Take a field trip and write a report on observations	10 points
- Write a term paper	50 points
- Classroom attendance	03 points
- Negotiate with the instructor one or more projects of interest to you	10-50 points

Evaluation and Agreement

A = 350 points or more B = 275-349 points C = 200-274 points

D or F: [No D or F contracts accepted]

I have read the requirements for earning points toward a grade in this course. I would like to contract for a grade by earning a minimum of points, The activities I have elected to complete to earn points are the following [List activities and corresponding points on the back of this page].

I understand that I can change my contract to try for a higher or lower grade until 15 March. This change must be approved by the instructor. All work on this contract must be performed to the quality standards set by the teacher. The teacher agrees to give me feedback on a timely basis regarding the quality of all work completed.

Teacher Signature: _____

Student Signature: _____

Class Symposium

Students are asked to write a term paper or to complete a research project during the term. The papers must be completed prior to the last week of class. During this week, class sessions are devoted to students presenting their papers to small groups of peers [e.g., 4-6 students]. The presentations should not be done by having people read or talk about their papers to peers. This process is too passive and typically does not engage those present. Rather, individuals leading groups should be assigned the following *presentation processes* to use [i.e., They can be rotated across groups by the instructor].

- *Copies of papers are passed out in advance to small group participants:* Everyone in the group receives a copy of the paper. Their task is to critique it before the session and to come prepared with 4-5 comments and questions about the content. The person who wrote the paper asks people to share their comments and listens to what is said. Afterwards, the student who wrote the paper responds to the comments. Next, specific questions people in the group had are raised and the individual who wrote the paper as well as other group members can respond.

- *Executive summary of the paper is prepared:* Students in the small groups are given a two page executive summary of the paper. They are asked to read it and to write comments, questions, as well as things they would like to have additional information about. These are shared in turn with the presenter using the same processed illustrated above.

- *Poster session on papers:* The person presents a poster session that highlights the key points in the paper and/or research project. Members of the small group are given time to examine the poster and to write questions and comments. These are shared with the presenter who listens to what is said and responds.

After the small group sessions, each presenter reports back to the class on what was learned from the comments and questions of people in the small group. The instructor should reserve a few minutes at the end to respond.

Debate Formats

Conflicts of opinion are inevitable in education. Sometimes they arise on their own while at other times teachers may decide to create them. Debates are one way to create some controversy as well as sharpen students' abilities to think independently and critically about issues. An important concern in having a debate is getting students access to materials associated with particular controversies. They can investigate issues by gathering information for themselves or materials packaged by commercial publishers can be used.

There are a variety of formats for engaging students in a debate. Two that in my experiences work well are Assigned Role Debates and Cooperative Controversies.

Assigned Role Debates

I have found a variation on a strategy suggested by Marguerite Egan [1990] helpful in getting students to participate in a debate. Roles are assigned to participants to guide and direct what they are supposed to do and to allow the debate to unfold in an orderly manner.

Two groups of three students each are formed and assigned one of the following roles within each group; A Presenter, Logical Thinker, and *Challenger.* Each group takes one side of an issue. While each person is responsible for representing their roles, the members of each group should work together as a team in preparing for the debate.

I typically ask students to work as a team and gather information relevant to the debate. Each person then reads the information taking notes on themes, facts, and other points that might help them play their role. They then share what they would like to say at a team meeting. [The independent preparation is designed to insure that everyone reads the information the group has gathered.] Members of each group are encouraged to listen to each others ideas at the team meeting and then to help each other organize their roles so that they will present a consistent and united front. They should then rehearse their parts and *fine tune* what they will say.

Presenter: The presenter states how his or her side views the issue. This introduction is generally brief and gives an introductory overview of the issue. The presenter may use notes but should be familiar enough with the material to present in a conversational tone. This role generally takes from 2 to 5 minutes.

Logical Thinker: The logical thinker is possibly the most difficult role. This student must provide relevant information to reinforce the statements the presenter made at the beginning of the debate. Those in the role of Logical Thinkers must have a good working knowledge of the group's position. During the debate, the Logical Thinker may take from 5 to 15 minutes to present depending on the evidence needed to support what the presenter said.

Challenger: The Challenger is responsible for leading the arguments against the other team. Students in this role will be required to listen well, think quickly, uncover logical flaws in what is said and identify opinions that are disguised as facts. It is important that each adversary challenge the information presented by the other side and not the personal qualities of the person presenting them.

A given debate might consist of the following interchanges between pro and con teams with a coin toss determining who goes first.

Round I: [15-20 minutes]

a.] *Position 1:* The Presenter brings forth the propositions of for his or her side of the issue.

b.] *The Logical Thinker on the Position 1 team* supports the presenter's statements with evidence.

c.] *Position 2:* The presenter on this side puts forth his or her perceptions of the issue.

d.] *The Logical Thinker on the Position 2 team* shows why the presenter holds this position by presenting relevant evidence.

e.] *The Challenger from the Position 1 team* may direct several questions to the other side or point out errors noted in the issue as presented.

f.] *The Challenger from the Position 2 team* gets a chance to do the same.

Round II: [10-15 minutes]

After this initial exchange, the debate is opened up. In turn the Presenters and Logical Thinkers can present additional information to support their views. The Challengers can question or take exception to what was said.

Round III: [10-15 minutes]

The remaining members of the class are instructed to develop questions and comments designed to clarify what was said or to get each team to justify further what was said. Thus, after the initial and rebuttal stage, class members are invited to share their questions and comments. Each team must respond to the questions and issues class members are raising.

At the end of the third round, the audience votes via secret ballot on which side did the better job of representing its position. To show that I am nonbiased, I typically give a bag of M&M's to each side. Their victory after all, should be a moral one.

The class should be told that the debate is a way to present information that is relevant to the content of the course. Thus, they should treat it as a presentation on issues, take notes, and participate in what is going on. This latter point is something worth repeating regardless of the student centered format used. *It is important to establish norms that students can learn from each other and that the activity is not something designed to fill time.* To reinforce this point, exam items are based on the content or further assignments build upon what happened in the debate.

The teacher should monitor what is happening but stay out of the debate. Once the debate has begun, no further interference is necessary. Often the students will have prepared trains of thought, and interruptions may spoil the points that they are developing. Instructors should only respond after the debate has ended and only to add information or points of view that were omitted by either side.

Cooperative Controversies

This format for a debate can be used in relatively small as well as large classes [Johnson, Johnson, & Holubec, 1990]. It differs from a more traditional debate format in the following manner. Instead of having two debate teams and an audience, everyone in class becomes part of a debate team. In addition, instead of preparing just one side, everyone prepares to discuss both sides of the issue. Thus, at an appropriate point in the debate, people switch sides. Finally, the goal is not to *win* a debate but for students to help each other learn. *Desired outcomes include participants learning as much as possible about each others' point of view and to gain new insights on the issue.*

The steps in setting up a cooperative controversy are:

- *The instructor presents a controversial question that is to be argued.* For example: Should birth control be made available to adolescents without parental knowledge or permission? Should gasoline be rationed to restrict the use of cars and thus cut down on emissions harmful to the atmosphere? Are people better off financially under a Democratic or Republican president? Should the peaceful use of atomic energy be curtailed?

- *Students are instructed to prepare arguments for and against the position.* If they have sufficient background information, and the issue does not involve extensive preparation, class time can be devoted to doing this. Normally, students will have to prepare outside of class. Some faculty members have them turn in the notes they used to develop their arguments as a check on any outside of class preparation.

- *Teams are assigned to debate the pro and con sides of the issue for the initial round.* The teams circle their chairs with multiple small groups formed around the classroom.

- *Each side presents its arguments while the other listens and takes notes.* The other side is allowed to ask questions of clarification after each presentation but arguments are not allowed. [15-20 minutes]

- *The teams switch roles and the process is repeated.* They can be given a few minutes to meet before doing this. [10-15 minutes]

- *Afterwards, students are asked to list on a sheet of paper,* "3-4 things I learned from the other side" and "questions I have about the topic." [5 minutes]

- *Both teams meet to share what they learned* and to help each other answer the questions. [10 minutes]

- *Toward the end of the session, the teacher polls the class for questions that remain to be answered.* In addition, the instructor checks to see if anyone has the information, offers an opinion or refers the students to a source that can answer the question.

Helping Trios

Students are given a problem to solve, a decision to make, or to develop an application of course content. . After writing out their plan or a modification to it that was prepared in class or before class, students are placed in groups of three and asked to assume one of the three roles:

- A *presenter* who describes his or her initial plan or modification to an existing plan for applying course principles.

- A *consultant* who helps the presenter to clarify what they want to do. Consultants should listen, ask questions, and if necessary suggest options for how the presenter might want to proceed.

- An *observer* who focuses on the nature and quality of the interaction between the presenter and consultant. The observer keeps time and notes problems in the interaction (e.g., lack of listening, consultant being too pushy, etc.). Observers should not tell the presenter exactly what to do and they must avoid sounding judgmental (e.g., "That was a stupid thing to say.").

The discussion occurs in three rounds with each student having the opportunity to play each one of the three roles. Ten to fifteen minutes are allowed for each round. The observer keeps time and uses the last two minutes to comment on the interaction between the presenter and consultant. At the end of this period, participants then switch roles. Everyone is given a chance to play each role once.

An important goal is for class members to help each other develop their ideas for the assignment. In class, the instructor can observe the groups to identify issues that need further clarification and/or afterwards ask group members to suggest ideas they did not understand. This activity also teaches students how to express their plans, how to consult, and it allows class members to develop their communication and interpersonal relationship skills.

Independent Study/Research Projects

Depending upon the discipline, such activities include Senior theses, as well as Master's and Dissertation projects. They also may include reviews of the literature, working on a research project with a faculty member, or writing a short story or book. Such activities may be quite extensive or pursued as a smaller project in a methods course. There are several things that faculty can do to enhance the quality of such experiences for themselves and their students. A good place to begin is to listen to what students across disciplines say are important components of effective teacher- student relationships under such conditions.

A checklist of helpful teacher behaviors is described in Self-Reflection Activity 8-1. They were developed from a review of the literature on good practices for working *one on one* with students [Grasha, 1995]. As you read the items, think about how many apply to a recent experience you have had supervising students on an independent research project.

In addition to paying attention to the components of effective supervision when working *one on one* with students, it is also important to take time beforehand to discuss the project in detail.

- *The nature and scope of the project must be discussed.* Sometimes students underestimate the amount of time and energy a project will take and thus need a reality check.

- *Give students an opportunity to tell you what they expect from you.* Typically they need you to be available to consult with them during certain time periods and to provide needed guidance and direction. This latter issue is very important. One of the goals of teaching in Cluster 4 is to develop students' capabilities as self-directed scholars. This means that you will want to act as a consultant and resource person more often than not. Explain how you see the latter roles and that you are likely to be less prescriptive when working with them.

- *Pay attention to the learning styles of the students with whom you are working.* To encourage the Independent and Collaborative learning styles you may have to talk to students about how they prefer to learn and the demands of working in an independent manner. Some may have to be gradually introduced to these styles while others may be ready to assume them immediately.

- *Make sure that all expectations, deadlines, descriptions of the project, authorship of any publications that may emerge, are put in writing.* Giving students a memo of understanding and inviting comments if issues in the memo are not clear is in my experience very helpful. Both you and the student should sign a final version of the memo. This helps to insure that misunderstandings do not occur later on. And if they do, it is easy to refer back to the original memo to check agreements.

Self-Reflection Activity 8-1
A Checklist of Helpful Faculty Behaviors
for Supervising Students

Think of one or more recent independent study or research projects you recently supervised. Check the items that applied to how you worked with those students. Only check an item if you can think of at least one specific example of how it appeared in the relationship.

_____ Focused on the needs of students.

_____ Took the time to discover the strengths and weaknesses of students.

_____ Provided frequent feedback to students.

_____ Gave feedback in a nonthreatening manner.

_____ Noted verbally or in written form both the positive and negative aspects of a student's performance.

_____ Stated clear expectations for students.

_____ Helped students set clear goals for the project.

_____ Was flexible in helping students to set goals for the project.

_____ Encouraged students to ask questions.

_____ Gave clear answer to questions.

_____ Was approachable and available to students.

_____ Provided clear directions and guidelines for students.

_____ Demonstrated concern and respect for the students I supervised.

_____ Encouraged the use of good research and scholarly skills.

_____ Was a good model for demonstrating scholarly behaviors.

_____ Was trustworthy and possessed good judgment as a supervisor.

_____ Encouraged the development of independent problem solving skills.

_____ Posed questions and problems that make students think deeply about issues.

_____ Able to elicit discussions and quality interactions with students.

_____ Was an advocate for students and their projects.

_____ Tried to be pleasant and helpful when working with students.

_____ Did not alienate students.

_____ Provided professional encouragement and support.

_____ Was enthusiastic about working with students.

_____ Maintained good rapport with students.

_____ Showed students that I was interested in their progress on the project.

List 2-3 aspects of effective supervision listed above that you checked or perhaps did not check that you must work on in the future?

Jigsaw Groups

This process has students teaching each other a part of total assignment. The following elements are a part of this teaching strategy.

- *Depending upon the material you want to cover, students are assigned to small groups of three to five students.* Each student completes an overnight assignment to prepare one-third to one-fifth of an assignment.

- *In class, they take turns teaching other members of the group the information they researched.* Those presenting are encouraged to be creative in how they present content. Those listening to the presentation are encouraged to ask questions to clarify points and to have the presenter elaborate on issues. When each member of the group is finished, everyone has the information to complete the assignment.

- *All members of the class are involved in a Jigsaw group during a given session.* They may all have the same content to teach each other or different groups may have different assignments. In the latter case, a spokesperson from each group can brief the class on what was presented in their group.

  When different content is taught in each group, members become knowledgeable about a topic. After working in their groups, two groups with different topics can be combined. Each group then teaches the other. This can occur during the same class session and/or during the one that follows.

- *Issues and questions that were not dealt with in a satisfactory manner in the Jigsaw Groups* can be addressed by the instructor or as part of a general class discussion.

This is often a helpful device for students to teach each other information in the textbook or to develop a position on some issue. For example, students might be asked how a problem solving process could be used find new solutions to the sale of illegal drugs. Members of the class are then divided into Jigsaw Groups of three members. Each person would be responsible for preparing a short 10 minute presentation on how components of a problem solving process applies to the issue of illegal drugs. Different people would examine the components of establishing a good problem definition, generating alternative solutions, or how to use criteria to select the best solution. Afterwards, each member of the group, or the group as a whole, would write-up a possible solution to the issue using the information they gained in the Jigsaw Groups.

Or, each of three major themes in a story could be analyzed by different students who then present their analysis to the group at large. Similarly, each of several important elements in designing a bridge could be researched by different students who then present what they found to members of their team. This process is quite flexible and applicable to a variety of disciplines.

Laundry List Discussions

- *Ask students to develop a laundry list of topics for discussion* based upon assigned readings or their reactions to information presented in class.

- *Divide the class into several groups of 3 to 5 students. Try to set the groups up in a more or less random fashion.* This can be done by having everyone in class take a number and forming groups based on a random selection of numbers. Or, have people count off from left to right 1, 2, 3 for three person groups, 1-4 and 1-5 for four and five person groups. Have everyone with the same numbers form a group to work together. This allows people who have not had a chance to work together to do so and increases the chance that the groups will have various levels of ability represented.

- *Have each group select a recorder.* Their task is to monitor the discussion and to note important points that are made in writing. Tell the recorders to report back to the class later about the outcomes of the discussion.

- *Assign the small groups different items from the laundry list and have them develop a position on the issue.* To do so, groups first have each member share whatever knowledge and ideas they have about the issue discussed. Those listening should be encouraged to ask questions for clarity and for additional information. Allow about 15 to 20 minutes for this part of the process.

- *After sharing their knowledge about the topic, the groups then take an additional 10 to 15 minutes to try and integrate the ideas that were generated into a common position.* The recorders then report to the entire group on the outcomes of the discussion. Those listening can comment on what the recorders said and the instructor can offer additional ideas including ways that his or her experiences support or refute what was said.

Learning Pairs

Learning Cells

- *Students are divided into pairs.* Everyone receives a topic from the text or outside reading to prepare for a particular class session. This preparation typically occurs outside of class. Students prepare questions for their partners to answer that deal with basic facts and knowledge, applications, critical thinking, and problem solving and decision making. Depending upon the topic, students can develop at least one question for their partners in each of the latter categories or the questions can be limited to fewer categories.

Questions for this process also can be developed in a generic manner [cf., King, 1993]. Students can be introduced to the following options as a place to begin the process of writing questions.

- What is the main idea of.....?
- How does ... affect ....?
- Why is .... important?
- What is a new example of ....?
- Explain why ....
- Explain how ....
- What conclusions can be drawn about ....?
- What is the difference between .... and ....?
- How are .... and .... similar? Different?
- How could I use .... to .... ?
- What are the strengths and weaknesses of ....?

Learners should be informed that the above are ideas for where to begin. They should be encouraged to be creative in developing questions. To insure that students take developing questions seriously, developing questions should be treated as a writing assignment with credit given. To help learners see creative possibilities for questions, the instructor also can develop a list of the top five or so questions from each session. These are posted for students to see or are placed on a handout that everyone in class receives.

In addition, exam items can be based in part on the questions that students developed for their learning cells. The questions are collected afterwards and then critiqued. Credit is assigned and the questions returned along with comments on how they can improve their questions.

• *Students work in pairs asking each other questions for about one-half of the class period.* The instructor can walk around the room and monitor the interactions or later ask individuals to suggest one or two major issues raised in their dyads.

This process works best when used several times during a term. In this way, students have an opportunity to respond to feedback and to improve the questions they ask. To help maintain interest, and to avoid interpersonal difficulties, pairs should be rotated each time this process is employed.

A variation of this technique is to have two or three different reading assignments distributed among members of the class. Outside of class, students must then prepare questions and a short presentation on the material. In class, students with different assignments are paired. Part of the time in the learning cell is spent with one student explaining what he or she read and then asking the other person questions. The roles are then reversed with the other student explaining and then questioning a partner.

About 20-25 minutes of class time should be devoted to the first option and 35-40 minutes when the second one is employed. The teacher can walk around and observe what is occurring in each group. Afterwards, the instructor polls the class for questions that people had trouble answering, suggests how he or she might have answered it, and then responds to additional issues students have about the content.

Think-Pair-Share

• A question that has broad implications or that demands some thought to develop a response is raised. Such questions may ask for applications of course content, how it could be employed to analyze a situation, or ways course material might be used to develop a conclusion about some issue.

• Students are given a few minutes to think through an appropriate response. This time also can be spent writing a response. Students then turn to a partner and share their responses.

• Afterwards, the student in each pair could join another pair to share ideas or different students might volunteer to comment on how they responded in front of the entire class. Consequently, everyone gets a chance to learn by reflection and verbalization.

This is a rather easy process to use and is particularly useful in getting a discussion going in a large class.

Dyadic Encounters

While students might individually work on a issue, they also can jointly work with each other in pairs to complete a task. Allison King [1993] suggests several activities for working in pairs. They include:

• *Generating examples:* Students working in pairs think up one or more new examples of a concept presented in class or in the text.

• *Developing scenarios:* Students develop a specific scenario of how and where a particular concept or principle can be applied.

• *Flowcharting:* Students sketch a flowchart showing how a procedure or process discussed in class or in the text works.

• *Predicting:* Given certain principles or concepts, students write down their own predictions about what might happen in a specific situation.

• *Developing rebuttals:* Students individually develop rebuttals for arguments presented in the lecture and then pair up with another student to argue for and against the issue.

- *Constructing tables/graphs:* Students develop a table or draw a graph representing the information presented.

- *Analogical thinking*: A metaphor or analogy for a principle or procedure is proposed.

- *Problem posing:* A real-world problem is developed related to a particular concept or principle. Students exchange their problem with their partner who then tries to solve it.

- *Developing critiques:* Students develop a critique of a common practice or the information presented in class, the text, or an outside reading.

- *Pair summarizing/checking*: Students work in pairs. One partner summarizes what has been presented. The other listens and checks for errors correcting his or her partner when mistakes are noted.

Modular Instruction

Modular instruction is based on the offering of individual units that cover major content areas of a course (Johnston, 1975; McKeachie, 1978). Each module is a curriculum package designed for self-study. The modules are usually large, with each requiring several hours of the student's time. The instructor's role is limited to developing the modules and to monitoring their use. Audiovisual or computer tutorial aids may be used, but they are not essential. Some modules may be set up for groups of students to complete together.

A module could include combinations of several of the following elements:

- Selections from a book or several articles to read.
- A case study to analyze using the information from the readings.
- A videotape to watch on a topic within the module.
- A study guide to complete on the videotape.
- Presentations in class or elsewhere on campus to attend.
- Directions for a research project or short paper.
- A topic that must be researched and presented to a small group of students during a designated time period.
- Instructions to interview someone knowledgeable about a topic and to write a short report.
- A critical analysis of an article.
- A computer program to use on a project.
- A requirement to learn how to use a computer program.
- Instructions and resources to pursue to develop particular skills.
- Small group projects and activities.

The construction of a module can be quite flexible and include as many of the above elements or others as needed. Students are typically assigned points for completing each module and are required to do a fixed number during a term. The modules might organize the entire course or they can be used to supplement other class activities.

The following steps are used in developing modules:

- *Specific goals are established and stated* for what students are expected to learn.

- *A rationale for the module is stated.* This includes the value of a particular unit and explains to students why it is beneficial for them to achieve the stated objectives.

- *A pretest is constructed to determine what competencies each student possesses* on the information and skills covered in the module.

- *Instructional activities are designed to help students acquire the competencies stated in the objectives.* Important here is the use of options so that the student may choose among different learning modes as illustrated above.

- *Deadlines for completing various modules are established* as well as how many of them participants must complete during a term.

- *A post-test is given to assess the student's learning from the module.* Typically students are required to achieve a minimum level of competency before being allowed to progress to the next module.

Panel Discussion

Panel discussions give students a chance to become experts on some aspect of the content. It also provides them with an opportunity to test their "expertise" in discussions with other panel members and the audience. Like a debate, panel discussions allow both sides of an issue to be explored. *Unlike a debate, each member of the panel is responsible for assuming the roles of Presenter, Logical Thinker, and Challenger.* The teacher is responsible for selecting the issue that will be discussed and to moderate the discussion. A process suggested by Egan [1990] is described in the following paragraphs.

- *Two teams are formed of 4-6 students each.* They are assigned or volunteer to take one side of an issue.

- *As with a debate, the teams hold an initial meeting and members agree to find information related to the topic.* The readings and other information are then shared among all members of the group.

- *At a subsequent meeting, each team decides what aspects of the topic each member will be responsible for becoming the team's expert on.* That person will probably want to seek and read additional information related to his or her area of expertise.

- *How much reading and research teams do to prepare their topics varies.* The information they need might be limited to that found in the textbook and other course related readings. Or, they could be asked to explore other sources for information. In the spirit of developing their self-directed learning skills, they should explore additional sources of information including contacting people with expertise in an area.

- *The panel discussion consists of four phases:*position presentation, clarification of team's position,free-form discussion, and audience response.

The four phases of a panel discussion include:

1.] Presentation of Position

All participants make a short presentation of one aspect of their team position. The purpose of the first is to provide the rest of the class with an introduction to the topic and a short statement of the issues involved. It also allows participants to state positions for the benefit of either team so that the points at issue are clear. The length of each presentation will depend on the number of students on the panel and the time available, but *one-fourth to one-third of the class session for all of the presentations should be devoted to the presentation of positions*. Each member of team will present some aspect of the issue. However, the first presenter has the primary responsibility of introducing the issue in general.

The individual presentations should begin with a concise statement of the main points followed by a brief summary of the evidence that supports each of the points. The evidence can be logical, empirical, experiential, or based on the opinions of experts. The presentation should then end with a restatement of the primary assertions to summarize the major focus of the position.

2.] Clarification of Team's Positions

This is a question and answer session between the teams. The purpose is to allow each side to clarify the other team's position. Panelists should be instructed that only questions of clarification are appropriate at this point. Challenges, rebuttals, and a general discussion are not permitted. However, this phase does allow each team to begin pinning down the other team as to the specifics of their position. *This phase is usually quite short, with 8-10 minutes allocated to it.*

3.] Free-form Discussion among Panel Participants

Here panel members can raise additional points, counterpoints, challenge what others are saying and generally discuss the issue. Members of the panel should be instructed to deal with the main issues as they perceive them. Discussions of trivial points or tangential issues are not appropriate and the moderator should keep them out of the discussion. In other words, students should begin the free-form phase with the primary points of disagreement. All members of the panel should be encouraged to participate and the teacher as moderator should ask individuals who are silent to share a point of view. *Ten to fifteen minutes can be spent in this stage of the discussion.*

4.] Audience Response

As with the debate format, *students in the audience must be reminded that the panel discussion contains content that they will be responsible for knowing.* Thus, they should treat it as a presentation of that information, take notes, and develop questions and comments about what they are hearing.

After the free-form discussion, questions that audience members have should be addressed to specific individuals. Otherwise, questions put to the entire group are usually handled by the most vocal member rather than by the person who made the initial comment. Some free-form dialogue should be permitted between the audience and panelists, but a number of different comments and questions should be encouraged.

Sometimes it helps to give the members of the class a minute to think about a comment or question and to write it down. Thus, if they are slow to respond, the moderator can call on individual members of the class to see what they have to say.

The teacher as moderator should keep a low profile during the class session. The students and what they have to say is figural. Sitting with the class usually works well as does having all remarks of panelists and the class directed to members of the panel. Following the final phase of the discussion, the moderator can provide an overview of what was said, suggest points that were not raised, and generally clarify a point or two that was not clear.

Some instructors like to grade the participation of each member of the panel. Others simply give a certain number of points for the overall job each team did to each team member. And in some classes, participating in a panel discussion is one of the interaction requirements for the course and a notation is made indicating that it was fulfilled or a grade of satisfactory or unsatisfactory is assigned. *Regardless of what evaluation scheme is used, it is important to give the team as well as individuals feedback on what was done well and not so well.* The general nature of such comments periodically should be shared with the class.

Position Papers

Two Minute Papers

A popular writing process is the use of one-minute papers [Cross and Angelo,1988; Angelo and Cross,1993]. Many faculty report that it is one of the most significant classroom methods they have ever used. Such enthusiasm aside, I have found that it is valuable but a one- minute paper typically takes longer to complete. Thus, it is best to allow students to write for at least two- minutes on one of the following topics:

a.] A position they have on an issue or controversy raised in class.

b.] Something they liked or disliked about an assignment or classroom activity.

c.] New insights they gained from an assignment or discussion of text content.

d.] Positive implications of an assignment or text material for their everyday lives.

Responses can be placed on one side of a large index card or on half a sheet of paper. Class members might share their papers with a partner, selected students might share with the entire class, or the papers are collected without comment by the instructor. It helps to summarize the themes in student reactions at the beginning of the next class session.

Two-minute papers work best when used to help students express ideas and when they are not graded. Assigning grades has a tendency to stifle the nature and quality of the reactions students have.

In-Depth Position Papers

More extensive position papers can be employed as a critical thinking activity and to help students learn how to integrate the views of authorities and their own ideas into a cohesive point of view. Given the discussion in Chapter 5 about the dualist orientation of students, asking them to develop and justify a position on an issue encourages higher level modes of thinking. Typically teachers create issues they want students to take a position on and to allow them to select one that interests them.

A variation on this process is to have two students work on a *for* or *against* position on an issue. When the paper is written, they exchange them and write a critique of each other's position. Essentially they assume the roles of the *Logical Thinker* and *Challenger* described in the earlier section on debate formats. After exchanging their written comments [and providing the teacher with a copy], the students meet to discuss their mutual reactions. Such meetings often occur during a class session that is designed to have students meet with a partner to discuss each of their reactions to the papers. As a wrap-up for such sessions, the instructor might ask participants to indicate what they learned most from the comments of a peer.

Evaluating position papers is sometimes a problems for teachers. The major concern is how to treat everyone fairly. As one faculty member told me, "I don't want them to think that I am dissatisfied with their position or somehow attacking them for taking a particular point of view." Peter Beidler [1993] offers one way to think about evaluating the points of view that students develop. He demands that student writing be "bold, clear, well-developed, unified, organized, and cohesive" [p. 23].

Students are told that their papers should:

> a.] Be free of grammatical, spelling, punctuation errors.
> b.] Assertively present their points.
> c.] Be written in an understandable way.
> d.] Use lots of supportive evidence and examples to back up the points being made.
> e.] Possess a strong central idea and an orderly plan of support for it.
> f.] Have transitions between their major points.

If students are not sure whether their writing is in line with such criteria, they are encouraged to use the teacher as a consultant and resource person to discuss and obtain feedback on a draft of the paper. Students receive a grade of *A* if each of the six elements listed above are present. Beidler also informs students that he will tell them which of the six he was not satisfied with and why their grade was adjusted accordingly. The criteria listed not only help teachers evaluate position papers but give students a sense of control over obtaining a favorable evaluation.

Another approach to grading position papers is reported by John Murray [1990]. He distributes five points according to the following criteria.

> "*1 or 2 points*—a paper that parrots text's or classroom discussion and shows little or no effort. *3 points*—a paper that demonstrates an honest attempt at dealing with the topic. *4 or 5 points*—a paper that shows effort and reflective thought on the topic. A *5* would require some originality or creativity of ideas" [p. 152].

Practicum

A practicum provides an opportunity for students to meet and discuss their work in settings where they are using discipline related knowledge. This can include field research, cooperative education work placements, clinical practice, student teaching, internships, personal growth and development projects and a variety of other activities. The goals of a practicum include sharing ideas, gaining additional ideas for how to handle situations, providing social support, and learning how to conceptualize their experiences.

Learning to conceptualize what they are doing is a very important function of a practicum. When working in applied settings, it is easy to get lost in the day to day routines and the tasks that must be completed. Stepping back to look at those tasks and activities from a philosophical or theoretical point of view is very important. Several things help to achieve this latter objective.

- *Students should present some aspect of what they are doing in the form of a case study.* This case study should include background information on the setting and task, key people who were involved, and the goals and objectives of the activity. The presentation should include supporting documentation, photos, videotapes, and other materials that help participants obtain a realistic view of what was done.

- *The presentation should be organized around critical decisions, choices, and problems that were encountered.* The presenter should stop when such issues arise and ask how others would have handled a situation. What was actually done is then shared and discussed.

- *Presenters should articulate the philosophical, theoretical, and other conceptual issues* inherent in their work.

- *Books, articles, and other readings that present a conceptual base to the work that students are doing should be available to participants.* Presenters should make use of such materials when pointing out the philosophical, theoretical, and other conceptual issues present in what he or she was doing.

  In a practicum on counseling or clinical work, the views of theorists in the field can be integrated into a justification for interventions that were made. Similarly, students working as interns in business and industry on biochemical, physics, engineering, and other hard science projects should bring in relevant theoretical issues their work touches upon.

- *Participants should keep journals to record important observations and significant learnings from the experience.* A summary of important insights and lessons learned should be prepared at the end of the term and distributed to all members of the practicum.

The teacher's role is to organize the practicum, select topics and individual projects that will be discussed on a given day, and to try to remain in the background. Outside of running a topical session on issues important to everyone in the group, the teacher should allow students to present and discuss their work.

In my experience, one of the best ways to design a practicum is to poll the students who will participate beforehand and have them suggest ideas and topics. An alternative is to have a skeleton design ready and to have students help fill it in during an initial session. A practicum works best when it meets the needs of participants. Thus, their preferences should be taken into account.

Round Robin Interviews

Judy Gay [1995] uses round robin interviews to allow small groups of students to develop ideas on issues by interviewing each other. After the interviews are completed, the themes that emerged in the interviews are assembled. This process has the following components.

- *The class is divided evenly into groups of 4 or 6 people.*

- *If there is a odd number of participants in the class, assign the extra person the task of observing how the process is working in each group.* The observer reports back at the conclusion of the interviews and class discussion on how well the round robin interview process appeared to work

- *Write 4 or 6 different questions related to the general topic under consideration.* Thus, if the topic of managing diversity in the classroom is under consideration, the questions for a four member group might be: [1.] What types of diversity do teachers have to take into account in the classroom? [2.] How do stereotypes of people and/or their capabilities affect the way that instructors are likely to teach? [3.] What strategies could teachers use to manage diversity in a positive manner? [4.] What responsibilities do students have for helping a teacher manage diversity in class.

- *Assign each member of the group one of the questions.* Allow them 4 to 5 minutes to write their own responses to the interview questions they were assigned.

- *Group members will then interview each other on the questions they were assigned.* This is done by pairing people within a group who have different questions [i.e., individual with question 1 meets with the person who has question 2 while the participant who has question 3 interviews the person with question 4]. Allow 6-8 minutes for each dyad to complete the interviews [i.e., each person has 3-4 minutes]. Every takes notes on what is said. Rotate one member of each group clockwise to interview someone with a different question. Do so until everyone discusses each question.

- *Each person highlights the themes that emerged in the interviews they conducted.* People assigned the same question in different groups then get together to develop overall themes. These are reported back to the class and then the instructor solicits additional ideas, comments, and points of clarification.

Self-Discovery Activities

Self-reflection is a very important part of learning. Our reflections become the raw materials for developing more complex and comprehensive views about a the world around us. A number of devices encourage self-reflection and encourage students to gain insights into themselves, their disciplines, and the applications of content within a discipline. For example, the results of questionnaires students fill out, writing a personal narrative, the outcomes of a personality test, critical thinking questions, attempts to solve a problem, stories about personal experiences that relate to the content area of a course, analyzing a research or scholarly article, a laboratory experiment, and a variety of other things provide students with experiences that can be related to issues within their disciplines.

David Kolb [1984] suggests that four processes are involved in self-reflection and discovery. They are listed below along with important or critical questions that I find helpful in getting people to think much more deeply about the experience.

- *Having a concrete experience:* This experience can be anything that potentially relates to the content of a discipline. Included here are such diverse things as participating in a laboratory experiment, reading a book or article, interacting with friends, completing a questionnaire, taking a test, and any number of other things.

- *Reflecting on those experiences:* Thinking about the experience. Replaying the entire experience or particular aspects of it back in our *minds eye.*
  Critical Questions:
  What events occurred? What incidents stand out for me? What was I doing? What were other people doing? How did events relate to one another?

- *Conceptualizing the experience:* Here discipline related ideas, concepts and principles are used to understand the experience. Essentially a personal model of what transpired is developed.
  Critical Questions:
  What concepts and principles in this field help me to understand what happened? What do my reactions say about my attitudes and values? What emotions was I experiencing?

- *Testing the model or theory:* The practical applications of what was learned is considered. It might involve following up our observations with an experiment, inventing something, or perhaps giving ourselves suggestions for what to do in the future.
  Critical Questions:
  What are the implications of what happened for my life? What are the practical applications of what I have learned? How can what I learned help me to understand other issues such as ____? What are the limitations of what I have learned? How does what I've learned suggest I should think or behave differently in the future?

To maximize a students understanding of an experience, devices that encourage self-discovery should be processed by having students answer questions such as those shown above. This helps students to consider in more detail what their responses mean and how they can be used to broaden their understanding of issues.

The scenario below provides one illustration of how the process suggested above can be employed.

Scenario: The Invisible Police Officer:

In a course dealing with applications of psychology, I had students describe to a partner a stressful experience. Afterwards, they answered the critical questions that applied to their experience in writing and then shared them with a partner. To illustrate what I wanted them to do, I related the following incident that had occurred to me earlier in the term. Since they were present to have witnessed the aftermath [i.e., my showing up 25 minutes late for class, it had added meaning].

Concrete Experience: I left home at 9:15 for my 9:30 class. I was obviously going to be 5-10 minutes late and found myself driving faster than usual. At an intersection noted for its long red light, I took a chance. I looked to my left and right, saw no one coming, and drove ahead. Unfortunately, Officer Webb witnessed the event, pulled me over, and quickly wrote a ticket. I arrived to class 25 minutes late after telling students earlier how important it was to be on time for class.

Reflecting on those experiences: I reviewed what had occurred and answered the question "How did events relate to one another?" I replayed the connections between leaving the house late and my behaviors as a driver.

Conceptualizing the experience: I answered the critical question, "What concepts and principles in this field help me to understand what happened?" My answer was that stress often leads people to adopt simplistic but problematic responses to situations. It also creates *tunnel vision* where important aspects of a problem or situation fail to get our attention. Thus, I used poor judgment, bad driving habits, and was not alert to the presence of a police officer.

Testing the model or theory: I focused on the question "What are the practical applications of what I have learned?" My response was to get up earlier and leave home with at least thirty minutes to spare.

While many learning tasks involve all of the components described above, some may emphasize the involvement of one or two components more than the others. Thus, writing poetry would involve processes of reflection and conceptualizing experiences to a larger degree than would fixing an automobile engine. The important point is that self-discovery is an active experiential and intellectual process.

Small Group Work Teams

Here students work on a course related project or in an independent study in teams. The teams function autonomously and the instructor often helps to form the teams and to facilitate the selection of a topic. The teams are then responsible for organizing themselves, determining when they will meet, and structuring the task.

The issues involved in supervising individuals mentioned earlier in Table 6-10 also apply to faculty members working with teams. Teams have the same needs for supervision as do individuals working on independent projects. In the context of the Cluster 4 teaching, the best role to assume is that of a consultant and resource person. A strong instructor *presence* is not required and students must shape the nature and quality of their *encounters* with each other.

In addition to the suggestions above, students need to be familiar with the group process issues discussed in Chapter 7. Sharing the materials in that chapter with them and encouraging students to process how they work together is very helpful. Finally, high performance and self-directed work teams in business settings have been studied to determine what makes them function well. [cf., Larson and LaFasto,1989; Wellins, et al., 1991]. The characteristics of such groups as well as the classroom implications of Larson and Lafasto's work are discussed in the following paragraphs.

1.] Clear and Elevating Goals

Goals were clearly stated and everyone on the team knew what they were. They also were able to tell as the group's work unfolded to what degree the goals were being achieved. Such groups were clear about their priorities and believed that what they were doing was important to the group as well as other people.

> *Implications for Classroom Group:* Have student teams work on establishing clear goals and objectives for a task.

2.] Results-Driven Structure

The way groups were organized to do their work was appropriately structured for the type of task they were going to achieve. Groups engaged in problem solving needed a high degree of trust among their members. Those engaged in creative processes needed to give themselves and their members autonomy. They had to be free of organizational pressures and constraints. Tactical teams needed clarity with everyone knowing how, when, where, and what they were supposed to do.

> *Implications for Classroom Groups:* Teams members need to discuss what they need from each other and the teacher in order to work well on the task.

3.] Competent Team Members

Effective work groups have the right mix of people who have the skills and abilities to accomplish a task.

> *Implications for Classroom Groups:* Students can self-select or the teacher can assign them to teams based on knowledge about what skills and abilities the task demands. This will help to get people with the right skills into the proper group, but it may not be sufficient. If the entire class is working on projects in small groups, there may not be enough people with the needed skills to go around.
>
> Therefore, team members must take some responsibility for insuring that they have the skills and abilities that are needed. Have team members discuss the skills and abilities they would need to achieve their goal. Ask them to be objective in determining which of those skills and abilities they already possess, what they need to acquire, and whether additional people might be needed to join the team.
>
> Make the team responsible for obtaining what they need. They should address the issue of how to acquire needed skills and/or how to recruit additional people to join the group. Those additional members might be people outside the class who periodically meet with the group to share expertise in an area. Groups might advertise for people with certain skills on a bulletin board posted in class. Some trading between various work teams on a temporary or permanent basis can then be arranged.
>
> Or, the team may decide that the project has to be shaped a little differently than they initially thought. Thus, they need to reexamine their goals and perhaps renegotiate the task with the instructor.

4.] Collaborative Climate

Team members must trust each other to work well together. Trust builds when individuals keep their commitments to do work, they show up for team meetings, and support and encourage other members. It is important that team members recognize that it takes effort to develop collaborative working relationships. In that respect, small group work teams are not unlike other relationships involving two or more people. Collaboration is something that must be developed and is not a natural outcome of putting people together.

> *Implications for Classroom Groups:* The suggestions for developing effective group processes described in Chapter 7 can help members to achieve the latter goal. In particular, discussing how well they work together and what they must do individually and collectively in the future to continue to function helps to create a collaborative climate.

5.] Unified Commitment

Good work groups have *team spirit* and are willing to spend time and energy to achieve a goal. Like trust in a relationship, a group cannot will itself to have team spirit. It develops over time as the team works on a project and meets with success and recognition for their efforts.

> *Implications for Classroom Groups:* Have groups break the larger task into smaller elements. Thus, as they complete each element, a partial sense of accomplishment from working together is achieved. Such *mini-successes* are very helpful in building *team spirit.* Also, requiring that teams periodically process how they work together helps to pull them together as a group. They begin to see how individual efforts and activities help the group produce a product.

6.] External Support and Recognition

Promises of help, praise, rewards, obtaining needed resources, and recognition from a broader audience [e.g. teacher, peers, consumers of the group's product, etc.] are important sources of support and recognition.

> *Implications for Classroom Groups:* Having groups periodically report on their progress in class and/or in meetings with the teacher also allows them to gain needed recognition for their efforts as a group. Asking groups to pay attention to the group maintenance functions mentioned earlier [cf., Table 6-2] also allows individuals as well as the group to obtain recognition for accomplishments to date.

7.] Standards of Excellence

The team is interested doing the best possible job it can. A mediocre performance on the part of individuals and the team is not tolerated.

> *Implications for Classroom Groups:* Having a set of criteria that the final product should meet is helpful in developing standards of excellence. Thus, the group should spend some time in preliminary discussions focusing on "how we will know that the outcome of our work will produce a high quality product."

8.] Principled Leadership

Such leaders have a vision of the future, a desire to move beyond the status quo, and the ability to get others excited about "what could be." Such leaders view themselves as changing "what is" and working on making a difference in the future. They also are fair, impartial, willing to confront and resolve issues, and are open to new ideas and information. They create a climate where problems can be solved and decisions can be made in the context of group interactions.

Implications for Classroom Groups: Groups should list the criteria [including those described above that are considered important] they believe they need in a leader. Each member then describes how the criteria fit them. Such descriptions should include examples of how they have displayed those characteristics in the past. Out of such discussions, the person who is most likely to be a good leader is identified. My experience is that students are more willing to serve as a group's leader after such a discussion because they can see the connection between the characteristics they possess and the needs of the task. Other members also see who the best person for the job is likely to be.

Student Journals

The use of student journals has become a prominent feature of courses across the curriculum. They are probably best used to help students think creatively and to foster critical thinking about issues in their lives. They also help students to develop writing skills and to become less anxious about the process of writing. There are several ways that journals can be employed to provide a learning experience for students. Two approaches described here are conceptual journals and group journals.

Conceptual Journals

Gary Shulman [1993] and his colleagues use journal assignments to help empower learners. That is, to foster the readiness, willingness, and ability of students to construct their own knowledge. Faculty who empower learners seek to facilitate discovery, excitement, and a personalized learning experience [Glasser, 1990]. The journal then becomes a device to help students achieve the latter objectives.

Shulman suggests that keeping journals to empower students has three basic stages.

- *Observation and Description:* A journal entry begins with some aspect of or an event in students' lives that they believe may be related to the course content. It is described with attention to factual information regarding what occurred.
  Example:
  "I did poorly on my History exam. I kept telling myself that I'll never recover from this setback and that I'm going to get a poor grade in the course. I'm really stressed out about this."

- *Conceptual Linkage:* Here the student relates the event or some aspect that was just described to topics or terms discussed in class or in the assigned readings. The student must not simply restate the topics or define the terms, but instead show how they explain, control, predict, or provide insight into the observation.

Example:
"We are reading about the ideas of Albert Ellis on irrational thought processes and I think I'm guilty of drawing an arbitrary inference [i.e., that just because I did poorly on one exam I'm guaranteed a bad grade in the course. How I think about something definitely affects how I feel in this instance."

- *Conceptual Insight for the Future:* Here the student describes why knowledge regarding the topics or terms used to analyze the observation is useful or valuable. This section is usually written in the future tense and is intended to help the student generalize his or her learning to other situations.
  Example:
  "The test was not the only time I formed an arbitrary inference. I also did it when my girlfriend and I broke up and when I was laid off from my part-time job. I need to be aware of this tendency to think this way in the future. It will probably hold me back from doing something about a problem and will undoubtedly help to keep me feeling miserable."

Each part of the journal entry should be relatively brief [i.e., a few sentences to a short paragraph]. It is probably best that it be kept to no more than a single page in a spiral notebook. *Other groundrules are that they should be dated and written in a legible and coherent fashion.* If the journal is to be graded, then the teacher should provide a page of constructive feedback and personal reaction. Included should be suggestions for how students can complete a set of high-quality entries in the future.

In using the approach of Gary Shulman and his colleagues, I have found the following things are useful. One is that improvements in future performance can also be achieved by having several observations from past journals as a model for them to follow also helps them. Also, checking journals early on in a course to get students moving in the right direction helps.

Grading a journal that students use to conceptualize their learning is a difficult process. In my experience it helps if criteria for grading them are developed. How well the journal conforms to the groundrules should be one part of the grade. Another is the degree to which students use course content to analyze their observations. Sometimes students mention concepts they think may apply but do little to connect them. At other times, they do a good in-depth analysis of an observation.

I find that assigning points to a journal project helpful. If the journal is worth 50 points towards a course grade, then up to 25 points are allocated depending upon how well the journal followed the groundrules. Similarly, the remaining 25 points are distributed depending upon my perceptions of how coherent and in-depth t they analyzed their observations.

Group Journals

Because students can learn significant things by interacting with peers, Anna Bolling [1994] uses group journals to improve writing and comprehension of information. To work well, authority must be shifted away from the instructor with students allowed to create a dialogue with peers through their contributions to a community dialogue. This dialogue takes place in the journal. The elements in developing a group journal she used in a writing class included the following things:

- *The class was divided into small groups of 4-5 students during the third week of the term.* The composition of the groups was based upon observations of the students' public and private writing styles. Thus, writing ability as well as sociocultural factors were taken into account. Each group included at least one accomplished writer, one less skilled writer, and diverse members by age, gender, or ethnic background.

- *Each group was given a journal.* On the first page each member's name and the order in which the journal was to progress were displayed graphically like a clock. The student whose name appeared at *high noon* made the first entry, followed by the other group members in clockwise fashion.

- *Each student responded to a question Anna Bolling provided.* They did so by taking turns. The student took the journal home, answered the question, and brought it to the next class period. The journal was then given to the next student on the *clock face.*

- *After all the group members had written their responses, the journal was forwarded to the instructor for review and comment.* The schedule of response and return ensured that she received the group journals every two weeks for review.

- *On successive assignments, students at different positions on the clock face got to respond first.* Thus, the person located at *high noon* was not overburdened.

- *The questions for the initial assignment were:* a.] What have you learned from the assigned readings at this point in the semester? b.] Based on your readings so far, what do you consider the most important concept [s] you have learned?

This process used a different kind of interaction than students were used to having. Instead of a face to face verbal exchange, students interacted through their writing. Each group member had the opportunity to read the entries of other members of the group. Anna Bolling reports that, "Although the students attempted to add new information, they also incorporated ideas suggested by preceding entries and occasionally made direct comments to other group members" [p. 50]. She observed that such entries were quite different than those made by students in her class who kept individual journals. The latter group typically wrote simple statements of agreement with the text authors and personal reminiscences.

Students reported that better comprehension of the course material occurred because they read each other's comments and in many cases reread them. Thus, they became immersed in the concepts and theories covered in the class.

Epilogue

Themes and Variations

The teaching processes of Clusters 3 and 4 highlight the Facilitator and Delegator styles of teaching. Consequently, they become more student-centered than those in Cluster 1. Small group learning processes are emphasized as well as opportunities for independent work and study. However the degree to which each element is present varies and there are other characteristics that allow distinctions to be made between each of the clusters. For example:

Cluster 3

The instructors' *presence* is clearly in the design and implementation of the group and other student-centered instructional activities of this cluster. Materials are selected or designed by the teacher [e.g., case studies, laboratory projects, role plays] and faculty members actively participate by helping to guide and direct the work of students, by observing students working together and/or by answering questions and clarifying issues as their efforts are processed in class. In effect, the instructor creates relatively tight boundaries and structures within which the students work and interact. When processing the outcomes of students' work, the teachers often shares their expertise, model by illustration and direct action, and function as a consultant and resource person.

An important goal of Cluster 3 teaching is to help students acquire foundational knowledge through student-centered teaching activities. That is, information and skills considered the core content of a discipline are taught by having learners assume more initiative and responsibility for their learning [Rockwood, 1994;1995]. The teacher establishes a learning environment in which students can acquire basic knowledge and skills.

Whether working alone or in small groups the instructor largely controls the process through which students learn and the product of their activity. An accounting task, for example, may require students to find an acceptable solution within a specific time period or budget. A humanities task may direct the groups' attention to the examination of the imagery of a poem. A physics project may ask students to consider whether a mechanical device can create more energy than it uses. In such cases, students explore these issues with each other, share their opinions, and consider the views of various authorities. One or more acceptable answers, however, clearly exist. *Thus, the authority of the teacher to evaluate the appropriateness of the group's outcome is an important part of such methods.*

Overall, teachers using the methods of Cluster 3 rely more on a Facilitator, Personal Model, and Expert blend of styles to strike a balance between letting students go and pulling them back into the fold. The teacher's *presence* becomes figural in *encounters* with students. The blend of teaching styles in Cluster 3 assumes that students need a *gentle hand to guide them* through the complexities of intellectual and interpersonal development. This assumes that most students not only need a roadmap but a guide for helping them to develop their skills as self-directed, self-initiated learners. When used well, the instructional processes of Cluster 3 stress a Collaborative style of learning as well as the Participant or "good classroom citizen" and the Independent learning styles.

Cluster 4

The primary blend of teaching styles are the Delegator, Facilitator, and Expert. The teachers' *presence* is not as pervasive as it is in the teaching methods of Cluster 3. While the general structure for a class session [e.g., class symposium, debates, small group work teams] is influence by the instructor, students spend more time preparing to participate either working alone or in small groups. They also are allowed to work with the content individually and/or in small group settings. And when working together in class on some activities [e.g., helping trios, learning pairs], instructors allow them the freedom to explore issues for themselves.

Thus, the teaching styles of Cluster 4 stress the development of an Independent learning style to a higher degree than do the methods of Cluster 3. Students are required to use their capacity as self-initiated, self-directed learners much more extensively. The student-centered nature of the instruction also encourages and reinforces Collaborative and Participant learning styles.

Checking in with the teacher on tasks and projects is encouraged but when and how students do this is much more flexible than it is in Cluster 3. Typically this occurs when students believe they need additional advice or assistance. Thus, the teacher enters the role of a consultant or resource person much more at the initiation of students than is typical of the methods in Cluster 3. Flexible boundaries and structures for how, when, and where students work together are established. In effect, faculty members strive to be much more nondirective when working with students than they do in Cluster 3.

One outcome of this nondirective approach is that it recognizes that knowledge is a social construct and learning a social process. Students do not simply learn what the teacher has deemed important. In one-on-one encounters with their instructors, for example, learners help to define the acceptability of the product of their discussions. Here, the ultimate authority on what is acceptable does not solely rest with faculty members. Discussions about content issues among students or with teachers in one-on-one encounters may yield new information, ideas, and points of view. The latter emerge through interactions with peers or with teachers What emerges is often something that neither party could predict in advance would occur. In such cases, faculty members are not the only ones who can determine whether ideas are appropriate or useful. The authority for doing this is shared with students.

Helping Students to Understand the Teaching Processes Employed

Regardless of whether the emphasis is on Cluster 3 or 4 teaching processes, the methods used and the roles of the teacher and students are different than is the case in traditional courses. Many will come expecting your course to be run essentially like others they have taken. Some will be delighted that this is not the case while others will become anxious and frustrated. *Thus, I believe it is important for students to make an informed choice about whether or not they want to take the course.* The students need information about the course and the teaching processes employed.

One way I do this is to spend the entire first class session discussing the syllabus and the teaching and learning processes that will be used. This is done in the following manner.

- I begin by presenting a brief five minute overview of the course and a conceptual rationale for the design.

- Students then read the syllabus and respond in writing with *potential likes, potential dislikes, and questions,*

- They are assigned to small groups of 3-5 students and share their reactions for ten minutes. A recorder in each group lists the major issues students identified.

- Afterwards, I poll each of the small groups and list on the board or overhead their *potential likes, dislikes, and questions. When* everything has been listed, I then comment on what they think they will like, dislike, and answer any questions.

I find the comments of students on the latter activity can be categorized in the following way. The majority like the change in teaching and learning. A few find that my approach reinforces processes they have experienced in other classes. Others are concerned about the amount of time a course using active and student-centered learning processes will take. Some are afraid of talking in groups or have concerns about the length of writing assignments and working in groups. If my experiences are typical, then others will probably have similar reactions from their students.

It is important to respond to such concerns. I typically begin by focusing on the *potential likes* and affirm students for identifying the things I also like about the course [i.e., with tongue in cheek of course]. For the *potential dislikes* I try to clarify any misconceptions and acknowledge that sometimes students are anxious about new ways of teaching and learning. The *questions* they have are answered as best I can at the moment. I tell students that to judge the class adequately they may have to experience a few sessions. Everyone is invited to sample several sessions to see if the instructional processes will be as unpleasant as a few of them believe.

In my Evening Division courses that run for three hours once a week, I use the first two hours of the first session to teach using active and student-centered teaching processes. The last hour is taken up discussing the syllabus. I find that this also shows students that such learning processes can be enjoyable and productive. Furthermore, I have employed the first hour of a day school course to teach content in a nontraditional manner and give students the syllabus to read between sessions. The syllabus is then discussed during the next class session.

Finally, to insure that everyone understands what is involved after sampling class sessions and reading and discussing the syllabus, I have them complete the course agreement form shown on the next page. Students take it home to read and think about whether or not they can meet the expectations for the course. They bring it back the following class session and any questions they have are then answered. *I make it clear that the expectations are not arbitrary but necessary for me to do a good job.*

In addition to communicating expectations and testing commitment to the course, the agreement is helpful when students fail to meet a class requirement. It reminds them that they agreed to do certain things and legitimizes a conversation with me on the reasons why their performance is deficient. An additional benefit is that people do not come back at the end of the term saying; "I didn't know I had to do......." Or, "I was unaware that attendance was a requirement for this class." Students are surprisingly responsible about signing the form. They typically ask questions about course activities and requirements before signing on the dotted line.

A Sample Course Agreement

Please place your initials next to each item and put your signature at the end.

1.] I acknowledge that I have read the syllabus and any initial assignment sheets and that I completely understand all of the course requirements. I acknowledge that the instructor and/or his assistants have answered my questions about what is required and the learning processes to be used in this course. *I know that I am responsible for keeping up to date and will not use "I forget" or "I didn't know it was due today" as an excuse.*

2.] I am responsible for asking questions when I do not understand the content covered. *I will not use," I didn't understand/know" as an excuse for not completing an assignment on time. It is my responsibility to bring all questions, comments, and reactions to this course that affect my ability to learn to the attention of the instructor.*

3.] I will inform the instructor in advance if I am going to miss a class. Furthermore, I cannot miss more than three class sessions this term and receive full credit for the course. *Because it affects my ability to participate, I will not come late to class.*

4.] I understand that this class will use active learning and collaborative learning teaching process. This will require much more preparation and involvement on my part than other classes I have taken.

5.] I am responsible for putting course deadlines on my calendar and for meeting them. I will get course assignments turned in no later than the deadlines whether or not I will be in class that day unless I receive permission in advance.

6.] I understand that no credit will be given for assignments turned in after the deadlines on the assignment sheets unless those deadlines were extended by the instructor. I also acknowledge that the in-class work on assignments is a key part of the assignments. *Unless otherwise specified on the syllabus or an assignment sheet, I must be in class to receive full credit for all assignments.*

7.] I understand that if inclement weather closes school and/or otherwise interferes with class being held, the instructor may extend the deadlines for assignments.

8.] The instructor understands that many students work outside of class. However, I will not use my job as an excuse for not meeting any of the requirements for this class. If the job is interfering, then I need to examine if I am trying to work too many hours, taking too many credit hours, or otherwise trying to do too much.

9.] I acknowledge that the instructor is not responsible for the decisions I have made for to spend my time. This includes my participation in extracurricular activities, my job, my social life, or waiting until the last moment to complete assignments. My life is my responsibility and I will not blame the teacher for my failures to meet course requirements.

Signature:_____

Creating Dynamic Instructional Scripts

Many of the strategies for teaching discussed in Chapters 6 and 8 could be used as the design for an entire course [e.g., case study method, teacher of the day, small group work teams] Or, a teacher could sample among various methods to use within a class session to provide variety in the instructional processes. What methods are chosen ought to relate to the elements in the integrated model of teaching and learning style discussed in Chapter 4. Thus the selection of teaching strategies should be sensitive to encouraging and reinforcing certain learning styles, the capability of students, the needs of the teacher to control the instructional process, and the willingness of a faculty member to work on interpersonal rapport with and among students.

To do such things means juggling a number of balls simultaneously. A device that I have taught to college faculty in workshops is the use of *instructional scripts*. A script provides a structure for organizing a class session to include active learning and student-centered teaching processes. Like the script for a play, an instructional script specifies what will be done including any necessary *stage directions*. The components of a script are:

- *A Time Line:* Specifies what activity and instructional process is scheduled to occur during a given period of time.

- *Outline of Content to be Covered:* Provides a sketch of critical points that must be raised.

- *Stage Directions:* Reminders to move around the room, to ask questions, tell a story, and do almost anything else that is easily forgotten.

- *Instructional Processes:* The instructional process from Clusters 1-4 that will be employed during a given time frame is shown.

- *Diversity Check:* The primary teaching and learning style that is emphasized during a given block of time. This helps to insure that different styles of learning are addressed and that variety in styles of teaching occur.

An example of an *instructional script* for teaching a session in my graduate seminar on college teaching appears in Table 8-7. The topic for that session was the integrated model of teaching and learning styles. Such scripts are helpful in organizing and structuring a session. In particular, they are an excellent way to check on what teaching and learning styles are emphasized. In addition, they help to organize a class session into 15-20 minute content blocks where different teaching and learning styles can be employed.

Overall, *instructional scripts* help someone become more systematic in designing a session. In turn this provides a multidimensional experience for students that enhances how and what they learn. Compared to courses taught without variety in the instructional process, those with variety have higher levels of course achievement, are more satisfied with their courses, and show up for class more often [Rau and Sherman-Heyl, 1990; Ryberg, 1986; Hersey, Blanchard, Caracushansky, 1992].

Table 8-7
An Instructional Script

Time Line	Content	Stage Directions	Teaching Processes	Diversity Check
8:00--8:15	Need for a conceptual base in our teaching/Five components of a conceptual base to teaching.	Stand at overhead.	Mini-Lecture	Expert Teaching Style/ Dependent Learning Style
8:15-8:40	Participants personalize the elements in a conceptual base.	Sit at table with class. Share two assumptions I make at an appropriate time.	Two-Minute Paper. *Question:* "What are 2-3 assumptions about teaching and learning that appear in your classes?" Think-Pair-Share [5 minutes] Participants share insights in large group. [18 minutes]	Facilitator-Delegator/ Teaching Styles and Independent Collaborative-Participant Learning Styles
8:40-9:00 5 minute break at 9:00	Intro to elements of teaching style. Video showing examples of teaching styles.	Overhead with 5 teaching styles on it. Class asked to identify styles in video in their notes.	Mini-Lecture Technology-Based Presentation Teacher-Centered Discussion	Expert/ Dependent Facilitator/ Independent/ Participant
9:05-9:25	Participants take Teaching Styles Inventory			Delegator/ Independent
9:25-9:50	Scores shared. Class profile developed. Lessons learned processed	Stand at overhead and ask questions as students respond.	Teacher-Centered Questioning/ Discussion	Facilitator/ Participant-Collaborative

Using the Instructional Hub Model

While scripts can help to introduce variety within a given class session, a course organization I designed labeled the "Hub Model" helps with providing active and student-centered learning experiences across sessions. I have used this model in 240 student sections of my introductory course as well as in classes with 40-60 students. Let me describe the model as it occurs in my introductory class. *The details of the content I teach are not the important issue here. Rather, the process by which the content is taught is the part that transfers across disciplines.*

The class meets for an hour three times a week. On two of those days, the students attend a common class session where I provide in-class active learning and student-centered activities. On the third day, the students sign up to participate in several outside of class small group modules. Each module is organized around a specific topic and is designed to encourage critical thinking, small group discussion, self-discovery, and to enhance the ability of students to learn with and from each other. The outside of class modules may meet during class time or at other time periods during the day [i.e., from 8 am until 8 PM]. Some like the library and language lab modules described below can be completed at any time students have access to the facility.

There are several things that make this model work effectively.

- *The use of a cadre of 6-8 junior and senior undergraduate majors who teach the outside of class modules.* Early on in my career, I decided that I could not teach very well active learning and student-centered processes by myself. I needed help and the use of undergraduate majors was a solution I pursued. The students must have taken at least one course from me, have a 3.2 overall GPA, and be willing to work six hours a week on course related activities.

- *The students are trained to work with class members one-on-one as well as to run a variety of discussion and small group activities.* They begin to work with me approximately 4 months before the course begins. During this period of time, they meet to discuss teaching strategies and the design of the outside of class course modules they will teach or coordinate. In return, the students learn important teaching skills, they get to work with a senior faculty member, and they earn course credits in a undergraduate teaching assistant practicum they take. I also get to know them well and can write well informed letters of recommendation for them.

- *A point system is used to earn credit in the course.* Students are generally required to complete 8 of the outside of class modules during the term. They earn 10 points for each of the modules they successfully complete.

- *Each classroom module is designed to take about 50 minutes.* Others like the library readings and the language lab tapes can take up to a couple of hours to complete.

- *A module often has a prework assignment and students typically write and discuss issues within a module.* All work is graded on a pass fail-system. The library readings and language lab tapes have a study guide that students must complete. Other modules involve case analyses, written observations of demonstrations, brief position papers, written responses that demand critical thinking, as well as small and large group discussion processes.

- *A series of modules for a topic are held over a two week period.* In the introductory course, this is typically the amount of time spent on a particular topic.

- *Many of the active and student-centered teaching processes in Clusters 3 and 4 are used during the sessions.* Students become familiar with them having taken at least one course from me and through the training period and the weekly staff meetings we have.

Overall, the use of undergraduate teaching assistants has worked well. The major benefit is that I can teach using a variety of instructional strategies and thus expose students to different teaching and learning styles. Course evaluations have been very positive and students have commented favorably on the performance of the teaching assistants.

Initially, the courses are much more difficult to set up. However, when I began, I did only half of the term using the model. Over time, enough materials were developed to do an entire academic quarter. The most important thing about using it is to have good people working for you. Thus, I am very careful who I allow to join the staff. I generally have students apply, I interview them, and select the best to serve as an undergraduate teaching assistants.

Concluding Comments

It is my hope that readers will have found the information in this book useful for enhancing their approach to instruction as well as understanding themselves and their students better. The instructional processes outlined in this book are of course not the only ones that are available to college teachers. Those covered represent a sample of those that fit the structure of the integrated model. The important point, however, is not to get bogged down in what techniques to use. Rather, it is essential that we first examine who we want to become as teachers, our philosophies of teaching, and how such things relate to among other things our learning and teaching styles. The latter three concerns will always be present regardless of what directions college teaching processes take in the future. *Then as now, and in so many different ways, teaching in college will continue to be a matter of style.*

References

Andrews, J.A. [1980]. The structure of teacher questions. *Journal of Professional and Organizational Development. 2,* 129-163.

Andrews, J.A. [1981]. Teaching format and student style: Their interactive effects on learning. *Research in Higher Education, 14,* 161-178.

Angelo, T.A. & Cross, K.P. [1993]. *Classroom assessment techniques: A handbook for faculty* [Second Edition]. San Francisco: Jossey-Bass.

Ashcraft, M.H. [1994]. *Human memory and cognition.* New York: Harper-Collins.

Atkinson, R.C. [1975]. Mnemotechnics in second language teaming. *American Psychologist, 30,* 821-828.

Baddeley, A. [1986]. *Working memory.* Oxford, UK: Oxford University Press.

Bandura, A. [1971]. *Social learning theory.* New York: General Learning Press.

Bandura, A. [1986]. *Social foundations of thought and action:* A social-cognitive theory. *37,* 122-147.

Barrett, E. [1992]. *Multimedia, hypermedia, and the social construction of knowledge.* Cambridge, MA: MIT Press.

Barron, A.E., & Orwig, G.W. [1993]. *Multimedia techniques for training.* Englewood Cliffs, NJ: Libraries Unlimited.

Baxter-Magolda, M. [1992]. *Knowing and reasoning in college: Gender-related patterns in student development.* San Francisco: Jossey-Bass.

Beidler, P.G., & Biedler, G.M. [1993]. What's your horse: Motivating college students. *Journal on Excellence in College Teaching. 4,* 9-26.

Belenky, M.B., Clinchy, B.M., Goldberger, N.R., & Tarule, J.M. [1986]. *Women's ways of knowing.* New York: Basic Books.

Berliner, D.C. [1986]. In pursuit of the expert pedagogue. *Educational Researcher, 15*[7], 5-13.

Blake, R.R.,& Mouton, J.S. [1986]. From theory to practice in interface problem solving. In S. Worchel & W. Austin [Eds.], *Psychology of intergroup relations.* Chicago: Nelson-Hall.

Bolling, A. [1994]. Using group journals to improve writing and comprehension. *Journal on Excellence in College Teaching, 5,* 47-54.

Bonwell, C.C., & Eison, J.A. [1991]. *Active learning: Creating excitement in the classroom.* ASHE-ERIC Higher Education Report No. 1. Washington, DC: The George Washington University, School of Education and Human Development.

Boring, E., [1950]. *A history of experimental psychology.* New York: Appleton-Century-Crofts.

Bridges, W. [1980]. *Transitions: Making sense of life's changes.* Reading, MA: Addison-Wesley.

Britton, B.K., & Tesser, A. [1991]. Effects of time-management practices on college grades. *Journal of Educational Psychology, 83,* 405-410.

Bruffee, K.A. [1993]. *Collaborative learning: Higher education, interdependence, and the authority of knowledge.* Baltimore, MD: The Johns Hopkins University Press.

Campbell, D.E. [1986]. Helping learners learn: A study of learning preferences, teaching styles, and learning systems. *Proceedings of the 1986 Air·Force Conference on Technology in Training and Education, II,* 30-45. Montgomery, AL: United States Air Force Training Center.

Campbell, D.E., & Davis, C.L. [1990]. Improving learning by combining critical thinking skills with psychological type. *Journal on Excellence in College Teaching. 1,* 39-51.

Cashdan, S. [1988]. *Object relations therapy: Using the relationship.* New York: Norton.

Christensen, R.C., & Hansen, A.J. [1987]. *Teaching and the case method.* Boston, MA: Harvard Business School Publishing,

Claxton, C.S., & Smith, W.F. [1984]. *Learning Styles: Implications for improving educational practices.* ASHE-ERIC Higher Education Report No. 4. Washington, DC: The George Washington University, School of Education and Human Development.

Conrad, J.M., & Conrad, P.L. [1993]. Small groups and research projects in science. *College Teaching, 41,* 43-46.

Cooper, S.E., & Miller, J.A. [1991]. MBTI learning style-teaching style discongruencies. *Educational and Psychological Measurement, 51,* 699-706.

Cross, L.H., Frary, R.B., & Weber, L.J. [1993]. College grading: Achievement, attitudes, and effort. *College Teaching, 41,* 143-152.

Cross, K.P., & Angelo, T.A. [1988]. *Classroom assessment techniques: A handbook for faculty.* Ann Arbor, MI: National Center for Research to Improve Postsecondary Teaching and Learning.

Crow, M.L. [1980]. Teaching as an interactive process. In K.E. Eble [Ed.], *Improving teaching styles.* San Francisco, CA: Jossey-Bass.

Curwin, R. L. & Fuhrmann, B.S. [1975]. *Discovering your teaching self: Humanistic approaches to effective teaching.* Englewood Cliffs, NJ: Prentice-Hall.

Czikszentimihalyi, M. [1990]. *Flow: The psychology of peak experience.* New York: Harper-Collins.

Dahlin, A. [1994]. The teacher as reflective professional. *College Teaching,. 42,* 57-61.

Davis, J.R. [1993]. *Better teaching, more learning: Strategies for success in postsecondary settings.* Phoenix, AZ: ORYX Press.

Davis, T.M., & Murrell, P.H. [1993]. *Turning teaching into learning: The role of student responsibility in the collegiate experience.* ASHE-ERIC Higher Education Research Report No. 1. Washington, DC: The George Washington University, School of Education and Human Development.

Dillon, J.T. [1988]. *Questioning and teaching: A manual of practice.* New York: Teachers College Press.

Dillon, J.T. [1990]. *The practice of questioning.* London: Routledge.

Druckman, D., & Bjork, R. [1991]. Modeling expertise. In D. Druckman &R. Bjork [Eds.] *In the mind's eye: Enhancing human performance.* Washington, DC: National Academy Press.

Egan, M.L. [1990]. Taking sides: Methods, systems, and techniques for the teaching of controversial issues. Sluice Dock, CA: Duskin.

Eagly, A.H., & Johnson, B.T. [1990]. Gender and leadership styles: A meta-analysis. *Psychological Bulletin, 108:* 233-256.

Eagly, A.H., & Karau, S.J. [1991]. Gender and the emergence of leaders: A meta-analysis. *Journal of Personality and Social Psychology, 60,* 685-710.

Eble, K.E. [1980]. Teaching styles and faculty behavior. In K.E. Eble [Ed.], *Improving teaching styles.* San Francisco: Jossey-Bass.

Eisenstaedt, R.S., Barry, W.E., & Glanz, K. [1990]. Problem-based learning: Cognitive retention and cohort traits of randomly selected participants and decliners. *Academic Medicine, 9,* 11-12.

Eison, J. [1980]. Grades: What do they tell? *Teaching-Learning Issues, 10,* 3-26.

Eison, J. [1991, February]. *Characteristics of learning oriented and grade oriented students and faculty.* Presentation at 2nd annual Southwest Ohio Consortium on Higher Education Conference on Teaching and Learning. Dayton, OH.

Ellis, A., & Dryden, W. [1987]. *The practice of rational-emotive therapy.* New York, NY: Springer.

Ellis, H.C., & Hunt, R.R. [1993]. *Fundamentals of cognitive psychology* [5th Edition]. Madison, WI: William C. Brown.

Evans, G. [1984]. Metaphors as learning aids in university lectures. *Journal of Experimental Education, 56,* 91-98.

Fisher, B.A. [1980]. *Small group decision making.* New York: McGraw-Hill.

Firestone, B. [1993, March]. *Understanding ourselves and others through psychological type.* Workshop presentation at 4th annual Lilly Conference on College Teaching-West. Lake Arrowhead, CA.

Frederick, P. [1981]. The dreaded discussion: Ten ways to start. *Improving College and University Teaching, 29,* 109-114.

Frick, W.B. [1987]. The symbolic growth experience. *Journal of Humanistic Psychology, 27,* 406-423.

Fuhrmann, B.S., & Grasha, A.F. [1983]. *A practical handbook for college teachers.* Boston, MA: Little-Brown.

Gay, J. [1995, August]. *Managing diversity in the classroom.* Presentation at annual Summer Academy on College Teaching, Allenberry, PA.

Glaser, W. [1990]. *The quality school.* New York: Perennial Library.

Gossard, H. [1966]. Wide, wide world. *Ramparts Magazine, 22,* 45-47.

Granrose, J.T. [1980]. Conscious teaching: Helping assistants develop teaching styles. In K.E. Eble [Ed.], *Improving teaching styles.* San Francisco: Jossey-Bass.

Grasha, A.F. [1972]. Observations on relating teaching goals to student response styles and classroom methods. *American Psychologist, 27,* 144-147.

Grasha, A.F. [1975]. A planning sequence to assist faculty in selecting alternative course designs. *Educational Technology, 15,* 9-16.

Grasha, A.F. [1977]. *Assessing and developing faculty performance: Principles and models.* Cincinnati, OH: Communication and Education Associates.

Grasha, A.F. [1983]. Learning styles: The journey from Greenwich Observatory [1796] to the college classroom [1983]. *Improving College and University Teaching, 32,* 46-53.

Grasha, A.F., Ichiyama, M., & Kelley, D. [1986, August]. *Psychological size and distance in student-teacher, parent, and peer relationships.* Paper presented at annual meeting of the American Psychological Association, Washington, DC.

Grasha, A.F., & Kirschenbaum, D.S. [1986]. *Adjustment and competence: Concepts and applications.* St. Paul, MN: West.

Grasha, A.F. [1987a]. *Practical Applications of Psychology* [Third Edition]. Boston, MA: Little-Brown.

Grasha, A.F. [1987b]. Short-term coping strategies for managing faculty stress. In P. Seldin [Ed.], *A Sourcebook on faculty stress.* San Francisco: Jossey-Bass.

Grasha, A.F. [1988, October]. *Learning styles in adult education.* Paper presented at National Conference on Teaching Adults: Myths and Realities. Cincinnati, OH.

Grasha, A.F. [1989, September & November]. *Faculty stress and coping strategies.* Presentations at Council of Independent Colleges workshop series on faculty stress, Athens, GA: & Boston, MA.

Grasha, A.F. [1989]. *Holistic stress management: A self-study manual.* Cincinnati, OH: Communication and Education Associates.

Grasha, A.F. [1990a]. Using traditional versus naturalistic approaches to assessing learning styles in college teaching. *Journal on Excellence in College Teaching, 1,* 23-38.

Grasha, A.F. [1990b]. The naturalistic approach to learning styles. *College Teaching, 3,* 106-109.

Grasha, A.F. [1990c]. Practical poetry: Using metaphors to evaluate academic programs. *The Journal of Staff, Program, & Organizational Development, 1,* 23-32.

Grasha, A.F. [1990d, November]. *Practical strategies for using learning styles in the classroom.* Workshop presentation at 10th annual Lilly Conference on Teaching and Learning, Miami University, Oxford, OH.

Grasha, A.F., & Gardener, A. [1991, October]. *The relationship of psychological size and distance to teaching style in classrooms and 1:1 teaching.* Presentation at annual meetings of Northeast Region Society of Teachers of Family Medicine, Cincinnati, OH.

Grasha, A.F. [1992, October]. *The role of historical and conceptual assumptions about teaching and learning in course design.* Presentation at conference on New Directions in Medical Education, University of Cincinnati Department of Family Medicine, Cincinnati, OH.

Grasha, A.F. [1993, November]. *Metaphors we teach and learn by.* Workshop presentation at 13th annual Lilly Conference on College Teaching, Miami University, Oxford, OH.

Grasha, A.F. [1994]. A matter of style: The teacher as expert, formal authority, personal model, facilitator, and delegator. *College Teaching,. 42,* 142-149.

Grasha, A.F. [1995a]. The role of cognitive processes in dispensing errors: A conceptual analysis.[*ICT Technical Report 0395,* 1-93.] Cincinnati, OH: University of Cincinnati. Institute for Consultation and Training,

Grasha, A.F. [1995b]. *Practical applications of psychology* [Fourth Edition]. New York: Harper-Collins.

Grasha, A.F. [1995, March]. *How to become an OSCAR winning teacher.* Keynote address at 7th annual Lilly Conference on College Teaching-West,Lake Arrowhead, CA.

Grasha, A.F. [1995e]. *Instructors manual: Practical applications of psychology.* New York: Harper-Collins.

Grasha, A.F. [1995f], November]. *Up close and personal: The dynamics of one on one teaching.* Workshop presentation at 14th annual Lilly Conference on College Teaching, Miami University, Oxford, OH.

Grasha, A.F. [1996]. Optimism and pessimism in the college classroom. *College Teaching.* In Press.

Haden-Elgin, S. [1989]. *Success and the gentle art of verbal self-defense.* Englewood Cliffs, NJ: Prentice-Hall.

Hadley, T. [1993, September]. *UC students: What are they like?* Presentation at 5th annual Graduate Student-New Faculty Orientation workshops, University of Cincinnati, Cincinnati, OH.

Halpern, D. [1989]. *Thought and knowledge: An introduction to critical thinking.* Hillsdale, NJ: Lawrence-Earlbaum.

Harrisberger, L. [1990]. *Temperament types in the college classroom.* Workshop presentation at Department of Psychology seminar on teaching and learning styles, University of Cincinnati, Cincinnati, OH.

Harvey, O.J., & Schroder, H.M. [1963]. Cognitive aspects of self and motivation. In O.J. Harvey [Ed.]. *Motivation and social interaction: Cognitive determinants.* New York: Ronald Press.

Hersey, P.K., & Blanchard, K. [1992]. *Management of organizational behavior: Utilizing human resources.* Englewood Cliffs, NJ: Prentice-Hall.

Hersey, P.K., & Blanchard, K., Caracushansky, S. [1992]. Variations in teaching style on course outcomes. In P.K. Hersey & K. Blanchard, [Eds.], *Management of organizational behavior: Utilizing human resources.* Englewood Cliffs, N.J.: Prentice-Hall.

Hildebrand, M. [1972]. How to recommend promotion for a mediocre teacher without actually lying. *Journal of Higher Education, 43,* 44-62.

Hoff-Macan, T., Sahani, C., Dipboye, R.L., & Phillips, A.P. [1990]. College students' time management: Correlations with academic performance and stress. *Journal of Educational Psychology, 82,* 760-768.

Hruska-Riechmann, S., & Grasha, A.F. [1982]. The Grasha-Riechmann Student Learning Style Scales: Research findings and applications. In J. Keefe [Ed.], *Student learning styles and brain behavior.* Reston, VA: NASSP.

Hutchings, P. [1993]. Windows on practice: Cases about teaching and learning. *Change,* November/December, 14-21.

Janzow, F., & Eison, J. [1990]. Grades: Their influence on students and faculty. *New Directions for Teaching and Learning.* San-Francisco: Jossey-Bass.

Johnson, D.W., Johnson, R.T., & Holubec, R.J. [1990]. *Circles of learning: Cooperation in the classroom.* [Third Edition]. Edina, MN: Interaction Book Company.

Johnson, D.W., Johnson, R.T., & Smith, K.A. [1991]. *Cooperative learning: Increasing college faculty instructional productivity.* ASHE-ERIC Higher Education Report No. 4. Washington, D.C.: George Washington University, School of Education and Human Development.

Johnson, J.L. [1992]. *A manual of learning styles: Scales for use with college students.* Portland, ME: University of Maine Testing and Assessment Center.

Johnston, J.M. [1975]. *Behavior research and technology in higher education.* Springfield, IL: Charles C. Thomas.

Jung, C.G. [1960]. The structure and dynamics of the psyche. In R.F.C. Hull [Translator], *Collected works, [Vol. 8].* Princeton, NJ: Princeton University Press.

Jung, C.G. [1976]. Psychological types. In R.F.C. Hull [Translator], *Collected works, [Vol. 1].* Princeton, NJ: Princeton University Press.

Kanfer, F.H., & Goldstein, A.P. [1991]. *Helping people change.* New York: Pergamon.

Keefe, J.W. [1982]. *Student learning styles and brain behavior.* Reston, VA: NASSP.

King, A. [1993]. From sage on the stage to guide on the side. *College Teaching, 41,* 30-36.

King, P.M., Kitchener, K.S., & Wood, P.K. [1985]. The development of intellect and character: A longitudinal-sequential study of intellectual and moral development in young adults. *Moral Education Forum, 10,* 1-13.

Kloss, R.J. [1994]. A nudge is best: Helping students through the Perry scheme of intellectual development. *College Teaching, 42,* 151-158.

Kolb, D. [1984]. *Experiential learning.* Englewood Cliffs, NJ: Prentice-Hall.

Kiersey, D., & Bates, M. [1984]. *Please understand me.* Del Mar, CA: Prometheus Nemesis Books.

Kirschenbaum, D.S., Malett, S.D., & Humphrey, L. [1982]. Specificity of planning and maintenance of self-control: A one year follow-up of a study improvement program. *Behavior Therapy, 13,* 232-242.

Knowles, M., & Knowles, H. [1959]. *Introduction to group dynamics.* NY: Association Press.

Kraft, R.E. [1976]. An analysis of student learning styles. *Physical Education, 22,* 23-30.

Kurfiss, J.G. [1988]. *Critical thinking: Theory, research, practice, and possibilities.* ASHE-ERIC Higher Education Report No. 2. Washington, D.C.: Association for the Study of Higher Education.

Lahey, R. [1994]. The occult and science. Colloquium presentation, Department of Psychology, University of Cincinnati, Cincinnati, OH.

Lakoff, G., & Johnson, M. [1980]. *Metaphors we live by.* Chicago, IL: University of Chicago Press.

Lawrence, G. [1982]. *People types and tiger stripes* [Second Edition]. Gainesville, FL: CAPT.

Lambiotte, J., & Dansereau, D. [1988]. Effects of knowledge maps and prior knowledge on recall of science lecture content. *Journal of Experimental Education, 60,* 189-201.

Langer, E. [1989a]. *Mindfulness.* Reading, MA: Addison-Wesley.

Langer, E. [1989b]. Minding matters. In L. Berkowitz [Ed.]. *Advances in experimental social psychology.* New York: Academic Press.

Larson, C.E., & LaFasto, F.M.J. *Teamwork: What must go right/what can go wrong.* Newbury Park, CA: Sage Publications.

Lee, C.R. [1992]. Thinking historically—thinking critically. *Teaching Forum, 4,* 1-3.

Lowman, J. [1984]. *Mastering the techniques of teaching. San* Francisco: Jossey-Bass.

Lowman, J. [1994]. Professors as performers and motivators. *College Teaching. 42,* 137-141.

Lowman, J. [1995]. *Mastering the techniques of teaching* [Third Edition]. San Francisco: Jossey-Bass.

Macan, T.H., Sahani, C., Dipboye, R.L., & Phillips, A.P. [1990]. College students' time management: Correlations with academic performance and stress. *Journal of Educational Psychology, 82,* 760-768.

Mann, R., Arnold, S.M., Binder, J., Cytrunbaum, S., Newman, B.M., Ringwald, J., & Rosenwein, R. [1970]. *The college classroom: Conflict, change, and learning.* New York: John Wiley & Sons.

McCaulley, M.H. [1981]. Jung's theory of psychological types and the Myers-Briggs Type Indicator. In P. McReynolds [Ed.], *Advances in personality assessment [Vol. V].* San-Francisco: Jossey-Bass.

McConnell, A.R., Bill, C.M., Dember, W.N., & Grasha, A.F. [1993]. Personality through metaphor: Optimism, pessimism, locus of control, and sensation seeking. *Current Psychology, 12, 1*95-215.

McDaniel, T.R. [1985]. The ten commandments of motivation. *Clearing House, 59,* 19-23.

McKeachie, W.J. [1978]. *Teaching tips: A guidebook for the beginning college teacher.* Lexington, MA: D.C. Heath & Co.

McKeachie, W.J., Chism, N., Menges, R., Svinicki, M., & Weinstein, C.E. [1994]. *Teaching tips: Strategies and theory for college and university teachers.* Lexington, MA: D.C. Heath & Co.

Milton, O., Pollio, H.R., & Eison, J. [1986]. *Making sense of college grades.* San Francisco: Jossey-Bass.

Montauk, S.L., & Grasha, A.F. [1992, October]. *Using learning styles in medical education.* Workshop presentation at annual meeting of the Northeast Regional Society of Teachers of Family Medicine, Lancaster, PA.

Montauk, S.L, & Grasha, A.F. [1993]. *Adult HIV outpatient care: A handbook for clinical teaching.* Kansas City, MO: Society of Teachers of Family Medicine.

Murray, J.P. [1990]. Better testing for better learning. *College Teaching, 38,* 148-152.

Myers, I.B. [1987]. *Introduction to type.* Palo Alto, CA: Consulting Psychologists Press.

Myers, I.B. [1990]. *Gifts differing.* Palo Alto, CA: Consulting Psychologists Press.

Nelson, C. [1989]. Skewered on the unicorn's horn: The illusion of the tragic trade-off between content and critical thinking in the teaching of science. In L. Crow [Ed.], *Enhancing critical thinking in the sciences.* Washington, DC: Society of College Science Teachers.

Nelson, C. [1991, November]. Critical thinking in the classroom. Workshop presentation at 11th annual Lilly Conference on College Teaching, Miami University, Oxford, OH.

Neustadt, R.E., & May, E.R. [1986]. *Thinking in time: The uses of history for decision makers.* New York: The Free Press.

Perkins, D.N. [1986]. *Knowledge as design.* Hillsdale, NJ: Erlbaum.

Perkins, D.N. [1987]. Knowledge as design: Teaching thinking through content. In Baron, J.B. & Sternberg, R.J. [Eds.], *Teaching thinking skills: Theory and practice.* New York: W.H. Freeman and Company.

Perry, W. [1970]. *Forms of intellectual and ethical development in the college years: A scheme.* New York: Holt, Rinehart & Winston.

Perry, W. [1981]. Cognitive and ethical growth: The making of meaning. In A. Chickering [Ed.], *The modern American college.* San Francisco: Jossey-Bass.

Peterson, C. & Bossio, L. [1992]. *Health and optimism.* New York: Free Press.

Polezynski, J., & Shirland, I. [1977]. Expectancy theory and contract grading combined as an effective motivational force for college students. *Journal of Educational Research, 70,* 33-35.

Pollio, H. [1986, Fall]. Practical poetry: Metaphoric thinking in science, art, literature and nearly everywhere else. *Teaching Learning Issues.* Knoxville, TN: *University of Tennessee Learning Resource Center.*

Prochaska, J.O. [1991]. Prescribing the stages and levels of change. *Psychotherapy, 28,* 463-468.

Prochaska, J.O., DiClemente, C.C., & Norcross, J.C. [1992]. In search of how people change. *American Psychologist, 47,* 1102-1114.

Quenk, N. [1993]. *Beside ourselves: Our hidden personality in everyday life.* Palo Alto, CA: CPP Books.

Rau, W., & Sherman-Heyl, B. [1990]. Humanizing the college classroom: Collaborative learning and social organization among students. *Teaching Sociology, 18,* 141-155.

Raven, B. [1992]. A power/interaction model of interpersonal influence: French and Raven thirty years later. *Journal of Social Behavior and Personality, 7,* 217-244.

Riechmann, S., & Grasha, A.F. [1974]. A rational approach to developing and assessing the construct validity of a student learning style scales instrument. *Journal of Psychology, 87,* 213-223.

Reinsmith, W.A. [1992]. *Archetypal forms in teaching: A continuum.* Westport, CN: Greenwood Press.

Reinsmith, W.A. [1994]. Archetypal forms in teaching. *College Teaching, 42,* 131-136.

Richards, J.P., & McCormick, C.B. Effect of interspersed conceptual prequestions on note-taking in listening comprehension. *Journal of Educational Psychology, 80,* 592-594.

Richlin, L., & Cox, M.D. [1991]. The scholarship of pedagogy. *Journal on Excellence in College Teaching. 2,* 1-8.

Richlin, L., & Manning, B. [1995]. *Improving a college/university teaching evaluation system: A comprehensive, developmental curriculum for faculty and administrators* [Second Edition]. Pittsburgh, PA: Alliance Publishers.

Roberts, J. [1985, March]. The keyword method: An alternative vocabulary strategy for developmental college readers. *Reading World.*, 34-38.

Rockwood, H. [1994]. Learning that encourages discovery. *College Teaching, 42,* 166.

Rockwood, H. S. [1995]. Cooperative and collaborative learning. *The National Teaching and Learning Forum, 4,* 4-5.

Rogers, C. [1969]. *Freedom to learn.* Columbus, OH: Merrill.

Rosenheck, M.B., Levin, M.E., & Levin, J.R. [1989]. Learning botany concepts mnemonically: Seeing the forest and the trees. *Journal of Educational Psychology, 81,* 196-203.

Ryan, M. P. [1984]. Conceptions of prose coherence: Individual differences in epistemological standards. *Journal of Educational Psychology, 76,* 248-258.

Rysberg, J.A. Effects of modifying instruction in a college classroom. *Psychological Reports, 58,* 965-966.

Salzmann, J., & Grasha, A.F. [1991]. Psychological size and distance in manager-subordinate relationships. *Journal of Social Psychology, 131,* 629-646

Sand, J. [1994]. *Student perceptions of teaching styles: The relationship to course outcomes.* Unpublished senior thesis. University of Cincinnati, Cincinnati, OH.

Sass, E.J. [1989]. Motivation in the college classroom: What students tell us. *Teaching of Psychology, 16,* 86-87.

Scerbo, M., Warm, J.S., Dember, W.D., & Grasha, A.F. [1992]. The role of time and cuing in a college lecture. *Contemporary Educational Psychology, 17,* 312-338.

Seldin, P. [1991]. *The teaching portfolio.* Boston, MA: Anker Publishing.

Seligman, M.E. P. [1991]. *Learned optimism.* New York: Knopf

Seligman, M.E.P. [1994]. *What you can change and what you can't.* New York: Knopf.

Short, G.J. & Grasha, A.F. [1995]. The relationship of MBTI dimensions to perceptions of stress and coping in managers. *Journal of Psychological Type, 32,* 13-22.

Shulman, G.M., McCormack, A., Luechauer, D.L., & Shulman, C. [1993]. Using the journal assignment to create empowered learners: An application of writing across the curriculum. *Journal on Excellence in College Teaching. 4,* 89-104.

Shulman, L.S. [1987]. Knowledge and teaching: Foundations of the new reform. *Harvard Educational Review, 57*[1], 1-22.

Sontag, S. [1989]. *AIDS and its metaphors.* New York: Farrart, Straus and Giroux.

Sternberg, R. [1993]. The practical intelligence of improving teaching. *The National Teaching and Learning Forum, 2,* 1-3.

Stuart, J., & Rutherford, R.J.D. [1978]. Medical student concentration during lectures. *Lancet, 2,* 514-516.

Swartz, P. [1976]. *Learning styles of nursing students in a small college.* Unpublished report, Gwynedd-Mercy College, 1976.

Toma, A.G., & Heady, R.B. [1996]. Take-two testing. *College Teaching,* In Press.

Toppins, A.D. [1987]. Teaching students to teach themselves. *College Teaching, 35,* 95-99.

Wales, C.E., & Nardi, A. [1982]. Teaching decision making with guided design. *IDEA Paper No 9.* Manhattan: KA: Kansas State University, Center for Faculty Evaluation & Development.

Ward, A.W. [1994]. *Multimedia and learning.* Alexandria, VA: National School Boards Association.

Watson, D.L., & Tharp, R.G. [1993]. *Self-directed behavior.* Pacific Grove, CA: Brooks/Cole.

Walvoord, B. [1990]. *Thinking and writing in college.* Urbana, IL: National Council of Teachers of English.

Weinberg, G. [1984]. *Self-creation.* Englewood Cliffs, NJ: Prentice-Hall.

Weiner, B. [1986]. *An attributional theory of motivation and emotion.* New York: Springer-Verlag.

Wellins, R.S., Byam, W.C., & Wilson, J.M. [1991]. *Empowered teams: Creating self-directed work groups that improve quality, productivity, and participation.* San Francisco: Jossey-Bass.

Welty, W.M. [1989, July/August]]. Discussion method teaching: How to make it work. *Change,* 40-49.

Weltzien, O.A. [1994]. Two great professors: Formidable intellects with an abiding affection for students. *College Teaching, 42,* 124-130.

Wrightsman, L.S. [1992]. *Assumptions about human nature.* Newbury Park, CA.: Sage Publications.

Subject/Author Index